The Shopaholic's Guide to Buying Online

Patricia Davidson

CAPSTONE

Free subscription offer

www.thesiteguide.com

www.thesiteguide.com, described by Condé Nast's *Glamour.com* as 'The web's best shopping directory', is the online version of The Shopaholic's Guide to Buying Online where you'll find direct links through to all the websites reviewed, plus regular online shopping features and updates and news of the latest site launches.

We're delighted to offer you a year's free subscription to *www.thesiteguide.com* (normally £9.99) to thank you for purchasing this book. To take this up you need to click on to the site and subscribe. When you're prompted for a Media Code just use the password you'll find at the end of the introduction to Chapter 28, The Beauty Specialists and you'll be able to use the Guide online.

Acknowledgments

My thanks to Andrew, Sholto and Calum for your patience (most of the time). To Sally Smith at John Wiley for making it happen. To my agent Kate Hordern for her encouragement and support and to my daughter Kirstie – the best Shopaholic of them all.

About the Author

After twelve years in international designer fashion mail-order, Patricia Davidson started *www.thesiteguide.com*, an online upmarket fashion, beauty and lifestyle website directory. She's a regular contributor to Condé Nast's *easylivingmagazine.com* and has also been published on online shopping in other women's titles. She lives in Buckinghamshire with her husband, three children and two dogs.

Contents

The Shopaholics Guide to Buying Online

I think that most people would agree with me that shopping is one of the pleasures of life. No, I don't mean the washing powder, dog food type of shopping but the sort that's enjoyable and always makes you feel good, such as your favourite fragrance, the latest fashion, gifts, books, dvds, music, tickets to that hot new show, tickets to Hawaii.

The days when you used to have to trek out to the shops for these are now well past. Just about everything is available online. You may go out to the shops because you prefer to, or you've lots of free time, but you certainly don't need to. There are hundreds of thousands of websites just waiting for you to buy from and there's the first problem. Just how much time do you have to spend searching?

If you can't stand searching, or don't have the time to search, or don't know how to you'll probably give up long before you find what you're looking for.

It goes like this: After being offered over 100,000 options on your favourite search engine (and that's being optimistic), and after being sent down endless byways to yet more search engines and shopping directories pretending to lead you directly to your product of choice, you'll probably have had enough. Now there's a much easier way.

What you'll find in this book are quite simply the best sites available, brought together under one roof, from household names to hidden gems you almost certainly won't have heard of. So you don't have to search because it's all been done for you. These are the ones you'll want to use over and over again, for gifts, for your home, for yourself. Well laid out and offering a classy service.

There are so many great online shops to discover. You can buy fashion, shoes, handbags, top brand cosmetics, skincare and gorgeous bath and body products, flowers, gifts, gadgets, food and wine online alongside the computers, printers, cameras, tvs, dvds, books and cds that you probably already know about. You can book your tickets to the theatre, your flights to Venice and find out where to have your clothes altered. You can shop from anywhere in the World and take delivery anywhere in the World. The World Wide Web has made the globe a much, much smaller place.

You can also save a great deal of money online. Your computer, your camera, your washing machine or fridge will almost certainly be cheaper by anything up to 30% (and sometimes more) than anything you could find offline, and those stores that have always promised to match the lowest price you can come up with can do so no longer.

All you need to do to get the best price is to use the Comparison Website guide in Chapter 77 at the back of this book. You'll be amazed at what you can save and you'll find out how to do it step by step.

You'll also discover all the information that's in this book on the website at *www.thesiteguide.com* where you can click straight through to whatever you're looking for in each category. Inevitably the site will update faster than when there'll be a new edition of the book, so do use it as well.

So for a little bedtime reading and a lot of temptation just turn the pages and read on. You'll be amazed and delighted at what you can find online.

Why Shop Online?

The first reason is obvious; convenience, convenience, convenience. Why even consider going out to shop when you can have most things delivered to your door, frequently only the day after you place your order?

You can also place your order whenever you feel like it. Whether it's 4 am in the morning or 11 pm at night, 24 hour service is there, ready and waiting for you.

The second reason is time saving. No longer do you have to drive to the shops, find somewhere to park, wait your turn and then waste time putting up with that over friendly assistant trying to offload something he's been having trouble selling to anyone else.

You choose when you want to shop and how long you want to spend doing it and no one can slow you down.

The third reason for shopping online is choice. It would simply not be possible to go round and find in the shops the kind of comprehensive selection you can see almost instantly online, even if you had a month, which most of us don't. You can look at as many or as few products as you want and see the full details and specification for each and every one.

You may well find that in some cases there's too much choice. You'll certainly never be limited in the way that you can be in the shops.

Finally the fourth reason for shopping online is price. As I've already said, the high street stores can very rarely compete (although they're now trying very hard), mainly because without an offline retail presence the overheads are so much lower and the cost benefit can be passed on to you.

Having said that, don't expect to buy your new pair of Gucci shoes cheaper on the internet than in the store. You can find lots of bargains for designer goods online but not (or very rarely) new season's collections. In terms of top quality fashion and accessories, convenience is what you get by buying online, not usually discounts.

Are you Secure?

You pay for just about everything you buy online with a credit card and before you hand this over you need to be sure of the following:

a) That the retailer you're buying from has a secure server.

b) That you can contact them if something goes wrong.

Most shopping sites use a kind of virtual shopping basket into which you can place what you want to buy and then take it to the checkout when you've finished. You'll need to be on a website that operates with a secure server to know that your details are safe.

To know that you're going into a secure server when you pay there'll be a key, or lock at the foot of your browser which will appear locked when you've clicked on 'checkout'. At the same time your retailer's web address will change from *http://www* to *https://www*. This shows that the site is secure. It also shows you that your credit card details will be encrypted between your computer and the retailer's server.

If none of this happens give the retailer a call to check before you hand over your credit card details. If in any doubt, don't buy.

Just to demonstrate, click on to *www.thewhitecompany.com* next time you're online and place something in your shopping basket. Then click on 'checkout'. You'll immediately see the tiny closed padlock in the bottom right hand corner of your screen (browser), and the address line change to https. That's what you're looking for from now on.

Website Information

The best websites will give you clear and easy categories and customer information (delivery, returns, contact info) right on the Home Page so you don't have to waste time clicking through long flash intros which slow down your search for that perfect product. After all, you're interested in buying from them, not seeing endless images for products you don't want.

Just for example, take a look at *www.eluxury.com* and *www.neimanmarcus.com*, two top US websites offering every designer from Marc Jacobs to Manolo Blahnik with Louis Vuitton and Christian Dior in between. There they are on the front page, ready and waiting for you to browse and buy with clear information about delivery, returns and every other question you can think of just one single click away. No 'clever' flash intros, no extra Home Page; no nonsense, just straight to what you want to buy.

Using this Book

All the websites included in the guide have been looked at carefully not only for the service and products they offer, but also for how easy the retailers make it for you to shop.

For almost every website you'll find something like the following:

Site Usability:	★★★★★	Based:	UK
Product Range:	★★★★★	Express Delivery Option?	(UK) Yes
Price Range:	Luxury/<u>Medium</u>/Very Good Value	Gift Wrapping Option?	Yes
Delivery Area:	Worldwide	Returns Procedure:	Down to you

In all cases the stars range from ★★★★★ to ★★★ and I'll explain as follows:

Site Usability:

How quick and easy is it for you to click round the website and get to the products you're looking for?

How quickly can you get to information on delivery, returns, whether or not gift wrapping is offered and how to contact the retailer?

Are the pictures clear and attractive?

Is there adequate information about every product offered?

Product Range:

How much choice there is on the website. Fewer stars here do not mean a lower quality product, just a smaller range.

Price Range:

This is just a guide so you know what to expect.

Delivery area:

Does the retailer deliver to the UK, EU Countries or Worldwide?

Based:

This tells you where the retailer is based, so you'll know straight away if you're going to be charged for duty or extra shipping costs.

Express Delivery Option:

Can you have your order tomorrow? Some websites are very quick anyway but this is specifically for where next day or express service is offered, usually within the country where the retailer is based.

Gift Wrapping Option:

Do they or don't they?

Returns Procedure:

'Down to you' means you pack it up and pay to send it back.

'Free' means just that and they may even collect it from you.

'Complicated' means that they want you to call them and tell them you're sending your order back. This normally only applies where the product you've ordered is particularly valuable.

More about returns below.

Returns

Are you put off by the thought of having to send something back? Well don't be. It's a fact of life with catalogue and online shopping and if you're not set up for it by now there are some shortcuts to make it easier.

Firstly, when you place an order either print out a copy of the confirmation (which will give you your order number and details) and keep it in a file or folder, or create a new email folder and then just drag the confirmations into it. This is much the easier option.

For example: In Outlook Express you could click on File at the top of the browser, then New, then Folder and call your new folder something like Web Orders. When you receive an email related to an outstanding order you've placed you left click on it, hold the left click button down and drag your email to your new folder.

In that way you'll keep everything together and know what you're waiting for and you'll have the links ready to use if you need to contact the retailer. Once your goods have arrived and you're happy with them you can delete the relevant email/s.

If this sounds a bore I promise you that it's not. It's quick and easy and if you have a problem or question you won't need to revisit the website, you can just click on 'reply' or their email link to contact them.

Here are some tips that will make returns much easier:

1 Always keep the packaging that your goods arrive in, just in case, plus the returns form and instructions that should be with it.
2 Keep a few large padded envelopes at home plus some wide packing tape and a black permanent marker.
3 On your next visit to the Post Office take some of the Recorded Delivery slips so you can, if you need to, fill them in at home and save time later.
4 Keep a file of your returns slips to secure them in one place and throw them out once you know that you've received your refund/replacement.

There are some retailers who ask you to phone them or fill in a form before returning goods to them. If this is the case I have marked them as returns: complicated. It's a bore but it usually means that the item you're returning is of particular value, and it's important you follow the instructions you're given to make sure you get your exchange/credit.

Rejoice when a retailer offers free returns. Hopefully this will become the norm. After all, the better the service, the more we'll buy from them.

Some facts and figures

Everyone remembers *boo.com*. Huge investment: Huge publicity: Huge crash.

That was just one example of what happened roughly seven years ago. 'It's over', everyone said. 'The dot.com bubble has burst'. It's the end.

Well how wrong could they be? Ok it took a while to come back and get going again but the dot.com boom is now unstoppable.

Take a look at these figures:

In the US, where web shopping got going much earlier than in the UK, online retail shopping now accounts for approximately 9% of the total market. It's expected that there will be a 20% growth in 2006 over the previous year, taking the online retail sales spend to over $200 billion.

In the UK, with a far smaller market, it's expected that 10% of all retail sales will be placed online in

2006, totalling over £30 billion, or a 56% increase over the £19.2 billion spent in 2005 (IMRG). This compares with offline retail which is practically at a standstill.

As potential online customers become more confident about security, as more retailers offer their goods online and online services improve; such as price comparison availability, express delivery and worldwide shipping, there will be more and more reasons to shop online. Add to this the improving speed of broadband connections (not to mention the increase in the numbers of homes with broadband rather than dial-up connections) and you can understand why the above growth will continue.

It has to be said that bricks and mortar retailers who have not yet jumped on the web shopping bandwagon are almost certainly going to be left behind.

So as you can see, retail online is no longer a bubble, it's a behemoth and it's definitely coming your way. Are you ready for it?

Section 1

Fashion at a Click

This, without doubt, is an area of online shopping that from a slow start is going to grow and grow. Now that luxury brands Gucci, Tiffany and Louis Vuitton are all online plus high street brands such as River Island, Topshop and French Connection more retailers must surely follow. The high street retailers are definitely ahead here and you can find some excellent basics and 'one season' fashion pieces from their cleverly designed websites.

At the top end of the market you can see a marked and surprising difference in the quality of the websites and the photographs. Some 'designer' retailers have gone to tremendous trouble to show you several views of each carefully pictured item, including close-up detail, which makes it much easier to make your decision to buy. Their websites are really beautifully designed. Others expect you to spend hundreds of pounds on a dress that looks as if it's been photographed in a slightly darkened room. Hopefully these will improve soon.

Just a note on buying from websites not based in your country: You will almost certainly have to pay duty. Shipping is unbelievably fast and many orders arrive in four or five days. I've given you information about the international sizing differentials and be warned. When I say the sizing is small it means the sizing is small so SIZE UP. Needless to say it usually depends on the type of garment you order. Don't be put off by this.

The hardest things of all to fit are dresses, because they have to be right all the way up. You're most likely to have to send those back unless you already know the retailer and your correct size. Next are skirts and trousers. Easiest are loose fitting items (of course) and best are tops, t-shirts and knitwear.

Now it's totally up to you. If you want to choose something up to the minute and excellent value from a store such as Mango or Warehouse you can. And if you want to go for broke and buy that absolutely mouthwatering caramel Boogie bag by Celine you can do that too. Happy Shopping. Yes you guessed it. I'm after that one.

Chapter 1

LuxuryBrands Online

If you thought you'd save money by staying at home and avoiding Harvey Nichols, Bond Street, Knightsbridge and the rest, you can forget it. Rejoice in the fact that luxury brand accessories from labels such as Tods, Celine and Marc Jacobs are now available online together with Tiffany, Gucci, Mulberry, Louis Vuitton, Blumarine, Missoni, Marni, Max Mara and many other mainstream designers, just waiting for you to click through to their websites.

Having said all that, the 'Superbrands', particularly outside the US, are being slow about putting themselves properly online (and when I say properly I mean so that you can buy from them directly). All praise to retailers such as Net-a-porter, Browns, Matches and Linea for enabling you to buy a selection from some top designers wherever you are in the world – you'll find the ranges available are growing all the time.

You can visit the luxury international brands at their expensively designed websites, such as *www.chanel.com*, *www.fendi.com*, *www.loewe.com* and *www.celine.com*, see the runway collections and find out where your nearest stockist is, but you can't buy anything online at the moment. Personally I think that this is totally understandable with the clothing collections, where fit would be extremely difficult and returns a nightmare, however, they could offer us their accessories, now couldn't they? Inevitably it will happen, so keep your fingers crossed and watch this space.

To find a particular designer go to the Quick Brand Directory at the back of this book and you'll see which websites they're available from. You'll find some online retailers offer the same designers, however the clothes they're offering online will almost certainly be different.

Sites to Visit

www.allegrahicks.com

This is, as you would expect, a really beautifully designed website offering some unusual and contemporary clothes and accessories designed by Allegra Hicks, who specialises in translating oriental themes into western style using strong organic patterns and colour. Her fashion collection is aimed at the woman who travels a lot and needs stylish clothes that can work in many climates, as well as travel and pack easily.

Site Usability:	★★★★	Based:	UK
Product Range:	★★★★	Express Delivery Option?	(UK) No
Price Range:	Luxury/Medium/Very Good Value	Gift Wrapping Option?	No
Delivery Area:	Worldwide	Returns Procedure:	Down to you

www.anyahindmarch.com

Anya Hindmarch's collection of beautiful, unique and sometimes quirky handbags and small accessories have long been glossy magazine fashion editor's favourites. They're totally different and very special, always carrying her signature bow logo somewhere whether they're on her clever picture bags or richly coloured leather tassled Marissa. Her chic Bespoke Ebury handbag is available in several colourways and is only made to order, with your personalised inscription inside. Alternatively go for Be a Bag, where you send the image of your choice which will then be used on one of her handbags.

Site Usability:	★★★★	Based:	UK
Product Range:	★★★	Express Delivery Option?	(UK) No
Price Range:	Luxury/Medium/Very Good Value	Gift Wrapping Option?	No
Delivery Area:	Worldwide	Returns Procedure:	Down to you

www.boodles.co.uk

Gorgeous modern jewellery: The real thing. Some things you might just imagine buying for yourself and others you'd probably rather have bought for you, like the divine Asscher cut diamond earrings that they don't even tell you the price of. Have a look round anyway, you might just be tempted. I should warn you though, there's almost nothing here for under £1000. Everything is gift wrapped and they'll ship all over the world.

Site Usability:	★★★★	Based:	UK
Product Range:	★★★★	Express Delivery Option?	(UK) Yes
Price Range:	Luxury/Medium/Very Good Value	Gift Wrapping Option?	Yes
Delivery Area:	Worldwide	Returns Procedure:	Down to you

www.brownsfashion.com

The new Browns website is not only very clear and easy to browse round but also offers a mouthwatering list of contemporary designers including Lanvin, Balenciaga, Missoni and Paul Smith plus Dolce & Gabbanna, Roberto Cavalli, Ann Demeulemeister and Issa. There are several views of each item plus lots of essential information and size charts. Look here too for your next Luella handbag fix (or Fendi or Marni) or pair of heels (Christian Louboutin or Marc Jacobs).

Site Usability:	★★★★	Based:	UK
Product Range:	★★★★	Express Delivery Option?	(UK) No
Price Range:	Luxury/Medium/Very Good Value	Gift Wrapping Option?	No
Delivery Area:	Worldwide	Returns Procedure:	Down to you and complicated

www.dunhill.com

In 1893 Alfred Dunhill inherited his father's saddlery business on London's Euston Road and developed a luxurious line of accessories. The first collection included car horns and lamps, leather overcoats, goggles, picnic sets and timepieces. Over a hundred years later Dunhill is one of the leading makers of English luxury accessories for men and here you can choose from their range which includes luggage, briefcases, washbags, wallets, diaries and belts, ties and cufflinks.

Site Usability:	★★★★	Based:	UK
Product Range:	★★★	Express Delivery Option?	(UK) No
Price Range:	Luxury/Medium/Very Good Value	Gift Wrapping Option?	No
Delivery Area:	UK	Returns Procedure:	Down to you

www.dvflondon.com

Diane von Furstenberg. How can you resist? Check out the latest arrivals in each new season's collection. Order one of her famous wrap dresses, skirts, tops or trousers and take a look at the catwalk pictures for this season or last. This is an extremely innovative website but when you take into account the style of the clothes on offer it works very well once you've learned how to get round it.

Site Usability:	★★★★	Based:	US
Product Range:	★★★	Express Delivery Option?	(UK) Yes
Price Range:	Luxury/Medium/Very Good Value	Gift Wrapping Option?	Yes
Delivery Area:	Worldwide	Returns Procedure:	Down to you/Complicated

www.escada.com

You'll probably be surprised at the range of clothes and accessories available on Escada's extremely pretty website where you'll find both the Escada and Escada Sport brands; from seriously beautiful and seriously expensive cocktail and evening dresses, skirts, jackets, shirts and knitwear to stylish sporty casualwear plus handbags, belts, small leather goods and fragrance. They'll be happy to gift wrap and send your order out on your behalf – if you can bear to give anything here away.

Site Usability:	★★★★★	Based:	EU
Product Range:	★★★★	Express Delivery Option?	(UK) No
Price Range:	Luxury/Medium/Very Good Value	Gift Wrapping Option?	Yes
Delivery Area:	EU	Returns Procedure:	Contact them to arrange

www.forzieri.com

Florence based Forzieri offers a wide range of products from some world famous designers such as Gucci, Miu Miu, Dolce and Gabbana, Fendi and Gianfranco Ferre and you can choose from the highest quality leather jackets and shoes, bags, briefcases and wallets, gloves, scarves, belts, jewellery and other accessories, all for both men and women. It's a beautifully laid out website and they'll deliver fast all over the world.

Site Usability:	★★★★★	Based:	Italy
Product Range:	★★★★★	Express Delivery Option?	(UK) Yes
Price Range:	Luxury/Medium/Very Good Value	Gift Wrapping Option?	Yes
Delivery Area:	Worldwide	Returns Procedure:	Down to you

www.gina.com

Gina was first established in 1954 and named after Gina Lollobridgida. Now it's run by the three Kurdash brothers (the sons of the founder, Mehmet Kurdash) who continue to design totally exquisite shoes, so if you want the couture look and a seriously special pair of shoes then click no further. Here you'll find a truly wonderful collection of beautiful, sexy shoes in the softest leather and with out-to-lunch and dinner heels. There's a price to match as you would expect, but the shoes are definitely worth it and they'll last a long time. You'll also find a small selection of handbags.

Site Usability:	★★★★	Based:	UK
Product Range:	★★★★	Express Delivery Option?	(UK) No
Price Range:	Luxury/Medium/Very Good Value	Gift Wrapping Option?	No
Delivery Area:	Worldwide	Returns Procedure:	Down to you

www.gucci.com

Leading the way for 'superbrand' designers to come online Gucci has opened up its website for online accessory orders. As you would expect the website is very modern and beautiful (and heartstoppingly expensive) and the products irresistible. You can buy handbags, luggage, men and women's shoes and gifts, such as key rings and lighters, on the site. Don't expect them to offer clothes, at least not for a while, as the fit would be very difficult and returns far too high.

Site Usability:	★★★★★	Express Delivery Option?	(UK) Yes
Product Range:	★★★★★	Gift Wrapping Option?	Yes/Automatic
Price Range:	Luxury/Medium/Very Good Value	Returns Procedure:	Down to you
Delivery Area:	Worldwide most places		

www.lineafashion.com

Linea started life as a boutique in London's Hampstead, offering designer wear from around the world. The shop is now online, with the range clearly photographed so you can see each item properly. Included are collections from international designers such as Blumarine, Celine, Etro, Gharani Strok, Juicy Couture, Missoni and Emanuel Ungaro, plus handbags and shoes by Hogan, Tods and Celine. If you're in a buying mood this could be a very dangerous site to visit.

Site Usability:	★★★★	Based:	UK
Product Range:	★★★★★	Express Delivery Option?	(UK) Yes
Price Range:	Luxury/Medium/Very Good Value	Gift Wrapping Option?	No
Delivery Area:	Worldwide	Returns Procedure:	Down to you/Complicated

www.louisvuitton.com

Louis Vuitton's unmistakable, chic and covetable (and luxuriously expensive) handbags are now available online directly through their quick and clear website. So you don't have to go into one of their stores anymore and ask for help and information, you'll find everything you could possibly need to know here, such as interior details, care and sizing. Once you've selected your country you'll find which styles are available to you; simply choose the design you like and go shop.

Site Usability:	★★★★★	Based:	UK
Product Range:	★★★★★	Express Delivery Option?	(UK) Yes
Price Range:	Luxury/Medium/Very Good Value	Gift Wrapping Option?	Automatic
Delivery Area:	Worldwide	Returns Procedure:	Down to you

www.luluguinness.com

'Be a glamour girl, put on your lipstick', is the phrase welcoming you to this elegant website, from which exquisite handbags and accessories from famous British designer Lulu Guinness can now be shipped to you wherever you are. With unique styling, sometimes very quirky, sometimes just plain gorgeous and a selection of cosmetic bags in stylish prints to take you anywhere, this is a website you should take a look at if you're in the mood for a treat or special gift.

Site Usability:	★★★★	Based:	UK
Product Range:	★★★	Express Delivery Option?	(UK) No
Price Range:	Luxury/Medium/Very Good Value	Gift Wrapping Option?	No but everything is beautifully packaged
Delivery Area:	Worldwide	Returns Procedure:	Down to you

www.matchesfashion.com

Luxury designer boutique Matches are famous for offering a unique, personal service together with a mouthwatering choice of designers such as Dolce & Gabbana, Bottega Veneta, Chloe, Christian Louboutin, Lanvin, Marc Jacobs, Missoni and Stella McCartney. You can now find this excellent service and the full range of designers online, where you can place your order directly through their website or search through their entire season's Lookbook, then call for availability when you find something you like. They'll be delighted to help you choose the essential pieces for each season.

Site Usability:	★★★★★	Based:	UK
Product Range:	★★★★	Express Delivery Option?	(UK) Yes
Price Range:	Luxury/Medium/Very Good Value	Gift Wrapping Option?	Yes
Delivery Area:	Worldwide	Returns Procedure:	Down to you

www.mikimoto-store.co.uk

Mikimoto is a name synonymous with beautiful and luxurious pearls (they've been in business for over 100 years) and now you can buy a selection of their best selling jewellery online. Prices start at around £120 for a pair of timeless pearl studs, and go up to around £2000 for their Tahitian pearl and pink sapphire pendants and earrings. Everything is beautifully gift wrapped and you can have your order within 48 hours.

Site Usability:	★★★★★	Based:	UK
Product Range:	★★★	Express Delivery Option?	(UK) Yes
Price Range:	Luxury/Medium/Very Good Value	Gift Wrapping Option?	Yes
Delivery Area:	Worldwide	Returns Procedure:	Down to you

www.mulberry.com

Mulberry's style signatures, of soft vegetable dyed leather, characterful detailing and robust hard wear haven't changed, but the designs certainly have under design director Stuart Vevers who creates beautiful modern handbags in colourful leathers and with fine detailing. Although the Roxanne is now Mulberry's fashion classic handbag – always available in seasonal colours, the shapes become more contemporary each season with the introduction of stylish designs, deep new colours and interesting trims. Buy one if you can.

Site Usability:	★★★★★	Based:	UK
Product Range:	★★★★	Express Delivery Option?	(UK) No
Price Range:	Luxury/Medium/Very Good Value	Gift Wrapping Option?	No
Delivery Area:	Worldwide	Returns Procedure:	Down to you

www.net-a-porter.com

This is the uber fashionista's website, where you'll find the most impressive range of designer clothes and accessories available online, and a retailer that's becoming increasingly well known for its clever buying, excellent service and attractive packaging. So if you're looking for something special with a designer label, such as Marc Jacobs, Alexander McQueen, Burberry, Roland Mouret, Alberta Feretti, Marni, Jimmy Choo or Paul Smith (the list goes on and on) you should definitely have a look here.

Site Usability:	★★★★★	Based:	UK
Product Range:	★★★★★	Express Delivery Option?	(UK) Yes
Price Range:	Luxury/Medium/Very Good Value	Gift Wrapping Option?	Yes
Delivery Area:	Worldwide	Returns Procedure:	Free using their DHL service

www.paulsmith.co.uk

One of the most successful and internationally well known British designers, with several collections including Paul Smith Black, Jeans and fragrance, his website is, as you would probably expect, different and idiosyncratic. Here you'll find a selection of his jeans, shoes, knitwear, t-shirts, and accessories plus a small amount of tailoring, and there are several clear views of each item. This is also a great place for gifts for Paul Smith fans.

Site Usability:	★★★★★	Based:	UK
Product Range:	★★★★	Express Delivery Option?	(UK) Yes
Price Range:	Luxury/Medium/Very Good Value	Gift Wrapping Option?	Yes
Delivery Area:	Worldwide	Returns Procedure:	Down to you.

www.smythson.com

Smythson is famous as the Bond Street purveyors, for over a century, of absolutely top quality personalised stationery and accessories, including diaries, leather journals, albums and frames and gold edged place cards. They also have a luxurious small collection of briefcases, wallets and small leather goods at totally frightening prices. They'll ship to you anywhere in the world. You need to allow 21 days for delivery unless you need something urgently, in which case call them.

Site Usability:	★★★★★	Based:	UK
Product Range:	★★★★	Express Delivery Option?	(UK) No
Price Range:	Luxury/Medium/Very Good Value	Gift Wrapping Option?	No
Delivery Area:	Worldwide	Returns Procedure:	Down to you

www.tannerkrolle.co.uk

Tanner Krolle, launched in 1856, is one of London's oldest and finest luxury leather goods houses and all of the brand's bespoke bridle leather pieces are still hand-crafted in London. In addition to their traditional luggage Tanner Krolle also produces beautiful handbags, shoes and small leather goods. You need to call 0207 823 1688 to order and you can expect excellent service.

Site Usability:	★★★★	Based:	UK
Product Range:	★★★	Express Delivery Option?	(UK) Yes
Price Range:	Luxury/Medium/Very Good Value	Gift Wrapping Option?	No but luxury packaging is standard
Delivery Area:	Worldwide	Returns Procedure:	Down to you

www.theofennell.com

Theo Fennell is famous as the jewellery designer of stars such as Elton John. His modern diamond studded crosses and keys are recognised the world over, together with his solid silver Marmite lids and Worcester Sauce bottle holders. Nothing on this website is inexpensive but you'll find some extremely beautiful and unique designs, and if you buy anything you can be sure it will be exquisitely presented. Browse the site and see if you're tempted.

Site Usability:	★★★	Based:	UK
Product Range:	★★★★	Express Delivery Option?	(UK) No
Price Range:	Luxury/Medium/Very Good Value	Gift Wrapping Option?	Yes
Delivery Area:	Worldwide	Returns Procedure:	Down to you

www.tiffany.com

Exquisite and expensive: The two words that sum up one of the World's most luxurious jewellery emporiums. Anything in the signature Tiffany blue box is sure to make a perfect present, from the smallest piece of Elsa Peretti or Paloma Picasso jewellery to wonderful classic diamonds and pearls. Beautiful Tiffany glass candlesticks, bowls and stemware, the new Tiffany fragrance in its lovely glass bottle or christening gifts for a new baby, it's all available online.

Site Usability:	★★★★★	Based:	UK
Product Range:	★★★★★	Express Delivery Option?	(UK) Yes
Price Range:	Luxury/Medium/Very Good Value	Gift Wrapping Option?	Yes/Automatic
Delivery Area:	UK and USA	Returns Procedure:	Down to you

Chapter 2

General Fashion Online

The Boutiques   Fashion Retailers

Here the choice is much, much better (and improving constantly) and you can buy your complete new season's wardrobe without ever having to leave home. You may choose to buy your basics online and your special items in the shops, but you don't have to. There's enough selection here so that if you're too busy at work to go out shopping for clothes, you live far away from the shops or you want to be able to shop in peace without your three young children beside you, you can, because online you can shop at any time of day or night.

Somewhere between the luxury brands and the high street stand a wealth of fashion choices, some from retailers who operate only as mail order and others who have retail outlets as well, so if you don't want to pay top brand designer prices, nor do you want to shop in the High Street, then this is definitely the place for you. Most of them will ship worldwide.

The beauty of this is also that you can pick and choose from several retailers within a very short space of time. You can buy your basics from *www.marksandspencer.com* or *www.landsend.co.uk* and then move swiftly on to more individual websites such as *www.peruvianconnection.com*, *www.pantalonchameleon.com* and *www.artigiano.co.uk* where you'll find the pieces to put your new look together.

Then you can buy your 'I can't live without it' handbag from Gucci in Luxury Brands and your 'this season only' fashion pieces from High Street retailer Top Shop. Having had a good look round at what's available you'll know where you can find the perfect shoes to pull everything together (*www.paulsmith.co.uk* maybe) and you can order those too. Can't resist those up to the minute Jimmy Choo or Gina sandals? Go for it.

Just a word about sizing: I'm sure that you're fully aware that there is no standard sizing for clothing retailers (even though they try and tell us there is). Having worked in the fashion industry for some years it always amazed me how every single retailer is slightly different and not only that, they'll be different from season to season (and in the worst cases from garment to garment). The best way to avoid having to send clothes back is to know your measurements, check the measurements in the retailer's sizing charts and then allow a little.

It seems to work out that the younger the age group the retailer is aiming at; the smaller the sizing. Don't let this put you off, however. Another of the joys of buying online is that you don't have to trek back to the shop if you want to send something back, nor do you have to make a feeble excuse as you meet the steely gaze of the shop assistant or manager, who really doesn't want your clothes back and may treat you a bit like a criminal. Returns are just an everyday part of buying online and most of the time they couldn't be easier.

The Boutiques

The small online boutiques, who are usually beautiful small offline boutiques as well, tend to offer a highly edited selection of delectable clothes and accessories and often some lifestyle products as well. They're extremely hard to find if you don't know where to look, but well worth a browse through for pretty and unusual pieces.

You'll usually find that everything has a specific handwriting which is a result of all the pieces being selected by just one person (very often the boutique owner), so you'll find quirky, stylish and contemporary or retro collections at each boutique, all following the same theme. You'll either love it or not. One of the great things here is that you can put your whole look together, or just select a single piece to give a new feel to what you already own (and then wait for everyone to ask where you found it).

Don't forget that these are not places where the stock is constantly replenished. If you find something you like, snap it up. It may not be there next week (or tomorrow even) and there's nothing more annoying then to have seen something, waited a couple of days to buy and then found it's gone for good, and you probably won't find it anywhere else. Buy it straight away – you can always return it.

These are also very good places to find special gifts for your fashionista friend, an unusual scarf perhaps, or a beaded buckle belt. Will you tell her where you found it or keep it a secret? Of course, it's up to you.

Take a look through the websites opposite and see if you're tempted.

Sites to Visit

www.anusha.co.uk

Here's a boudoir style online boutique where you can buy pretty and indulgent designer pieces, from clothes, luxurious loungewear, vintage-inspired jewellery and unique accessories to pampering gifts. When your order arrives it'll be beautifully wrapped in layers of fuchsia tissue paper and finished off with a feather butterfly and chocolate brown Anusha label. So come here for a treat for yourself or perfect presents. They deliver worldwide and in the UK you need to allow five to seven days.

Site Usability:	★★★★	Based:	UK
Product Range:	★★★	Express Delivery Option?	(UK) No
Price Range:	Luxury/Medium/Very Good Value	Gift Wrapping Option?	Yes
Delivery Area:	Worldwide	Returns Procedure:	Down to you

www.boxinthepost.com

Box in the Post is a fashion mail order service and website boutique, delivering everything in a stylish yet simple box. Launched in Spring 2005, Box promises 'non High Street', original yet stunning clothes, an extremely friendly and efficient service and a personal touch with its customers. Run as a chic boutique, stock is updated all the time throughout the season so keep coming back to find something new.

Site Usability:	★★★★	Based:	UK
Product Range:	★★★	Express Delivery Option?	(UK) No
Price Range:	Luxury/Medium/Very Good Value	Gift Wrapping Option?	No
Delivery Area:	Worldwide	Returns Procedure:	Down to you

www.cocoribbon.com

Calling itself London's lifestyle boutique, Coco Ribbon offers a selection of contemporary clothing by designers such as Collette Dinnigan, Rebecca Taylor and Cynthia Vincent, pretty, modern lingerie and swimwear, a small but beautiful range of handbags and jewellery plus gorgeous and unusual girly gifts and candles. There's a lot to choose from here and the range is constantly updated so you need to return regularly for another browse.

Site Usability:	★★★★	Based:	UK
Product Range:	★★★★	Express Delivery Option?	(UK) Yes
Price Range:	Luxury/Medium/Very Good Value	Gift Wrapping Option?	Yes
Delivery Area:	Worldwide	Returns Procedure:	Down to you

www.little-london.com

Here you'll find a boutique style atmosphere trying to mirror that of the retailer's boutiques in the South of England with deep colours and gilt framed mirrors. It does take you quite a while to get to the clothes themselves but as they offer a selection by Max Mara, Issa London, Calvin Klein Jeans and Missoni to name but a few, and the range is growing all the time, it's worth a look round. Expect very good service.

Site Usability:	★★★		Based:	UK
Product Range:	★★★		Express Delivery Option?	(UK) Yes
Price Range:	Luxury/Medium/Very Good Value		Gift Wrapping Option?	Yes
Delivery Area:	Worldwide		Returns Procedure:	Down to you

www.max-oliver.co.uk

If you're in the mood for a visit to a small but beautiful boutique where you'll find unusual, personally chosen clothes, accessories and homewares you probably won't find anywhere else, then stop by here. Max Oliver is quite simply a treasure trove of beautiful French and vintage inspired pieces including dresses, skirts, jackets and coats, cushions, crockery and accessories and there are never large quantities of anything, so if you see something you like, snap it up fast.

Site Usability:	★★★		Based:	UK
Product Range:	★★★		Express Delivery Option?	(UK) No
Price Range:	Luxury/Medium/Very Good Value		Gift Wrapping Option?	No
Delivery Area:	Worldwide		Returns Procedure:	Down to you

www.my-wardrobe.com

This is a really well laid out designer clothing and accessories website (with lots of designers you'll have found it difficult to buy online before) including FrostFrench, Cacharel, Ann Louise Roswald, Sara Berman, Tocca and See by Chloe. For each item you can see several different views plus a close-up of details such as embroidery and prints and there's excellent description and commentary under 'My-Advice'. When you spot something you like they'll recommend other items to go with it.

Site Usability:	★★★★★		Based:	UK
Product Range:	★★★★		Express Delivery Option?	(UK) Yes
Price Range:	Luxury/Medium/Very Good Value		Gift Wrapping Option?	Automatic
Delivery Area:	Worldwide		Returns Procedure:	Free of Charge

www.noangel.co.uk

No Angel offers glamorous partywear, corsets, funky casualwear and a very good selection of evening footwear (from the inexpensive to designer prices) plus handbags and jewellery. At the moment the accessories are definitely the best part of the collection and, bearing in mind how hard it is to find a good choice of evening accessories online, you should take a look round. You can buy Gift Vouchers here as well and they ship only to the UK.

Site Usability:	★★★	Based:	UK
Product Range:	★★★	Express Delivery Option?	(UK) No
Price Range:	Luxury/<u>Medium</u>/Very Good Value	Gift Wrapping Option?	No
Delivery Area:	UK	Returns Procedure:	Down to you

www.pantalonchameleon.com

You'll discover colourful, dressy, modern and fun clothing from this unusual London boutique offering an individual collection you won't find anywhere else. They're particularly good if you have a special event to go to and you like long, pretty skirts which they match with embroidered tops and knitwear and some stunning shoes. You can finish off your outfit from their selection of beaded jewellery and other small accessories.

Site Usability:	★★★★★	Based:	UK
Product Range:	★★★★	Express Delivery Option?	(UK) Yes
Price Range:	Luxury/<u>Medium</u>/Very Good Value	Gift Wrapping Option?	No
Delivery Area:	Worldwide	Returns Procedure:	Down to you.

www.plumo.co.uk

At Plumo you'll always find something different and interesting, from a gold trimmed basket to a floral print tote. They also offer homeware, clothes and accessories including shoes and jewellery. It's not a huge collection but beautifully edited to be feminine and chic at the same time. There are some lovely gift ideas here as well and express delivery and gift wrapping are just two of the services offered.

Site Usability:	★★★★	Based:	UK
Product Range:	★★★	Express Delivery Option?	(UK) Yes
Price Range:	Luxury/<u>Medium</u>/Very Good Value	Gift Wrapping Option?	Yes
Delivery Area:	Worldwide	Returns Procedure:	Down to you.

www.shopatanna.com

With stores based in London, Norfolk & Suffolk, Anna is an innovative boutique offering clothes and accessories by Betty Jackson, Seven, Issa London, Orla Kiely, Gharani Strock and lesser known designers such as Day and Noa Noa. It's an eclectic and modern collection, combining elegance and quirkiness and the designers are being added to all the time, so keep checking back.

Site Usability:	★★★★★	Based:	UK
Product Range:	★★★★	Express Delivery Option?	(UK) Yes
Price Range:	<u>Luxury</u>/Medium/Very Good Value	Gift Wrapping Option?	Yes
Delivery Area:	Worldwide	Returns Procedure:	Down to you

www.voyage-paris.com

This is a pret-a-porter collection from Paris (though based in London) of modern dresses and separates in line with each season's fashion trends and regularly updated. You'll find unusual skirts and dressy tops plus some trousers and basics. If you want you can use the services of their 'celebrity stylist' (or personal shopper) to help you put your look together. You need to check back to see the new styles and don't delay if you want to order if you're over a size 12.

Site Usability:	★★★★	Based:	UK
Product Range:	★★★	Express Delivery Option?	(UK) No
Price Range:	Luxury/Medium/Very Good Value	Gift Wrapping Option?	No
Delivery Area:	UK	Returns Procedure:	Down to you

www.valentineandfrench.co.uk

At the Valentine and French boutique there's a treasure trove full of accessories, home treats and gift ideas such as glamorous clutch bags, unusual and beautifully fragranced body products, cashmere separates and pretty jewellery. This is a very attractively designed website and you'll discover all the products under headings such as 'Stepping Out', 'Staying In', 'Little Pleasures', and 'Jewellery Box'.

Site Usability:	★★★★	Based:	UK
Product Range:	★★★	Express Delivery Option?	(UK) No
Price Range:	Luxury/Medium/Very Good Value	Gift Wrapping Option?	No
Delivery Area:	Worldwide	Returns Procedure:	Down to you

Fashion Retailers

This is where you'll find all the fashion retailers with either a large presence offline (in other words, like Kew, a chain of stores, or alternatively a Mail Order catalogue such as Boden), or both and you'll probably have heard of most if not all of them. They're experienced at sending goods out to you, their websites are usually very well designed and the service speedy and helpful.

At most of these websites the collections will be continually updated, with stores such as Kew receiving deliveries throughout the season, so you need to keep checking back to see what's just come in. They'll also (usually) carry a greater number of each item, and reorder something that's popular when they see it going fast. Some websites are very good at telling you what's available, what's coming back into stock and when, for each item in each colour and size.

There's quite a range of online stores here, from the quirky French label APC, to Matches' idiosyncratic brand Freda, modern/classic Artigiano, colourful and fun Boden and unusual clothes at Evisu and a wide range of prices as well. The best for smart clothes are definitely Artigiano, Hobbs, Evening Dresses (as you'd expect) and Freda, but with everything from jeans to full length gowns you really need to sit down with your cup of coffee (or preferably glass of wine), at a time when you'll be undisturbed and have a good look through.

Sites to Visit

www.agnesb.com

You may not necessarily like the music they play you on this unusual but cleverly designed website but you can still buy your perfect fitted white shirts, superbly designed t-shirts and chic trousers here from this famous French designer offering addictive quality and cut. It isn't the easiest site to get round if you want to place a quick order but if you're an Agnes b addict (and there are many of them) then this is the place to be.

Site Usability:	★★★	Based:	France
Product Range:	★★★★	Express Delivery Option?	(UK) No
Price Range:	Luxury/Medium/Very Good Value	Gift Wrapping Option?	No
Delivery Area:	EU	Returns Procedure:	Down to you

www.apc.fr

You will need quite a fast Broadband connection to get the best out of this unusually designed French website offering high quality and well priced chic designer separates. Collections are offered as complete 'looks' from the outerwear to the basics. You see everything at once as if it's hanging in your cupboard then click on the individual items to buy. You'll find each new seasons essentials here as well as their jeans and accessories collections for men, women and children,

Site Usability:	★★★	Based:	France
Product Range:	★★★★	Express Delivery Option?	(UK) No
Price Range:	Luxury/Medium/Very Good Value	Gift Wrapping Option?	No
Delivery Area:	Worldwide	Returns Procedure:	Down to you

www.artigiano.co.uk

At Artigiano you could buy your whole wardrobe without even going to another website. The emphasis is fairly classic with shapes easy rather than very fitted and standard sizing (not small). You'll find lovely knitwear, from fine to chunky, excellent t-shirts and tops, trousers in a selection of styles and fabrics and unique jackets and outerwear you can't buy anywhere else. There's some very good leather and suede as well. The collection is updated four times a year.

Site Usability:	★★★★★	Based:	UK
Product Range:	★★★★	Express Delivery Option?	(UK) Yes
Price Range:	Luxury/Medium/Very Good Value	Gift Wrapping Option?	Yes
Delivery Area:	Worldwide	Returns Procedure:	Free using Royal Mail

www.boden.co.uk

It would be surprising if you hadn't already seen the Boden catalogue. It's everywhere, with Johnnie Boden's inimitable style (and commentary) all over it. Provided you like his colourful style the clothes have their own relaxed appeal which is popular with a lot of people. If you're into minimalist chic black don't go there. If you like your pinks, blues, greens and reds then certainly have a browse. There's a mini Boden and menswear as well.

Site Usability:	★★★★	Based:	UK
Product Range:	★★★★	Express Delivery Option?	(UK) Yes
Price Range:	Luxury/Medium/Very Good Value	Gift Wrapping Option?	No
Delivery Area:	Worldwide	Returns Procedure:	Down to you

www.eveningdresses.co.uk

This is a large collection of classic, elegant, full length and cocktail dresses ranging in price from around £150 to £700. The main collection shown is held in stock and provided they have your chosen colour and size they'll rush it to you by express delivery, so the next time you have a special event to go to and no time to shop you don't need to panic. Alongside their own collection they offer dresses by Alfred Sung and Dessy which can take longer to deliver.

Site Usability:	★★★★	Based:	UK
Product Range:	★★★★	Express Delivery Option?	(UK) Yes if dress is in stock
Price Range:	Luxury/Medium/Very Good Value	Gift Wrapping Option?	No
Delivery Area:	Worldwide	Returns Procedure:	Down to you

www.evisu.com

Evisu is the brainchild of Japanese jean junkie Yamane who came up with the idea in the 1980s to use reconditioned sewing machines and make new 'vintage style' jeans with old Japanese handicraft traditions. Every pair of Evisu jeans is made from 100% Japanese indigo dyed denim and features 23 details which makes each pair unique. In the really fun and funky online store there are all the Evisu ranges including Heritage, Donna, Mens Mainline, Evisu (European Edition), Kizzu and Shoos.

Site Usability:	★★★★	Based:	UK
Product Range:	★★★	Express Delivery Option?	(UK) No
Price Range:	Luxury/Medium/Very Good Value	Gift Wrapping Option?	No
Delivery Area:	Worldwide	Returns Procedure:	Down to you

www.fredafashion.com

You'll no doubt be delighted to know that top designer store Matches of Wimbledon has now launched its own collection online, with a beautifully finished and wearable selection of each season's essentials, including chic coats, jackets, skirts, trousers, tops and knitwear, all beautifully in line with fashion's latest trends and all of which you'll probably want to buy immediately. Sizes are from 8–14.

Site Usability:	★★★★	Based:	UK
Product Range:	★★★★	Express Delivery Option?	(UK) Yes
Price Range:	Luxury/Medium/Very Good Value	Gift Wrapping Option?	Automatic
Delivery Area:	Worldwide	Returns Procedure:	Down to you

www.hobbs.co.uk

You may well already have shopped at Hobbs, for beautifully cut workwear, chic eveningwear or casual separates (not to mention their wide collection of shoes). You'll no doubt be pleased to learn that they're now offering an ordering facility on their website. All the items are put together as outfits so you can clearly see what works together and wherever you click, you'll get the details for that particular piece, whether it's a scarf, dress, cardigan or pair of shoes plus the size and colour choices. It's an excellent collection and delivery takes about three days.

Site Usability:	★★★★★	Based:	UK
Product Range:	★★★★	Express Delivery Option?	(UK) No
Price Range:	Luxury/Medium/Very Good Value	Gift Wrapping Option?	No
Delivery Area:	UK	Returns Procedure:	Down to you

www.landsend.co.uk

This famous mail order company originated in the US and offers a wide range of high quality and well priced casual and classic clothing and accessories all over the World. They're very good for outerwear such as fleece and parkas and you can be sure that you'll get value for money, good quality and great service. They also offer some very well priced cashmere in a range of colours.

Site Usability:	★★★★★	Based:	UK (this website)
Product Range:	★★★★★	Express Delivery Option?	(UK) Yes
Price Range:	Luxury/Medium/Very Good Value	Gift Wrapping Option?	Yes
Delivery Area:	Worldwide	Returns Procedure:	Down to you

www.lauraashley.com

Becoming more up to date by the day (although still retaining some of the feminine influences we've come to associate with this long standing retailer), at Laura Ashley there are some really good tops and knitwear, shirts, skirts, trousers and accessories. Alongside this, and possibly the strongest part of the website, is the home accessories and furniture section, where you can choose everything from pretty gift ideas to handcrafted cabinet furniture and lots of decorating advice.

Site Usability:	★★★	Based:	UK
Product Range:	★★★	Express Delivery Option?	(UK) No
Price Range:	Luxury/Medium/Very Good Value	Gift Wrapping Option?	No
Delivery Area:	UK but there are Global sites as well	Returns Procedure:	Down to you

www.orvis.co.uk

Originally a company specialising in fishing equipment, Orvis have now developed their brand to offer a full clothing and accessories range for men and women. You'll find a high quality classic range here from Donegal tweed jackets to quilted, microfibre coats plus knitwear, shirts, polos, t-shirts and accessories, all in a wide choice of colours. There's hardwearing footwear here too plus the Barbour Collection.

Site Usability:	★★★★★	Based:	UK (this website)
Product Range:	★★★★★	Express Delivery Option?	(UK) Yes
Price Range:	Luxury/<u>Medium</u>/Very Good Value	Gift Wrapping Option?	Yes
Delivery Area:	Worldwide	Returns Procedure:	Down to you

www.poetrycollection.co.uk

Poetry is a new, fresh collection of clothing online, offering a very good selection of tops and fine knitwear in a modern range of colours, tailoring, pretty skirts and dresses, all using mainly natural fibres. The prices are reasonable and sizes go from 10 to 24 in just about everything. This is a beautifully photographed and easy to get round website, and you can see several different pictures of everything offered.

Site Usability:	★★★★★	Based:	UK
Product Range:	★★★★	Express Delivery Option?	(UK) Yes
Price Range:	Luxury/<u>Medium</u>/Very Good Value	Gift Wrapping Option?	No
Delivery Area:	EU	Returns Procedure:	Down to you

www.peruvianconnection.com

Each season Peruvian Connection offers a richly photographed collection of ethnic style separates (with some classics) using Peruvian alpaca and jewel coloured pima cotton. The look is very elegant, matching their unusually coloured tops and fine knitwear with gorgeously patterned skirts. They also offer specialist patterned jackets and sweaters, and lovely beaded jewellery plus scarves and bags. You'll find excellent quality with quite steep prices.

Site Usability:	★★★★★	Based:	UK
Product Range:	★★★★	Express Delivery Option?	(UK) Yes
Price Range:	<u>Luxury</u>/<u>Medium</u>/Very Good Value	Gift Wrapping Option?	Yes
Delivery Area:	Worldwide	Returns Procedure:	Down to you

www.sunandsand.co.uk

This is a great t-shirt store, offering a wide range of colours and styles, all in high quality natural cotton with everything from boat necks and scoop necks to this season's must-have nautical stripes (and even these in several different shapes). Prices are not cheap, expect to pay upwards of £27 for a basic short sleeved tee, but you know that the quality you'll be getting will be excellent. The website is very simply designed and there's little information about their services.

Site Usability:	★★★	Based:	UK
Product Range:	★★★	Express Delivery Option?	(UK) No
Price Range:	Luxury/<u>Medium</u>/Very Good Value	Gift Wrapping Option?	No
Delivery Area:	UK	Returns Procedure:	Down to you

www.thelinenpress.co.uk

As far as linen clothing goes I think there are two sorts of people, those who love it and those who don't. It is a pain to iron usually and always creases the minute you put it on (but then it's supposed to, isn't it?), but at least you can now find linen that washes beautifully and doesn't shrink as it used to. The Linen Press have a range of men's and women's clothing in soft, wearable twill weave, fine garment washed linen, natural cotton stretch baby cord and fleecy pure cotton.

Site Usability:	★★★	Based:	UK
Product Range:	★★★	Express Delivery Option?	(UK) No
Price Range:	Luxury/<u>Medium</u>/Very Good Value	Gift Wrapping Option?	No
Delivery Area:	Worldwide	Returns Procedure:	Down to you

www.toastbypost.co.uk

Toast has long been well known for simple, beautifully made clothes in natural colours and natural fabrics – the range of separates includes skirts, tops, knitwear and trousers and you'll also find nightwear and gowns, beachwear and a small collection of bed linen. Don't expect lots of bright colours here, you won't find them. This designer is about quiet, easy style. Their photographs are really beautiful and they offer still life pictures as well as model pics which is extremely helpful.

Site Usability:	★★★★	Based:	UK
Product Range:	★★★	Express Delivery Option?	(UK) No
Price Range:	Luxury/<u>Medium</u>/Very Good Value	Gift Wrapping Option?	Yes
Delivery Area:	Worldwide	Returns Procedure:	Down to you

www.trehearneandbrar.com

This must surely be the most beautiful collection of pashminas and shawls available. Don't expect cheap prices here and don't expect to be able to see them all online, either. You need to email them or call for a brochure. (Hopefully they'll be online soon although it would be very difficult to show their constantly changing range). Their collection includes plain, dyed to order, lined and reversible shawls, plus blankets and exquisite beaded shawls and all are of the best quality you can find.

Site Usability:	★★★	Based:	UK
Product Range:	★★★	Express Delivery Option?	(UK) No
Price Range:	<u>Luxury</u>/Medium/Very Good Value	Gift Wrapping Option?	No
Delivery Area:	Worldwide	Returns Procedure:	Down to you

www.wallcatalogue.com

If you haven't already heard of Wall but you like beautifully made, easy to wear clothing in unusual fabrics, then you should take a good look at this well photographed website. It's a very different and attractive range of modern flattering separates in muted colours such as barley, oyster, pale grey and black, of course, for winter. The clothes aren't inexpensive but you're buying into real quality and the service is excellent.

Site Usability:	★★★★★	Based:	UK
Product Range:	★★★★	Express Delivery Option?	(UK) No
Price Range:	Luxury/Medium/Very Good Value	Gift Wrapping Option?	No
Delivery Area:	Worldwide	Returns Procedure:	Down to you

www.wraponline.co.uk

At Wrap you'll find modern separates in each season's colours attractively photographed on real models so you can not only see the clothes very well but there's lots of atmosphere too. There's always a very good selection of tops, knitwear, trousers and skirts using mainly natural yarns such as cotton, silk and cashmere and you can see how they all work together. You can also tell at a glance whether what you want to order is in stock or not. Check out the new accessory range of casual bags and belts. There are separate websites for the UK, USA and Germany.

Site Usability:	★★★★	Based:	UK
Product Range:	★★★★	Express Delivery Option?	(UK) Yes
Price Range:	Luxury/Medium/Very Good Value	Gift Wrapping Option?	No
Delivery Area:	Worldwide	Returns Procedure:	Down to you

Chapter 3

Knitwear Store

There are some excellent online retailers who sell only knitwear, frequently cashmere and cashmere blends and the competition is fierce so you can find some really good prices too. Don't be deceived, however, like everything else you get what you pay for and if you want something that's going to last season after season you'll probably have to pay a bit more.

You'll find everything from extremely chic and contemporary styling from retailers such as Brora and Pure Collection with the prettiest colours to choose from, to very classic, often Scottish based classic cashmere retailers offering you the staple designs of V neck, crew neck or round neck cardigans for men and woman. All these are usually excellent and it totally depends on what sort of look you want.

Some of the fashion retailers mentioned before also have very good collections of knitwear and cashmere, so you should have a look through there as well, particularly as they usually work in with the overall colours of their collections each season. In particular look at Hobbs, Kew and Poetry Collection for stylish, well made and not overpriced knits.

Just a note for the shopaholic: You'll probably have great difficulty here if you're intending to just buy for someone else so prepare to be tempted. Don't say I didn't warn you.

Sites to Visit

www.belindarobertson.com

Award winning Belinda Dickson is a knitwear designer whose international reputation for quality, colour and modern eclectic style has earned her the affectionate title of 'Queen of Cashmere'. On her website you'll find her two different labels, the White Label collection, offering affordable but beautifully designed cashmere and her signature 'Cashmere Couture' range of the finest cashmere, made exclusively in Scotland, and sparkling with Swarovski crystals and satin trims, all available in up to 120 colours.

Site Usability:	★★★★	Based:	UK
Product Range:	★★★★	Express Delivery Option?	(UK) Yes
Price Range:	Luxury/Medium/Very Good Value	Gift Wrapping Option?	Yes
Delivery Area:	Worldwide	Returns Procedure:	Down to you

www.brora.co.uk

Brora was established in 1992 with the aim of offering classic fine quality Scottish cashmere with a contemporary twist, with prices that offer real value for money. Although they are now definitely not the cheapest they offer some of the best quality available, and in designs and a selection of colours that you won't find anywhere else. The pictures are beautifully clear and you'll find them hard to resist. The collection extends to men, children and babies.

Site Usability:	★★★★★	Based:	UK
Product Range:	★★★★	Express Delivery Option?	(UK) Yes
Price Range:	Luxury/Medium/Very Good Value	Gift Wrapping Option?	Yes
Delivery Area:	Worldwide	Returns Procedure:	Down to you

www.cashu.co.uk

Here's cashmere for men and women at quite irresistible prices and a very attractive range of colours where you'll find fine, v neck cardigans for £57 and ballet wraps for £69. At these prices this website is certainly worth a browse. How do they do it? According to them it's because they're buying direct from the manufacturer and only offering the range online. Obviously you're not paying for the highest grade of cashmere here but at these prices you should have a look.

Site Usability:	★★★★	Based:	UK
Product Range:	★★★	Express Delivery Option?	(UK) No
Price Range:	Luxury/Medium/Very Good Value	Gift Wrapping Option?	No
Delivery Area:	UK	Returns Procedure:	Down to you

www.designsoncashmere.com

This company is based in Edinburgh and offers real Scottish, mostly two ply cashmere so the prices will be more than on some other websites offering single ply cashmere sourced overseas. The styles are mostly classic and the range of colours isn't huge but if you want your cashmere to come from Scotland this could be the place to buy. They'll ship to you all over the world, shipping is free (worldwide) and they offer a currency converter if you're ordering from overseas.

Site Usability:	★★★★	Based:	UK	
Product Range:	★★★	Express Delivery Option?	(UK) No but Worldwide delivery is free	
Price Range:	Luxury/Medium/Very Good Value	Gift Wrapping Option?	No	
Delivery Area:	Worldwide	Returns Procedure:	Down to you	

www.eric-bompard.com

French knitwear retailer Eric Bompard offers a really pretty and unusual collection with chic styling and some different colours. Remember to click on the tiny Union Jack in the bottom right hand corner unless your French is very good. They have some very attractive designs in a wide range of colours that you won't find anywhere else so do have a look here. They'll ship to anywhere in the EU and you need to allow 6–8 days for delivery.

Site Usability:	★★★★★	Based:	France	
Product Range:	★★★★	Express Delivery Option?	(UK) No	
Price Range:	Luxury/Medium/Very Good Value	Gift Wrapping Option?	No	
Delivery Area:	EU	Returns Procedure:	Down to you	

www.johnsmedley.com

John Smedley is a family owned business originally established in 1784 and specialises in the highest quality fine gauge knitwear. It's definitely expensive but unbeatable for quality and fit, and whether you want a simple shell to wear underneath a jacket or a modern cut fine merino cableknit top with the perfect neckline and three quarter sleeves; it's better to buy just one piece from here than several cheaper versions. Buy two if you can. You really won't regret it.

Site Usability:	★★★★	Based:	UK	
Product Range:	★★★	Express Delivery Option?	(UK) No	
Price Range:	Luxury/Medium/Very Good Value	Gift Wrapping Option?	No	
Delivery Area:	Worldwide	Returns Procedure:	Down to you	

www.claireid.com

A site with a really different, fun and quirky feel offering modern pure cotton knitwear in unusual styles and a good range of colours. There's a made to measure bespoke service offered plus a colour advisory service. Some of the pictures are at strange angles which makes it hard to see the products clearly (which is a shame), but everything is designed to be easy to wear and sizing goes from 8 to 24, so whatever your size or shape (or if you're expecting) you may well find something.

Site Usability:	★★★★	Based:	UK
Product Range:	★★★	Express Delivery Option?	(UK) No
Price Range:	Luxury/Medium/Very Good Value	Gift Wrapping Option?	No
Delivery Area:	Worldwide	Returns Procedure:	Down to you

www.npealworks.com

Here's beautiful soft cashmere in modern designs and colours. Well priced as well. If you've never visited N Peal's shop at the bottom of Burlington Arcade and you love cashmere (don't we all?) you should certainly have a look round their website, which is beautifully designed, clean and clear and extremely tempting. Their aim is to despatch everything within 48 hours of receiving your order and they'll send to anywhere in the World. They also offer a specialist cashmere cleaning and mending service.

Site Usability:	★★★★★	Based:	UK
Product Range:	★★★	Express Delivery Option?	(UK) No
Price Range:	Luxury/Medium/Very Good Value	Gift Wrapping Option?	No
Delivery Area:	Worldwide	Returns Procedure:	Down to you

www.purecollection.com

This is chic, high quality cashmere in a wide range of styles with the emphasis on modern shapes and new season's colours. Alongside their less expensive range they also offer 'Superfine' cashmere at a higher price which is perfect for layering or wearing on its own. The delivery and service are excellent and the prices are very good too. If you want something particular in a hurry call to make sure it's in stock and you can have it the next day.

Site Usability:	★★★★★	Based:	UK
Product Range:	★★★★	Express Delivery Option?	(UK) Yes
Price Range:	Luxury/Medium/Very Good Value	Gift Wrapping Option?	Yes
Delivery Area:	Worldwide	Returns Procedure:	Free

Also check out these websites for knitwear

Website Address	You'll find it in
www.ctshirts.co.uk	Mens shirts, ties and Accessories
www.thewhitecompany.com	In The Bedroom

Chapter 4

Shop the High Street

Very much ahead in the online retailing stakes, the high street is well represented, and you can find some extremely well priced basics and fashion pieces from these websites. They're great for taking designer level fashion pieces and turning them into something affordable. Sometimes you'll be amazed at the similarities between what they're offering and what was just very recently on the catwalk, but that's their major skill so take advantage of it. They're also very good at showing you the different trends and how to put them together. You may not want to become a 'fashion victim' and take up each season's looks but if you did, this would be a good place to find out how.

The other advantage if you're not a small size is that you can shop from these (mostly) younger brands without feeling in the slightest bit out of place as you might in the store, or in the fitting rooms. You can try on as many things as you like (none of that, 'just four items at a time' business) and if you want to experiment with putting together this season's latest trends and colours you can. In private.

Some of the high street retailers are very good for basics if you don't want to go for the latest looks. You can try *fcukbuymail.co.uk* for their fine gauge knitwear and t-shirts, *riverisland.co.uk* for jeans and modern trousers (although most of them have quite a low rise) and *monsoon.co.uk* for pretty skirts. Try lots of different looks to see what works for you but avoid being too obvious. If the trend is for full skirts try them with a simple top. If you want to buy the latest military jacket then pair it with jeans to let people know you're not taking the look too seriously. After all, no shopaholic wants to be thought of as a fashion victim, do they? Perish the thought.

You'll notice that quite a few of the high street retailers think that anything beyond a small size is not worth bothering with. Thankfully they're not all like that and some go up to an 18 or higher. So have a browse, check out the trends and enjoy.

Sites to Visit

www.debenhams.com

When I look at some of the 'trend' clothing offered by Debenhams and in particular their 'Designers for Debenhams' section (think Betty Jackson, Jasper Conran, Ben de Lisi, John Rocha etc), and even though I'm well aware that I'm not getting the quality of fabric or make I'd get if I bought the real thing (if I could afford it) I simply can't resist. Ok so maybe you'll only wear some of the items for one season but if you fancy trying a new trend this is a very good place to buy for men, women and children.

Site Usability:	★★★★	Based:	UK
Product Range:	★★★★★	Express Delivery Option?	(UK) No
Price Range:	Luxury/Medium/<u>Very Good Value</u>	Gift Wrapping Option?	No
Delivery Area:	UK	Returns Procedure:	Down to you

www.dorothyperkins.co.uk

Dorothy Perkins clothes and accessories are modern and amazingly well priced using some natural fabrics and with sizing from 8-22 for most items. You'll find most of the wearable new looks each season plus some colourful knits, tops and accessories. Take a good look at the start of the season if you're likely to want something here as once a product has sold out they probably won't replace it, however they offer new styles online each week.

Site Usability:	★★★★	Based:	UK
Product Range:	★★★	Express Delivery Option?	(UK) Yes
Price Range:	Luxury/Medium/<u>Very Good Value</u>	Gift Wrapping Option?	No
Delivery Area:	UK	Returns Procedure:	Down to you

www.fcukbuymail.co.uk

A company where the words young, funky and high street come straight to mind but you can find some very good basics here, in particular their knitwear and t-shirts which are well priced, good quality and available in a range of colours. French Connection is definitely not cheap but delivers good quality, up to the minute styling for men and women and is well worth taking a look at each season for new, modern additions to your wardrobe.

Site Usability:	★★★★	Based:	UK
Product Range:	★★★★	Express Delivery Option?	(UK) Yes
Price Range:	Luxury/<u>Medium</u>/Very Good Value	Gift Wrapping Option?	No
Delivery Area:	Worldwide	Returns Procedure:	Use their free service

www.jeans-direct.co.uk

If you're a fan of wearing jeans you should take a look at this website, where there's a wide choice by Levi, Ben Sherman, Wrangler, Diesel and Duchesse. Personally I think you really have to know your size in each brand to be sure you won't have to send them back, but obviously you can try lots of different styles at home which is a great benefit (particularly if you're not a size 8/10, like me, and would prefer to try on in private).

Site Usability:	★★★	Based:	UK
Product Range:	★★★	Express Delivery Option?	(UK) No
Price Range:	Luxury/<u>Medium</u>/Very Good Value	Gift Wrapping Option?	No
Delivery Area:	EU	Returns Procedure:	Down to you

www.kew-online.com

From the same family as Jigsaw, Kew offers modern, versatile, well priced separates in a wide choice of colours and styles. There's a very good selection on this website, and there are some great tops and fine knitwear plus easy jackets and skirts. They sometimes take quite a while for each new season's collection to be available online so be patient. It'll be worth it.

Site Usability:	★★★★	Based:	UK
Product Range:	★★★★	Express Delivery Option?	(UK) Yes
Price Range:	Luxury/<u>Medium</u>/<u>Very Good Value</u>	Gift Wrapping Option?	No
Delivery Area:	Worldwide; call for international	Returns Procedure:	Down to you

www.mango.com

Spanish label Mango offers inexpensive, up-to-the minute clothes and accessories which they'll ship to you just about anywhere in the world. Their clever, modern website shows you everything at a glance. With jackets at around 60 euros and t-shirts from around 13 euros you can find plenty here to help you get the latest look without breaking the bank. Delivery is from Spain but is most of the time almost unbelievably quick.

Site Usability:	★★★★	Based:	Spain
Product Range:	★★★★★	Express Delivery Option?	(UK) No
Price Range:	Luxury/Medium/<u>Very Good Value</u>	Gift Wrapping Option?	No
Delivery Area:	Worldwide	Returns Procedure:	Down to you

www.marksandspencer.com

You've probably already shopped here from their huge online range of just about everything clothing related, from outerwear, tailoring, casualwear and accessories, lingerie, swimwear, shoes – the list just goes on and on. What's really great about this website now is that you'll find the special collections available too, such as Autograph, Per Una and Limited Collection where you can shop from the more contemporary designs and make your choice from everything that's available, rather than what's just in the small store near you.

Site Usability:	★★★★★	Express Delivery Option?	(UK) Yes
Product Range:	★★★★★	Gift Wrapping Option?	No
Price Range:	Luxury/Medium/Very Good Value	Returns Procedure:	Free to store or their Freepost service
Delivery Area:	UK		

www.missselfridge.co.uk

An integral part of the high street since the 60's, Miss Selfridge has always been a mainstay for young, modern style. There's nothing quiet about the clothes offered here but plenty of information and guidance on how to put together the latest looks and the background to the trends. They do go up to a size 16 but most of the clothes are designed for smaller sizes. They only deliver to the UK and offer express delivery for just £1 more than their standard service.

Site Usability:	★★★★	Based:	UK
Product Range:	★★★★	Express Delivery Option?	(UK) Yes
Price Range:	Luxury/Medium/Very Good Value	Gift Wrapping Option?	No
Delivery Area:	UK	Returns Procedure:	Freepost or to their stores but complicated

www.monsoon.co.uk

With its well known presence on the high street almost everyone has heard of Monsoon, offering attractive, not inexpensive but still good value clothing including some extremely wearable and different occasionwear. Sizing in a lot of cases goes up to a 20. The childrenswear selection is smaller but no different with really pretty clothes, mainly for younger girls, including candy coloured skirts and tops, sugar striped swimwear and the prettiest partywear.

Site Usability:	★★★★★	Based:	UK
Product Range:	★★★★	Express Delivery Option?	(UK) No
Price Range:	Luxury/Medium/Very Good Value	Gift Wrapping Option?	No
Delivery Area:	UK	Returns Procedure:	Down to you

www.principles.co.uk

With an easier to wear selection than some of the high street retailers Principles offers a stylish, well priced collection of separates, dresses and coats on their attractively designed website. They clearly show some of the trends of the season and have picked out pieces that go well together for each look. You'll find dresses, skirts, tops, jeans, knitwear, some very attractive tailoring and occasionwear and a petite collection which goes from size 6-16.

Site Usability:	★★★★	Based:	UK
Product Range:	★★★★	Express Delivery Option?	(UK) Yes
Price Range:	Luxury/Medium/Very Good Value	Gift Wrapping Option?	No
Delivery Area:	UK	Returns Procedure:	Freepost or return to store but complicated

www.riverisland.co.uk

If you're looking for the latest combat trousers, sparkly or decorated jeans or flirty tops (and you're no larger than a size 12, sorry) then take a look round here. They seem to get more modern each season, however they do have some coats, parkas and jackets that would be wearable for a lot of ages and they also have a casual, modern menswear collection. The site is very quick and easy to use and their help desk with all the delivery information is excellent.

Site Usability:	★★★★★	Based:	UK
Product Range:	★★★★	Express Delivery Option?	(UK) Yes
Price Range:	Luxury/<u>Medium</u>/Very Good Value	Gift Wrapping Option?	No
Delivery Area:	UK	Returns Procedure:	Down to you

www.savagelondon.com

For t-shirt collectors this is the place to be, with t-shirts and tops of all shapes and sizes and an enormous range of colours but here's the main point – you get to customise your t-shirt, top or hoody specifically for you (or whoever you want to give one to). Just select your design, choose your style (raw edge, long sleeve etc) then the colour. On some you can choose the text or word as well. The website is very busy but the instructions are clear once you get the hang of how things work.

Site Usability:	★★★★	Based:	UK
Product Range:	★★★★	Express Delivery Option?	(UK) No
Price Range:	Luxury/<u>Medium</u>/Very Good Value	Gift Wrapping Option?	No
Delivery Area:	Worldwide	Returns Procedure:	Down to you

www.tedbaker.co.uk

Fast expanding global brand Ted Baker offers well made and innovative clothing on a clever but slightly distracting website where you don't really feel that you get close to the clothes and there's lots of music (which you can turn off, of course). Don't expect cheap here, you won't find it. What you will find is modern, mainly understated fashion, totally in line with each season's trends. Also watches, accessories, fragrance and a small collection of homewares.

Site Usability:	★★★	Based:	UK
Product Range:	★★★	Express Delivery Option?	(UK) No
Price Range:	Luxury/<u>Medium</u>/Very Good Value	Gift Wrapping Option?	No
Delivery Area:	Worldwide	Returns Procedure:	Down to you

www.topshop.co.uk

This is the place to go if you want the latest fashions at the best prices and definitely the place to go if you can't stand the scrum of the shops. Can't afford Marc Jacobs or Miu Miu? Go straight to Top Shop, and if you can't bear the heaving crowds in the store, desperately seeking the last pair of the latest and absolutely must have heels in your size, you can order them online and have them sent to you by express delivery. A fashionista could surely ask for no more than this.

Site Usability:	★★★★	Based:	UK
Product Range:	★★★★★	Express Delivery Option?	(UK) Yes
Price Range:	Luxury/Medium/<u>Very Good Value</u>	Gift Wrapping Option?	Yes
Delivery Area:	UK	Returns Procedure:	Down to you

www.wallis-fashion.com

Wallis offers a small selection from its stores on the website and just about everything goes up to a size 20, so styles on the whole are easier to wear for most people. They give clear information right from the start about each and every product, right down to washing information, fabric content and sizing as well as telling you about each season's looks and how to put them together. They aim for 48-hour delivery in the UK with the option of express delivery.

Site Usability:	★★★★★	Based:	UK
Product Range:	★★★	Express Delivery Option?	(UK) Yes
Price Range:	Luxury/<u>Medium</u>/Very Good Value	Gift Wrapping Option?	No
Delivery Area:	UK	Returns Procedure:	Freepost or return to store

www.warehouse.co.uk

Warehouse have re-launched their website to offer an even more addictive online shopping experience. Products go live on a daily basis so there's lots to choose from and you need to check back on a regular basis. Collections come in sizes 6–16 together with competitions, trends and features in their Ware-Style section and email newsletter. They offer 2-day delivery throughout the UK and ROI and the website is ultra user friendly so logon now and take a look.

Site Usability:	★★★★	Based:	UK
Product Range:	★★★	Express Delivery Option?	(UK) Yes
Price Range:	Luxury/Medium/<u>Very Good Value</u>	Gift Wrapping Option?	No
Delivery Area:	UK	Returns Procedure:	Freepost or return to store

www.whitestuff.com

This young, urban clothing company sells casual sporty lightweight gear in the summer months for guys and girls, plus trendy skiwear in the winter (hence the name). There are colour options for just about all the clothes, from the Flawless T to the Java Jive pant and you can see straight away what's available in stock or what you'll have to wait for. This isn't a huge collection but it's fun and well priced and definitely worth having a look at.

Site Usability:	★★★★	Based:	UK
Product Range:	★★★	Express Delivery Option?	(UK) Yes
Price Range:	Luxury/Medium/<u>Very Good Value</u>	Gift Wrapping Option?	No
Delivery Area:	Worldwide	Returns Procedure:	Freepost or return to store

Chapter 5

Tall and Plus Size Clothing

nline this is another area that's growing all the time, with retailers beginning to realise that the market for sizes from 16 upwards is a huge one and only the foolish ignore it (I'll apologise right now for any puns – really not intended).

Having said that there are still a lot of clothing websites that won't take you much further than a UK size 14 and who wants to trawl through them all finding the ones that not only size up, but also get it right? It's not just a matter of going up a few sizes but in the same way that petite ranges need completely different measurements; shoulder and cuff openings, jacket lengths and trouser hem widths (rather than just the inseam measurements) the same is true of larger clothes. Those who go beyond a UK size 16 really need to know what they're doing so they can offer not just a stylish and attractive range but also one that will fit properly.

Of course in the US they really know what they're doing which is why I've suggested you also look at two US based sites *www.llbean.com* and *www.eddiebaur.com*. Both these are expert at offering a wide range of sizes for all types of garments. I would steer clear of ordering anything too fitted which would be more likely to need to be returned (unless you see a jacket that you simply have to try, needless to say) but their ranges of shirts, outerwear, knitwear, tops and some of their trousers are simply superb.

Remember that if you ship from the US to other countries you will no doubt have to pay extra shipping and duty but these companies are used to shipping all over the World and when you look at the prices that you would have to pay in the UK for the comparable quality you get in the US you really should give it a go.

I hope very much that there will be more quality plus size retailers coming online in the not too distant future, in the meantime take a look through the websites below and enjoy the fact that you can eliminate the shops that don't offer your size and shop from the best of the rest from home.

Please note that all the sizes mentioned are basic UK sizes. For international conversions go to the Clothing Size Conversions at the end of this book

Sites to Visit

www.cinnamonfashion.co.uk

Cinnamon specialises in clothing for sizes 16–34 and stocks casual wear, tailoring and occasionwear plus sportswear and swimwear. You'll find lots of continental brands such as Chalou, Melli Mel, Doris Streich, Yoek, Samoon and BS Casuals plus designers such as Kirsten Krog and Charles and Patricia Leicester. They're happy if you call them for advice on what works with what and will deliver to you anywhere in the world. Call them to ask for express delivery.

Site Usability:	★★★★	Based:	UK
Product Range:	★★★	Express Delivery Option?	(UK) Yes
Price Range:	Luxury/Medium/Very Good Value	Gift Wrapping Option?	No
Delivery Area:	Worldwide	Returns Procedure:	Down to you

www.grayandosbourn.co.uk

This is a really excellent selection of designer separates, from labels such as Basler and Gerry Weber plus their own well priced Gray and Osbourn range. Most items are available in sizes 12 to 22 and some go up to 26. The range is essentially classic but in tune with each season and you can dress here from holiday/cruise, country weekends, smart tailoring, tops and accessories to really chic eveningwear. Delivery is by courier within 7–10 days and UK and Channel Islands only.

Site Usability:	★★★★★	Based:	UK
Product Range:	★★★★	Express Delivery Option?	(UK) No
Price Range:	Luxury/Medium/Very Good Value	Gift Wrapping Option?	No
Delivery Area:	UK	Returns Procedure:	Down to you

www.longtallsally.co.uk

As someone who's always been quite a bit (a lot) shorter than they'd really like to be, when I click onto this modern, stylish website I always wish (fleetingly) that they offered clothes I could wear as well (foolish, I know, but there it is). Here there's a stylish range of clothes for women over 5ft 8in from casual to smart and everything in between. Also swimwear and a very small selection of maternity wear. Everything is beautifully photographed. They'll ship worldwide and offer an Express service to the UK.

Site Usability:	★★★★	Based:	UK
Product Range:	★★★★	Express Delivery Option?	(UK) Yes
Price Range:	Luxury/<u>Medium</u>/Very Good Value	Gift Wrapping Option?	No
Delivery Area:	Worldwide	Returns Procedure:	Freepost or return to store but complicated

www.rowlandsclothing.co.uk

The first Rowlands shop opened in Bath in 1983 with the aim of providing a range of high quality, reasonably priced, smart casual classic country clothing. From their successful mail order catalogue they've now put their collection online with a simple, easy to use website offering smart coats and jackets, dresses and a selection of separates from day to evening. Sizing is 10 to 22 (24 for some items). They aim to deliver within 7–10 days.

Site Usability:	★★★★	Based:	UK
Product Range:	★★★★	Express Delivery Option?	(UK) No
Price Range:	Luxury/<u>Medium</u>/Very Good Value	Gift Wrapping Option?	No
Delivery Area:	UK	Returns Procedure:	Down to you

www.spirito.co.uk

This is the top end of the online plus size clothing ranges offering a very high quality selection in sizes 10–20 including smart daywear, knitwear, casualwear and evening wear. Everything is beautifully made in Italy and smartly photographed to make you really want to buy as you would expect from Artigiano's sister company. Shoes, accessories and jewellery are from the main Artigiano ranges and footwear goes up to a size 9.

Site Usability:	★★★★★	Based:	UK
Product Range:	★★★★	Express Delivery Option?	(UK) Yes
Price Range:	Luxury/<u>Medium</u>/Very Good Value	Gift Wrapping Option?	No
Delivery Area:	Worldwide	Returns Procedure:	Free with Royal Mail

Also visit these websites for tall and plus size clothing

Website Address	You'll find it in
www.dorothyperkins.co.uk	Shop the High Street
www.principles.co.uk	Shop the High Street
www.wallis-fashion.com	Shop the High Street
www.llbean.com	Shop America
www.eddiebaur.com	Shop America
www.landsend.co.uk	Fashion Retailers
www.claireid.com	Fashion Retailers
www.poetrycollection.co.uk	Fashion Retailers
www.marksandspencer.com	Fashion Retailers

Chapter 6

Shop America

If you don't have time to go out looking round the shops and you can't find it online where you are, then consider making your next purchase from the US, but without the jet lag, of course.

Ordering is normally very easy, you will pay extra delivery charges but you won't pay US tax. You will probably also have to pay duty but you'll probably still find the prices are very good. The speed at which your order will reach you may well surprise you, with FedEx and UPS taking just a couple of days to anywhere in the world.

Just a word of advice. If you're not sure about the size you're ordering go up. You're much less likely to have to send back something if it's slightly too big than if it's too small.

For clothing size conversions, US clothes are usually one but can sometimes be two sizes down from the UK. So a US 8 will be a UK 10 or 12. The only way to be sure about clothing measurements is to look at the size guides, measure yourself and then allow a bit. Please refer to page 463 for the US/UK/Europe sizing conversions.

Women's Shoe Size Conversions

UK	3.5	4	4.5	5	5.5	6	6.5	7	7.5	8	8.5
EU	36.5	37	37.5	38	38.5	39	40	41	42	43	43.5
US	6	6.5	7	7.5	8	8.5	9	9.5	10	10.5	11

Men's Shoe Size Conversions

UK	7	7.5	8	8.5	9	9.5	10	10.5	11	11.5	12
EU	40.5	41	42	42.5	43	44	44.5	45	46	46.5	47
US	7.5	8	8.5	9	9.5	10	10.5	11	11.5	12	12.5

Sites to Visit

www.abercrombie.com

This is where the young chic American denim brigade shop for their jeans, jackets and tees. The style is very 'Casual Luxury' and they even call it that. Take a look around if you can tear yourself away from the outstanding photographs of the most beautiful models (mostly men). Prices are good and delivery is very fast. The quality is excellent. Sizing is SMALL particularly for fitted items so if in any doubt go up a size.

Site Usability:	★★★★★	Based:	US
Product Range:	★★★	Express Delivery Option?	(UK) No
Price Range:	Luxury/Medium/Very Good Value	Gift Wrapping Option?	No
Delivery Area:	Worldwide	Returns Procedure:	Down to you

www.ae.com

Not as expensive as Abercrombie (and not quite so well known, particularly over here), American Eagle offers a wide selection of colourful, young, modern, casual clothing extremely popular across the pond and I wish they were just down the road here, too. Think preppy striped shirts, humorous and sporty t-shirts and great jeans, hoodies and jackets plus some camis and underwear and a good range of shoes. Thankfully they have no problem in shipping to you anywhere in the world using USPS Global Express Mail.

Site Usability:	★★★★★	Based:	US
Product Range:	★★★★	Express Delivery Option?	(UK) No
Price Range:	Luxury/Medium/Very Good Value	Gift Wrapping Option?	No
Delivery Area:	Worldwide	Returns Procedure:	Down to you

www.brooksbrothers.com

Here you'll find quite expensive, beautifully made classic clothes for both men and women and they have no problem shipping to you anywhere in the world. The quality really is excellent and for a perfect classic cardigan or pair of trousers you'll be hard put to find anywhere better, particularly if you've tried them and know their look. The website is beautifully photographed and easy to go round and delivery is speedy.

Site Usability:	★★★★★	Based:	US
Product Range:	★★★★★	Express Delivery Option?	(UK) No
Price Range:	Luxury/Medium/Very Good Value	Gift Wrapping Option?	No
Delivery Area:	Worldwide	Returns Procedure:	Down to you

www.eddiebaur.com

Eddie Baur is one of those American companies who show how it really should be done. Their site is attractive to look at, easy to get round, offers great products, good prices (not cheap but good value) and they'll ship to you anywhere in the world. No wonder Vogue US picks some of their products as the 'must haves' of the season. From clothing, to swimwear, performance walking boots, accessories and some very, very good sporting luggage you won't go wrong here.

Site Usability:	★★★★★	Based:	US
Product Range:	★★★★★	Express Delivery Option?	(UK) No
Price Range:	Luxury/Medium/Very Good Value	Gift Wrapping Option?	No
Delivery Area:	Worldwide	Returns Procedure:	Down to you

www.goclothing.com

You have been warned. There's so much to look at on this website that it takes a while to load and yes, they do ship internationally. You'll almost certainly discover something you like, from C & C California t-shirts to funky belts and bags and a whole host of clothing labels including allen b jeans, Tracy Reese, Cathering Malandrino, Lilly Pulitzer and a lot you'll probably never have heard of.

Site Usability:	★★★★	Based:	US
Product Range:	★★★★★	Express Delivery Option?	(UK) No
Price Range:	Luxury/Medium/Very Good Value	Gift Wrapping Option?	Yes
Delivery Area:	Worldwide	Returns Procedure:	Down to you

www.grahamkandiah.com

If you're going anywhere hot in the near future you have to take a look at this website now, where you can choose from the most attractive sarongs, kaftans, wraps and bikinis plus t-shirts and totes, all in a wonderful treasure trove of fabrics with names such as Tiger, Riviera, South Beach, Jungle, Havana and

Bahia. Yes the retailer is based in the US but it's quick and easy to order and they'll deliver to you anywhere in the World.

Site Usability:	★★★★	Based:	US
Product Range:	★★★	Express Delivery Option?	(UK) No
Price Range:	Luxury/Medium/Very Good Value	Gift Wrapping Option?	Yes
Delivery Area:	Worldwide	Returns Procedure:	Down to you

www.llbean.com

You'll be hard put to see a more comprehensive collection of very well priced, quality clothing including outerwear, fleece, shirts, trousers and snow sport clothing, luggage, outdoor gear, swimwear, footwear and accessories. They're particularly good for their cold weather shirts which are extremely reasonable. Have a browse. It's hard to get away without buying something.

Site Usability:	★★★★★	Based:	US
Product Range:	★★★★★	Express Delivery Option?	(UK) No
Price Range:	Luxury/Medium/Very Good Value	Gift Wrapping Option?	No
Delivery Area:	Worldwide	Returns Procedure:	Down to you

www.neimanmarcus.com

Every designer from YSL to Marc Jacobs and accessories from Manolo Blahnik to Tods is offered at this top level US store, with a brilliantly laid out website showing beautiful modern pictures of absolutely everything. The downside is you'll have to pay duty on top of the designer prices (if you're not based in the US) but it's worth having a look at some of the American designers, and well worth checking out the trends from season to season. If you want to place an international order you need to call them on 1 888 888 4757.

Site Usability:	★★★★★	Based:	US
Product Range:	★★★★★	Express Delivery Option?	(UK) No
Price Range:	Luxury/Medium/Very Good Value	Gift Wrapping Option?	Yes
Delivery Area:	Worldwide	Returns Procedure:	Down to you

www.shopbop.com

Here is just about the full collection from Juicy Couture, including the velour and cashmere collections, plus brands such as Diane von Furstenberg, Chip and Pepper, Marc by Marc Jacobs and Seven for all Mankind. Brands that you can find here but you really have to look for them. They offer standard UPS delivery plus the worldwide express service which will only take 2–3 days.

Site Usability:	★★★★★	Based:	USA
Product Range:	★★★★★	Express Delivery Option?	(UK) No
Price Range:	Luxury/Medium/Very Good Value	Gift Wrapping Option?	No
Delivery Area:	Worldwide	Returns Procedure:	Down to you

www.stuartweitzman.com

If you've purchased Stuart Weitzman shoes before you'll already know that they're chic, comfortable and beautifully well made, sometimes very modern but always with a wearable option. This is one of the best shoe stores online although they don't make it easy for you to buy outside the US. You can buy them in some shoe shops (mainly in London) and you can also buy them direct from the US website. Currently they only accept American Express but this may change so watch this space.

Site Usability:	★★★★★	Based:	US
Product Range:	★★★★★	Express Delivery Option?	(UK) No
Price Range:	Luxury/Medium/Very Good Value	Gift Wrapping Option?	No
Delivery Area:	Worldwide	Returns Procedure:	Down to you

www.sundancecatalog.com

Inspired (and initiated) by Robert Redford, Sundance is a truly American catalogue which has now become a worldwide online store. You'll discover wonderful jewellery by American craftsmen, a wide range of high quality classic American clothing including shirts, tops and ts, skirts and trousers, ranch style boots, home accessories (gorgeous quilts and throws) and lots of ideas for gifts.

Site Usability:	★★★★★	Based:	USA
Product Range:	★★★★★	Express Delivery Option?	(UK) No
Price Range:	Luxury/Medium/Very Good Value	Gift Wrapping Option?	Yes
Delivery Area:	Worldwide	Returns Procedure:	Down to you

www.swimwearboutique.com

This is a really excellent swimwear boutique offering great labels such as Gottex and Gideon Oberson which for some reason are almost impossible to buy here. When you're placing your order you'll notice that one of the clever features of the site is the 'availability' box which shows up as soon as you've chosen your style, size and colour and tells you when you can have your order. They offer quick worldwide delivery but you'll have to pay duty if you're outside the US.

Site Usability:	★★★★★	Based:	US
Product Range:	★★★★	Express Delivery Option?	(UK) No
Price Range:	Luxury/Medium/Very Good Value	Gift Wrapping Option?	No
Delivery Area:	Worldwide	Returns Procedure:	Down to you

www.travelsmith.com

This US based website must be the ultimate online travel clothing store. They offer a really comprehensive and well priced range of travel clothing and accessories for men and women, from outerwear including washable suede, tailoring and safari jackets to easy care separates, hats, swimwear and luggage. You can't place your order directly online for International delivery but you can fax it to them at 001 415-884-1351 and they'll send it to you anywhere in the world.

Site Usability:	★★★★★	Based:	US
Product Range:	★★★★★	Express Delivery Option?	(UK) No
Price Range:	Luxury/<u>Medium</u>/Very Good Value	Gift Wrapping Option?	No
Delivery Area:	Worldwide	Returns Procedure:	Down to you

www.trunkltd.com

This is for t-shirt addicts only. This funky US based website sells collectible t-shirts, camis and jackets emblazoned with classic rock and roll art – think the Beatles, Alice Cooper, Blondie, Frank Zappa, Fleetwood Mac and Janis Joplin. Be careful before you get too excited, some of these, embellished with Swarovski crystals, are definitely collector's items with steep prices so you need to have a good look through. They'll deliver to you anywhere in the world.

Site Usability:	★★★★	Based:	USA
Product Range:	★★★★	Express Delivery Option?	(UK) No
Price Range:	<u>Luxury/Medium</u>/Very Good Value	Gift Wrapping Option?	No
Delivery Area:	Worldwide	Returns Procedure:	Down to you

www.victoriassecret.com

The US based mail order lingerie company that uses world famous models. Seductive pictures of bronzed beauties don't detract from the fact that here is probably one of (if not) the best selections of lingerie in the world. When you consider the size of the American market that's probably not surprising; but what's great is that you can order from anywhere in the world.

Site Usability:	★★★★★	Based:	US
Product Range:	★★★★★	Express Delivery Option?	(UK) No
Price Range:	Luxury/Medium/<u>Very Good Value</u>	Gift Wrapping Option?	Yes
Delivery Area:	Worldwide	Returns Procedure:	Down to you

Chapter 7

The Sportswear Option and Travel Clothing

If you're a real fitness/sports addict you don't need to go to your local sports shop to search out your casual clothes or kit any more, as there are some excellent shops online, offering you a huge selection of t-shirts, hoodies, track pants and trainers plus gymwear and accessories. If you want to pay a lot of money for new season's Adidas, Nike or Reebok you can, or if you want to go the much cheaper route you can do that as well.

If, on the other hand, you're a bit of a couch potato (like me, most of the time) who just likes to look sporty and to have a few 'designer' sportswear pieces in your wardrobe (to relax in, of course), or you just like to wear the odd Quicksilver or O'Neill jacket on the slopes, you can find all that here too.

It couldn't be easier if you live in London to wander down Carnaby Street or pay a visit to Covent Garden and visit the huge sports brand shops there. However, if like most people, you don't have the time, or maybe you live miles (or even thousands of miles) from London, you can shop online for whichever brand takes your fancy. I'll say it again. It couldn't be easier.

As I've said in all the other clothing sections do make allowances for the different sizing of all the brands here. The younger the store the smaller they seem to make the clothes. If you're in doubt as to whether you're a size 12 or a size 14 then you have two options. You can either try both sizes and know that you'll have to send one back or you can allow a bit and go for the larger size. The first option is obviously the most advantageous as although you'll have the bore of returning something you're almost certain to be able to get the right size at first hit.

As regards travel clothing again there's a very good choice, and one of the major advantages is that you can buy your lightweight gear from somewhere like *www.rohan.co.uk*, your mosquito repellent and dry wash from *www.blacks.co.uk* and your anti malaria tablets from one of the pharmacies listed in the Health and Beauty section (where you'll find they're much less expensive than buying from your local chemist). So if you don't have a lot of time you can see everything available and order very quickly.

Sites to Visit

www.asquith.ltd.uk

If you haven't yet given up on your New Year's resolution of getting fitter, or you want something to stimulate you into getting on with it, then have a look here. Asquith offer an unusual collection of clothes for Yoga, Pilates (and, yes, lounging around in) in a lovely selection of colours including candy, coral, aqua and dewberry, wrap tops, capri pants, camisoles and t-shirts. There's excellent information about each item, from what it's made of, to sizing and washing instructions.

Site Usability:	★★★★		Based:	UK
Product Range:	★★★		Express Delivery Option?	(UK) Yes
Price Range:	Luxury/<u>Medium</u>/Very Good Value		Gift Wrapping Option?	No
Delivery Area:	Worldwide		Returns Procedure:	Down to you

www.blacks.co.uk

If you or any member of your family has ever done any camping, walking or hiking (or climbing) you'll probably already have visited Blacks, where they offer a well priced (rather than 'designer') range of clothing and accessories and good value skiwear in season. You can buy waterproof jackets and trousers, lots of fleece, tents, poles, footwear and socks and great gifts such as Cybalite torches, Kick and Huntsman knives and tools and Garmin compasses.

Site Usability:	★★★★★		Express Delivery Option?	(UK) No
Product Range:	★★★★		Gift Wrapping Option?	No
Price Range:	Luxury/<u>Medium</u>/Very Good Value		Returns Procedure:	Down to you
Delivery Area:	UK			

www.casall.co.uk

Next time you feel like being active, get the gear, so that a) you feel you look the part, which always helps and b) you've spent all that money so you really better make it pay. Casall have a very good range of sportswear for women from classic easy pieces which would be great for golf (or just looking chic and stylish), great separates for yoga and the real thing for the gym. Have a look round even if you're not feeling all that energetic – you might get inspired.

Site Usability:	★★★★	Based:	UK
Product Range:	★★★	Express Delivery Option?	(UK) Yes
Price Range:	Luxury/Medium/Very Good Value	Gift Wrapping Option?	No
Delivery Area:	UK	Returns Procedure:	Down to you

www.crewclothing.co.uk

This is a really attractive and modern website with a constantly expanding range, offering all the Crew gear, from the full collection of sailing inspired clothing to lots of other choices including hard wearing footwear, faux fur jackets and gilets (resist them if you can) and excellent travel bags, gloves, hats and socks. They offer standard and next day UK delivery and same day in central London if you order by 12pm. They'll also ship worldwide.

Site Usability:	★★★★★	Based:	UK
Product Range:	★★★	Express Delivery Option?	(UK) Yes
Price Range:	Luxury/Medium/Very Good Value	Gift Wrapping Option?	No
Delivery Area:	Worldwide	Returns Procedure:	Down to you

www.extremepie.com

There are enough sportswear brands here to sink a ship from famous brands such as O'Neill, Quicksilver, Animal, Vans, Billabong, RipCurl, Addict, Extreme and Reef plus loads more that you may not have heard of. This is definitely a good site for anyone who's addicted to sport, or just wants the sporty look (and for gifts for sporty people). They also sell snowboards, skateboards, wetsuits, accessories and sunglasses by Animal and Roxy.

Site Usability:	★★★★	Based:	UK
Product Range:	★★★★	Express Delivery Option?	(UK) Yes
Price Range:	Luxury/Medium/Very Good Value	Gift Wrapping Option?	No
Delivery Area:	Worldwide	Returns Procedure:	Down to you

www.fatface.com

When you first take a look at the fatface.co.uk website you may be a little disconcerted. It's certainly not like most others with pictures and type all being used to reinforce Fatface's idiosyncratic 'cool' active style. But it works together. You'll find a wide selection of tops and t-shirts, jackets and fleece, denim and sweats, all in unique fabrics and style and their more often than not muted colour palette.

Site Usability:	★★★★	Based:	UK
Product Range:	★★★★	Express Delivery Option?	(UK) Yes
Price Range:	Luxury/Medium/Very Good Value	Gift Wrapping Option?	No
Delivery Area:	Worldwide	Returns Procedure:	Down to you

www.figleaves.com

Figleaves' collection of activewear now includes designers such as Calvin Klein, Puma, Elle, Candida Faria, Venice Beach and Tommy Hilfiger and the range is growing all the time. You'll find bright colour and good shapes here (with lots of stretch) and if you haven't tried figleaves's service before now you should certainly give it a go as it really is excellent and worldwide shipping is free. As Figleaves' main area of business is lingerie you'll also be able to buy your sports bras here as well.

Site Usability:	★★★★★	Based:	UK
Product Range:	★★★★	Express Delivery Option?	(UK) Yes
Price Range:	Luxury/Medium/Very Good Value	Gift Wrapping Option?	Yes
Delivery Area:	Worldwide	Returns Procedure:	Use their returns service

www.jdsports.co.uk

As one of the largest UK sports retailers there is, as you'd expect, a huge range of sports shoes including Nike, Puma, Reebok, Lacoste and Adidas. Their clothing ranges are also extensive and taken from the same brands and the ordering system is extremely easy to use. With each pair of shoes (or each item of clothing) they show you other items to go with. Clever or what? They aim to make delivery within five working days of receipt of your order.

Site Usability:	★★★★★	Express Delivery Option?	(UK) No
Product Range:	★★★★	Gift Wrapping Option?	No
Price Range:	Luxury/Medium/Very Good Value	Returns Procedure:	Down to you
Delivery Area:	UK		

www.nomadtravel.co.uk

The next time you feel like taking off on safari or into the jungle take a look at this website, which offers a good, highly edited range of efficient and well priced travel clothing including lightweight trousers, zip-offs and vented shirts, base layer fleece and thermals as well as lots of advice on travel health depending on where you're going, with particular reference to malaria and also on travelling with children. You can place your order to the EU online and elsewhere by contacting them and they offer 48-hour delivery in the UK

Site Usability:	★★★★★	Express Delivery Option?	(UK) 48 hour service
Product Range:	★★★★	Gift Wrapping Option?	No
Price Range:	Luxury/Medium/Very Good Value	Returns Procedure:	Down to you
Delivery Area:	Worldwide		

www.puma.com

Puma have now launched their website so they can offer pretty well their full range to you online. As a great fan of their unbelievably comfortable footwear (so comfortable I've become an addict) this is great news. Whereas on most sports websites you'll find just a small part of the range, now you can choose from all the styles and all the colourways. Delivery is within 1–3 days unless you select Royal Mail Special Delivery, in which case you can have your order the day after you place it.

Site Usability:	★★★★★	Based:	UK	
Product Range:	★★★★	Express Delivery Option?	(UK) Yes	
Price Range:	Luxury/Medium/Very Good Value	Gift Wrapping Option?	No	
Delivery Area:	EU most countries	Returns Procedure:	Down to you	

www.rohan.co.uk

Specialists in easy care (easy wear, easy wash and dry) travel clothing, Rohan offer trousers, shirts, underwear and accessories for men and women. You select depending on the type of activity, clothing or climate and there's a very good selection, lots of information and fast service. If you're planning a visit to the jungle this is an excellent website as you can buy not only your clothing but also clever washbags, microfibre towels, dry wash, travel bottles and lots of other accessories.

Site Usability:	★★★★	Based:	UK	
Product Range:	★★★★	Express Delivery Option?	(UK) Yes	
Price Range:	Luxury/Medium/Very Good Value	Gift Wrapping Option?	No	
Delivery Area:	Worldwide	Returns Procedure:	Down to you	

www.routeone.co.uk

Route One is a young, committed, independent store aimed at inline skate and skateboard riders but having such a large selection of shoes, clothing and accessories by brands such as Converse, Atticus, Fenchurch, Billabong and Carhatt (and, I have to confess, loads of others I haven't heard of) it's bound to appeal to anyone who likes a contemporary, sporty look. The service is speedy and reliable.

Site Usability:	★★★★	Based:	UK	
Product Range:	★★★★	Express Delivery Option?	(UK) Yes	
Price Range:	Luxury/Medium/Very Good Value	Gift Wrapping Option?	No	
Delivery Area:	Worldwide	Returns Procedure:	Down to you	

www.sandstormbags.com

Sandstorm offers an excellent range of heavy duty luggage and accessories, perfect for your next safari (or actually wherever you want to go). All are hand made by skilled Luo tribesmen from Lake Victoria in Kenya and each bag is cut from water-resistant, 18oz, 100% cotton canvas and natural cow hide with double stitched stress points and solid brass fittings. The range includes travel bags, travel accessories, business bags, handbags and cool bags and all in a selection of colours.

Site Usability:	★★★	Based:	UK	
Product Range:	★★★	Express Delivery Option?	(UK) No	
Price Range:	Luxury/Medium/Very Good Value	Gift Wrapping Option?	No	
Delivery Area:	Worldwide	Returns Procedure:	Down to you	

www.sport-e.com

Part of Littlewoods Online, this is the place to find discounted sports shoes by Nike, Adidas, Puma, Reebok, Converse and Lacoste. Also sportswear, sports bras and sports equipment. There's a good selection; delivery is free if you spend over £100 and returns are free as well, so if you really don't want to spend too much but you still like to have that 'designer' look you may well find your answer here.

Site Usability:	★★★★★	Based:	UK
Product Range:	★★★★	Express Delivery Option?	(UK) No
Price Range:	Luxury/<u>Medium</u>/Very Good Value	Gift Wrapping Option?	No
Delivery Area:	UK	Returns Procedure:	Free of charge

www.sheactive.co.uk

Here's a website just for women, covering sports such as fitness, cycling, rock climbing, skiing and swimming. They don't offer any products that are adaptations of men's sportswear and just go for the best that's been specifically designed for women. There's a very good selection, whether you're a dedicated sportswoman or just want the look. Brands include Puma, Adidas, Berghaus, Bolle, Helly Hanson and Salomon.

Site Usability:	★★★★★	Based:	UK
Product Range:	★★★★	Express Delivery Option?	(UK) Yes
Price Range:	Luxury/<u>Medium</u>/Very Good Value	Gift Wrapping Option?	No
Delivery Area:	Worldwide	Returns Procedure:	Free of charge

www.shoe-shop.com

Puma, Asics, Nike, Adidas and Reebok are just some of the many brands you can choose from, whatever your sport. If you're a lounge lizard and just want to look modern (and like being comfortable) you'll find all the latest styles here too. They do sell other types of shoes but their strength is definitely at the sporty end. Beware of wearing your sports shoes too much though, you'll never be able to wear your killer heels again with ease.

Site Usability:	★★★★★	Based:	UK
Product Range:	★★★★★	Express Delivery Option?	(UK) No
Price Range:	Luxury/<u>Medium</u>/Very Good Value	Gift Wrapping Option?	No
Delivery Area:	Worldwide	Returns Procedure:	Down to you but select their good value returns paid option.

www.sweatybetty.com

Another website to get you going, where you can choose from an excellent and stylish range of clothes for the gym and for yoga, available in basic colours such as black, grey and pink. They also offer sleek (and minimal) beachwear, chic and well priced skiwear plus accessories such as leg and arm warmers and books on yoga. Postage is free on orders over £50 (UK) and they'll deliver Worldwide.

Site Usability:	★★★★	Based:	UK
Product Range:	★★★	Express Delivery Option?	(UK) No
Price Range:	Luxury/<u>Medium</u>/Very Good Value	Gift Wrapping Option?	No
Delivery Area:	Worldwide	Returns Procedure:	Down to you

www.travellinglight.co.uk

Order your hot weather travel clothing here at any time of the year. There's an excellent range for men and women here if you're planning to go trekking or on safari plus smart/classic, easy to wear separates, tailoring and eveningwear. In their casualwear section there are shorts, bermudas and capri pants plus lots of tops and t-shirts. They also have accessories such as lightweight luggage, Bolle and Oakley sunglasses and sun hats.

Site Usability:	★★★★★	Based:	UK
Product Range:	★★★★	Express Delivery Option?	(UK) Yes
Price Range:	Luxury/<u>Medium</u>/Very Good Value	Gift Wrapping Option?	No
Delivery Area:	Worldwide	Returns Procedure:	Free of charge

www.w1style.co.uk

An excellent website offering new and current brands such as Quicksilver, Miss Sixty, Roxy, O'Neill, Bench, Billabong, Diesel and FCUK in an easy to view format. Although most of the items offered are brand new current season's stock (and new stock is regularly being added to the site) there are also some very good reductions. They will ship to North America as well as Europe and all items are shipped from Gibralter.

Site Usability:	★★★★	Based:	Gibralter
Product Range:	★★★★★	Express Delivery Option?	(UK) Yes
Price Range:	Luxury/<u>Medium</u>/Very Good Value	Gift Wrapping Option?	Yes
Delivery Area:	EU and North America	Returns Procedure:	Down to you

www.wildlifeonline.com

Wildlife Clothing offers a range of leisurewear, footwear and accessories for people with active lifestyles, bringing together a selection of products from international brands such as Armor Lux from Brittany Camper and Hispanitas footwear from Spain, Dockers, Merrell and Sebago from the United States, Oska from Germany, Kipling from Belgium and Joules, Jack Wills, Quayside, Orla Kiely, Musto and Seasalt from the UK. Allow 7–10 days for delivery although they aim to despatch all items much faster.

Site Usability:	★★★★★	Based:	UK
Product Range:	★★★★	Express Delivery Option?	(UK) No
Price Range:	Luxury/Medium/Very Good Value	Gift Wrapping Option?	Yes
Delivery Area:	Worldwide	Returns Procedure:	Down to you

Also check out this website for travel clothing

Websites Address   **You'll find it in**

www.travelsmith.com   Shop America

Chapter 8

Handbag Addicts Only

Y̶ou can tell a great deal by a person's handbag. Whether they care about fashion for example, or if they just want something to carry everything around in. Personally, as a shopaholic and a handbag addict I don't understand why anyone would want to miss out on the fix of having at least one great bag (several, preferably).

You may not be able to afford to buy this season's fashion statement bag – Luella, Miu Miu, Jimmy Choo *et al* but bearing in mind some of the great copies and less expensive brands around there's no excuse not to pay attention to the accessory that speaks more about you than just about anything else.

If it's a designer buy you're after then a full lineup is waiting for you in Luxury Brands Online including Gucci, Prada, Fendi, Jimmy Choo, Chloe, Luella, Louis Vuitton, Marc Jacobs, Marni, Tanner Krolle and Bottega Veneta. Not seconds, not copies, not auction items or bin ends but the real McCoy. Sometimes you'll find earlier season's stock at discounted prices. Just about all the accessory websites will ship all over the world. In other words, this is a shopaholic's paradise.

If you don't want to go to the designer end of the spectrum then check out the offerings at the websites below where the prices are much more reasonable but the handbags still shout style. And if you're in any doubt about your current clutch then take a good look here and invest now. This is one case of when in doubt do.

Just a couple more words before you launch into your next shop. Be careful. Don't go off on a search for that Louis Vuitton tote on a search engine and not make absolutely certain that you're buying the real thing. There are loads and loads of websites out there waiting to rip you off. The only people who should be selling discounted designer handbags are either those who are buying from accredited resellers (in other words ends of lines and over stocks they've been allowed to sell) or the designers themselves at the end of their seasons: No one else. So take care.

This is not to try and warn you off buying designer merchandise online but just to make sure that you have enough information to ensure you make a good, safe purchase. The World Wide Web is absolutely wonderful if you know how to use it – it can also lead you down some paths where you probably don't want to go.

And also

Small Accessories

You know; all those things you need to put into that chic handbag you've just bought, your wallet, gloves (if you wear them, including the luxurious warm lined ones) chic make-up bag, smart key ring etc plus all the other clutter that always manages to force the thing you're really looking for down to the bottom of your bag, unless you're extremely organised, of course.

There are some names you'll recognise here, such as Mulberry and Pickett and some I'm sure that you'll never have heard of before. The idea is to keep things simple and elegant without spending the earth, unless you want to.

Some of the websites below offer the full range, from your new handbag to that matching leather fobbed key ring. Others specialise in just one or two areas. The aim is to give you as wide a choice as possible of all the gorgeous accessories online. So you can pick and choose. Go on and treat yourself.

Sites to Visit

www.alicecaroline.co.uk

Not your usual range of leather handbags and purses here but something just a little bit different to tempt you when you want a new colourful handbag fix but don't want to shell out the earth. These are fabric bags which would be perfect for summer and evenings with oriental, silk and funky prints and names such as Glamour Girls and Shoes. There are matching large and small purses and they'd all make great gifts for style conscious girls.

Site Usability:	★★★★	Based:	UK
Product Range:	★★★	Express Delivery Option?	(UK) Yes
Price Range:	Luxury/<u>Medium</u>/Very Good Value	Gift Wrapping Option?	No
Delivery Area:	Worldwide	Returns Procedure:	Down to you

www.angeljackson.co.uk

From the glamorous Ultimate Day Bag in black, cocoa, green or gold, to the woven leather Polanski you'll find an irresistible collection of extremely well priced and well made handbags here, plus weekenders, purses and day to evening clutches. You can see all the items in a lot of detail with close-up and different view photographs. Call them for mail order until their online shopping facility is up and running.

Site Usability:	★★★	Based:	UK
Product Range:	★★★	Express Delivery Option?	(UK) No
Price Range:	Luxury/Medium/Very Good Value	Gift Wrapping Option?	No
Delivery Area:	Worldwide	Returns Procedure:	Down to you

www.belenechandia.com

Simple, classic, soft leather handbags in a choice of colours with names such as Rock Me, Hold Me and Take Me Away by accessory label Belen Echandia. Choose your style of handbag, check out the measurements and detailing and then use their semi-bespoke service to select your particular choice of leather, from croc finish to metallics and brights to neutrals. These are definitely at the luxury end of the market with prices starting at about £400 but extremely beautiful, unique and different and investments that'll last you for years.

Site Usability:	★★★★	Based:	UK
Product Range:	★★★	Express Delivery Option?	(UK) Yes
Price Range:	Luxury/Medium/Very Good Value	Gift Wrapping Option?	Yes
Delivery Area:	Worldwide	Returns Procedure:	Down to you

www.billamberg.com

From Bill Amberg's London studio the accessories team design a seasonal collection of very modern bags and luggage for men and women in carefully selected fine leathers and suedes with names such as Rocket Bag, Trafalgar Tote and Supernatural. You won't find his full range online but just a small collection which also gives you a very good idea of his individual style. You can also buy jewellery boxes and briefcases here along with his range for the shooting enthusiast.

Site Usability:	★★★	Based:	US
Product Range:	★★★	Express Delivery Option?	(UK) No
Price Range:	Luxury/Medium/Very Good Value	Gift Wrapping Option?	No
Delivery Area:	Worldwide	Returns Procedure:	Down to you

www.branded.net

Handbags, wallets and purses by Gucci, Christian Dior, Fendi, Dolce & Gabanna and Prada, all at discounted prices and from recent seasons' collections. The site is based in London UK and they'll ship all over the World. You always have to be careful when buying discounted designer labels in case they're not the real thing, however there are a number of re-sellers (at present) particularly in Italy who are able to sell on ends of lines and overstocks of real designer products and these are what you'll find here.

Site Usability:	★★★★	Based:	UK
Product Range:	★★★★	Express Delivery Option?	(UK) No
Price Range:	Luxury/Medium/Very Good Value	Gift Wrapping Option?	Yes
Delivery Area:	Worldwide	Returns Procedure:	Down to you

www.bravida.co.uk

Bravida offers a collection of simple, stylish handbags made by Italian craftsmen in very high quality leather. You may not be buying into a famous brand here, but many of the handbags are really chic and with prices starting at around £130 they're very good value. There are contemporary and classic bags plus a small collection of wallets. They'll ship worldwide and offer an express service.

Site Usability:	★★★	Based:	UK
Product Range:	★★★	Express Delivery Option?	(UK) Yes
Price Range:	Luxury/Medium/Very Good Value	Gift Wrapping Option?	No
Delivery Area:	Worldwide	Returns Procedure:	Down to you

www.kanishkabags.co.uk

This is a lovely, ethnically inspired collection of clothes and accessories and you're unlikely to find it in the shops. You'll discover beaded and quilted handbags (plus unusual straw totes in the summer), different and well priced jewellery, beautifully embroidered and colour woven shawls plus beaded silk and cotton kaftans, so if you like something totally unique you may find it here.

Site Usability:	★★★	Based:	UK
Product Range:	★★★	Express Delivery Option?	(UK) No
Price Range:	Luxury/Medium/Very Good Value	Gift Wrapping Option?	No
Delivery Area:	Worldwide	Returns Procedure:	Down to you

www.jandmdavidson.com

J & M Davidson design and produce beautiful quality and extremely expensive leather goods and clothing, including some very chic handbags and small accessories in lovely leathers and different colours. Their website is quite simple and the pictures small and not as good as they could be, however, don't be fooled. Anything you buy from them will be real designer quality, superbly made and will last you a long time.

Site Usability:	★★★	Based:	UK
Product Range:	★★★★	Express Delivery Option?	(UK) No
Price Range:	Luxury/Medium/Very Good Value	Gift Wrapping Option?	No
Delivery Area:	Worldwide	Returns Procedure:	Down to you

www.julieslaterandson.co.uk

You can certainly find these products on other websites (passport covers, address books, purses, luggage tags and the like), however probably you'd have to search long and hard to find the colour ranges offered here which include pistachio, aubergine, meadow blue, hot pink and carnation. Everything is beautifully pictured in detail so you'll know exactly what you're ordering. Delivery is worldwide with an express option for the UK and they'll gift wrap for you as well.

Site Usability:	★★★★	Based:	UK
Product Range:	★★★	Express Delivery Option?	(UK) Yes
Price Range:	Luxury/Medium/Very Good Value	Gift Wrapping Option?	Yes
Delivery Area:	Worldwide	Returns Procedure:	Down to you

www.lizcox.com

Liz Cox offers a very British collection of bags and luggage using exclusive fabrics, bridle and saddle leathers, and she's well known for her use of exotic patterns and innovative designs. Her shops are based in Bath and Notting Hill, London and you can now buy a selection of her range online. Prices are definitely not cheap, so make sure you're a colourful patterned bag sort of person before you invest (although you can buy her gorgeous leathers as well here). Call for gift wrapping and express delivery.

Site Usability:	★★★	Based:	UK
Product Range:	★★★	Express Delivery Option?	(UK) No
Price Range:	Luxury/Medium/Very Good Value	Gift Wrapping Option?	No
Delivery Area:	Worldwide	Returns Procedure:	Down to you but you need to tell them first

www.ollieandnic.com

Ollie & Nic's Vintage Chic collection conjures up the romance and nostalgia of yesteryear, featuring rich shades of merlot, midnight, tan and forest green. Brooches and corsages decorate bags and boudoir-inspired accessories, with the styling a mixture of old and new using tweed, fine needlecord, crochet, leather and their signature print. Think of antique flea markets, an undiscovered attic or your grandmother's jewellery box and you can imagine the look.

Site Usability:	★★★★	Based:	UK
Product Range:	★★★	Express Delivery Option?	(UK) No
Price Range:	Luxury/Medium/Very Good Value	Gift Wrapping Option?	No
Delivery Area:	Worldwide	Returns Procedure:	Down to you

www.orlakiely.com

Orla Kiely designs unique, instantly recognisable clothes and accessories, using bold and colourful patterns that are always fresh and appealing. On her website there is a small selection from her ready-to-wear clothing range, but a much wider choice of her unusual, attractive and highly functional accessories, including handbags, purses and luggage. They'll deliver anywhere in the world.

Site Usability:	★★★★		Based:	UK
Product Range:	★★★		Express Delivery Option?	(UK) No
Price Range:	Luxury/Medium/Very Good Value		Gift Wrapping Option?	No
Delivery Area:	Worldwide		Returns Procedure:	Down to you

www.osprey-london.co.uk

Osprey create beautifully crafted handbags and small leather accessories in high quality leathers, all designed by Graeme Ellisdon in Florence. The range includes classic and business handbags (but think modern business, so although they'll take all the papers you need to carry, they look like great bags as well), plus the London Collection of contemporary bags in tune with what's happening each season. They'll deliver anywhere in the world and offer an express service in the UK.

Site Usability:	★★★★		Based:	UK
Product Range:	★★★		Express Delivery Option?	(UK) Yes
Price Range:	Luxury/Medium/Very Good Value		Gift Wrapping Option?	No
Delivery Area:	Worldwide		Returns Procedure:	Down to you

www.pierotucci.com

I'm sure that you'd agree with me that if you really had your choice you'd be on that plane to Florence to choose your next Italian leather handbag, wallet or fur trimmed pair of gloves, however, if that's just not possible you should have a look at this Florence based website, where you can choose from classic, beautifully made Italian styling. They offer UPS express shipping to anywhere in the World.

Site Usability:	★★★★		Based:	Italy
Product Range:	★★★★		Express Delivery Option?	(UK) Yes
Price Range:	Luxury/Medium/Very Good Value		Gift Wrapping Option?	No
Delivery Area:	Worldwide		Returns Procedure:	Down to you

www.tabitha.uk.com

At Tabitha you can see some extremely covetable, not overpriced but very unusual bags and accessories in a choice of coloured leathers and metallics. There's lots to choose from, from the studded Angel Bag, to the chic Go Less Lightly bag with loads of pockets and buckles and my definite favourite the Lost Weekend Bag, just irresistible in ice white glazed leather. To order you need to complete their online form and email it back to them.

Site Usability:	★★★★		Based:	UK
Product Range:	★★★		Express Delivery Option?	(UK) No
Price Range:	Luxury/Medium/Very Good Value		Gift Wrapping Option?	No
Delivery Area:	Worldwide		Returns Procedure:	Down to you

Also visit these websites for handbags and small accessories

Website Address	You'll find them in
www.artigiano.co.uk	Fashion Retailers
www.debenhams.com	Fashion Retailers
www.anyahindmarch.com	Luxury Brands Online
www.lineafashion.com	Luxury Brands Online
www.luluguinness.com	Luxury Brands Online
www.mulberry.com	Luxury Brands Online
www.net-a-porter.com	Luxury Brands Online
www.gucci.com	Luxury Brands Online
www.forzieri.com	Luxury Brands Online
www.tannerkrolle.co.uk	Luxury Brands Online
www.pickett.co.uk	Mens Shoes and Accessories

Chapter 9

Shoes to Party In

nd to go shopping in, run for the train in, go to work in, go out to lunch in, go to the bar in, go simply anywhere in.

Like handbags, shoes say a lot about you. You need the right ones for you, for fashion, for what you're wearing and where you're going and the time of year. They can be more complicated than handbags, in fact, and can wreck your whole outfit if they're wrong – and haven't we all had that feeling?

However, help is at hand. You can find the shoes to take you to the ball online and you can spend from the totally ridiculous to the acceptable (well nearly). Beware shopaholics. If you're a shoe addict too this could really be your downfall.

Don't be scared of buying shoes online. Unlike clothing shoes usually (and I mean usually so don't blame me if someone's out of line) stay true to size. If you're a size 4/37/6.5 Artigiano you'll be the same size at Gina, or Pantalon Chameleon etc. If in doubt you can ask them if their shoes are standard, wide or narrow fitting. If narrow take a half size up.

Just in case you're in doubt, here are the size conversions for UK, European and US women's shoes

US	5.5	6	6.5	7	7.5	8	8.5	9	9.5
UK	3	3.5	4	4.5	5	5.5	6	6.5	7
European	36	36.5	37	37.5	38	38.5	39	39.5	40

Sites to Visit

www.dune.co.uk

Here you can buy from a range of trendy, affordable and stylish shoes and accessories including glitzy sandals, dressy pumps and flats, modern casual shoes and ballerinas and excellent boots. As well as all of this there are handbags, belts and sunglasses. The website is well photographed and easy to use and provided you place your order before 10am you'll receive it the next day.

Site Usability:	★★★★	Based:	UK
Product Range:	★★★	Express Delivery Option?	(UK) Yes
Price Range:	Luxury/Medium/Very Good Value	Gift Wrapping Option?	No
Delivery Area:	UK	Returns Procedure:	Down to you

www.espadrillesetc.com

Whether or not you're an espadrilles fan, if you're going on holiday you really should take a look at this summer shoe website, where there's every colour, fabric and style you can think of to choose from, including soft coloured suede and brightly coloured fabric espadrilles, plus some very pretty sandals, brightly coloured beach bags and totes and children's espadrilles as well. They'll be happy to ship to you anywhere in the world

Site Usability:	★★★★	Based:	Spain
Product Range:	★★★	Express Delivery Option?	(UK) No
Price Range:	Luxury/Medium/Very Good Value	Gift Wrapping Option?	No
Delivery Area:	Worldwide	Returns Procedure:	Down to you

www.faith.co.uk

In 1964 Samuel Faith established Faith shoes with the aim of combining style and affordability and he seems to have succeeded. You'll discover some extremely modern styles here plus some that are far more classic and they're all at very reasonable prices (you'll probably find yourself shopping without having intended to, particularly from their boots range). Faith Solo is the most avant-garde part of the collection and there are also some extremely well priced fun leather handbags.

Site Usability:	★★★★	Based:	UK
Product Range:	★★★	Express Delivery Option?	(UK) No
Price Range:	Luxury/Medium/Very Good Value	Gift Wrapping Option?	No
Delivery Area:	UK	Returns Procedure:	Down to you

www.floydshoes.co.uk

You won't find this collection of well priced shoes in any retail outlets (at least not at the time of writing) as they're currently only offered on this website and at regional fairs. All the shoes here are designed by Janice Floyd, who created her company in 2002 with the idea of producing distinctive, fashionable and elegant but fun shoes at an affordable price. There's also a small range of handbags in a selection of great colours.

Site Usability:	★★★★	Based:	UK
Product Range:	★★★	Express Delivery Option?	(UK) No
Price Range:	Luxury/<u>Medium</u>/Very Good Value	Gift Wrapping Option?	No
Delivery Area:	Worldwide	Returns Procedure:	Down to you

www.frenchsole.com

If you've been looking for the perfect ballet flat to update your spring/summer or autumn/winter wardrobe you need search no more. French Sole are well known for offering a wide range of styles, from the classic two-tone pump to this season's must-have animal print and metallic versions and each season they bring out new styles. They also offer high quality, well priced driving shoes in a range of colours from the palest pink nubuck to gold leather.

Site Usability:	★★★★	Based:	UK
Product Range:	★★★	Express Delivery Option?	(UK) No
Price Range:	Luxury/<u>Medium</u>/Very Good Value	Gift Wrapping Option?	No
Delivery Area:	Worldwide	Returns Procedure:	Down to you

www.helenbateman.com

Winner at the 2002 Footwear Awards for Customer Service this Edinburgh based shoe designer offers a pretty and unusual selection of shoes for all occasions. There's a great deal of choice from beaded Shantung silk evening shoes and stylish sandals to funky espadrilles in a range of colours. One of the great advantages of ordering shoes here is the amount of information on each style, from fit to fabric and heel height plus different views. As well as the shoes you'll find modern, well priced bags, must-have belts with beaded buckles and unusual scarves and jewellery.

Site Usability:	★★★★★	Express Delivery Option?	(UK) Yes
Product Range:	★★★★	Gift Wrapping Option?	No
Price Range:	Luxury/<u>Medium</u>/Very Good Value	Returns Procedure:	Down to you
Delivery Area:	Worldwide		

www.kurtgeiger.com

For some reason shoe designers have been extremely slow to get themselves online. Kurt Geiger is one of the top retailers leading the way and its ranges include not just Kurt Geiger but also Carvela, Emma Hope and Gina. Expect to find everything from high fashion to modern classic and young contemporary and a wide range of prices. They only deliver to the UK currently and offer an express service.

Site Usability:	★★★★★	Express Delivery Option?	(UK) Yes
Product Range:	★★★★	Gift Wrapping Option?	No
Price Range:	Luxury/Medium/Very Good Value	Returns Procedure:	Down to you
Delivery Area:	UK		

www.parallelshoes.com

Currently you have to call Parallel to order their shoes, however this is such a good collection, the website is well laid out and you can see all the designs really clearly so they're well worth having a look round. Shoes are divided up into 'Casual and Sporty', 'Evening and Dressy', 'Classic', 'Sexy and Feminine' and there are handbags (by designers such as Blumarine and Francesco Biasia) and belts as well. Next day delivery is standard.

Site Usability:	★★★★	Express Delivery Option?	(UK) Yes
Product Range:	★★★★★	Gift Wrapping Option?	No
Price Range:	Luxury/Medium/Very Good Value	Returns Procedure:	Down to you
Delivery Area:	UK		

www.prettyballerinas.com

Established in 1918 to make ballet shoes Pretty Ballerinas offer a wide selection of colours and prints including animal prints (zebra, leopard, or tiger) metallics, sequins, prints such as purple butterflies and fuchsia, green or blue satin. When you look at the site you need to be aware that all the prices are in Euros so you'll need to do the conversion to pounds, dollars or whatever currency you want to buy in. They're happy to ship to you anywhere in the world.

Site Usability:	★★★★	Based:	UK
Product Range:	★★★	Express Delivery Option?	(UK) No
Price Range:	Luxury/Medium/Very Good Value	Gift Wrapping Option?	No
Delivery Area:	Worldwide	Returns Procedure:	Down to you.

www.sand-monkey.com

If you fancy a change from run-of-the-mill synthetic flip-flops you should take a look at this collection of 'Sand monkeys' – leather sandals with cute, stylish and funky finishes including beads and shells, originally designed on a luxury safari camp in Kenya's Masai Mara to be worn by the camp's clients. You can now have them sent to you anywhere in the world and by express delivery if you ask specially nicely.

Site Usability:	★★★★	Based:	UK
Product Range:	★★★	Express Delivery Option?	(UK) Yes on request
Price Range:	Luxury/Medium/Very Good Value	Gift Wrapping Option?	No
Delivery Area:	Worldwide	Returns Procedure:	Down to you

www.scorahpattullo.com

If your taste is for the very (I mean very) high heeled and extremely modern then come and take a look round Scorah Puttullo, where their latest collections are just waiting to be delivered to you by high speed courier anywhere in the World. The emphasis is on the latest up to date styles, from flats and sandals to dressy heels so if you're looking for something new this season you may well find it here.

Site Usability: ★★★★	Based: UK
Product Range: ★★★	Express Delivery Option? (UK) No
Price Range: Luxury/Medium/Very Good Value	Gift Wrapping Option? No
Delivery Area: Worldwide	Returns Procedure: Down to you

www.schuhstore.co.uk

At schuhstore.co.uk there are lots of pairs of shoes from a wide choice of labels to choose from at very good prices. There are always some very modern styles and others extremely over colourful but there's such a large range here you'll surely discover something to suit. You can select from each range (boots, for example) whether you want high heel, mid heel, low heel or flat and the zoom feature allows you to get really close up to each product. You can also search by brand, style, price and what's new. They offer a 365 day returns policy for shoes returned in perfect condition.

Site Usability: ★★★★	Based: UK
Product Range: ★★★★★	Express Delivery Option? (UK) No
Price Range: Luxury/Medium/Very Good Value	Gift Wrapping Option? No
Delivery Area: UK	Returns Procedure: Down to you

www.strutshoes.co.uk

For those of you who really like (and presumably can walk in) the highest killer heels this is probably the place for you, where chic and very sophisticated sum up the style. There's nothing for the fainthearted here but if you like to make an impression you should definitely take a look round. The shoes are very dressy and there are some wonderful boots here you probably won't find anywhere else. There's a small but gorgeous range of handbags as well.

Site Usability: ★★★★	Based: UK
Product Range: ★★★	Express Delivery Option? (UK) Yes
Price Range: Luxury/Medium/Very Good Value	Gift Wrapping Option? No
Delivery Area: EU	Returns Procedure: Down to you

www.ugsandkisses.co.uk

The extraordinarily comfortable and popular Ugg boot from Australia is now available on this website, which offers the full range in both the short and tall versions and in a choice of colours. They also sell baby Uggs and sheepskin rugs and handcrafted reversible scarves and wraps. There's lots of information on how to care for your Uggs including Ugg Shampoo which you can order.

Site Usability:	★★★★★	Based:	UK
Product Range:	★★★	Express Delivery Option?	(UK) No
Price Range:	Luxury/<u>Medium</u>/Very Good Value	Gift Wrapping Option?	No
Delivery Area:	Worldwide	Returns Procedure:	Down to you

www.vivaladiva.com

This is an online store that's growing like Topsy with more and more styles and designers being added each season. You'll find couture shoes by Beatrix Ong, Cavalli, Sergio Rossi and Emma Hope, their Boutique collection with names such as LK Bennett and Hobbs plus much less expensive ranges like Schuh, Ecco and Converse. It's a fun website to take a look at with a lot of attitude and the shoes are displayed very clearly. Shoes range from £25 to £300. Watch out for new designers being included.

Site Usability:	★★★★★	Express Delivery Option?	(UK) Yes
Product Range:	★★★★	Gift Wrapping Option?	Yes/Automatic
Price Range:	<u>Luxury</u>/Medium/Very Good Value	Returns Procedure:	Free of charge by courier or Royal Mail
Delivery Area:	UK		

Also visit these websites for shoes

Website Address	You'll find them in
www.artigiano.co.uk	Fashion Retailers
www.boden.co.uk	Fashion Retailers
www.pantalonchameleon.com	Fashion Retailers
www.gina.com	Luxury Brands Online
www.gucci.com/uk	Luxury Brands Online
www.net-a-porter.com	Luxury Brands Online
www.paulsmith.co.uk	Luxury Brands Online
www.stuartweitzman.com	Shop America

Chapter 10

The Lingerie Dilemma

To bare or not to bare? Full cup, half cup, lacy or sporty, strappy or no straps at all, pink, white, yellow, brown, black, navy, red, floral, striped, leopard print, heart print or no print at all and that's just for the bras.

Probably because underwear is something you do really prefer to try on at home and it's very easy to send out and return if necessary, lingerie is one of the fastest growing and most successful areas of online shopping. Joy for the shopaholic. There's real choice from a selection of great sites offering quick (and often free) delivery and an excellent service all round. No longer are you limited to what's in stock at any given time in your local lingerie shop or department store. You can see everything. The choice is almost overwhelming.

I've only included here retailers that sell from their stock. There are one or two on the Internet who only order in and whose service is bad, bad, bad. There should be enough here for even the most ardent bra collector so I suggest that you stay with these sites.

And on to ...

What'll you be wearing on the beach next summer?

There are some people (or so I've heard) to whom slipping into a micro string bikini (is there such a thing?) is just as easy as pulling on their size 8 (UK) jeans and a t-shirt. Well lucky them is all I can say.

To those perfectly normal shopaholics who hate trying on new swimwear in a cramped changing room, well before they've had a chance to do that 100 hours in the gym (just joking), and before they've either exposed themselves to some colour enhancing rays or a fake tan, these websites offer a great alternative.

Not only is there a very good choice but you can try your selection on at home and make sure you're happy rather than making an off-the-cuff decision in a shop that you may regret and a) sheepishly take back or b) not take back and never wear.

As many of the lingerie retailers sell properly sized swimwear you should have no problems in ordering online, whether you're looking for a bikini, tankini or flattering one piece so there's no excuse from now on. You can look great on the beach (or by the pool, whatever) and enjoy the shopping experience, as you should.

Sites to Visit

www.agentprovocateur.com

Joseph Corre and Serena Rees opened the first Agent Provocateur shop in December 1994 and have never looked back. The look is overt and sexy and you'll find just that on their extremely unusual website, where their gorgeous lingerie is displayed with attitude on the most perfect bodies. Don't come here if you're looking for something in a size larger than a 36E or if you want a website where ordering is easy, it's not until you've got used to it. Do come here if you love their products and don't want to have to go out to find them.

Site Usability:	★★★	Based:	UK
Product Range:	★★★★	Express Delivery Option?	(UK) No
Price Range:	Luxury/Medium/Very Good Value	Gift Wrapping Option?	No but packaging is very attractive
Delivery Area:	Worldwide	Returns Procedure:	Down to you

www.barenecessities.co.uk

Barenecessities.co.uk is an excellent site offering a range of lingerie and swimwear from brands such as Fantasie, Aubade, Prima Donna and Lejaby plus La Perla hosiery. They stock all items where possible and their size range is from A to HH/JJ. They also stock mastectomy lingerie and swimwear and really care about their service so give them a call if you want to ask them any questions. They don't pretend to offer a huge range in any area but what they offer is well worth a look.

Site Usability:	★★★★	Based:	UK
Product Range:	★★★★	Express Delivery Option?	(UK) Yes
Price Range:	Luxury/Medium/Very Good Value	Gift Wrapping Option?	Yes
Delivery Area:	Worldwide	Returns Procedure:	Down to you

www.belladinotte.com

This is a very smiley website with very smiley models showing really pretty nightwear, lingerie and tops. Italian silk and wool (washable) blend tops come in modern colours such as chocolate, aubergine and (of course) black. Lingerie is by Chantelle and Lejaby and their range of wool and silk thermals, sleeveless, short sleeved and long sleeved, frequently trimmed in lace and in white, ivory, black and, on occasion, garnet, could certainly be worn as tops.

Site Usability:	★★★★	Based:	UK
Product Range:	★★★★	Express Delivery Option?	(UK) Yes
Price Range:	Luxury/Medium/Very Good Value	Gift Wrapping Option?	Yes
Delivery Area:	Worldwide	Returns Procedure:	Down to you

www.bodas.co.uk

Much loved by glossy magazine fashion editors for its modern minimal style, at Bodas you won't find loads of lace or extra details but just chic, seamfree and form fitting lingerie with a choice of colours, beautifully photographed and including briefs, camisoles, vests, crop tops and a small range of swimwear in season. Just a word of warning, they don't really offer anything much beyond a 36D, so if you're looking for a larger size this is not the place for you.

Site Usability:	★★★★★	Based:	UK
Product Range:	★★★	Express Delivery Option?	(UK) Yes
Price Range:	Luxury/Medium/Very Good Value	Gift Wrapping Option?	No
Delivery Area:	Worldwide	Returns Procedure:	Down to you

www.bonsoirbypost.com

Here's very pretty nightwear from Bonsoir by Post, ranging from soft dreamy cotton, to Italian lace and pure silk in a range of colours. Be warned though, if your taste is for black or neutral you won't find much of it here, but colours such as ash, heather, pale blue and white. There's also a small range of loungewear, including Yoga pants, fluffy towels and bath robes plus scented candles, mules, beaded slippers and bedsocks.

Site Usability:	★★★★	Based:	UK
Product Range:	★★★	Express Delivery Option?	(UK) Yes
Price Range:	Luxury/Medium/Very Good Value	Gift Wrapping Option?	Yes
Delivery Area:	Worldwide	Returns Procedure:	Down to you

www.bravissimo.com

Bravissimo was started to fill the niche in the market created by those who aren't looking for lingerie or swimwear in minute sizes. They offer a wide selection of lingerie in D to JJ cup plus bra-sized swimwear in D to J cup, making it the essential site for the fuller figure. You'll find strappy tops and sports bras and fitting advice as well. Their service is really excellent and if you have any queries you can email them and they'll come back to you immediately. They'll ship to you speedily anywhere.

Site Usability:	★★★★★	Based:	UK
Product Range:	★★★★	Express Delivery Option?	(UK) Yes but you need to call them
Price Range:	Luxury/Medium/Very Good Value	Gift Wrapping Option?	No
Delivery Area:	Worldwide	Returns Procedure:	Free

www.contessa.org.uk

Contessa has a superb selection of bras and briefs in every colourway and style you can think of. You can choose by brand, style, size or colour or to make matters even easier just click on your size on the Home Page and everything that they have in stock can be viewed straight away. The emphasis here is very much on price and they frequently have some excellent offers. They'll ship worldwide and giftwrap your order as well.

Site Usability:	★★★★★	Based:	UK
Product Range:	★★★★	Express Delivery Option?	(UK) Yes
Price Range:	Luxury/Medium/Very Good Value	Gift Wrapping Option?	Yes
Delivery Area:	Worldwide	Returns Procedure:	Down to you

www.elingerie.uk.net

This is a really calm, well photographed and easy to find your way round website, offering brands such as Rigby and Peller, Chantelle, Janet Reger, Huit, Freya, Splendour, Panache and lots more. The products are all very easy to see although I suggest you search for your size rather than pick on a range and find it's not available for you. There's also lots of help for men buying lingerie as gifts, plus a gift wrap service.

Site Usability:	★★★★	Based:	UK
Product Range:	★★★★	Express Delivery Option?	(UK) No
Price Range:	Luxury/Medium/Very Good Value	Gift Wrapping Option?	Yes
Delivery Area:	Worldwide	Returns Procedure:	Down to you

www.elishalauren.co.uk

Sizing here is from AA to J and you'll find a full range including everyday bras, smooth styles, shapewear, bridal lingerie, basques and corsets plus maternity and sports bras. Ranges stocked are Ballet, Charnos, Panache, Naturana, Braza, Nubra and Ultimo. So if you want to take a look around on a website that is calm and easy to go round and order from, try this one. They also offer some very good discounts from time to time.

Site Usability:	★★★★	Based:	UK
Product Range:	★★★	Express Delivery Option?	(UK) No
Price Range:	Luxury/Medium/Very Good Value	Gift Wrapping Option?	No
Delivery Area:	Worldwide	Returns Procedure:	Down to you

www.figleaves.com

If you can't find it here, you may well not be able to find it anywhere else as this is definitely one of the best collections of lingerie, swimwear and sportswear available online. Almost every lingerie brand name is offered, from DKNY, Dolce and Gabbana and Janet Reger to Sloggi, Gossard and Wonderbra and delivery is free throughout the World. All sizes are covered from the very small to the very large and there's a huge choice in just about every category.

Site Usability:	★★★★★	Based:	UK
Product Range:	★★★★★	Express Delivery Option?	(UK) Yes
Price Range:	Luxury/Medium/Very Good Value	Gift Wrapping Option?	Yes
Delivery Area:	Worldwide	Returns Procedure:	Free in the UK

www.glamonweb.co.uk

This is quite an unusual website with some slightly strange translations (probably due to the fact that they're electronic, rather than done by real people) offering lingerie, hosiery and nightwear by La Perla, Marvel and Malizia. This is beautiful and luxurious lingerie as you would expect with prices to match, and I would suggest that you make sure that you know your La Perla size before you order as the sizing is not standard. If in doubt you can email or call their customer service team.

Site Usability:	★★★★	Based:	UK
Product Range:	★★★★	Express Delivery Option?	(UK) Yes
Price Range:	Luxury/Medium/Very Good Value	Gift Wrapping Option?	No
Delivery Area:	Europe	Returns Procedure:	Down to you

www.glamorousamorous.com

You'll find some quite different lingerie here – think animal print and marabou trim from Frankly Darling, Kitten cami and suspenders from Discover Mademoiselle and a lace bustier and thong from Bacirubati and you'll get the kind of idea – extremely glam in other words. There's a 'Lingerie and Gift Guide' with help for men buying presents and everything arrives in a silk organza bag, wrapped in tissue paper scented with Provencal lavender.

Site Usability:	★★★★★	Based:	UK
Product Range:	★★★★	Express Delivery Option?	(UK) Yes
Price Range:	Luxury/Medium/Very Good Value	Gift Wrapping Option?	Yes
Delivery Area:	Worldwide	Returns Procedure:	Down to you

www.heavenlybodice.com

This is a lingerie website particularly good for gifts and particularly from him to her. You can choose from a wide range of designers, from Charnos and Warners to Naughty Janet and Shirley of Hollywood. There's an excellent selection of bridal lingerie, a separate section for larger sizes, swimwear by

Fantasie, Panache and Freya and gifts by price band or in the 'Naughty' category. There's also a gift guide specifically for men.

Site Usability:	★★★★	Based:	UK
Product Range:	★★★★	Express Delivery Option?	(UK) No
Price Range:	Luxury/Medium/Very Good Value	Gift Wrapping Option?	Yes
Delivery Area:	Worldwide	Returns Procedure:	Down to you

www.hush-uk.com

Hush-uk.com has a really well designed and beautifully photographed website where there are lots of clothes for going to sleep in or just for lounging around, with nightdresses, pyjamas and gowns, vest tops, t-shirts and sloppy joes and also kaftans and sarongs for the beach and sheepskin slippers. In their gift ideas section you can combine various items to be wrapped up together and they offer Gift Vouchers as well.

Site Usability:	★★★★	Based:	UK
Product Range:	★★★★	Express Delivery Option?	(UK) Yes
Price Range:	Luxury/Medium/Very Good Value	Gift Wrapping Option?	Yes
Delivery Area:	Worldwide	Returns Procedure:	Down to you

www.janetreger.co.uk

On Janet Reger's beautiful, dark website, there's the most gorgeous selection of lingerie, where the prices are definitely not for the faint hearted. Once you've picked the style you like you can immediately see all the other items in the range plus colourways and size options (don't expect large sizes here). This brand is totally about luxe and glamour so be prepared to spend a small fortune, but on absolutely wonderful quality and style.

Site Usability:	★★★★★	Based:	UK
Product Range:	★★★★	Express Delivery Option?	(UK) Yes
Price Range:	Luxury/Medium/Very Good Value	Gift Wrapping Option?	Yes
Delivery Area:	Worldwide	Returns Procedure:	Down to you

www.ladybarbarella.com

Specialising in exclusive vintage pieces, decadent silks and burlesque styles, plus designs aimed at the many of us who can't fit into a 32B, at Lady Barbarella you can browse through a delightful selection of less available designers including Damaris Evans, Emma Benham, Frankly Darling, FleurT, Spoylt and Yes Master plus many more. This is a very prettily and cleverly designed website well worth a look if you like something a bit different.

Site Usability:	★★★★	Based:	UK
Product Range:	★★★	Express Delivery Option?	(UK) Yes
Price Range:	Luxury/Medium/Very Good Value	Gift Wrapping Option?	Yes
Delivery Area:	Worldwide	Returns Procedure:	Down to you

www.lasenza.co.uk

La Senza is an own brand lingerie retailer originally based in Canada and also well established in the United Kingdom. You'll find a large choice of lingerie and nightwear ranging from beautiful basics to seriously sexy styles as well as bra accessories. Their site is clear and easy to use. It's great to know that retailers are actually catering for those who want something larger than a C cup as sizes also go from 30A to 38F. Yes you can buy colours, plunge bras and diamante trimmed bras even if you're a DD or above and you'll also find cleavage enhancers, extra bra straps and strap extenders here as well.

Site Usability:	★★★★★	Based:	UK
Product Range:	★★★★★	Express Delivery Option?	(UK) Yes
Price Range:	Luxury/Medium/<u>Very Good Value</u>	Gift Wrapping Option?	Yes
Delivery Area:	Worldwide	Returns Procedure:	Down to you

www.myla.com

Of course, chocolate body paint may be just what you're looking for, along with some of the more risqué items offered on this sexy lingerie website (I'll say no more) but if what you're looking for is really beautiful feminine lingerie then just click into their lingerie section and ignore the rest. They also offer suspenders, thongs, feather boas, silk mules, camis and baby dolls and sizing goes up to a 36E in some parts of the range.

Site Usability:	★★★★	Based:	UK
Product Range:	★★★	Express Delivery Option?	(UK) Yes
Price Range:	<u>Luxury/Medium</u>/Very Good Value	Gift Wrapping Option?	No
Delivery Area:	Worldwide	Returns Procedure:	Down to you

www.rigbyandpeller.com

You may know their shop just round the side of Harrods where you can be properly fitted for your next bra and choose from a chic selection of lingerie. If you can't get to Knightsbridge you can now see the range on their website, where they offer a wide range of brands such as Aubade, Lejaby, La Perla and their own, and a superb service. They endeavour to despatch all orders within 48 hours and will send to you anywhere in the World.

Site Usability:	★★★★	Based:	UK
Product Range:	★★★★	Express Delivery Option?	(UK) Yes
Price Range:	<u>Luxury/Medium</u>/Very Good Value	Gift Wrapping Option?	Yes
Delivery Area:	Worldwide	Returns Procedure:	Down to you

www.sassyandrose.co.uk

If you're a collector of gorgeous nightwear (and definitely one of those who likes to look glam when she goes to bed rather than the novelty t-shirt kind) you should have a browse here at a colourful range of camisoles, chemises, nightdresses, kaftans and pjs in high quality but well priced silk and embroidered cotton. If you want delivery outside the UK you need to call them and they aim to ship everything within two days.

Site Usability:	★★★	Based:	UK
Product Range:	★★★	Express Delivery Option?	(UK) No
Price Range:	Luxury/<u>Medium</u>/Very Good Value	Gift Wrapping Option?	No
Delivery Area:	Worldwide	Returns Procedure:	Down to you

www.silkstorm.com

The next time you're looking for something out of the ordinary take a look here at Silk Storm – an online lingerie boutique offering luxury French and Italian brands with collections including Aubade, Valery, Argentovivo, Cotton Club and Barbara. Everything is beautifully photographed and the sizing help is excellent although don't expect anything to go much above a 36D. They're aiming this very much at men buying lingerie for their ladies with sexy pictures and gorgeous gift wrapping.

Site Usability:	★★★★	Based:	UK
Product Range:	★★★	Express Delivery Option?	(UK) Yes
Price Range:	Luxury/<u>Medium</u>/Very Good Value	Gift Wrapping Option?	Yes
Delivery Area:	Worldwide	Returns Procedure:	Down to you

www.sophieandgrace.co.uk

Sophie and Grace offer top quality lingerie, nightwear and swimwear including the bridal ranges of Honeymoon Pearls and Verde Veronica where you'll find garters, bras and briefs, basques and nightgowns with touches such as embroidered lace and pearl straps. This is a very different and luxurious range of lingerie and you'll no doubt want some to take away on honeymoon as well. Delivery is free and everything is automatically tissue wrapped and gift boxed.

Site Usability:	★★★★	Based:	UK
Product Range:	★★★	Express Delivery Option?	(UK) Yes
Price Range:	<u>Luxury/Medium</u>/Very Good Value	Gift Wrapping Option?	Yes
Delivery Area:	UK Call them for Overseas	Returns Procedure:	Down to you

www.the-lingerie-company.co.uk

Based in Hinkley in Leicestershire, this retailer offers lingerie by a multitude of designers including Berlie, Chantelle, Charnos, Warners, Rigby and Peller and Gossard. Swimwear is by Aubade, Footprints and Fantasie. It's a very simply designed website (and very pink) with an excellent search facility so you can pick exactly what you're looking for. Expect a high level of personal service and quick delivery.

Site Usability:	★★★★	Based:	UK
Product Range:	★★★★	Express Delivery Option?	(UK) No
Price Range:	Luxury/<u>Medium</u>/Very Good Value	Gift Wrapping Option?	No
Delivery Area:	Worldwide	Returns Procedure:	Down to you

www.tightsplease.co.uk

Whether you want fishnets and crochet tights, bright colours, knee highs, stay-ups, stockings or footsies you'll find them all here plus leg warmers, socks and flight socks, maternity and bridal hosiery. This website really caters for all your hosiery needs and with names such as Aristoc, Pretty Polly and Charnos offered you should never run out again. As an extra benefit delivery is free in the UK and takes only 1–2 days.

Site Usability:	★★★★★	Based:	UK
Product Range:	★★★★★	Express Delivery Option?	(UK) Automatic
Price Range:	Luxury/Medium/Very Good Value	Gift Wrapping Option?	No
Delivery Area:	Worldwide	Returns Procedure:	Free

www.vollers-corsets.com

This is quite simply an amazing collection of corsets, both for underwear and outerwear. The sexy and feminine designs include ruched velvet, satin, lace, leather, beaded brocade, gold and silver fabric, moiré and tartan and with flower, feather, lace and velvet trims. Sizes go from an 18 to 38 waist or you can have a corset specially made for you. There are corsets perfect for weddings and special occasions and most are available in a range of colours.

Site Usability:	★★★★★	Based:	UK
Product Range:	★★★★★	Express Delivery Option?	(UK) Yes
Price Range:	Luxury/Medium/Very Good Value	Gift Wrapping Option?	No
Delivery Area:	Worldwide	Returns Procedure:	Down to you

www.wolfordboutiquelondon.com

Wolford are world famous for their top quality hosiery, bodies, tops and lingerie and you can now purchase their collection online, through their London South Molton Street shop. The range includes sexy and beautifully photographed seasonally inspired pieces and is being updated all the time. Wolford are definitely not the cheapest for any part of their range but everything is of the highest quality and well worth an investment.

Site Usability:	★★★★	Based:	UK
Product Range:	★★★★★	Express Delivery Option?	(UK) Yes
Price Range:	Luxury/Medium/Very Good Value	Gift Wrapping Option?	No
Delivery Area:	Worldwide	Returns Procedure:	Down to you

Also check out this website for lingerie and swimwear

Website Address	You'll find it in
www.victoriassecret.com	Shop America

Swimwear and Resortwear

Sites to Visit

www.heidiklein.com

Heidi Klein offer really beautiful holidaywear, from chic bikinis and one piece swimsuits to kaftans, skirts, tops and sarongs and the collection is available all the year round. Currently it's a small range as the website is quite new but new collections are being added each season and there's certainly enough here to put all the essentials together you could need for your next trip away to the sun. There's a same day delivery service in London

Site Usability:	★★★★	Based:	UK
Product Range:	★★★	Express Delivery Option?	(UK) Yes
Price Range:	Luxury/Medium/Very Good Value	Gift Wrapping Option?	Yes
Delivery Area:	Worldwide	Returns Procedure:	Down to you

www.kikoy.com

For holidays and trips abroad you'll definitely want to know about this colourful website, offering fine cotton and muslin shorts, kaftans, cover-ups, trousers, hats and bags plus beach towels. There are some excellent summer/holiday gift ideas here but if you see something you want in a hurry give them a call to make sure that they have it in stock. If they do, they'll ship it to you for next day delivery. They're happy to deliver to you anywhere in the world.

Site Usability:	★★★★	Based:	UK
Product Range:	★★★	Express Delivery Option?	(UK) Yes
Price Range:	Luxury/Medium/Very Good Value	Gift Wrapping Option?	No
Delivery Area:	Worldwide	Returns Procedure:	Down to you

www.sexykaftans.com

There were so many kaftans around last summer that you're almost certainly aware by now that this is a must-have for summer holidays. Whether they're in fashion or not (and I'm sure they will be for a while) they're great for wearing over a swimsuit when you want something with a bit more cover than a sarong. Here's an excellent collection, long, short, colourful or neutral and beautifully embroidered. You'll definitely find yours here. Delivery is worldwide.

Site Usability:	★★★	Based:	UK
Product Range:	★★★	Express Delivery Option?	(UK) Yes
Price Range:	Luxury/Medium/Very Good Value	Gift Wrapping Option?	No
Delivery Area:	Worldwide	Returns Procedure:	Down to you

www.simplybeach.com

At last, a really great website devoted just to swimwear and including designer brands Melissa Obadash, Gideon Oberson and Wahine with swimsuits and bikinis in all shapes and sizes. There's a wide range of accessories as well including cover-ups, towels, beach bags and inflatables and direct links through to their other website where you'll find everything for scuba diving and snorkelling. Get ready for your next beach holiday and take a good look round.

Site Usability:	★★★★★	Based:	UK
Product Range:	★★★★	Express Delivery Option?	(UK) Yes
Price Range:	Luxury/<u>Medium</u>/Very Good Value	Gift Wrapping Option?	No
Delivery Area:	Worldwide	Returns Procedure:	Down to you

www.splashhawaii.com

Not for the faint hearted, this Hawaii based site (lucky things) really only sells bikinis (and diddy ones at that), but there's a very good choice so if you fit into the bikini category it's well worth having a look. Billabong, Roxy and Tommy Hilfiger are just some of the brands available plus US designers you may well not have heard of. They'll ship worldwide but if you take my advice you'll make that special journey and go and collect yours.

Site Usability:	★★★★	Based:	Hawaii
Product Range:	★★★	Express Delivery Option?	(UK) No
Price Range:	Luxury/<u>Medium</u>/Very Good Value	Gift Wrapping Option?	No
Delivery Area:	Worldwide	Returns Procedure:	Down to you

Also check out these websites for swimwear and resortwear

Website address	You'll find it in
www.barenecessities.co.uk	Lingerie
www.bravissimo.com	Lingerie
www.figleaves.com	Lingerie
www.heavenlybodice.com	Lingerie
www.sophieandgrace.co.uk	Lingerie
www.the-lingerie-company.co.uk	Lingerie
www.grahamkandiah.com	Shop America
www.swimwearboutique.com	Shop America
www.victoriassecret.com	Shop America

Chapter 11

What to Wear with a Bump

Where do you go for great maternity clothes? Do you want to go searching around in the shops, where you'll find some horrifically expensive clothes you'll only be wearing for a few months? (Well ok, maybe a few times for a few months but even so ...). Or would you rather look at maternity retailers where you'll find something much less expensive, that almost certainly won't make you feel good, at a time when you definitely need everything you can to make you feel your best as you get larger and larger (and I know about this).

It very much depends of course on what sort of lifestyle you lead. If you work full time you'll probably need smart clothes to take you right up to just before you're due to produce. You may likewise do a lot of entertaining. Or you may live out in the country and need great jeans, tops and jackets and just a few smart things.

Now that there are so many maternity stores online you can find all the smart and casual clothes you could possibly need without any trouble, from the extremely glamorous to simple, easy and comfortable and from the really quite expensive to the very well priced.

A few years ago you had to search for great maternity shops and if you'd left it rather late (until you really couldn't make do with your current wardrobe) you'd have to go round the shops and exhaust yourself in the process. Now of course the beauty of the internet is that you can just sit back, click round and make all your choices online. With next day delivery being an option at most of the sites your new clothes will be with you almost immediately.

So enjoy these excellent websites whose main aim in life is to make your life easy at a time when you certainly need it to be, and to help you to look your best at the same time.

Sites to Visit

www.bjornandme.co.uk

For choice and value you'd find it hard to beat this website, where the clothes are divided up into sections such as Outdoor and Exercise wear/Formalwear/Petite/Tall and Plus Size. There's also swimwear and lingerie, so whether you're looking for a pair of soft white linen trousers or something for the Oscars, you'll almost certainly find it here – the evening and occasionwear is particularly good. This is international designer styled maternity wear and a very good collection.

Site Usability:	★★★★	Based:	UK
Product Range:	★★★★	Express Delivery Option?	(UK) Yes
Price Range:	Luxury/Medium/Very Good Value	Gift Wrapping Option?	No
Delivery Area:	Worldwide	Returns Procedure:	Down to you

www.blossommotherandchild.com

Blossom caters for the fashion conscious expectant mum, with a collection of glamorous dresses and separates which combine high-end fashion with comfort and functionality without sacrificing quality and style. You'll also find customised jeans by brands such as Rock and Republic and James. They use an assortment of luxurious fabrics such as silk-cashmere, voile and fluid and matte jersey and expand the collection continuously – summer 2006 saw the launch of their first swimwear line and they'll shortly be launching babywear.

Site Usability:	★★★★	Based:	UK
Product Range:	★★★★	Express Delivery Option?	(UK) Yes
Price Range:	Luxury/Medium/Very Good Value	Gift Wrapping Option?	No
Delivery Area:	Worldwide	Returns Procedure:	Down to you

www.bumpsmaternity.com

Bumps Maternity was established several years ago to offer stylish and out of the ordinary maternity wear from occasion dressing to casual and holiday. It's only available online and consists of a fun, well photographed range. This is not a huge selection but definitely merits clicking through as most items are very good value and they'll ship all over the World. You can buy maternity lingerie and plus size clothes here as well.

Site Usability:	★★★★	Based:	UK
Product Range:	★★★	Express Delivery Option?	(UK) Yes
Price Range:	Luxury/Medium/Very Good Value	Gift Wrapping Option?	No
Delivery Area:	Worldwide	Returns Procedure:	Down to you

www.cravematernity.co.uk

This is a well designed, friendly and clearly photographed website offering well cut and versatile separates and dresses in good fabrics and at reasonable prices. You'll find tailoring, eveningwear and casual separates all aimed at the busy woman who wants to carry on with her normal life and look smart throughout her pregnancy and afterwards. This is a website just for maternity clothes so you're not going to be sidetracked by the children's clothes and accessories you'll find on so many other sites here.

Site Usability:	★★★★	Based:	UK
Product Range:	★★★	Express Delivery Option?	(UK) No
Price Range:	Luxury/Medium/Very Good Value	Gift Wrapping Option?	No
Delivery Area:	Worldwide	Returns Procedure:	Down to you

www.formes.com

Formes is a French company offering beautifully styled 'designer' pregnancy wear and selling all over the world. You won't find their full collection here, but an edited range and it's well worth looking through. Unlike a lot of the maternity shops here you'll find all the information you could possibly want, from complete product detailing to fabric content and full measurements plus very clear pictures.

Site Usability:	★★★★★	Based:	UK
Product Range:	★★★★	Express Delivery Option?	(UK) No
Price Range:	Luxury/Medium/Very Good Value	Gift Wrapping Option?	No
Delivery Area:	Worldwide	Returns Procedure:	Down to you

www.hommemummy.co.uk

This is where to come if you're looking for simple, elegant maternity wear that will travel well and look great all the time as everything is made from soft, comfortable, luxury jersey, stretch lace and cord, from tops to trousers and skirts. You can also buy the Essential Maternity Wardrobe here which includes a go-anywhere trouser, elegant wrap top and glamorous versatile dress. There are really good line drawings of all the items to go with the photos so you can see the shapes more clearly.

Site Usability:	★★★★	Based:	UK
Product Range:	★★★	Express Delivery Option?	(UK) Yes
Price Range:	Luxury/Medium/Very Good Value	Gift Wrapping Option?	No
Delivery Area:	Worldwide	Returns Procedure:	Down to you

www.isabellaoliver.com

Isabella Oliver is a maternity wear company for pregnant women who love clothes. Their sexy designs in soft jersey fabrics have signature style details like ruching and wrapping to flatter new curves. Every item arrives gift wrapped and their brochure and website include style tips to pick up on the season's trends. Isabella Oliver also offers lingerie, loungewear, sophisticated sleepwear, chic outerwear, and sun and swimwear, plus gift vouchers from £30. Call them if you want some expert advice.

Site Usability:	★★★★★	Based:	UK
Product Range:	★★★	Express Delivery Option?	(UK) Yes
Price Range:	Luxury/Medium/Very Good Value	Gift Wrapping Option?	Yes
Delivery Area:	Worldwide	Returns Procedure:	Free

www.jojomamanbebe.co.uk

This is a really pretty website offering a very good choice for expectant mothers, babies and young children. The drop-down menus on the home page take you quickly and clearly to everything you might be looking for, whether it's maternity occasionwear or safety gates for young children. There's a good range of maternity underwear and swimwear as well. They have some very good gift ideas and offer gift vouchers and gift boxes as well to make your life easier.

Site Usability:	★★★★★	Based:	UK
Product Range:	★★★★	Express Delivery Option?	(UK) No
Price Range:	Luxury/Medium/Very Good Value	Gift Wrapping Option?	No
Delivery Area:	Worldwide	Returns Procedure:	Down to you

www.pushmaternity.com

The Push boutique in Islington specialises in designer maternity wear and a high level of customer service. Now you can buy the collection online from labels such as Earl Jean, Tashia, Alex Gore Brown, Cadeau, Citizens of Humanity, Leona Edmiston (gorgeous jersey dresses) and Juicy Couture. There's maternity hosiery and chic baby bags here as well. Select from next day or standard delivery (UK though they ship overseas as well) and if you have any queries don't hesitate to give them a call.

Site Usability:	★★★★	Based:	UK
Product Range:	★★★	Express Delivery Option?	(UK) Yes
Price Range:	Luxury/Medium/Very Good Value	Gift Wrapping Option?	No
Delivery Area:	Worldwide	Returns Procedure:	Down to you

www.seraphine.com

Find excellent maternity wear here on this really prettily photographed website where the collection is stylish and different and the prices reasonable. You can choose from the latest looks, maternity essentials and glamorous partywear and as well as all of this there's lingerie by Elle Mcpherson, Nougatine and Canelle, gorgeous layettes for newborn babies and Tommy's Ts. Delivery takes up to five working days; you'll find postage costs for the UK and EU on the website and email them for elsewhere.

Site Usability:	★★★★	Based:	UK	
Product Range:	★★★★	Express Delivery Option?	(UK) No	
Price Range:	Luxury/Medium/Very Good Value	Gift Wrapping Option?	No	
Delivery Area:	Worldwide	Returns Procedure:	Down to you	

www.serendipity-online.com

A very unusual and attractively designed website offering designer maternity wear from Earl Jean, Chiarakruza, Belly Basics, Bella Materna, C&C California and Kate Spade, to name but a few. Calling themselves 'the one stop online boutique for hip mums and their babies', Serendipity Online offer an excellent service with standard, next day and even same day delivery for central London. This really is the designer end of maternity wear and it's an extremely good collection.

Site Usability:	★★★★	Based:	UK	
Product Range:	★★★★	Express Delivery Option?	(UK) Yes	
Price Range:	Luxury/Medium/Very Good Value	Gift Wrapping Option?	No	
Delivery Area:	UK	Returns Procedure:	Down to you	

www.tiffanyrose.co.uk

Here you'll find smart and quite unusual maternity wear including dresses and chic separates. It's quite a small range but very stylish so if you're looking for something for a special occasion you should have a click round. There are also beautiful maternity wedding dresses and a sale area where there are usually some very good discounts. They deliver worldwide and offer a next day and Saturday delivery service for the UK.

Site Usability:	★★★★	Based:	UK	
Product Range:	★★★	Express Delivery Option?	(UK) Yes	
Price Range:	Luxury/Medium/Very Good Value	Gift Wrapping Option?	No	
Delivery Area:	Worldwide	Returns Procedure:	Down to you	

Also check out these websites for maternitywear

Website Address	You'll find it in
www.bloomingmarvellous.co.uk	Baby and Toddler Clothes
www.mamasandpapas.co.uk	Baby and Toddler Clothes
www.figleaves.com	Lingerie and Swimwear

Chapter 12

Sunglasses

To hold your hair back, look cool in, keep the wind out of your eyes, hide your face or even to keep the sun out of your eyes (yes really, I hear that some people do wear them for that). Sunglasses have become an essential fashion statement and if you believe what the designers tell you you'll be buying a new pair each season (to go with your new wardrobe, of course).

You can often get a better deal buying your sunglasses online than buying them in the shops but no matter how much a certain pair calls to you, you need to be sure that they're going to be right for you. Either they must be a make and shape you've had before, or you must be pretty sure that they will suit you and believe me they're all different and we're all different.

So to make this exercise as risk free as possible stay closely to what you've liked and what has suited you before and/or go to *www.unitedshades.com* and have a look at their 'choose the style to suit your face' guide, which is really excellent and advises on which shapes to buy for different faces, think round, square, oblong or oval. Then check out the prices on the sites below and 'stay cool'.

If you're a fan of sports' sunglasses and goggles you can find these here too with brands such as Oakley, Bolle and Spy together with replacement lenses for particular sports such as fishing, golf, tennis, shooting and skiing. You can also order prescription sunglasses, children's sunglasses and safety glasses on some of these websites.

Sites to Visit

www.shadestation.co.uk

For the cooler end of the market have a look round here, where the emphasis is on young, modern styles from brands such as Prada, Police, D & G, Diesel, Gucci and Armani and you'll find watches by some of these names as well. They stock the complete Oakley brand including glasses, accessories, goggles and watches plus replacement lenses and sunglass cases.

Site Usability:	★★★	Based:	UK
Product Range:	★★★	Express Delivery Option?	(UK) Yes
Price Range:	Luxury/Medium/Very Good Value	Gift Wrapping Option?	No
Delivery Area:	UK	Returns Procedure:	Down to you

www.ten-eighty.co.uk

By far the best thing about this site is their range of Oakley sunglasses and lenses. Whereas on most sites you'll be offered a style and that's it, here with their help you can create your own, particularly for sports use, and their service is really excellent. Persevere with this site although some of it is hard to read and you do have to scroll around a lot. It will be worth it. If you want extra advice don't hesitate to call them.

Site Usability:	★★★	Based:	UK
Product Range:	★★★	Express Delivery Option?	(UK) Yes
Price Range:	Luxury/Medium/Very Good Value	Gift Wrapping Option?	No
Delivery Area:	UK	Returns Procedure:	Down to you

www.the-eye-shop.com

This website is based in Chamonix in France (where you do need sunglasses a lot of the time, of course) and the list of brand names is fantastic, including Chanel, Dior, Diesel, Bolle, Oakley, Quicksilver and Valentino. They claim to hold almost everything in stock and delivery is free by UPS. You'll also buy from a very good selection of sport goggles here from brands such as Cebe, Oakley and Adidas plus binoculars and GPS systems.

Site Usability:	★★★★★	Based:	France
Product Range:	★★★★★	Express Delivery Option?	(UK) No
Price Range:	Luxury/Medium/Very Good Value	Gift Wrapping Option?	No
Delivery Area:	Worldwide	Returns Procedure:	Down to you

www.sunglasses-shop.co.uk

The Sunglasses Shop offers you free, express UK delivery (from the UK) and you can choose from designer brands Prada, Gucci, Chanel, Versace, Dolce and Gabbana, Dior and many more. They have a very comprehensive and modern range and if you click on the pair you like you not only get a close-up but also detailed pictures showing you what the side hinges and nose piece look like. You can shop by brand and by colour or select from their best sellers.

Site Usability:	★★★★★	Based:	UK
Product Range:	★★★★★	Express Delivery Option?	(UK) Yes
Price Range:	Luxury/Medium/Very Good Value	Returns Procedure:	Down to you
Delivery Area:	UK		

www.sunglassesuk.co.uk

Just about every brand of sunglasses is available from this UK site including Gucci, Chloe, Dolce and Gabbana, Moschino, Bolle and Prada. You can check out their best sellers or buy the same pair of sunglasses your favourite celebrity is wearing this year. It's a fun site with lots to see. They don't carry every style in stock and it's best to call them if you find something you really like.

Site Usability:	★★★★	Based:	UK
Product Range:	★★★★	Express Delivery Option?	(UK) No
Price Range:	Luxury/Medium/Very Good Value	Gift Wrapping Option?	No
Delivery Area:	UK	Returns Procedure:	Down to you

www.technical-gear.com

For sports and technical sunglasses and goggles look no further than this excellent website, where they offer brands such as Oakley, Bolle, Gargoyle, Action Optics and Spy; a full range of goggles for all sports activities and specific advice on which shades you need for driving, skiing, sailing, golf, fishing and many more activities

Site Usability:	★★★★★	Based:	US
Product Range:	★★★★★	Express Delivery Option?	(UK) No
Price Range:	Luxury/Medium/Very Good Value	Gift Wrapping Option?	No
Delivery Area:	Worldwide	Returns Procedure:	Down to you

www.unitedshades.com

This US based website has a comprehensive range of the latest sunglasses. Choose from Versace, Armani, Ferragamo, Givenchy, Gucci, Yves St Laurent and many more. With over twenty-five brands on offer you're sure to find something you like. Using FedEx shipping is extremely quick and you can take advantage of the discounts, wherever you are in the world. Don't forget, however that there will probably be tax and shipping costs on top.

Whatever you're thinking of buying you absolutely should have a look at their 'choose your sunglasses' area where they give advice on finding the right pair to suit your face. Everyone who sells sunglasses online should be doing this but most of them aren't yet (or they're hiding it) so congratulations to United Shades.

Site Usability:	★★★★★	Based:	US
Product Range:	★★★★★	Express Delivery Option?	(UK) No
Price Range:	Luxury/Medium/Very Good Value	Gift Wrapping Option?	No
Delivery Area:	Worldwide	Returns Procedure:	Down to you

Chapter 13

Jewellery and Watches

*A*s every good shopaholic knows buying jewellery for yourself is like buying a handbag: Therapy. What could possibly make you feel better? (Provided you can afford it, otherwise the guilt, the guilt).

You don't have to go for that enormous diamond, of course, there are a number of websites offering chic and inexpensive costume jewellery that'll make you feel satisfied. Some of these are general clothing sites as well and others, usually those offering real (and really expensive) jewellery are only jewellers and don't do anything else.

Ignore anyone who's offering you diamonds for less. There's no such thing and if you are going for the real thing buy the best quality you can possibly afford even if the stone is a little smaller.

Needless to say I'm not advising you choose your new diamond bracelet online – if you're going for a really expensive spend you have to be absolutely certain that you're not only buying the best, but getting the best service too. You'll definitely be safe if you shop online from somewhere like Tiffany, Theo Fennell or Boodles, all well known names with reputations based on design, quality and service. Be careful of splashing out elsewhere.

However, if you want something modern, fun and different, with semi-precious stones perhaps or the highest quality zirconias, you won't go wrong with the websites included here. The selection is excellent, you can usually get speedy delivery and the feelgood factor when you try on your new pair of earrings is high.

On to watches: You can find some real deals from a few high quality online retailers such as Blitz. Yes, you can actually buy that diamond edged Gucci for less than you'll find it in most shops and you'll get a very good service. However, as with all things online, be careful who you buy from and if you're buying a premium watch on the internet check with the retailer that the warranty period will be valid, and exactly who will be repairing the watch if this should become necessary.

Sites to Visit

www.absolutepearls.co.uk

This website was originally established in China and has now relocated to the UK to offer you quality cultured pearl necklaces, earrings and bracelets. There's a good selection from simple single strand necklaces to black Tahitian pearl and diamond pendants. If you want information about how to choose pearls and what makes them so special, you'll find it in their extremely comprehensive information centre, together with suggestions for gifts and their message card service.

Site Usability:	★★★★★	Based:	UK
Product Range:	★★★★	Express Delivery Option?	(UK) Yes
Price Range:	Luxury/Medium/Very Good Value	Gift Wrapping Option?	No
Delivery Area:	UK	Returns Procedure:	Down to you

www.astleyclarke.com

New online designer jewellery retailer Astley Clarke have a really attractive website, where you'll find the collections of New York and London based designers such as Coleman Douglas, Talisman Unlimited, Vinnie Day, Flora Astor and Catherine Prevost, some of which are exclusive to Astley Clarke. Prices start at around £100 and then go skywards. For gorgeous gifts or treats this is the perfect place, as everything arrives beautifully gift boxed and can be gift wrapped as well. There's also a collection for brides and bridesmaids.

Site Usability:	★★★★★	Based:	UK
Product Range:	★★★★★	Express Delivery Option?	(UK) Yes
Price Range:	Luxury/Medium/Very Good Value	Gift Wrapping Option?	Yes
Delivery Area:	UK	Returns Procedure:	Down to you

www.accessoriesonline.co.uk

Modern designer jewellery by Les Nereides, Butler and Wilson, Tarantino and Kleshna with a varied and attractive, well priced range. Click here when you want your next fashion jewellery fix or when you're looking for a treat for a friend and you'll definitely not be disappointed. Les Nereides in particular are really unusual and pretty, not cheap but always in line with the season.

Site Usability:	★★★★★	Based:	UK
Product Range:	★★★★	Express Delivery Option?	(UK) No
Price Range:	Luxury/<u>Medium</u>/Very Good Value	Gift Wrapping Option?	No
Delivery Area:	Worldwide	Returns Procedure:	Down to you

www.blitzjewellery.co.uk

The sister site to Blitz Watches, this is well worth having a look through if you're hunting for something new or for a gift. Prices range from the very reasonable up into the thousands with discounts shown for everything (although it's hard to compare like with like). Their watch discounts are very reliable but it's not as easy to get a direct comparison with the jewellery. Find what you want and compare prices on other sites for similar items. You may well do better here.

Site Usability:	★★★★★	Based:	UK
Product Range:	★★★★	Express Delivery Option?	(UK) Yes
Price Range:	<u>Luxury/Medium</u>/Very Good Value	Gift Wrapping Option?	Yes
Delivery Area:	UK	Returns Procedure:	Down to you

www.butlerandwilson.co.uk

Famous for their signature whimsical fashion jewellery you can now choose from a glamorous and well priced range online of necklaces, bracelets, earrings and brooches. Both costume jewellery and jewellery using semi-precious stones such as rose quartz, agate, amber and jade are available. You can choose from their range of very pretty printed and beaded handbags plus their collection of bridal jewellery and accessories.

Site Usability:	★★★★	Based:	UK
Product Range:	★★★★	Express Delivery Option?	(UK) No
Price Range:	Luxury/<u>Medium</u>/Very Good Value	Gift Wrapping Option?	No but everything is beautifully packaged
Delivery Area:	Worldwide	Returns Procedure:	Down to you

www.dinnyhall.com

Here you can see beautifully designed well priced modern jewellery from one of Britain's foremost jewellery designers. Every piece is hand crafted using traditional jewellery making techniques with high quality silver, gold and precious and semi-precious stones. If you haven't discovered her work up until now this is definitely the time to start collecting. This is a very clear and modern website where you can see all the products in each category at once which is extremely helpful.

Site Usability:	★★★★★	Based:	UK
Product Range:	★★★★	Express Delivery Option?	(UK) No
Price Range:	Luxury/<u>Medium</u>/Very Good Value	Gift Wrapping Option?	Yes
Delivery Area:	Worldwide	Returns Procedure:	Down to you

www.green-frederick.co.uk

If you love beautiful jewellery and the sparkle of diamonds but the real thing is slightly out of your range (like most of us) you'll need to spend some time on this wonderful website where there are 18ct gold necklaces, bracelets and earrings set with glittering hand cut cubic zirconias plus a wide range of real pearl jewellery. This is not cheap jewellery but superb quality at a very good price and it's very hard to tell the difference between the highest quality zirconias used here and the real thing.

Site Usability:	★★★	Based:	UK
Product Range:	★★★★	Express Delivery Option?	(UK) Yes
Price Range:	Luxury/<u>Medium</u>/Very Good Value	Gift Wrapping Option?	No
Delivery Area:	Worldwide	Returns Procedure:	Down to you

www.harriet-whinney.co.uk

Harriet Whinney specialises in pearl jewellery made to order and beautiful timeless pearl earrings, necklaces and bracelets. You can select from her ready made range or choose the quality of the pearl you want for your piece of jewellery and then select the type of clasp. There are also some extremely special pieces here such as baroque and South Sea pearls.

Site Usability:	★★★★	Based:	UK
Product Range:	★★★★	Express Delivery Option?	(UK) No
Price Range:	<u>Luxury</u>/Medium/Very Good Value	Gift Wrapping Option?	No
Delivery Area:	Worldwide	Returns Procedure:	Down to you

www.justdivine.co.uk

Just Divine is a collection of vintage inspired jewellery and gifts designed by Shelley Cooper of the USA, a fashion and jewellery historian whose passion for the past is reflected in her work. If you love vintage style jewellery you'll be spoilt for choice here. The website offers a limited edition of favourites from the huge range of designs in the main collection and highlights select pieces each month.

Site Usability:	★★★★★	Based:	UK
Product Range:	★★★	Express Delivery Option?	(UK) No
Price Range:	Luxury/<u>Medium</u>/Very Good Value	Gift Wrapping Option?	No
Delivery Area:	EU	Returns Procedure:	Down to you

www.kirstengoss.com

After studying jewellery design in South Africa Kirsten Goss moved to London and launched her own company where she currently creates exclusive, modern collections of jewellery using semi-precious stones and sterling silver. Having been featured by Harpers, Elle, Glamour and In Style and described as 'the next big thing' by the Sunday Times magazine this is definitely one to watch.

Site Usability:	★★★★	Based:	UK
Product Range:	★★★	Express Delivery Option?	(UK) Yes
Price Range:	Luxury/<u>Medium</u>/Very Good Value	Gift Wrapping Option?	No
Delivery Area:	Worldwide	Returns Procedure:	Down to you

www.linksoflondon.com

Links of London are well known for an eclectic mix of jewellery in sterling silver and 18ct gold, charms and charm bracelets, cufflinks, gorgeous gifts and leather and silver accessories for your home. Inevitably each season they design a new collection of totally desirable pieces (in other words, I want them) such as the 'Sweetie Rolled Gold Bracelet', or 'Annoushka' gold and ruby charm. This website is perfect for gifts and if you need something sent in a hurry they offer an express service worldwide.

Site Usability:	★★★★★	Based:	UK
Product Range:	★★★★★	Express Delivery Option?	(UK) Yes
Price Range:	<u>Luxury</u>/Medium/Very Good Value	Gift Wrapping Option?	Yes
Delivery Area:	Worldwide	Returns Procedure:	Down to you

www.lolarose.co.uk

This is a very unusually designed website, where you see all the products as on the pages of a book, however, it's very clever as well, as you can not only see everything very clearly but also view all the different colourways of the necklaces and bracelets made with rose quartz, white jade, green aventurine, mother of pearl and black agate. The prices for these beautifully designed pieces are very reasonable so it's well worth having a look.

Site Usability:	★★★★	Based:	UK
Product Range:	★★★	Express Delivery Option?	(UK) No
Price Range:	Luxury/<u>Medium</u>/Very Good Value	Gift Wrapping Option?	No
Delivery Area:	Worldwide	Returns Procedure:	Down to you

www.manjoh.com

On Manjo's attractively designed contemporary jewellery website, you'll find designers such as Izabel Camille, Benedict Mouret, Vinnie Day and Monica Carvalho and the list is regularly being added to. There are some unusual, wearable pieces incorporating semi-precious stones and freshwater pearls plus accessories such as keyrings by Bill Amberg. Everything is really clearly photographed and they offer next day and courier services plus worldwide delivery.

Site Usability:	★★★★★	Based:	UK
Product Range:	★★★	Express Delivery Option?	(UK) Yes
Price Range:	Luxury/Medium/Very Good Value	Gift Wrapping Option?	Yes
Delivery Area:	Worldwide	Returns Procedure:	Down to you

www.murrayforbes.co.uk

Based in Inverness in the Highlands of Scotland, Murray Forbes has an unusual selection of not overpriced jewellery online, comprising earrings, bracelets and necklaces, some quite traditional and some modern, using semi-precious stones, pearls, black and white diamonds and 9 or 18ct gold. The pictures are very clear and the details and information excellent. They offer free shipping and shipping insurance in the UK and will deliver worldwide.

Site Usability:	★★★★	Based:	UK
Product Range:	★★★	Express Delivery Option?	(UK) No
Price Range:	Luxury/Medium/Very Good Value	Gift Wrapping Option?	Yes
Delivery Area:	Worldwide	Returns Procedure:	Down to you

www.pascal-jewellery.com

Here's a collection of timeless stylish jewellery from a retailer that was originally established in Liberty of London about twenty-five years ago who you can now find in stores such as Harvey Nichols. As members of the National Association of Goldsmiths you can be sure that you're buying real quality. The collection is updated at least four times a year so you can be tempted regularly and prices start at around £50 (and average about £300).

Site Usability:	★★★★★	Based:	UK
Product Range:	★★★★	Express Delivery Option?	(UK) No
Price Range:	Luxury/Medium/Very Good Value	Gift Wrapping Option?	Yes
Delivery Area:	UK	Returns Procedure:	Down to you

www.piajewellery.com

Pia has a very quick and clever website where you can choose from their creative jewellery by type or browse page by page through their catalogue. The pictures of this modern, well priced jewellery range are extremely clear and definitely make you want to buy. There are natural stones such as carnelian, agate, labradorite and coral mixed with silver and turned into very wearable necklaces, earrings and bracelets. They also offer soft leather handbags, a small range of leather and shearling clothing and pretty scarves and shawls.

Site Usability:	★★★★★	Based:	UK
Product Range:	★★★★	Express Delivery Option?	(UK) Yes
Price Range:	Luxury/<u>Medium</u>/Very Good Value	Gift Wrapping Option?	Yes
Delivery Area:	Worldwide	Returns Procedure:	Down to you

www.selectraders.co.uk

This is a company based in Germany, offering a superb range of pearls including Akoya, South Sea and freshwater with a gorgeous choice of necklaces, earrings, rings, bracelets and pendants. Everything is beautifully and extremely clearly photographed with many views of the same item and you can choose pearls on their own or match them with diamonds and 18ct gold settings. They'll deliver all over the world.

Site Usability:	★★★★	Based:	Germany
Product Range:	★★★★★	Express Delivery Option?	(UK) No
Price Range:	Luxury/Medium/Very Good Value	Gift Wrapping Option?	No
Delivery Area:	Worldwide	Returns Procedure:	Down to you

www.stonedjewellery.co.uk

With its main boutique based in Nottingham, Stoned stocks a unique mix of local designers, directional London studios and Far Eastern pearl specialists. Everything offered is chic, stylish and beautifully photographed, of the highest quality and a mid price range with necklaces starting at around £100 and earrings at £55 (and going up steeply). You'll find designers such as Claire Henry, Dower and Hall and Monica Vinader plus others you probably won't have heard of before.

Site Usability:	★★★★	Based:	UK
Product Range:	★★★	Express Delivery Option?	(UK) No
Price Range:	Luxury/<u>Medium</u>/Very Good Value	Gift Wrapping Option?	Yes
Delivery Area:	UK	Returns Procedure:	Down to you

www.swarovski.com

You've almost certainly heard of Swarovski (and seen those tiny sparkling faceted glass animals and objects). You may also have passed their gloriously midnight-lit shops with glittering and stylish jewellery and accessories inside (and I mean really glittering). You'll no doubt be delighted to know that you can buy a wide selection online, all set with their signature crystals and extremely hard to resist.

Site Usability:	★★★★★	Based:	Germany
Product Range:	★★★★★	Express Delivery Option?	(UK) No
Price Range:	Luxury/<u>Medium</u>/Very Good Value	Gift Wrapping Option?	Yes
Delivery Area:	Worldwide	Returns Procedure:	Down to you

www.tictocsnrocks.co.uk

This is a collection of modern jewellery and designer watches at a range of prices from a retailer based in Devon. There are watches by Calvin Klein, D&G, Diesel, DKNY and Roberto Cavalli and jewellery by Angie Gooderham, Azuni, Philippe Ferrandis, Pilgrim and Taratata plus lots more. This would make a great place to find an accessory gift as they offer a gift wrapping service and they'll also ship worldwide.

Site Usability:	★★★	Based:	UK
Product Range:	★★★	Express Delivery Option?	(UK) No
Price Range:	Luxury/Medium/Very Good Value	Gift Wrapping Option?	Yes
Delivery Area:	Worldwide	Returns Procedure:	Down to you

www.treasurebox.co.uk

Here you'll find a wealth of costume jewellery from Butler and Wilson, Tarina Tarantino, Angie Gooderham and Les Nereides to name just a few, with the emphasis on what's in fashion right now. You can select your jewellery to go with each new season's look, and they're adding in new designers all the time. This is a really fun website where there's not only a lot of choice but also a great deal of information about the trends the pieces go with.

Site Usability:	★★★★	Based:	UK
Product Range:	★★★★	Express Delivery Option?	(UK) Yes
Price Range:	Luxury/Medium/Very Good Value	Gift Wrapping Option?	Yes
Delivery Area:	Worldwide	Returns Procedure:	Down to you

www.vanpeterson.com

This is a very small collection of extremely modern and unusual jewellery designed by Eric van Peterson, who opened his Walton Street jewellery store in 1981 to offer easily distinguished, modern/ethnic designs. It's certainly a highly edited selection of his range but hopefully it'll be increasing season on season.

Site Usability:	★★★	Based:	UK
Product Range:	★★★	Express Delivery Option?	(UK) No
Price Range:	Luxury/Medium/Very Good Value	Gift Wrapping Option?	No
Delivery Area:	Worldwide	Returns Procedure:	Down to you

www.blitzwatches.co.uk

Browse through the best brands such as Tag Heuer, Tissot, Baume and Mercier, Rolex and Cartier to name but a few. Place your order and you can have your delivery the next day. The pictures are beautifully clear and extremely tempting and on some watches there are substantial savings to be had which are clearly shown with each model. For some premium watches you receive the manufacturers warranty and for others the warranty is provided by Blitz.

Site Usability:	★★★★★		Based:	UK
Product Range:	★★★★★		Express Delivery Option?	(UK) Yes
Price Range:	Luxury/Medium/Very Good Value		Gift Wrapping Option?	Yes
Delivery Area:	UK		Returns Procedure:	Down to you/Complicated but these are valuable items so it's understandable

Also visit the following websites for jewellery

Website Address	You'll find it in
www.boodles.co.uk	Luxury Brands Online
www.net-a-porter.com	Luxury Brands Online
www.gucci.com	Luxury Brands Online
www.mikimoto-store.co.uk	Luxury Brands Online
www.theofennell.com	Luxury Brands Online
www.tiffany.com	Luxury Brands Online
www.peruvianconnection.com	Fashion Retailers
www.artigiano.co.uk	Fashion Retailers

Chapter 14

Leather, Shearling and Faux Fur

If you're anything like me your collection (yes I did say collection) of gloves, belts, leather jackets, soft shearling coats and gilets and faux fur stoles are incredibly important parts of your wardrobe. Whether they're stored away in the warmer months and then re-discovered as each winter approaches, or worn all year round (no not the shearling coat in July, I'm not that daft), each piece is looked at again and again with pleasure because these, like beautiful vintage clothing and real designer handbags, are things that last and last.

That's not to say, of course, that you might not feel (at any given time) that the time was right to make a tiny new investment and add a piece to your 'collection' but whatever you do, hold on to the rest unless the colour and shape are so outdated you know for sure you'll never wear it again and even then, think hard.

If you haven't yet started your collection and you're in the mood to make a purchase, there are several websites here you should visit. Consider buying Merino shearling if you want something understated and Toscana (the long haired shearling) if you want something very glam. Look for something a bit shaped to be stylish but don't go too far and whatever you do, don't buy something with a belt of any sort unless you're really really slim.

Then there's the issue of quality. If in any doubt ask the retailer to send you a swatch of the skin he's going to use for your coat so you can be sure. If he won't do this don't buy there. There are very different grades of leather and suede and particularly shearling and you only want to buy the best. It should be really, really soft and well coloured. If they don't state what type of suede they're using ask, although they should always tell you. Only buy goat suede. It is more expensive but it's a completely different material from the suede you find in some of the less expensive stores.

At the end of the day there's sometimes nothing better for the morale than pulling on a beautiful leather jacket, shearling gilet or suede coat. You immediately feel stylish, modern and (in my case) younger and what could be better than that?

Sites to Visit

www.dlux-ltd.co.uk

Dlux is a boutique mail-order company specialising in beautiful sheepskin and shearling collections. The collection is made of the highest quality soft and supple Merino and Toscana skins and there are two ranges, which they call Classic and Modern although everything is chic and stylish here whichever you choose. To order you need to download their Order Form and then email it to them. If you're in the mood for something luxuriously soft and warm this winter take a good look here.

Site Usability:	★★★★		Based:	UK
Product Range:	★★★		Express Delivery Option?	(UK) No
Price Range:	Luxury/Medium/Very Good Value		Gift Wrapping Option?	No
Delivery Area:	UK		Returns Procedure:	Down to you

www.ewenique.co.uk

This is a very attractive and comprehensive range of leather, suede and shearling coats and jackets for men and women plus flying jackets and accessories such as scarves and stoles, hats, hide bags, gloves and snuggly slippers. It's not as sophisticated as some of the leather websites as everything is photographed in still life, but the prices are reasonable and there's lots of information about each garment.

Site Usability:	★★★★		Based:	UK
Product Range:	★★★★		Express Delivery Option?	(UK) No
Price Range:	Luxury/Medium/Very Good Value		Gift Wrapping Option?	No
Delivery Area:	Worldwide		Returns Procedure:	Down to you

www.faux.uk.com

If you like to wrap yourself in something soft and furry, but you don't want to wear the real thing then here's a collection of the softest faux fur coats, jackets and shrugs plus gorgeous accessories, cushions and throws. These are perfect additions to winter evenings, whether you choose a jacket to go over your evening dress or an unbelievably soft throw to snuggle up in at home.

Site Usability:	★★★	Based:	UK	
Product Range:	★★★	Express Delivery Option?	(UK) Yes but you need to call them	
Price Range:	Luxury/Medium/Very Good Value	Gift Wrapping Option?	No	
Delivery Area:	Worldwide	Returns Procedure:	Down to you	

www.higgs-leathers.co.uk

This is an unsophisticatedly designed website (although improving all the time) with a really marvellous collection of leather, suede and shearling clothing. They obviously know what they're doing and offer very high quality items at reasonable (though not cheap) prices. Expect to pay around £900 for the best Toscana shearling full length coat. You need to call them to order to ensure that you take the right size.

Site Usability:	★★★★	Based:	UK	
Product Range:	★★★★	Express Delivery Option?	(UK) No	
Price Range:	Luxury/Medium/Very Good Value	Gift Wrapping Option?	No	
Delivery Area:	Worldwide	Returns Procedure:	Down to you	

www.hyde-online.net

Here's real designer quality, beautifully made leather, suede and shearling from a company that makes for some World famous designers. Nothing here is cheap but you definitely get what you pay for. You may not know the difference between the various types of suede and shearling, but they certainly do, and only use the highest quality skins. The focus is on modern styling but you'll also find some great classics that'll last you for years.

Site Usability:	★★★★	Based:	UK	
Product Range:	★★★★	Express Delivery Option?	(UK) No	
Price Range:	Luxury/Medium/Very Good Value	Gift Wrapping Option?	No	
Delivery Area:	Worldwide	Returns Procedure:	Down to you	

www.leatherglovesonline.com

This is a marvellous glove (surprise) retailer where the prices are excellent and they offer a speedy delivery service. You should have a good look round before it gets really cold out there. There are plain leather gloves with silk or cashmere linings, contrast stitched and extra long cuffs, fur and faux fur trims and linings and the warmest of all, lined in shearling.

Site Usability:	★★★★	Based:	US	
Product Range:	★★★★	Express Delivery Option?	(UK) No	
Price Range:	Luxury/Medium/Very Good Value	Gift Wrapping Option?	No	
Delivery Area:	Worldwide	Returns Procedure:	Down to you	

www.safigloves.com

I don't know if you're anything like me but the minute it gets cold I have to search through any and all of my winter coats and jackets for the gloves I left behind as, I'm sure you'll agree with me, cold hands are the worst. Anyway, here's a website that'll solve that problem for you with an excellent range, including gloves with fur cuffs and cashmere lining, silk lined gloves, fingerless gloves, driving gloves and gloves for kids of all ages.

Site Usability:	★★★★	Based:	UK
Product Range:	★★★	Express Delivery Option?	(UK) No
Price Range:	Luxury/<u>Medium</u>/Very Good Value	Gift Wrapping Option?	No
Delivery Area:	UK	Returns Procedure:	Down to you

www.wonderfulwraps.com

Established for over ten years, Wonderful Wraps has featured major UK retail outlets such as Harrods, Selfridges and Harvey Nichols in London and Saks Fifth Avenue and Neiman Marcus in the US. They offer a collection of sumptuous velvets, silk organzas, chiffons and tulles, satins, faux furs, marabous and other luxury wraps, stoles and capes, with styles ranging from luxurious embroidered organzas to classic angora throws. To place your order you need to call them.

Site Usability:	★★★	Based:	UK
Product Range:	★★★	Express Delivery Option?	(UK) No
Price Range:	<u>Luxury/Medium</u>/Very Good Value	Gift Wrapping Option?	No
Delivery Area:	Worldwide	Returns Procedure:	Down to you

Section 2

Men Only

There are lots of menswear shops on the web at all price ranges and although, just as for female fashion some want to try it on, feel it and wouldn't dream of ordering a shirt or tie online (let alone a suit) there are others who don't have the time, don't like to shop, live too far from the shops or just want something different. Either way you can find it all here, from a made to measure suit through a huge choice of shirts to outerwear, knitwear, ties, cufflinks and footwear.

For the online high street retailers check out 'Shop the High Street' in Fashion Fix, as most of the websites there, such as River Island and French Connection, offer menswear as well and you can find some very good, contemporary, well priced basics.

The difference in general with shopping for men is that on the whole it's much easier (sorry, maybe I shouldn't have said that). Sizing, particularly for shirts and definitely for ties is standard. A 15.5 neck shirt is the same whether you buy it from a Savile Row shop or from Marks and Spencer and ties; well if he wants a funny shaped tie I'd steer clear, personally.

Here are the best of the online menswear shops, both in the UK and elsewhere. Some will only ship to you here and others will deliver to anywhere in the world.

Chapter 15

Shirts, Ties, Cufflinks and Belts

There's a wonderful choice of men's shirts online - shirts were the first items of clothing that internet (usually catalogue) retailers experimented with and of course they worked, as it's easy to show all the different cuff and collar styles, colours, stripes and checks in a clear picture online.

Now it's not only the mail order specialists who are trying to get your business, but also some extremely up market (think Jermyn Street) names such as Hilditch and Key and T M Lewin. Some have very quick and beautifully designed websites and others don't (yet) but either way there's a huge range of prices and you can also find some very good deals that aren't in the shops.

I do know (having three men in my family), that they all like totally different things - colours, stripe widths, cuffs and collars and usually prefer to choose for themselves. However, if you do want to give your man a gorgeous shirt for his next birthday you'll certainly find a wide selection here and needless to say, he can always change it if he wants to.

Most of the shirt retailers also offer accessories such as cufflinks, belts, socks and ties and several have branched out into clothing ranges, cashmere knitwear, underwear and nightwear and on into trousers, casual and smart jackets and full business tailoring so you can have a browse through them as well.

Sites to Visit

www.coles-shirtmakers.com

Here you'll find high quality shirts with an excellent choice of fabrics and styles and an emphasis on finish. You can order from their standard selection or alternatively have your new shirt made exactly to your measurements (be careful here as of course you won't be able to return a bespoke shirt unless it's faulty). There's a discount system if you spend over a certain amount and a lot of information on how to order the perfect shirt. They also offer ties and cufflinks.

Site Usability:	★★★★	Based:	UK
Product Range:	★★★★	Express Delivery Option?	(UK) Yes
Price Range:	Luxury/Medium/Very Good Value	Returns Procedure:	Down to you
Delivery Area:	Worldwide		

www.ctshirts.co.uk

Well known for their colourful and well laid out catalogue now you can also order all their shirts, handmade shoes, ties and other accessories online. Their website is extremely attractive and easy to get round and the service offered excellent. A range of shirt qualities and styles are available and they frequently have special offers, and there's also a good selection of casual shirts and knitwear, tailoring, ladies shirts, cashmere knits and accessories and 'Tiny Tyrwhitt' clothing too.

Site Usability:	★★★★★	Based:	UK
Product Range:	★★★★★	Express Delivery Option?	(UK) Yes
Price Range:	Luxury/Medium/Very Good Value	Gift Wrapping Option?	Yes
Delivery Area:	Worldwide	Returns Procedure:	Down to you

www.curtisanddyer.co.uk

Curtis and Dyer do not have retail outlets, and so you may well find that their shirts sell online for quite a lot less than you would expect to pay for the quality. They also give you the opportunity of supplying them with your exact specification. Their shirt selector is really excellent. First you choose your fabric, then collar type, cuff type, neck measurement and then input your exact measurements if you want to, or use their standard sizing.

Site Usability:	★★★★★	Based:	UK
Product Range:	★★★★	Express Delivery Option?	(UK) No
Price Range:	Luxury/Medium/Very Good Value	Gift Wrapping Option?	No
Delivery Area:	UK	Returns Procedure:	Down to you

www.duchamp.co.uk

If the man in your life likes brightly coloured and unusual shirts and ties (probably best worn in the sunshine) and wonderful enamel cufflinks then this is a marvellous place to shop. Duchamp was originally started almost twenty years ago as a cufflink collection by designer Mitchell Jacobs and has now expanded into ties, shirts and other accessories. Nothing here is inexpensive but the quality and styling is as excellent as you would expect.

Site Usability:	★★★	Based:	UK
Product Range:	★★★★	Express Delivery Option?	(UK) No
Price Range:	Luxury/Medium/Very Good Value	Gift Wrapping Option?	No
Delivery Area:	Worldwide	Returns Procedure:	Down to you

www.gievesandhawkes.com

Situated at Number 1 Savile Row, London and established in 1785, Gieves and Hawkes have always stood for the very best in men's tailoring whether for formal evening wear, suiting or casualwear. On their website you can now not only find out a great deal about the brand, but also choose from their high quality range of shirts, belts and braces, cufflinks, shoes and ties.

Site Usability:	★★★★	Based:	UK
Product Range:	★★★	Express Delivery Option?	(UK) No
Price Range:	Luxury/Medium/Very Good Value	Gift Wrapping Option?	Yes
Delivery Area:	EU	Returns Procedure:	Down to you

www.harvieandhudson.com

Harvie and Hudson are a family-owned London shirtmaker and gentlemen's outfitter based in Jermyn Street, St James's and Knightsbridge. They offer a wide range of shirts online, from deep button down to classic striped, plain and check shirts, unusual colour combinations and excellent country shirts. You can have your shirt custom made by selecting from their fabrics and then choosing your cuff and collar style and you can order too from their selection of ties, links, socks and evening wear shirts and accessories.

Site Usability:	★★★★	Based:	UK
Product Range:	★★★★★	Express Delivery Option?	(UK) No
Price Range:	Luxury/Medium/Very Good Value	Gift Wrapping Option?	No
Delivery Area:	Worldwide	Returns Procedure:	Down to you

www.hilditchandkey.co.uk

Recognised as one of the longest established Jermyn Street retailers of mens shirts and accessories (as well as some women's shirts) Hilditch manages to give you a top of the range shopping experience without your having to leave home. Their shirts are not the cheapest, definitely, but if you order from them you'll be absolutely certain that you'll get the high quality you're paying for. They also offer silk ties and some clothing.

Site Usability:	★★★★★	Based:	UK
Product Range:	★★★★	Express Delivery Option?	(UK) No
Price Range:	Luxury/Medium/Very Good Value	Gift Wrapping Option?	No
Delivery Area:	Worldwide	Returns Procedure:	Down to you

www.josephturner.co.uk

Joseph Turner offer men's shirts, ties, cufflinks, sweaters, shoes and accessories with a wide choice in all areas and regular special offers. Their shoes are made for them by Loake. There's much more information than usual on sizing together with an alterations service. As with all the men's clothing websites they're extremely keen to offer something extra so you'll find cashmere sweaters, socks and belts here too.

Site Usability:	★★★★★	Based:	UK
Product Range:	★★★★★	Express Delivery Option?	(UK) No
Price Range:	Luxury/<u>Medium</u>/Very Good Value	Gift Wrapping Option?	No
Delivery Area:	UK	Returns Procedure:	Down to you

www.manning-and-manning.com

This is not one of the modern, beautifully photographed websites but what you will find here are not only classic 'Jermyn Street' style shirts but also their 'Stateside' fit which they recommend for more casual shirts. Here you choose your shirt measurements by going for their standard fit or inputting your own, then you select from a wide range of fabrics and finally the fit you want. Prices are high here but bearing in mind you'll end up with a totally unique shirt, if you're looking for the very best that's what you'll get.

Site Usability:	★★★	Based:	UK
Product Range:	★★★★★	Express Delivery Option?	(UK) No
Price Range:	<u>Luxury/Medium</u>/Very Good Value	Gift Wrapping Option?	No
Delivery Area:	Worldwide	Returns Procedure:	Down to you

www.thomaspink.co.uk

Thomas Pink has a slick and beautifully designed site offering shirts, clothing and accessories for men and women. There's an enormous amount of detail available for every product plus very clear pictures and a speedy search facility by pattern, style and finish. You can also buy scarves, knitwear, accessories and nightwear here and you'll know from the name that what you'll receive will be a very high quality product, beautifully packaged and extremely well made.

Site Usability:	★★★★	Based:	UK
Product Range:	★★★★	Express Delivery Option?	(UK) Yes
Price Range:	<u>Luxury/Medium</u>/Very Good Value	Gift Wrapping Option?	Yes
Delivery Area:	Worldwide	Returns Procedure:	Down to you

www.woodsofshropshire.co.uk

This is a shirt retailer with a difference, offering you high quality shirts, not cheap and not over priced, free and easy returns, worldwide delivery, extra collar stiffeners with every shirt plus complimentary silk knots with double cuff shirts. Roll your mouse over the shirt and tie pics and you can home in on the fabrics. You can buy large size shirts here too, up to a collar size 20. A great deal of thought has gone into this website and it shows, couple that with a well made shirt for £30 (at time of writing) and you have a website well worth a try.

Site Usability:	★★★★	Based:	UK
Product Range:	★★★★	Express Delivery Option?	(UK) No
Price Range:	Luxury/<u>Medium</u>/Very Good Value	Gift Wrapping Option?	No
Delivery Area:	Worldwide	Returns Procedure:	Down to you

Chapter 16

Suits etc

Your instant reaction may be that you (or the man in your life) wouldn't dream of buying a suit online but think again. Over the past couple of years the number of retailers expanding their online offers from just shirts (too easy, really) to complete tailoring for men has increased exceptionally fast and there's now a very good choice.

This is not, however, cheap suit heaven. As with everything you get what you pay for, and those who think that anything bought on the internet should be cheaper are mis-informed. Yes, that certainly applies to some areas, such as electricals, cds, dvds and books etc but it doesn't usually apply to clothing. Yes, you will find the occasional quality menswear site offering a discount they're not showing in their shops but this is usually because the internet is a very good place to sell off overstocks and you need to search them out.

If high quality ready made tailoring is what you're looking for then there are websites for you, many of which are based in London's Savile Row or Jermyn Street and although they have to be competitive (with other non West End of London websites) you'll be paying for and getting the best.

As my family is 50% Scottish I definitely had to include *www.kinlochanderson.co.uk* where the true Scot can find his new kilt, Prince Charlie or lovat tweed jacket and all the other accessories needed. This is probably only going to be of interest to those who already own a kilt (no don't experiment), know which tartan to wear (their own) and have the right sort of knees. It looks absolutely wonderful on the right person but it's not for the faint hearted and absolutely not as an experiment. Stick to your dinner jacket, please.

So if you're short of time, live overseas and like a British cut jacket or live and work far from the shops you should find a great selection here.

Sites to Visit

www.austinreed.co.uk

The choice on this website is growing every season, and now you can buy mens tailoring, shirts and ties, plus casual jackets, trousers and knitwear. The photography is very simple compared to most of the other men's websites and some of the products are quite hard to see. Balance this with the fact that you almost certainly know the name and the quality that it represents and you'll want to have a look round.

Site Usability:	★★★	Based:	UK
Product Range:	★★★	Express Delivery Option?	(UK) No
Price Range:	Luxury/Medium/Very Good Value	Gift Wrapping Option?	No
Delivery Area:	UK	Returns Procedure:	Down to you

www.crombie.co.uk

The Crombie name has been synonymous for over 200 years with high quality, hard wearing cloth and while that still continues the Crombie brand has been developed into an excellent collection of clothing for men and women, some of which you can find online. There's an extensive range for men, including the famous Crombie coat, blazers and jackets, shirts, ties and other accessories and some very good gift ideas. For women there's a much smaller range including some leather and suede.

Site Usability:	★★★★	Based:	UK
Product Range:	★★★★	Express Delivery Option?	(UK) No
Price Range:	Luxury/Medium/Very Good Value	Gift Wrapping Option?	No
Delivery Area:	Worldwide	Returns Procedure:	Down to you

www.englishtailor.co.uk

Don't expect a sophisticated modern website from this quality tailoring company. The site is very simple but the pictures are so large and clear you can practically feel the fabrics. Here you'll find high quality Harris Tweed jackets in a choice of weaves (with a large swatch to choose colours from), hacking jackets, cavalry twills, cords and moleskins. Everything here is very classic and reasonably priced and they're happy to ship worldwide.

Site Usability:	★★★★	Based:	UK
Product Range:	★★★	Express Delivery Option?	(UK) No
Price Range:	Luxury/Medium/Very Good Value	Gift Wrapping Option?	No
Delivery Area:	Worldwide	Returns Procedure:	Down to you

www.hackett.co.uk

Famous for using Jonny Wilkinson as their model as well as for great quality clothing, you can now buy from a selection of sportswear, tailoring, shirts and ties, great quality knitwear and outerwear online. In the Rugby Shop you can choose from a very good selection of striped rugby shirts and the Aston Martin Shop, with 'Aston Martin Racing by Hackett' socks, hats and brollies.

Site Usability:	★★★★	Based:	UK
Product Range:	★★★	Express Delivery Option?	(UK) No
Price Range:	Luxury/<u>Medium</u>/Very Good Value	Gift Wrapping Option?	No
Delivery Area:	UK	Returns Procedure:	Down to you/complicated

www.haggarts.com

Haggarts of Aberfeldy are one of the most famous Scottish tweed producers, having been in business since 1801 and they've now put their excellent country clothing catalogue online, so if you're one for the great outdoors (think shooting, hunting, fishing) this website is a must. Traditional coats, sports jackets and shooting waistcoats plus plus-twos, moleskins, cords and cavalry twills, hunter boots, caps and hats are just some of the items you can buy here (you can even buy your Sherlock Holmes hat as well).

Site Usability:	★★★	Based:	UK
Product Range:	★★★	Express Delivery Option?	(UK) No
Price Range:	Luxury/<u>Medium</u>/Very Good Value	Gift Wrapping Option?	No
Delivery Area:	Worldwide	Returns Procedure:	Down to you

www.hawesandcurtis.com

Hawes and Curtis were established in 1913, and are famous for being the creators of the backless waistcoat, which was worn under a tailcoat and was renowned for its comfort. Now on their excellently designed website you can choose from their range of classic and fashion shirts, ties, cufflinks, silk knots and boxer shorts. They also offer a range of women's classic, high quality shirts in three different styles.

Site Usability:	★★★★	Based:	UK
Product Range:	★★★	Express Delivery Option?	(UK) No
Price Range:	Luxury/<u>Medium</u>/Very Good Value	Gift Wrapping Option?	No
Delivery Area:	Worldwide	Returns Procedure:	Down to you

www.jamesjames.co.uk

Order your made to measure suit from James and James of Savile Row, London on their idiosyncratic website which very cleverly creates the ambience of a top London tailor. Choose from one of 20 high quality fabrics then select your jacket and trouser style and input your measurements. There's a clear measuring and style guide as you go through the selection process which makes the ordering process much easier than some. They aim to deliver in three weeks and they'll deliver worldwide.

Site Usability:	★★★	Based:	UK
Product Range:	★★★	Express Delivery Option?	(UK) No
Price Range:	Luxury/Medium/Very Good Value	Gift Wrapping Option?	No
Delivery Area:	UK	Returns Procedure:	Down to you

www.kinlochanderson.co.uk

The only place to buy a Scottish Tartan kilt is of course Scotland, but if you can't make it up there then you can order it online from Kinloch Anderson. (Don't mock, my husband's a Scot and looks great in his kilt). You need to know which tartan you want to order and they have an extensive selection to choose from. You can also buy all the necessary accessories including jackets and sporrans, skien dubh's (decorative knives), kilt pins, belts and footwear with kilts, jackets, sashes and accessories for ladies and children as well.

Site Usability:	★★★★	Based:	UK
Product Range:	★★★	Express Delivery Option?	(UK) No
Price Range:	Luxury/Medium/Very Good Value	Gift Wrapping Option?	No
Delivery Area:	UK	Returns Procedure:	Down to you

www.milanclothing.com

At Milan Clothing you'll find casual clothing from brands such as Fake London, Paul Smith, Pringle and Paul and Shark. There's a wide selection so you'll no doubt want to take advantage of the speedy search facility where you can search by brand, or type of clothing, or both. The pictures are very simple indeed because the range is changing all the time, however this is a very clear and easy to get round site and one of the best for casualwear.

Site Usability:	★★★★★	Based:	UK
Product Range:	★★★★★	Express Delivery Option?	(UK) Yes
Price Range:	Luxury/Medium/Very Good Value	Gift Wrapping Option?	No
Delivery Area:	Worldwide	Returns Procedure:	Down to you

www.mossdirect.co.uk

No this is not the place you can hire your dinner jacket, but an offshoot of the famous brand (and men's hire shop) retailing Moss Bros's own brand, plus Savoy Tailors Guild, De Havilland, Pierre Cardin and Baumler. You won't find an enormous range but a well designed website with some very good special offers and particularly good dress shirts (which is one of the things they're famous for, after all). Delivery is UK only and you need to allow ten days.

Site Usability:	★★★★	Based:	UK
Product Range:	★★★	Express Delivery Option?	(UK) No
Price Range:	Luxury/Medium/Very Good Value	Gift Wrapping Option?	No
Delivery Area:	UK	Returns Procedure:	Down to you

www.newandlingwood.com

In 1865 a Miss New and a Mr Lingwood founded the business which still bears their names. Now based in Jermyn Street, London, they're almost certainly the most traditional of the gentlemen's outfitters, supported by their own workrooms where they make their bespoke and ready made shirts, the finest quality piped pyjamas and bespoke shoes and boots. Their website offers a selection of classic, casual and fashion shirts, footwear from luxury boots to casual shoes and everything from velvet collared coats to eveningwear accessories. Expect high prices and the very best quality here.

Site Usability:	★★★★	Based:	UK
Product Range:	★★★★	Express Delivery Option?	(UK) No
Price Range:	Luxury/Medium/Very Good Value	Gift Wrapping Option?	No
Delivery Area:	Worldwide	Returns Procedure:	Down to you

www.oki-ni.com

Oki-ni is an independent, London-based design group, working in collaboration with a range of globally renowned brands and designers such as Aquascutum, Adidas, Evisu and Tanner Krolle to create products unique to Oki-ni and only available online from their website. You can choose from footwear, jeans, jackets and accessories all with an unusual designer twist. All items are available in limited numbers only so if you see something you like, order it fast.

Site Usability:	★★★★	Based:	UK
Product Range:	★★★	Express Delivery Option?	(UK) No
Price Range:	Luxury/Medium/Very Good Value	Gift Wrapping Option?	No
Delivery Area:	UK	Returns Procedure:	Down to you

www.orvis.co.uk

Originally a company specialising in fishing equipment, Orvis have now developed their brand to offer a full clothing and accessories range for men and women. You'll find high quality classic outerwear here from Donegal tweed jackets to quilted, microfibre coats plus knitwear, shirts, polos, t-shirts and accessories, all in a wide choice of colours plus hardwearing footwear here too and the Barbour Collection.

Site Usability:	★★★★★	Based:	UK
Product Range:	★★★★★	Express Delivery Option?	(UK) Yes
Price Range:	Luxury/Medium/Very Good Value	Gift Wrapping Option?	Yes
Delivery Area:	Worldwide	Returns Procedure:	Down to you

www.pakeman.co.uk

Here's an extensive range of good quality sensibly priced classic clothing from this Cotswold based retailer. For men you can choose from black tie tailoring, suits, flannels, cords and jeans, shirts and ties, belts, shoes, cufflinks and underwear. They offer a next day delivery service for items in stock and the emphasis is on service and quality. This is not a complicated website but one where there is high standard in every area so don't be put off by the simplicity of the pictures.

Site Usability:	★★★★	Based:	UK	
Product Range:	★★★★	Express Delivery Option?	(UK) No	
Price Range:	Luxury/<u>Medium</u>/Very Good Value	Gift Wrapping Option?	No	
Delivery Area:	Worldwide	Returns Procedure:	Down to you	

www.perlui.co.uk

This is an excellent designer menswear store offering designer ranges by Lacoste, Ralph Lauren, Tommy Hilfiger, Ted Baker and many more. You'll find good discounts in their end of season sales but otherwise they offer full price new season's stock. The collection is mainly casual and sportswear. You can also order from their Hackett range but you have to call them to do so.

Site Usability:	★★★★	Based:	UK	
Product Range:	★★★★	Express Delivery Option?	(UK) No	
Price Range:	<u>Luxury/Medium</u>/Very Good Value	Gift Wrapping Option?	No	
Delivery Area:	Worldwide	Returns Procedure:	Down to you	

www.racinggreen.co.uk

Famous for its well priced men's and ladies wear for several years Racing Green has now relaunched its website with a good range of menswear (sorry no ladies clothing) including shirts, tailoring (including dinner jackets and dress shirts) shoes and accessories. It's a very easy site to get round and much more classic than it used to be with smart pictures of a wide range of products. The prices are reasonable and the branding is very classy so definitely give it a try.

Site Usability:	★★★★★	Based:	UK	
Product Range:	★★★★	Express Delivery Option?	(UK) Yes	
Price Range:	Luxury/<u>Medium</u>/Very Good Value	Gift Wrapping Option?	No	
Delivery Area:	UK	Returns Procedure:	Down to you	

www.savilerowco.com

This is a really good and fast developing range of menswear, offering everything you could possibly need, including tailoring (and dinner jackets) a wide range of formal shirts, casual shirts, trousers and sweaters plus a full collection of accessories. The site is very clearly photographed and the order system is really easy. There are also some men's gift ideas here such as cashmere scarves and cufflinks.

Site Usability:	★★★★★	Based:	UK	
Product Range:	★★★★★	Express Delivery Option?	(UK) Yes	
Price Range:	Luxury/<u>Medium</u>/Very Good Value	Gift Wrapping Option?	No	
Delivery Area:	Worldwide	Returns Procedure:	Free	

www.stoneisland.co.uk

Trendy, relaxed and very well photographed, this website offers Stone Island and C.P casualwear (and some more formal jackets) plus outerwear, jeans, shirts, knitwear and accessories. This is an extremely fast and attractive website to look round. I wish we could say that about more of them. Be warned though; the products are not inexpensive, but high quality designer gear, so if you're looking for a cheap pair of casual jeans you'll be disappointed.

Site Usability:	★★★★★	Based:	UK
Product Range:	★★★	Express Delivery Option?	(UK) No
Price Range:	Luxury/Medium/Very Good Value	Gift Wrapping Option?	No
Delivery Area:	UK	Returns Procedure:	No

www.theclothesstore.com

Once you get past the flash intro, there are some excellent clothes by Burberry London, Nigel Hall, Lacoste, Puma and One True Saxon and 'Urban Menswear' by Fred Perry, Ben Sherman, Wrangler and Edge. The designer ranges are changing all the time. They also offer a funky collection from Converse and Kickers. They're happy to ship worldwide

Site Usability:	★★★	Based:	Channel Islands
Product Range:	★★★★	Express Delivery Option?	(UK) No
Price Range:	Luxury/Medium/Very Good Value	Gift Wrapping Option?	No
Delivery Area:	Worldwide	Returns Procedure:	Down to you

www.tmlewin.co.uk

This is one of the easiest sites to get round with simple drop down menus and clear pictures. They also frequently have some very good special offers. You can buy almost everything here, from formal tailoring to casual trousers and a good selection of accessories and there's a wide range of striped, check and solid coloured shirts with simple size and length options.

Site Usability:	★★★★★	Based:	UK
Product Range:	★★★★	Express Delivery Option?	(UK) No
Price Range:	Luxury/Medium/Very Good Value	Gift Wrapping Option?	No
Delivery Area:	Worldwide	Returns Procedure:	Down to you

Chapter 17

Shoes and Accessories

Don't be afraid of buying shoes online. You're usually well aware of your size and it'll be the same across just about all the makes. If you're ordering in from overseas check the sizing conversion tables below. The quality you can get online is excellent and there's lots of choice.

You can, of course, spend a fortune on your shoes and if you're looking for something really special I suggest you take a look at *www.gucci.com* or, *www.forzieri.com* where you'll find the 'designer' end of the market (and at 'designer' prices). However, you don't need to spend the earth and you can choose from a wide selection at all budgets.

When it comes to accessories, briefcases, small leather goods, cufflinks, belts, ties and the like, you need to take a good look through the men's websites listed above as well, as nearly all of them are adding to their accessories range regularly. Some of the best websites offering you everything are: *www.tmlewin.co.uk* and *www.ctshirts.co.uk* where the quality is high and the service excellent. You'll also find some very high quality accessories for gift ideas below.

International Shoe Size Conversion Table

UK	7	7.5	8	8.5	9	9.5	10	10.5	11	11.5	12
EU	40.5	41	42	42.5	43	44	44.5	45	46	46.5	47
US	7.5	8	8.5	9	9.5	10	10.5	11	11.5	12	12.5

Sites to Visit

www.aspinal.co.uk

Aspinal specialise in leather gifts and accessories and there's a wide choice of styles and colours in each section. In their 'Executive Folios and Cases' there are zipped document cases in a choice of eight colours, conference portfolios, leather ring binders, jotters and memos and leather document envelopes. There are lots of other gift ideas here as well, including stud boxes, leather journals and books, handmade by skilled craftsmen using age old traditional leather and bookbinding skills.

Site Usability:	★★★★★	Based:	UK
Product Range:	★★★★★	Express Delivery Option?	(UK) Yes
Price Range:	Luxury/<u>Medium</u>/Very Good Value	Gift Wrapping Option?	Yes
Delivery Area:	Worldwide	Returns Procedure:	Down to you

www.bexley.com

This is a French based website (although you'll probably be glad to know that there's an English translation) offering excellent shoes and accessories for men. Clearly and attractively photographed and easy to get round you can buy socks, formal and casual shoes, ties, shoe trees, polishing kits, belts and gloves at reasonable prices. Average shipping time for Europe is roughly one week and up to two weeks for the rest of the world.

Site Usability:	★★★★	Based:	France
Product Range:	★★★★	Express Delivery Option?	(UK) No
Price Range:	Luxury/<u>Medium</u>/Very Good Value	Gift Wrapping Option?	No
Delivery Area:	Worldwide	Returns Procedure:	Down to you

www.forzieri.com

Italian company Forzieri offers ties by Dolce & Gabbana, Kenzo and Versace (among others) belts by Gianfranco Ferre plus wallets, briefcases, leather travel bags and other accessories, very high quality shoes by Packerson, Mariano Campanile and Brunori and Forzieri's own brand where you'll expect to pay around £240. Very good descriptions are given about the products and their manufacturers and there are some excellent gift ideas as well.

Site Usability:	★★★★★	Based:	Italy
Product Range:	★★★★★	Express Delivery Option?	(UK) Yes
Price Range:	<u>Luxury/Medium</u>/Very Good Value	Gift Wrapping Option?	Yes
Delivery Area:	Worldwide	Returns Procedure:	Down to you

www.pickett.co.uk

Gloves, wallets, umbrellas, belts, briefcases and stud boxes are just some of the high quality, beautifully made men's accessories available on Pickett's website. If you've ever visited one of their shops you'll know that everything is the best you can buy and most items would make lovely gifts. Couple this with their distinctive dark green and orange packaging and excellent service and you can't go wrong, whatever you choose.

Site Usability:	★★★★	Based:	UK
Product Range:	★★★★	Express Delivery Option?	(UK) No
Price Range:	Luxury/Medium/Very Good Value	Gift Wrapping Option?	No but luxury packaging is standard
Delivery Area:	Worldwide	Returns Procedure:	Down to you

www.pierotucci.com

There's a very good range of briefcases and bags on this Florence based website from hard sided briefcases to slim portfolios, soft travel and duffle bags, wallets and belts. Everything is made in Italy (as you'd expect) and because it's an Italian brand (rather than a 'designer' brand) some of the prices are quite reasonable although you are looking at top Italian quality. They offer UPS express shipping to anywhere in the world.

Site Usability:	★★★★	Based:	Italy
Product Range:	★★★★	Express Delivery Option?	(UK) Yes
Price Range:	Luxury/Medium/Very Good Value	Gift Wrapping Option?	No
Delivery Area:	Worldwide	Returns Procedure:	Down to you

www.shiptonandheneage.co.uk

Shipton and Heneage have been trading for over twelve years and offer a very good, high quality collection of over 120 styles of shoe. You choose first from different types of shoes, such as brogues, country shoes, town shoes, Oxfords, extra wide and loafers and then make your choice from the selection of each that rapidly appears. They also have an excellent range of sailing shoes plus slippers, socks and accessories.

Site Usability:	★★★★★	Based:	UK
Product Range:	★★★★	Express Delivery Option?	(UK) Yes
Price Range:	Luxury/Medium/Very Good Value	Gift Wrapping Option?	No
Delivery Area:	Worldwide	Returns Procedure:	Down to you

www.shoesdirect.co.uk

For reasonably priced smart and casual shoes stop here, where you'll find Loake, Rockport, Gregson, Ecco, Clarks and Barker. Everything is very clearly shown and they couldn't make the order process easier. Some of their shoes go up to a UK size 16 which is really large, and if you're in doubt about which size to use their shoe size conversion chart is always available. They'll also tell you which shoes have extra width. Mainland UK deliveries are free for orders over £30.

Site Usability:	★★★★★	Based:	UK
Product Range:	★★★★★	Express Delivery Option?	(UK) No
Price Range:	Luxury/<u>Medium</u>/Very Good Value	Gift Wrapping Option?	No
Delivery Area:	UK	Returns Procedure:	Down to you

www.wellie-web.co.uk

Here's a website with a name that you won't forget quickly but if you're someone who spends a lot of time outdoors, particularly in wet weather, you'll find it indispensable. You can find a cheap pair of wellies here with prices starting at £22 and you'll also find some with flowers all over them (er, maybe not). However, this website specialises in the quality end of the market where a top notch pair of boots can set you back up to £200.

Site Usability:	★★★★	Based:	UK
Product Range:	★★★★	Express Delivery Option?	(UK) No
Price Range:	<u>Luxury/Medium</u>/Very Good Value	Gift Wrapping Option?	No
Delivery Area:	UK	Returns Procedure:	Down to you

Also visit the following websites for men's shoes and accessories

Website Address	You'll Find Them In
www.ctshirts.co.uk	Shirts, Ties, Cufflinks and Belts
www.josephturner.co.uk	Shirts, Ties, Cufflinks and Belts
www.dunhill.com	Luxury Brands Online
www.gucci.com	Luxury Brands Online
www.smythson.com	Luxury Brands Online

Chapter 18

Mens Toiletries

There probably isn't a brand of fragrance or grooming product that you can't find online and there are some excellent websites where you can get discounts and/or free delivery, such as *www.beautybay.com*, *www.strawberrynet.com* and *www.beautybase.co.uk*. Be aware that if you're ordering from overseas (for Strawberrynet, for example, who are based in Hong Kong) that you may well have to pay duty. So it's probably only worthwhile doing this if you're getting a good discount, or if you're buying something very different which you can't buy here.

Of course the real problem for shopaholics is that when you're browsing the fragrance websites (for men) you'll no doubt find something you like as well, as most of the websites, other than the ones dedicated to mens shaving and grooming, sell women's fragrances too, so if necessary grit your teeth and click on the 'men's fragrance' button.

Some of the websites I've included below carry the full range of well known products from makes such as Dior, Chanel, Lacoste etc - everything for everyone, as it were. What I've also included are those specialised websites who offer something a bit different - *www.carterandbond.co.uk* for modern (and traditional) mens grooming products and accessories, *www.jasonshankey.co.uk* who have an amazing range for both men and women including some products you probably won't have ever heard of (well I hadn't, anyway) and *www.theenglishshavingcompany.co.uk* who offer just exactly what you'd expect.

Sites to Visit

www.1001beautysecrets.com/beauty/caswell

I've included this website because here you can buy products from Caswell Massey, one of the America's oldest perfumers. If you'd like to try something different check out their excellent men's range including their Newport, Lime and Verbena fragrances. There's a full range of products from Cologne to soap to shower gel and with everything so smartly packaged they'd make great gifts as well.

Site Usability:	★★★★	Based:	US
Product Range:	★★★	Express Delivery Option?	(UK) No
Price Range:	Luxury/Medium/Very Good Value	Gift Wrapping Option?	No
Delivery Area:	Worldwide	Returns Procedure:	Down to you

www.aehobbs.com

This is a very simple website from a retailer who's been based in Tunbridge Wells for over 100 years. They offer traditional grooming and toiletry products from brands such as Truefitt and Hill, Woods of Windsor, Mason and Pearson and Kent from their barbershop and Klorane, Perlier and Olverum from their beauty department. They stock Zambesia Botanica as well, which is a special range for people who have very sensitive skin.

Site Usability:	★★★★	Based:	UK
Product Range:	★★★	Express Delivery Option?	(UK) No
Price Range:	Luxury/Medium/Very Good Value	Gift Wrapping Option?	No
Delivery Area:	Worldwide	Returns Procedure:	Down to you

www.carterandbond.com

Carter and Bond was established in 2002 to bring together the very finest male grooming products around. The simple to use secure website is home to over 600 products from more than 40 brands including Molton Brown, American Crew, Baxter of California, Geo F Trumper and Proraso. Whether you're looking for skin care, hair care, fragrance, shaving products or gift ideas you'll find it all here. Orders received by 2.30pm are despatched same day (to anywhere in the world) and gift wrapping is available for just 95p per item.

Site Usability:	★★★★★	Based:	UK
Product Range:	★★★★★	Express Delivery Option?	(UK) Available on orders over £100
Price Range:	Luxury/Medium/Very Good Value	Gift Wrapping Option?	Yes
Delivery Area:	Worldwide	Returns Procedure:	Down to you

www.jasonshankey.co.uk

If you're a fan of American Crew or Geezers hair products this is the place for you. There's also a phenomenal range of excellent products on this site from hair care and hair appliances to nail care, slimming products, men's grooming and hangover cures. They're also good for appliances – they claim to sell the most powerful hair dryer on the market although it's not always in stock, as well as GHD straighteners, Hairart T3 and Remington.

Site Usability:	★★★★	Based:	UK
Product Range:	★★★★	Express Delivery Option?	(UK) Yes
Price Range:	Luxury/<u>Medium</u>/Very Good Value	Gift Wrapping Option?	Yes
Delivery Area:	Worldwide	Returns Procedure:	Down to you

www.mankind.co.uk

This is definitely one of the best men's websites. It's modern, easy to use and has a great range of products, showcasing the very best and most innovative shaving, skin and hair care brands made for men and offering them in a way that makes buying simple, fast and fun. There are shaving products, skin basics and problem skin solutions as well as gift ideas here. Next day and standard delivery to the UK; worldwide delivery options and gift wrapping are all available.

Site Usability:	★★★★★	Based:	UK
Product Range:	★★★★★	Express Delivery Option?	(UK) Yes
Price Range:	Luxury/<u>Medium</u>/Very Good Value	Gift Wrapping Option?	Yes
Delivery Area:	Worldwide	Returns Procedure:	Down to you

www.trumpers.com

Established in 1875 in Curzon Street, Mayfair, this famous traditional London barber is well known for superb exclusive men's fragrances and grooming products. Think of fragrances such as Sandalwood, Bay Rum and Spanish Leather which all have matching soaps and body washes. Now you can buy the full range online plus an exclusive collection of ties and cufflinks and they'll be delighted to ship to you anywhere in the world.

Site Usability:	★★★★	Based:	UK
Product Range:	★★★★	Express Delivery Option?	(UK) Yes
Price Range:	<u>Luxury</u>/Medium/Very Good Value	Gift Wrapping Option?	Yes
Delivery Area:	Worldwide	Returns Procedure:	Free

www.theenglishshavingcompany.co.uk

At theenglishshavingcompany.co.uk you'll find the highest quality hand crafted razors and shaving sets plus travel sets, soaps, brushes and aftershaves from Geo Trumper, Edwin Jagger, D R Harris and

Molton Brown. You can read their 'shaving tutorial' in Useful Information plus razor shaving tips, so if you're tired of using your electric razor and want to turn traditional you'll definitely need this site.

Site Usability:	★★★★	Based:	UK
Product Range:	★★★★	Express Delivery Option?	(UK) No
Price Range:	Luxury/Medium/Very Good Value	Gift Wrapping Option?	Yes
Delivery Area:	Worldwide	Returns Procedure:	Down to you

Other websites to visit for mens toiletries

Website Address	You'll find them in
www.escentual.co.uk	Skincare and Cosmetics
www.penhaligons.co.uk	Skincare and Cosmetics
www.woodruffs.co.uk	Skincare and Cosmetics
www.boots.com	Skincare and Cosmetics
www.garden.co.uk	Skincare and Cosmetics

Section 3

Babies, Kids and Teens

*U*p to a certain age (probably no more than 8) you can choose everything for your children. At that stage you have two options. Leave them with someone at home (much preferable, if you can) and go out shopping for them or take the little darlings with you and put up with their endless boredom (fights), tiredness and hunger pretty well whatever their age (and believe me, I know, I've had three).

Now mine are in their late teens I can look back in amusement (and some horror) at the time when I took all three into Gap in Windsor and they decided, aged 4, 6 and 7 to have a major disagreement which involved a great deal of screaming and yelling. We quit Gap without buying anything – in any case I think I'd totally forgotten what I went there for in the first place.

I'm sure that this story will hit home with many of you. Nowadays (now that I'm an older mother) I hear this sort of tale with amazement. Why do people need to go shopping with their children when the shopping can come to them?

There are some really lovely baby and children's clothes available online (traditional and modern) and some which are beautifully designed and extremely good value as well. You can see far more in a short space of time than you ever could in the shops and if you want to you can let your children have a say without their having to be within ten yards of the till. And you can make the final decision without a riot.

Once they get to the age when they insist on choosing for themselves it's a completely different matter. There's no point in trying to force them to wear what they don't want to, it simply doesn't work and you certainly don't want to waste your money on clothes your children aren't ever going to put on, nor are you going to let them loose in the shops to come back with something ghastly, although I assure you there does come a stage where you have to blink and say nothing and pray they'll grow out of the floppy boarding trouser moment, they usually do.

There is a big cross over at age 15 or so, when they'll want to be buying from the High Street shops with the twenty somethings. Some of those websites I've repeated below and some they'll find in the High Street section above. This is when life becomes really expensive (you have been warned).

So your children too can have a browse through some of the childrenswear and teen websites and tell you what they want and then you can fight about it. But at least it'll be at home, where no-one else can hear and you can immediately pour yourself that stiff drink you'll certainly need.

Chapter 19

Baby and Toddler Clothes

ere you can really have fun. You get to choose, every single time, whether you want to put your baby into frills and lace or the simplest of babygros and no one can stop you. You may get some funny looks if you go too far down the frilly route but at the end of the day it's your choice.

If you're buying for your own newborn you'll want to check out the high quality but good value places where you can choose quantity and quality at the same time. After all, your friends and relations will be buying you (hopefully) beautiful expensive special things you might not buy yourself. So you need to visit retailers such as *www.bloomingmarvellous.co.uk*, *www.jojomamanbebe.co.uk* and *www.mamasandpapas.co.uk* where you'll find a wide choice, a pretty collection and good prices.

If your friends and family ask for recommendations as to where they should shop you could do no better then to point them at the gorgeous baby clothes at *www.rachelriley.com* or *www.thekidswindow.co.uk* where there are really exquisite designer baby and children's clothes (and of course prices to match).

You can also find lovely baby gifts here to give your friends when they produce, pretty sets and baskets containing baby clothes and bath goodies, gorgeous fleecy blankets, soft toys and nursery products. There are also presents for babies in the gift section, so if you're looking for something really special have a browse there as well.

Don't forget (I'm sure you won't) that you can buy all your nappies and baby food at the online supermarkets, and baby equipment from *www.johnlewis.com* and (believe it or not) *www.amazon.co.uk* plus lots of the websites listed below. There really is no need to trail round the shops unless you really, really want to.

Sites to Visit

www.aztecstore.com

Here you'll find a simple, pretty range of clothes and accessories for girls and boys up to age 8, with a separate section for babies and toddlers. There are dresses, ra-ra skirts, smock tops and capri pants, lovely trimmed cardigans and swimsuits with ruched frills and wraps to match (for the girls of course). For boys the selection is also traditional, with appliqued knitwear, gingham shorts and shirts and fun Hawaiian print swim trunks. Everything is reasonably priced.

Site Usability:	★★★★	Based:	UK
Product Range:	★★★	Express Delivery Option?	(UK) Yes
Price Range:	Luxury/Medium/Very Good Value	Gift Wrapping Option?	No
Delivery Area:	Worldwide	Returns Procedure:	Down to you

www.bloomingmarvellous.co.uk

Blooming Marvellous offer everything for the newborn baby, including sets of babygros and vests in pink or blue, pointelle blankets, bootees and padded outdoor suits. It's not a huge range for babies but what they specialise in are extremely well priced essential basics. You can sign up for their monthly email newsletter full of parenting advice and tips, promotions and competitions and you'll always get an excellent service here.

Site Usability:	★★★★★	Based:	UK
Product Range:	★★★★★	Express Delivery Option?	(UK) No
Price Range:	Luxury/Medium/Very Good Value	Gift Wrapping Option?	No
Delivery Area:	Worldwide	Returns Procedure:	Down to you

www.gagagoogoo.co.uk

I almost couldn't get past the name of this website but then when I had a look I could see they were offering something really original and clever (which almost certainly only the adults will understand). These are a range of baby and toddler t-shirts up to two years and packs of bibs with famous and witty sayings on them such as 'Go ahead and make my day' (Clint Eastwood), 'Here's looking at you, kid' (Humphrey Bogart) and 'I have nothing to declare but my genius', (Oscar Wilde).

Site Usability:	★★★★★	Based:	UK
Product Range:	★★★	Express Delivery Option?	(UK) Yes
Price Range:	Luxury/Medium/Very Good Value	Gift Wrapping Option?	No
Delivery Area:	Worldwide	Returns Procedure:	Down to you

www.hennabecca.co.uk

There's just one product here, and it's essential for anyone who's just had a baby and doesn't want to lose the chic, stylish look she's always worked hard to maintain. So: This bag not only looks good and comes in canvas, print and leather versions but it also works hard as the perfect baby bag with three detachable interior compartments, long zip pulls, bottle holder and loads of other special details.

Site Usability:	★★★★	Based:	UK
Product Range:	★★★	Express Delivery Option?	(UK) Yes
Price Range:	Luxury/Medium/Very Good Value	Gift Wrapping Option?	Yes
Delivery Area:	Worldwide	Returns Procedure:	Down to you

www.jojomamanbebe.co.uk

This is a really pretty website offering a very good choice for babies and young children. The drop-down menus on the home page take you quickly and clearly to everything you might be looking for, whether it's baby essentials, nightwear or towelling snugglers. They also have some excellent Polartec all in ones for colder weather. Delivery is free in the UK, there are some very good gift ideas and they offer gift vouchers and gift boxes as well.

Site Usability:	★★★★★	Based:	UK
Product Range:	★★★★	Express Delivery Option?	(UK) No
Price Range:	Luxury/Medium/Very Good Value	Gift Wrapping Option?	No
Delivery Area:	Worldwide	Returns Procedure:	Down to you

www.kentandcarey.co.uk

Kent and Carey have been in the business of supplying beautifully made, classic children's clothes for over fifteen years. For babies there are cute babygros and really sweet nightwear in pretty fabrics. For slightly older girls there are Peter Pan printed tops, tiered skirts and print tied trousers and for boys check shirts, long shorts and traditional 'growy up style' knitwear. The pictures are lovely and the prices are good as well.

Site Usability:	★★★★	Based:	UK
Product Range:	★★★	Express Delivery Option?	(UK) No
Price Range:	Luxury/Medium/Very Good Value	Gift Wrapping Option?	No
Delivery Area:	Worldwide	Returns Procedure:	Down to you

www.littletrekkers.co.uk

If this is the moment when you realise your newly walking (and getting into things and splashing in puddles) toddler is going to be getting wet and dirty, from now on you definitely ought to take a look here, where you'll find extremely good value waterproofs, from splashsuits to jackets and dungarees, plus skiwear and fleece for babies and kids up to age 8, weatherproof and summer pool footwear and lots of other ideas for babies and young children.

Site Usability:	★★★★★	Based:	UK
Product Range:	★★★★	Express Delivery Option?	(UK) Yes
Price Range:	Luxury/Medium/Very Good Value	Gift Wrapping Option?	No
Delivery Area:	Worldwide	Returns Procedure:	Down to you

www.mamasandpapas.co.uk

This company combines great attention to detail, high quality fabrics and pretty designs in their babywear section, covering everything from a gorgeous selection for the newborn which they've called 'welcome to the world', excellent well priced basics and exquisite and innovative clothes for girls and boys. This is really a beautifully photographed website offering loads of advice on what to buy. They only deliver to the UK but you can click through to their US based site.

Site Usability:	★★★★★	Based:	UK
Product Range:	★★★★	Express Delivery Option?	(UK) No
Price Range:	Luxury/Medium/Very Good Value	Gift Wrapping Option?	No
Delivery Area:	UK but US site available	Returns Procedure:	Down to you

www.muddypuddles.com

Waterproofs, wellies, thermal socks and booties, hats, gloves, brollies for tinies, ski wear and even a wellie peg on this innovative and clever site aimed at children up to five with a very few items going up to eight (such as ski tops). This is an absolutely essential website for just about anyone with young children so take a good look round as you could easily give some of the flowered wellies, funny socks and bootees as gifts.

Site Usability:	★★★★	Based:	UK
Product Range:	★★★★	Express Delivery Option?	(UK) No
Price Range:	Luxury/Medium/Very Good Value	Gift Wrapping Option?	No
Delivery Area:	Worldwide	Returns Procedure:	Down to you

www.ollipops.com

Here you'll find really cute soft baby shoes by Starchild and Bobux, enchanting bibs (before they've eaten) by Beautiful Bibs and a selection of Hopscotch dressing up outfits and hats, plus lots of other unusual products for babies and small children. It's a pretty, colourful and extremely busy website with lots of customer comments and information on the home page but the products themselves couldn't be clearer.

Site Usability:	★★★★	Based:	UK
Product Range:	★★★★	Express Delivery Option?	(UK) No
Price Range:	Luxury/Medium/Very Good Value	Gift Wrapping Option?	No
Delivery Area:	Worldwide	Returns Procedure:	Down to you

www.rachelriley.com

The next time you're asked where someone could find something for your little one, point them in the direction of Rachel Riley, a truly lovely collection for infants, teens and grown ups as well. Everything is really exquisite with a marvellous attention to style and detail and as you'd expect, nothing is inexpensive. So if you can't afford to kit out your child totally from here, at least you can ask a Godmother or granny to contribute something really special.

Site Usability:	★★★★	Based:	UK	
Product Range:	★★★★	Express Delivery Option?	(UK) Yes	
Price Range:	Luxury/Medium/Very Good Value	Gift Wrapping Option?	No	
Delivery Area:	Worldwide	Returns Procedure:	Down to you	

www.serendipity-online.com

This is a really cute designer baby and maternity website where the baby clothes are by designers such as Coochie Cooture, Due Sorelle, Mandarin, Little Moon and Oink (Oink?). Anyway, I have to confess that it's a while since I was buying baby clothes and I don't know these labels at all, however the clothes are really pretty and they're not over priced so I would certainly consider buying here.

Site Usability:	★★★★	Based:	UK	
Product Range:	★★★	Express Delivery Option?	(UK) Yes	
Price Range:	Luxury/Medium/Very Good Value	Gift Wrapping Option?	No	
Delivery Area:	UK	Returns Procedure:	Down to you	

www.thebabyshoeshop.co.uk

The Baby Shoe Shop specialise in retailing soft shoes for babies and toddlers, from quality manufacturers such as Daisy Roots, Shoo Shoo, Pitter Patter, Inch Blue and Star Child. They also sell rubber wellies from Aigle and neoprene beach shoes from the wet suit factory. There are unbelievably cute ballet pumps with satin ribbons up to 24 months, a gorgeous choice of little soft shoes (some humorous, some just pretty) for boys and girls and kids' wet suit shoes for running in and out of the water.

Site Usability:	★★★★	Based:	UK	
Product Range:	★★★	Express Delivery Option?	(UK) No	
Price Range:	Luxury/Medium/Very Good Value	Gift Wrapping Option?	No	
Delivery Area:	UK	Returns Procedure:	Down to you	

www.thekidswindow.co.uk

Buy specialist children's clothing brands online here, from everyday clothing labels such as Catfish and Inside Out to top designer brands including Marie Chantal and Budishh. Clothes are available in sizes from newborn to 14 years and you can search on this website by age, gender, season and by brand.

You can choose next day or their standard 48 hour delivery and they'll ship to you pretty well anywhere in the World. Gift wrapping is also available.

Site Usability:	★★★★	Based:	UK
Product Range:	★★★★	Express Delivery Option?	(UK) Yes
Price Range:	Luxury/Medium/Very Good Value	Gift Wrapping Option?	Yes
Delivery Area:	Worldwide	Returns Procedure:	Down to you

Also check out this website for baby and toddler clothes

Website Address

www.bjornandme.co.uk

You'll find it in

What to wear with a bump

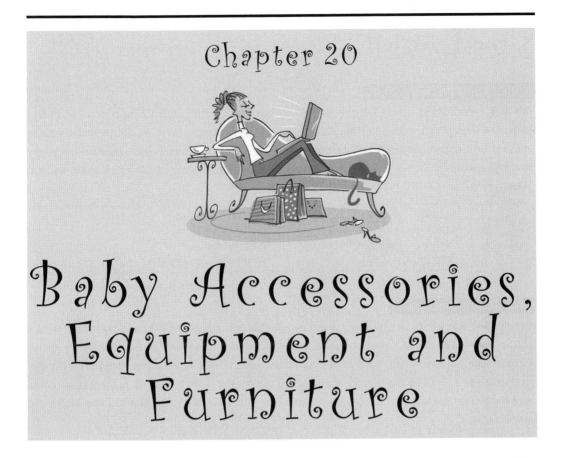

Chapter 20

Baby Accessories, Equipment and Furniture

Choosing exactly what accessories and equipment you'll need when you're expecting your first baby (and after that you'll be an expert, believe me) can be extremely confusing, not to say horrifically expensive. To make life easier before you start to buy you could check out one of the websites that exist to help you, such as *www.askbaby.com*, *www.babyworld.co.uk* or *www.raisingkids.co.uk* where you'll find lots of advice plus information on the types of equipment you'll need and what details you should look for when buying.

Alternatively you can go to *www.amazon.co.uk* and buy one of their baby advice books (you probably have already) which should give you all the information you want and probably a great deal more than you want.

The websites listed here all offer a range of accessories and equipment so allow yourself enough time to really have a good look through. When you find something you like before you're ready to buy make sure that you make a note of where you found it. It can be exasperating if you don't and have to search again. Also don't forget to do a price comparison to make sure that you're getting the best deal available, particularly for brand name buggies etc.

With regards to nursery furniture the sky really is the limit and some of what is offered here is truly unique and beautiful. Some items you'll probably be happy to buy yourself and others you'll definitely want to include in your Godmother/parent/granny gift list; at least, I would.

Sites to Visit

www.caboodle-baby.co.uk

This is a beautifully designed website where you can order birth announcements and christening invitations (and if you want something really special you can have these as ribbon tied scrolls in coloured card boxes), handmade photo albums and guest books to match the overall theme you've chosen plus keepsake boxes. Delivery is only within the UK and you need to allow four weeks for your order to arrive.

Site Usability:	★★★★★	Based:	UK
Product Range:	★★★	Express Delivery Option?	(UK) No
Price Range:	Luxury/Medium/Very Good Value	Gift Wrapping Option?	No
Delivery Area:	UK	Returns Procedure:	Down to you

www.happybags.co.uk

If you've just had a baby or you know someone who has it would be well worth your while taking a look at this website from a retailer specialising in baby bags. The kind of bag that holds all the paraphernalia you need if you go out, with multiple compartments to keep everything separate, that you can use as a shoulder bag if you want or attach to your high tech buggy. There are lots to choose from the Million Dollar Baby Bag (extremely expensive) to the excellent Skip Hop bag which comes in lots of colours.

Site Usability:	★★★	Based:	UK
Product Range:	★★★	Express Delivery Option?	(UK) No
Price Range:	Luxury/Medium/Very Good Value	Gift Wrapping Option?	No
Delivery Area:	Worldwide	Returns Procedure:	Down to you

www.kiddicare.com

Kiddicare is a large independent retailer of baby and nursery equipment and nursery furniture and claim to keep everything in stock ready to send out to you. You can buy Avent sterilisers and feeding bottles, Grobags, buggies and travel cots, high chairs, rockers and baby swings plus lots for the home including playpens, stair gates, cots, changing units and nursery furniture. Delivery is free to most of the UK and takes about four working days.

Site Usability:	★★★★★	Based:	UK
Product Range:	★★★★★	Express Delivery Option?	(UK) No
Price Range:	Luxury/Medium/Very Good Value	Gift Wrapping Option?	No
Delivery Area:	UK	Returns Procedure:	Down to you

www.kidsfabrics.co.uk

Here you can buy fabric for children's furnishings by the metre or as ready cut kits for curtains, cot bedding, and pillow cases. You can also order linings, header tape, voile and other accessories and order a selection of four samples which they'll send you free of charge. There's a wide selection of delightful fabrics for children with themes such as jungle/animals, appliqued and embroidered fabrics, fairytale, cars and helicopters, outer space, soldiers and teddies.

Site Usability:	★★★★	Based:	UK
Product Range:	★★★★	Express Delivery Option?	(UK) No
Price Range:	Luxury/Medium/Very Good Value	Gift Wrapping Option?	No
Delivery Area:	Worldwide	Returns Procedure:	Down to you

www.nurserywindow.co.uk

Once you arrive at this website you'll find it very hard to leave. There are some seriously lovely things here for children's rooms, from unusual bedding, moses baskets and high quality cots and furniture to gift baskets for new babies and everything is beautifully photographed. Just click on the area of their online shop you're interested in, enter, and you'll certainly be hooked. You can also buy matching fabric to the bedlinen. Nothing is cheap but it's all beautiful quality.

Site Usability:	★★★★★	Based:	UK
Product Range:	★★★★	Express Delivery Option?	(UK) No
Price Range:	Luxury/Medium/Very Good Value	Gift Wrapping Option?	No
Delivery Area:	Worldwide but ask for postage charges	Returns Procedure:	Down to you

www.preciouslittleone.com

Here's an excellent baby equipment website offering, amongst other things, footmuffs (which I haven't found anywhere else) pushchairs and accessories with lots of details to help you choose, car seats and a very good range for the nursery including the high quality Saplings range of furniture, most of which will take your child from baby to older years. You can also buy giant themed sticker sets for room decorating.

Site Usability:	★★★★★	Based:	UK
Product Range:	★★★★	Express Delivery Option?	(UK) No
Price Range:	Luxury/Medium/Very Good Value	Gift Wrapping Option?	No
Delivery Area:	Worldwide	Returns Procedure:	Down to you

Also visit these websites for baby accessories and equipment

Website Address	You'll find it in
www.bloomingmarvellous.co.uk	Baby and Toddler Clothes
www.mamasandpapas.co.uk	Baby and Toddler Clothes
www.thekidswindow.co.uk	Baby and Toddler Clothes

Chapter 21

Children's Clothes and Accessories to age 12

This is where it gets quite difficult. Just how long will they allow you to choose their clothes for them? Some children (as you may already know) start creating their own style at about age six or seven and nothing you can do will change their minds. Once they've established the type of clothes they like to wear and providing it's not too outrageous you may well want to choose the easy life and go along with them. Personally I would do just about anything to make life easier in this area, why create extra and unnecessary (and upsetting) hassle.

Anyway, this is not a book about parental advice so the troubleshooting is down to you. This is more about choices, and there are plenty of them from the cheap and cheerful end of the market to the designer end where you can spend a fortune.

You'll find all the options below. Most of the websites offer an excellent and speedy service and you can, of course, call them if you have any queries.

Sites to Visit

www.accessorize.co.uk

Just about as well known on the High Street as its sister shop Monsoon, Accessorize is the essential destination if you're looking for a gift for an older child or if your early teen and upwards needs (as in I NEED) a new pair of earrings, flip flops, party slip on shoes, scarf or bag. Not only are the prices extremely reasonable but the products are fun and modern. The stores themselves are usually heaving, so take advantage of the fact that you (or they) can now shop online.

Site Usability:	★★★★★	Based:	UK
Product Range:	★★★★	Express Delivery Option?	(UK) No
Price Range:	Luxury/<u>Medium</u>/Very Good Value	Gift Wrapping Option?	No
Delivery Area:	UK	Returns Procedure:	Down to you

www.childrenssalon.co.uk

This is a family run business operating out of their shop in Kent and offering designer children's clothes from 0-12 years from labels such as Oilily, Bengh Par Principesse, Oxbow, Gabrielle, Elle, Cacharel, Kenzo, Dior and loads more (and I mean loads). They also have the Petit Bateau range of underwear for boys and girls, nightwear and dressing up clothes and they specialise in a gorgeous range of christening gowns and accessories.

Site Usability:	★★★★★	Based:	UK
Product Range:	★★★★	Express Delivery Option?	(UK) Yes
Price Range:	<u>Luxury/Medium</u>/Very Good Value	Gift Wrapping Option?	No
Delivery Area:	Worldwide	Returns Procedure:	Down to you

www.clothes4boys.co.uk

Here you'll find, yes you guessed it, clothes just for boys, from 2-14 years old and including designers Ripcurl, Salty Dog, Eager Beaver, Regatta and Flyers. There really is a great choice with casual clothes from t-shirts to boarding trousers and football trousers, plus an excellent sale shop and some fun and funky swimwear. You can select to view their range by age or by designer.

Site Usability:	★★★★★	Based:	UK
Product Range:	★★★★	Express Delivery Option?	(UK) No
Price Range:	<u>Luxury/Medium</u>/Very Good Value	Gift Wrapping Option?	No
Delivery Area:	Worldwide	Returns Procedure:	Down to you

www.hopscotchdressingup.co.uk

Hopscotch have definitely got the childrens dressing up market sewn up with their lovely bright website full of dressing up box clothes from angels and fairies to witches and wizards, cowboys and indians to kings and queens and everything in between. There's no question that if your child has been asked to a fancy dress party and is determined to really look the part you absolutely have to visit here.

Site Usability:	★★★★★	Based:	UK
Product Range:	★★★★	Express Delivery Option?	(UK) Yes
Price Range:	Luxury/Medium/Very Good Value	Gift Wrapping Option?	No
Delivery Area:	Worldwide	Returns Procedure:	Down to you

www.kidscavern.co.uk

Kids Cavern is one of the top children's designer stores in the North West of England and their website covers children's wear over three departments from new born–3 years, 4–10 years and 11–16 years. Designers offered include Timberland, Moschino, DKNY, Burberry, Armani, Miniman, Dior and many more and they'll ship worldwide although outside the UK and USA you need to email them to find out how much your postage will cost.

Site Usability:	★★★	Based:	UK
Product Range:	★★★★	Express Delivery Option?	(UK) Yes
Price Range:	Luxury/Medium/Very Good Value	Gift Wrapping Option?	No
Delivery Area:	Worldwide	Returns Procedure:	Down to you

www.littlesky.co.uk

Little Sky specialise in children's branded surf, ski and fashion wear, footwear and accessories for kids 0–16 years. On their website there's a really good range of functional, fashionable and technical wear from brands including Quiksilver, Roxy, Billabong, O'Neill, Animal, Oxbow, Timberland, Kookai, Elle, Reef, Columbia, Trespass, Brugi and many more. In the summer you can find all you need for your holiday in the sun from bikinis, boardshorts and funky shirts to UV suits, rash vests and footwear and in winter they focus on skiwear and accessories.

Site Usability:	★★★★★	Based:	UK
Product Range:	★★★★	Express Delivery Option?	(UK) Yes
Price Range:	Luxury/Medium/Very Good Value	Gift Wrapping Option?	No
Delivery Area:	EU	Returns Procedure:	Down to you

www.pleasemum.co.uk

This is a company that was established in London in 1971, aiming to provide fashionable, unique and high quality childrens clothing. They now offer their excellent own brand collections online for children up to age 12/13 (and there are some really gorgeous outfits here, particularly for girls) plus designer childrenswear by Moschino, D & G, Armani, Versace and Roberto Cavalli. Do not expect to save money when you visit this website, it's definitely not cheap.

Site Usability:	★★★★	Based:	UK
Product Range:	★★★★	Express Delivery Option?	(UK) No
Price Range:	Luxury/Medium/Very Good Value	Gift Wrapping Option?	No
Delivery Area:	Worldwide	Returns Procedure:	Down to you

www.teddywear.com

Teddywear is a small internet boutique selling high quality children's clothes including brands such as Balu, Catimini, Marese, Miniman, Little Darlings, SULK, Chipie, Lili Gaufrette, Babar, Timberland, DKNY, Diesel, Confetti, Pampolina, and many more. You can search by age or brand and, as they update their stock regularly, keep coming back to see what's available. There's a really good selection here up to age 9/10 as well as a baby section.

Site Usability:	★★★★	Based:	UK
Product Range:	★★★★	Express Delivery Option?	(UK) No
Price Range:	Luxury/Medium/Very Good Value	Gift Wrapping Option?	No
Delivery Area:	Worldwide	Returns Procedure:	Down to you

www.theirnibs.com

The approach at Their Nibs is to offer a truly distinctive children's clothing collection to fill the gap between the national chains and independent retailers who stock all the usual brands. The collection, which includes lots of prints, is continually updated and inspiration comes from a variety of sources including their own in house, 'vintage collection'. There are some really pretty clothes for children aged 0–8 including perfect dresses for little flowergirls.

Site Usability:	★★★★★	Based:	UK
Product Range:	★★★★	Express Delivery Option?	(UK) No
Price Range:	Luxury/Medium/Very Good Value	Gift Wrapping Option?	No
Delivery Area:	Worldwide	Returns Procedure:	Down to you

www.wildchildfashions.com

With labels such as Lacoste, Paul Smith, Ted Baker, Hackett, Timberland, Diesel, DKNY, Nike and Guess you'll probably have to fight to keep your children off this website and warn your bank manager if you fail. Wildchild are a fairly new childrenswear company aiming to appeal to both children and parents (is such a thing possible?) and offer their ranges for girls and boys up to mid teens.

Site Usability:	★★★★★	Based:	UK
Product Range:	★★★★	Express Delivery Option?	(UK) Yes
Price Range:	Luxury/Medium/Very Good Value	Gift Wrapping Option?	No
Delivery Area:	Worldwide	Returns Procedure:	Down to you

Also visit these websites for childrens' clothes and accessories to age 12

Website Address	You'll find it in
www.boden.co.uk	Fashion Retailers
www.thekidswindow.co.uk	Baby and Toddler Clothes
www.monsoon.co.uk	Fashion Retailers

Chapter 22

Teen Shopping and Young Sportswear

Having three teenagers myself I know pretty well where they'd like to shop, how important it is to be wearing the right labels, to be cool amongst their friends, to wear what's trendy and what they feel comfortable in (at least that applies to two of them). At this point it's absolutely, totally and utterly useless to try and get them to wear what you want them to and even for high days and holidays it seems a struggle (yes, those are my children).

Of course, you may have the perfect kind of children who wear exactly what you tell them to all the time. In which case you're extremely lucky and I suspect total rebellion is just around the next corner.

Here are some excellent websites for teen clothing and sportswear that are modern, funky and in tune with the current look. You'll find sportswear from the 'right' labels and places where they can find the 'just launched' Pumas and Converse trainers. Places, in fact, where I'm sure your children will feel right at home.

There are some excellent High Street retailers who aren't yet on the web. Hopefully they'll follow the trend and join these sites soon. We'll be sure to let you know.

Sites to Visit

www.agirlsworld.co.uk

This really is a great shop for girls (and yes they stock some 'boyfriend's' clothes as well). With brands such as Amplified, Converse, Fenchurch, Fly, Heidi Seeker, Duck and Cover, Get Cutie and Paul Frank (don't worry, I haven't heard of most of them either) the teen girl in your family will definitely want to shop here. They also have accessories such as belts, scarves, socks, hats, bags, purses and footwear.

Site Usability:	★★★★	Based:	UK
Product Range:	★★★★	Express Delivery Option?	(UK) No
Price Range:	Luxury/Medium/Very Good Value	Gift Wrapping Option?	No
Delivery Area:	UK	Returns Procedure:	Down to you

www.cult.co.uk

This is definitely a website for those who want to wear something young and slightly different. Offering brands such as Alpha, Bench, Carhartt, Franklin and Marshall and Fenchurch the look is young, modern and colourful. Take a look at their 'what's hot' section to find out what they think you should be wearing this season. Delivery is free on orders over £20. Well worth a look.

Site Usability:	★★★★	Based:	UK
Product Range:	★★★★	Express Delivery Option?	(UK) No
Price Range:	Luxury/Medium/Very Good Value	Gift Wrapping Option?	No
Delivery Area:	Worldwide	Returns Procedure:	Use their free service

www.extremepie.com

Offering up to date surf/skate wear extremepie is the online brand name of Extreme Group who specialise in bringing together the best of this particular type of sportswear from around the World. There are enough brands to sink a ship from famous brands such as O'Neill, Quicksilver, Animal, Vans, Billabong, RipCurl, Addict, Extreme and Reef plus loads more that you may not have heard of. This is definitely a good site for anyone who's addicted to sport, or just wants the sporty look.

Site Usability:	★★★★	Based:	UK
Product Range:	★★★★	Express Delivery Option?	(UK) Yes
Price Range:	Luxury/Medium/Very Good Value	Gift Wrapping Option?	No
Delivery Area:	Worldwide	Returns Procedure:	Down to you

www.jobrowns.com

This is a really fun website, where you'll find very well priced contemporary sportswear for men and women. Think vintage style tops, ruffled shirts, sporty gilets and colourful polos and you'll get my drift. The pictures are extremely clear and there's plenty of description and information about each item. Alongside the clothing there are lots of accessories including sunglasses, jewellery, bags and purses and belts.

Site Usability:	★★★★	Based:	UK
Product Range:	★★★★	Express Delivery Option?	(UK) No
Price Range:	Luxury/Medium/<u>Very Good Value</u>	Gift Wrapping Option?	No
Delivery Area:	UK	Returns Procedure:	Down to You

www.missselfridge.co.uk

An integral part of the high street since the 60's, Miss Selfridge has always been a mainstay for young, modern style. There's nothing quiet about the clothes offered here but plenty of information and guidance on how to put together the latest looks and the background to the trends. They do go up to a size 16 but most of the clothes would suit better if they went no further than a small 12.

Site Usability:	★★★★	Based:	UK
Product Range:	★★★★	Express Delivery Option?	(UK) Yes
Price Range:	Luxury/<u>Medium</u>/Very Good Value	Gift Wrapping Option?	No
Delivery Area:	UK	Returns Procedure:	Freepost or to their stores but complicated

www.topman.co.uk

From their high quality premium suit collection right through to modern, inexpensive knitwear, t-shirts, casual trousers and well priced shirts this is an extremely popular website. You'll also find a funky shoe collection ranging from casual shoes to smart loafers to cowboy boots. It's a modern, young collection and one where you can find just about everything.

Site Usability:	★★★★★	Based:	UK
Product Range:	★★★★	Express Delivery Option?	(UK) Yes
Price Range:	Luxury/Medium/<u>Very Good Value</u>	Gift Wrapping Option?	Yes
Delivery Area:	UK	Returns Procedure:	Down to you

www.topshop.co.uk

Here's the place to go if you want the latest fashions at the best prices and definitely the place to go if you can't stand the scum of the shops. Can't afford Marc Jacobs or Miu Miu? Go straight to Top Shop, and if you can't bear the heaving crowds in the store, desperately seeking the last pair of plaited leather wedge sandals in your size, you can order them online and have them sent to you by express delivery. A fashionista could surely ask for no more than this.

Site Usability:	★★★★	Based:	UK
Product Range:	★★★★★	Express Delivery Option?	(UK) Yes
Price Range:	Luxury/Medium/<u>Very Good Value</u>	Gift Wrapping Option?	Yes
Delivery Area:	UK	Returns Procedure:	Down to you

www.urbanitystore.com

Urbanitystore is a hip, modern website offering young, urban sportswear for girls and boys. Brands include Pop Clothing, Ichi, Boxfresh, Power Puff Girls and loads more and include jeans, dresses, skirts, tops and jackets plus bags, belts and jewellery. They regularly have new stock in so it's worth while checking back if this is the kind of fashion for you.

Site Usability:	★★★	Based:	UK
Product Range:	★★★	Express Delivery Option?	(UK) No
Price Range:	Luxury/Medium/Very Good Value	Gift Wrapping Option?	Yes
Delivery Area:	Worldwide	Returns Procedure:	Down to you

Also visit these websites for teen shopping and young sportswear

Website Address	You'll find it in
www.fcukbuymail.co.uk	Shop the High Street
www.mango.com	Shop the High Street
www.w1style.com	Shop the High Street
www.riverisland.co.uk	Shop the High Street
www.warehousefashion.com	Shop the High Street
www.fatface.co.uk	The Sportswear Option

Chapter 23

The Young and Funky Beauty and Accessory Place

This is very much aimed at the female end of the market (sorry boys), but being the mother of a mid-teen (sorry again, dreadful expression but I'm sure you know what I mean), I know that they become 'collectors' very early on and although you want to encourage them to buy quality what they actually want is lots of this season's 'must-haves', earrings, belts, bracelets and bags (and the latest make-up) and so they need their own ranges at decent prices.

You won't find the bottom end of the market here, but a few clever retailers who manage to appeal to a variety of age groups and keep up to date with the trends. You'll probably have seen their names in other areas of this book but if it's your teen you're shopping for, or if your teen is shopping for herself and her friends, she'll want everything together just for her. I know this from a recent lecture from my daughter who, having seen an early draft of this book, asked 'but where's my section, you seem to have left me out?'

On the subject of young cosmetics this is just a fun place to find new and accessibly priced ranges from a number of brands, some of which I had never heard of before. However, having shopped with my daughter on numerous occasions (she now has more make-up than I do which sounds dreadful but isn't as bad as it sounds if you know what I mean) I know that brands such as Urban Decay, Pout,

Bloom, Benefit and Hard Candy have far more allure for a modern girl than the classics such as Lancome, Arden and YSL.

These cosmetics are young and they're fun and most won't break the bank. You can't stop them experimenting (you just have fights over how much eyeliner they're wearing) but you can steer them away from yours, thank heavens.

Sites to Visit

www.accessorize.co.uk

Accessorize is the essential destination if you're looking for a gift for an older child or if your early teen and upwards needs (as in I NEED) a new pair of earrings, flip flops, party slip on shoes, scarf or bag. Not only are the prices extremely reasonable but the products are fun and modern.

Site Usability:	★★★★★	Based:	UK
Product Range:	★★★★	Express Delivery Option?	(UK) No
Price Range:	Luxury/Medium/<u>Very Good Value</u>	Gift Wrapping Option?	No
Delivery Area:	UK	Returns Procedure:	Down to you

www.hqhair.com

The products on this fantastic website are growing by the day so I'm not even going to try and list them all here for you. However, alongside their excellent range of hair products and beauty accessories you'll also find a great range of modern cosmetics and skincare from names such as Pout and Urban Decay. Once you start shopping here it's almost impossible to stop. I know. I'm an addict.

Site Usability:	★★★★★	Based:	UK
Product Range:	★★★★	Express Delivery Option?	(UK) Yes
Price Range:	Luxury/<u>Medium</u>/Very Good Value	Gift Wrapping Option?	No
Delivery Area:	Worldwide	Returns Procedure:	Down to you

www.johnnylovesrosie.co.uk

Famous for their chic, modern collection of hair accessories, Johnny Loves Rosie has now branched out into a collection of small, beautifully detailed bags, flip flops and pretty bead jewellery. This is a small selection online, but how can you resist their carved marigold bobby pins, crystal hair clips and flower clips and elastics, featuring orchids, buttercups, hyacinths and carnations, in a variety of colours? They're simply a must for any hair conscious girl.

Site Usability:	★★★★	Based:	UK
Product Range:	★★★	Express Delivery Option?	(UK) No
Price Range:	Luxury/<u>Medium</u>/Very Good Value	Gift Wrapping Option?	No
Delivery Area:	Worldwide	Returns Procedure:	Down to you

www.mikeyjewellery.co.uk

If you've ever walked into Sprit in Selfridges you may have glanced at the crowds milling around the jewellery and accessory section. Well a large part of this belongs to Mikey, a well priced contemporary jewellery designer. Make a note here, if you have a daughter who loves to collect accessories (preferably that you've paid for) you may want to look at this website at dead of night just before Christmas or a Birthday as otherwise you'll definitely be spending more than you intend.

Site Usability:	★★★★★	Based:	UK
Product Range:	★★★★	Express Delivery Option?	(UK) Yes depending on how much you spend
Price Range:	Luxury/<u>Medium</u>/Very Good Value	Gift Wrapping Option?	No
Delivery Area:	UK	Returns Procedure:	Down to You

www.missgroovy.co.uk

There's a real mixture of products on offer here from YSL Touche Eclat and Hollywood Fashion Tape to cosmetics by Girlactik, Duwop, Eyeko and Principessa plus bath and body products, hair and nail care and lots of suggestions and advice. So if you're looking for something a bit different this would be a very good place to have a browse or to find an unusual gift. They'll ship worldwide and aim to despatch within a day.

Site Usability:	★★★★	Based:	UK
Product Range:	★★★	Express Delivery Option?	(UK) Yes
Price Range:	Luxury/<u>Medium</u>/Very Good Value	Gift Wrapping Option?	Yes
Delivery Area:	Worldwide	Returns Procedure:	Down to You

www.popbeauty.co.uk

Here's a new, young retailer offering a clever, well priced range of cosmetics online, with names such as Sparkling Emerald Eye Glimmer, Dust Delux and Yummy Sugar Shine lip gloss and all at accessible prices. They also have some very pretty gifts (which are not so inexpensive) but which arrive gift wrapped with a free make-up bag. This is a very colourful and well put together website which I'm sure will prove to be extremely tempting to any make-up addict.

Site Usability:	★★★★	Based:	UK
Product Range:	★★★	Express Delivery Option?	(UK) No
Price Range:	Luxury/Medium/<u>Very Good Value</u>	Gift Wrapping Option?	Yes for some of the gifts
Delivery Area:	Worldwide	Returns Procedure:	Down to You

www.temptationjewellery.com

This is a very young and funky website aimed, they say, at the stylish desk-bound professional but, I say, perfect for the jewellery collecting teen of almost any age as they have a wide range of well priced and modern earrings, necklaces and other accessories starting at around £10.00. They offer free UK delivery, an express service and gift wrapping and voucher options plus a fourteen day money back guarantee.

Site Usability:	★★★★		Based:	UK
Product Range:	★★★★		Express Delivery Option?	(UK) Yes
Price Range:	Luxury/Medium/Very Good Value		Gift Wrapping Option?	Yes
Delivery Area:	UK		Returns Procedure:	Down to you

Section 4
Pamper Yourself

Want to know where you can find a spa in your area with a swimming pool? Or just need the instant feel good fix of a small but beautiful (and not bank breaking) purchase – something from Jo Malone perhaps, or Molton Brown, Diptyque, Penhaligons, l'Artisan Parfumeur, Annick Goutal, Cote Bastide? The list goes on and on and here you can really enjoy having a browse, knowing that what you order will arrive beautifully packaged and every bit as good as it looks online.

This is also a great area for present giving, however much you want to spend. Frequently you're offered gift-wrapping and delivery to anywhere in the world as an added temptation. Now you won't find that in a shop, will you? (You should, but you don't). Nothing beats being given a glossy bag containing ribbon tied products from your favourite company, Penhaligons, Jo Malone or L'Occitane, or receiving them in the post. It's quite simply a joy. It doesn't matter what you're looking for, whether it's an unusual fragrance, your replacement lipstick or a packet of Nurofen. You can find practically everything online.

The beauty of buying all these products online is that it gives you more time being your real shopaholic self, trying out new fragrance and cosmetics at the beauty counters in the store. Don't think you'll see the new colours online at their best. You won't. Colour reproduction is extremely tricky at the best of times so don't expect to find that perfect shade of red you're looking for. No way. But once you've found it at a beauty counter, to replenish it? No problem. The same goes for fragrance. You have to try it out first in the store. Then order it online.

Chapter 24

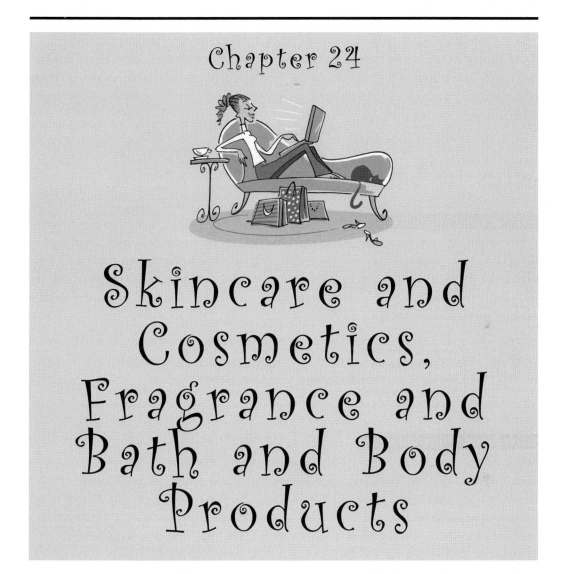

Skincare and Cosmetics, Fragrance and Bath and Body Products

This is a really well established area of online shopping partly because the goodies are so easy to package up and send, they're easy to have gift wrapped and sent on for you and, most importantly, it's where you can treat yourself, choose something beautiful and wait a very short while for it to arrive. So if you're having a down day or the children are giving you a hard time just spend a couple of minutes here and you'll feel better extremely fast.

As I've said before, there are really very few brands now that are not available online, partly due to the enthusiasm of retailers such as *www.spacenk.co.uk* and *www.hqhair.com* to offer you new and different products from all over the world and partly because once *www.boots.com* and *www.garden.co.uk* got going with all the major brands such as Chanel and Lancome others simply had to follow and try and do it better.

So why would you buy these products online, when the beauty counters are just there, waiting for your business? As usual, it's a time issue and if you're working or have young children you may well find it preferable to relax with a glass of wine and browse with no time constraints and no one trying to drag you away, I know I do. And where gifts are concerned these websites are the answer to a prayer if you're busy, as I'm sure you'll discover.

Sites to Visit

www.arranaromatics.com

If you want to find something a little unusual, beautifully presented and well priced than look no further than Arran Aromatics where you can discover bath and body products, candles and much more with names such as Laurel, Lili, After the Rain and Waterbabe. The packaging is very pretty and you can select from individual items such as room sprays, shower gels and bath soak grains or their excellent gift boxes and travel sets.

Site Usability:	★★★★★	Based:	UK
Product Range:	★★★★	Express Delivery Option?	(UK) Yes
Price Range:	Luxury/<u>Medium</u>/Very Good Value	Gift Wrapping Option?	No
Delivery Area:	Worldwide	Returns Procedure:	Down to you

www.bathandunwind.com

Bath & Unwind specialise in luxury products that help you to relax (and unwind) after a hard day's work. They aim to provide the highest quality bath and spa products from around the world including brands such as Aromatherapy Associates, Korres, Nougat, Burt's Bees and Jane Packer. Delivery is free (UK) provided you spend over a certain amount and they'll ship to you anywhere in the world. They also have a gift selector and an express service for the next time you forget that special present.

Site Usability:	★★★★	Based:	UK
Product Range:	★★★★	Express Delivery Option?	(UK) Yes
Price Range:	Luxury/<u>Medium</u>/Very Good Value	Gift Wrapping Option?	No
Delivery Area:	Worldwide	Returns Procedure:	Down to you

www.beautybase.com

Don't expect lots of pretty pictures on this cosmetics and fragrance site which carries hundreds of brand name products but little illustration. You need to know what you're looking for. There's fragrance by just about everyone you can think of including Annick Goutal, Boucheron, Carolina Herrera, Escada and Paul Smith. Skincare and make-up (not full selection) by Dior, Clarins, Guerlain and La Prairie and there are discounts on some products and very good service, so it's well worth seeing if they stock what you're looking for.

Site Usability:	★★★★	Based:	UK
Product Range:	★★★★	Express Delivery Option?	(UK) Yes
Price Range:	Luxury/Medium/Very Good Value	Gift Wrapping Option?	No
Delivery Area:	Worldwide	Returns Procedure:	Down to you

www.beautybay.com

This is a beautifully laid out website offering just about every fragrance with bath and body products to match and a small range of cosmetics and skincare, plus jewellery and fragrance giftsets (excellent for presents). Delivery is free on orders over £30, they'll ship to just about anywhere in the world and offer a next day service as well. What's particularly good here is that on many of the products you'll find yourself spending less than you expect. What more could you want?

Site Usability:	★★★★★	Based:	UK
Product Range:	★★★★	Express Delivery Option?	(UK) Yes
Price Range:	Luxury/Medium/Very Good Value	Gift Wrapping Option?	No
Delivery Area:	Worldwide	Returns Procedure:	Down to you

www.benefitcosmetics.com

You can find Benefit cosmetics in the major stores but you'll be hard put to see this complete range anywhere else online, and with tempting products such as Benetint, Lip Plump, Super Strength Blemish Blaster and Ooh La Lift how can you resist buying (too much probably) from this veritable candy store for the face? There's the cleverly packaged makeup, foundations, concealers and glitters, bodycare, skincare, accessories and a great gift selection.

Site Usability:	★★★★★	Based:	USA
Product Range:	★★★★	Express Delivery Option?	(UK) Yes
Price Range:	Luxury/Medium/Very Good Value	Gift Wrapping Option?	Yes
Delivery Area:	Worldwide	Returns Procedure:	Down to you

www.blisslondon.co.uk

Sign up for Bliss Beut e-mails and stay in the 'Glow'. Does that give you some idea of the tone from beauty online from New York and London's hottest spa? If you don't have the time to visit the spas themselves you can at least now buy the products online and relax at home with your own treatments, shower gels and shampoos with simple names like Body Butter, Rosy Toes and Glamour Glove Gel. Some of the products are reasonably priced but you'll also find some of their marvellous anti ageing products will set you back a bit. It'll be worth it though.

Site Usability:	★★★★	Based:	UK
Product Range:	★★★	Express Delivery Option?	(UK) Yes
Price Range:	Luxury/Medium/Very Good Value	Gift Wrapping Option?	No
Delivery Area:	Worldwide	Returns Procedure:	Down to you

www.boots.com

Not only can you buy your basic bathroom cupboard items here, plus fragrance from most of the major brands, but from their Brand Boutique you can also buy the full ranges from Chanel, Clarins, Clinique, Dior, Estee Lauder, Elizabeth Arden and Lancôme plus ultra modern brands Ruby and Millie, Urban Decay and Benefit. Delivery is free when you spend £40 and returns are free too. Their excellent service is simply not publicised enough.

Site Usability:	★★★★★	Express Delivery Option?	(UK) Yes
Product Range:	★★★★★	Gift Wrapping Option?	Yes
Price Range:	Luxury/Medium/Very Good Value	Returns Procedure:	Free
Delivery Area:	UK		

www.cosmeticsalacarte.com

Christina Stewart and Lynne Sanders, both creative cosmetic chemists, founded Cosmetics à la carte 30 years ago – the first made-to-measure make-up range. If you can't get to their Knightsbridge store you can order this range of 'makeup to fit' online with easy to see wide choices of colours for face, cheek, lip and eye products (including their wonderful Lip Glass) plus 'Skin Basics' skin treats and a great selection of brushes and other beauty accessories.

Site Usability:	★★★★★	Express Delivery Option?	(UK) No
Product Range:	★★★★	Gift Wrapping Option?	No
Price Range:	Luxury/Medium/Very Good Value	Returns Procedure:	Down to you
Delivery Area:	Worldwide		

www.crabtree-evelyn.co.uk

Well known and sold throughout the World, Crabtree & Evelyn offer a wide range of bath, body and spa products from classic fragrances such as Lily of the Valley to the ultra modern La Source. Everything is cleverly and attractively packaged and offered on their well designed and easy to use website. Particularly good as gifts are their pretty boxes containing miniatures of their most popular products.

Site Usability:	★★★★★	Based:	UK
Product Range:	★★★★★	Express Delivery Option?	(UK) No
Price Range:	Luxury/Medium/Very Good Value	Gift Wrapping Option?	No
Delivery Area:	Worldwide	Returns Procedure:	Down to you

www.cologneandcotton.net

This is a very special website offering some unusual and hard to find bath and body products and fragrance by Diptyque (If you haven't already tried their candles you really should, they're gorgeous), Cath Collins, La Compagnie de Provence (try their hand wash) and Cote Bastide. There are also fragrances by Annik Goutal, Coudray and Rosine and for the bathroom they have lovely fluffy towels and bathrobes.

Site Usability:	★★★★★	Based:	UK
Product Range:	★★★★	Express Delivery Option?	(UK) Yes
Price Range:	Luxury/Medium/Very Good Value	Gift Wrapping Option?	Yes
Delivery Area:	Worldwide	Returns Procedure:	Down to you

www.escentual.co.uk

Escentual carry what is probably the widest range of fragrance for men and women in the UK. Choose a fragrance or fragrance linked bath and body product and then search for it on this site – you're almost certain to find it. Bath and body products include Burberry, Bvlgari, Calvin Klein, Gucci, Guerlain, Rochas and Versace plus Crabtree and Evelyn, Tisserand and I Coloniali. Delivery is free on orders over £30 and they also offer free gift wrapping.

Site Usability:	★★★★★	Based:	UK
Product Range:	★★★★★	Express Delivery Option?	(UK) Yes
Price Range:	Luxury/Medium/Very Good Value	Gift Wrapping Option?	Yes
Delivery Area:	Worldwide	Returns Procedure:	Down to you

www.garden.co.uk

The Garden Pharmacy's list of top brands seems to be growing by the day. Here you'll find Chanel, Elizabeth Arden, Lancôme, Revlon, Clinique and Clarins online together with Vichy, Avene, Caudalie and Roc and spa products by I Coloniali, L'Occitane, Roger et Gallet and Segreti Mediterranei (and no doubt a few more will have appeared by the time you read this). The list of fragrances they offer is huge. They also offer free gift wrapping and 24 hour delivery.

Site Usability:	★★★★	Based:	UK
Product Range:	★★★★★	Express Delivery Option?	(UK) Yes
Price Range:	Luxury/Medium/Very Good Value	Gift Wrapping Option?	Yes
Delivery Area:	Worldwide	Returns Procedure:	Down to you

www.jomalone.co.uk

Most people when they think of Jo Malone think of her gorgeous and luxurious fragrance and bath and body products. Take a good look again at her attractively designed website, where you'll also find beautifully scented cleansers, serums and moisturisers and her facial finishers: finishing fluid and powder, lip gloss, blush and mascara, but beware; once you're on her site it's extremely hard to escape without buying. The service is excellent and everything is exquisitely packaged in her signature cream and black.

Site Usability:	★★★★★	Based:	UK
Product Range:	★★★★★	Express Delivery Option?	(UK) Yes
Price Range:	Luxury/Medium/Very Good Value	Gift Wrapping Option?	Yes
Delivery Area:	Worldwide	Returns Procedure:	Down to you

www.kennethturner.co.uk

White Flowers, Wild Garden, Magnolia Grandiflora and Rose (plus his Original fragrance) are some of the fragrances you'll find on this pretty website, presented as candles, tea lights, shower gel and body lotions, room colognes and pot pourri. His packaging, in flower printed blue and white boxes turn his products into perfect gifts and you'll find travel sets and prepared gift boxes here as well.

Site Usability:	★★★★	Based:	UK
Product Range:	★★★	Express Delivery Option?	(UK) Yes
Price Range:	Luxury/Medium/Very Good Value	Gift Wrapping Option?	Yes
Delivery Area:	Worldwide	Returns Procedure:	Down to you

www.laboutiquedelartisanparfumeur.com

If you're not already aware of this gorgeous collection of French fragrance and bath and body products by L'Artisan Parfumeur, with names such as Mure et Musc (blackberry and musk) and Figuier and Orchidee Blanche, then now's the time to discover this beautifully presented range and order it online. You'll also find such unusual ideas as their blackberry-shaped glass bottle, scented silk peonies and terracotta amber balls, all of which make exceptional gifts.

Site Usability:	★★★★	Based:	UK
Product Range:	★★★	Express Delivery Option?	(UK) Yes
Price Range:	Luxury/Medium/Very Good Value	Gift Wrapping Option?	Automatic
Delivery Area:	Worldwide	Returns Procedure:	Down to you

www.miam-miam.co.uk

I had to find this one out. Dorothy Day of miam-miam tells me that the name is the French equivalent of our 'yummy'. 'Because everything in my shop is yummy'. Take note, if you're passing through Edinburgh visit her shop, it certainly looks lovely. Anyway, you can buy your L'Occitane products from here wherever you are in the World, along with gorgeous hand stitched quilts from Une Histoire Simple and Blanc d'Ivoire and decorative wall clocks by Roger Lascelles.

Site Usability:	★★★★	Express Delivery Option?	(UK) Yes
Product Range:	★★★	Gift Wrapping Option?	Yes
Price Range:	Luxury/Medium/Very Good Value	Returns Procedure:	Down to you
Delivery Area:	Worldwide		

www.moltonbrown.co.uk

The range of Molton Brown's bath, skincare, makeup and spa products seems to increase daily and you want to try every single one. The packaging is lovely and the products not only look and smell wonderful but they are not overpriced. Delivery is quick and you quite often get sent delicious trial sized products with your order. A great site for gifts, travel size products and that extra body lotion and bath gel you simply won't be able to resist.

Site Usability:	★★★★★	Based:	UK
Product Range:	★★★★★	Express Delivery Option?	(UK) No
Price Range:	Luxury/<u>Medium</u>/Very Good Value	Gift Wrapping Option?	Yes
Delivery Area:	Worldwide	Returns Procedure:	Down to you

www.ormondejayne.co.uk

Sometimes you feel that you'd really like to find a new range of fragrance and candles, one that most people haven't heard of but one that's still totally luxurious and beautifully presented. That's exactly what you'll find here, with a unique range of fragrances such as the citrussy Osmanthus and floral Champaca. There are bath and body products to complement the fragrances plus the most beautiful candles and everything is gorgeously packaged.

Site Usability:	★★★★	Based:	UK
Product Range:	★★★	Express Delivery Option?	(UK) No
Price Range:	<u>Luxury</u>/Medium/Very Good Value	Gift Wrapping Option?	Yes
Delivery Area:	Worldwide	Returns Procedure:	Down to you

www.penhaligons.co.uk

Penhaligons offers fragrance, candles and bath and body products for perfect and luxurious gifts for men and women. Choose from classics Lily of the Valley, Elizabethan Rose or Bluebell or the more modern and spicy Malabah, Artemesia or LP No 9. Each fragrance is matched up to its own shower gel, soap, body lotion and candle. Gift-wrapping is gorgeous, free and they deliver worldwide.

Site Usability:	★★★★★	Based:	UK
Product Range:	★★★★★	Express Delivery Option?	(UK) Yes
Price Range:	<u>Luxury</u>/Medium/Very Good Value	Gift Wrapping Option?	Automatic
Delivery Area:	Worldwide	Returns Procedure:	Down to you

www.pout.co.uk

Pout is the perfect place for beauty junkies who want to enjoy and have fun with cosmetics. The whole range is clever and lighthearted through tongue-in-cheek product names such as 'Bite my Cherry' and 'Saucy Sadie' and packaging inspired by the founders' favourite items of underwear, gaining Pout the reputation as 'the underwear of make-up'. If this sounds slightly silly, don't be fooled, it's a really gorgeous, cleverly packaged range of cosmetics, makeup bags, great gifts and excellent beauty accessories. Take a look round now.

Site Usability:	★★★★★	Based:	UK
Product Range:	★★★★★	Express Delivery Option?	(UK) Yes
Price Range:	Luxury/<u>Medium</u>/Very Good Value	Gift Wrapping Option?	Yes
Delivery Area:	Worldwide	Returns Procedure:	Down to you

www.powderpuff.net

Next time you go looking to buy one of your regular beauty essentials have a look at this website, offering free delivery in the UK and a huge selection of products. It's been called 'The Daddy of all Beauty Sites' and you'd find it hard to disagree. You'll find brand names such as Lancôme, Clarins, Clinique and YSL plus GHD, Kerastase and Fudge together with skincare, cosmetics and fragrance and mostly at very good prices. They'll also deliver worldwide.

Site Usability:	★★★★	Based:	UK
Product Range:	★★★★	Express Delivery Option?	(UK) Yes
Price Range:	Luxury/Medium/Very Good Value	Gift Wrapping Option?	Yes
Delivery Area:	Worldwide	Returns Procedure:	Down to you

www.thesanctuary.co.uk

Just looking at this spa website makes you feel more relaxed, with its shades of blue background and the attractive, simple packaging of pampering products such as Sanctuary Salt Soak, Body Polisher and Eastern Massage and Body Oil. You can buy the full range of Sanctuary products here plus Gift Vouchers and information on treatments at the Covent Garden spa. For International orders you need to give them a call.

Site Usability:	★★★★	Based:	UK
Product Range:	★★★★	Express Delivery Option?	(UK) Yes
Price Range:	Luxury/Medium/Very Good Value	Gift Wrapping Option?	Automatic
Delivery Area:	Worldwide	Returns Procedure:	Down to you

www.skye-soap.co.uk

This is a really beautifully designed website offering natural aromatherapy soaps produced on the Isle of Skye. There isn't a huge range of products but if you like lovely, natural soaps and oils you'll want to buy from here, not only for yourself but also for your friends, from their selection of attractively packaged gift boxes. You'll discover fragrances such as Lavender, Lemon and Lime, Geranium, Patchouli, Sandalwood, Tea Tree and Orange for the soaps and essential oils plus gifts of bath bombs and soaks.

Site Usability:	★★★★	Based:	UK
Product Range:	★★★	Express Delivery Option?	(UK) No
Price Range:	Luxury/Medium/Very Good Value	Gift Wrapping Option?	No
Delivery Area:	Worldwide	Returns Procedure:	Down to you

www.spacenk.co.uk

Nars, Stila, Darphin, Laura Mercier, Eve Lom, Diptyque, Frederic Fekkai and Dr Sebagh are just some of the 60 plus brands offered on the website of this retailer, famous for bringing unusual and hard to find products to the UK (so you don't have to go to New York any more to buy your Frederic Fekkai shampoo: Shame). They're also an excellent place for gifts as they offer a personalised message and gift wrapping service and next day delivery if you need it. It's a well designed and easy to get round website with very clear pictures.

Site Usability:	★★★★★	Based:	UK
Product Range:	★★★★★	Express Delivery Option?	(UK) Yes
Price Range:	Luxury/Medium/Very Good Value	Gift Wrapping Option?	Yes
Delivery Area:	Worldwide	Returns Procedure:	Down to you

www.strawberrynet.com

Check to see if your favourite product is available on this Hong Kong based website where shipping is free and most products are discounted. There's a really huge range of designers, so big it's not worth trying to list. To be clear, as this site is based overseas you may well get charged duty, however delivery to anywhere in the world is free of charge and the discounts can be very good.

Site Usability:	★★★	Based:	Hong Kong
Product Range:	★★★★★	Express Delivery Option?	(UK) No
Price Range:	Luxury/Medium/Very Good Value	Gift Wrapping Option?	Yes
Delivery Area:	Worldwide	Returns Procedure:	Down to you

www.woodruffs.co.uk

This fragrance and gift retailer offers an excellent range of bath, body and fragrance products by Roger et Gallet, Diptyque, Kenneth Turner, Crabtree & Evelyn, Floris, Cath Collins and Jane Packer, to name but a few. They'll deliver anywhere in the world, offer an express delivery service for the UK and are happy to gift wrap for you. They also have unusual accessory ideas as well.

Site Usability:	★★★★★	Based:	UK
Product Range:	★★★★	Express Delivery Option?	(UK) Yes
Price Range:	Luxury/Medium/Very Good Value	Gift Wrapping Option?	Yes
Delivery Area:	Worldwide	Returns Procedure:	Down to you

Chapter 25

Hair, Nails and Beauty Accessories

There are lots of websites springing up offering ranges of hair care products plus the very latest in brushes, straighteners, dryers and every other possible accessory you can think of.

They're very good if you have a particular range that you like and it's hard to get where you live and for learning about the latest equipment 'must haves'. Some of them can make a big difference, such as ceramic hair brushes and really powerful hair dryers and it's well worth comparing the prices. All those listed are excellent for service (believe me, they've been tried and tested).

I have to mention *hqhair.com* here. This is a truly wonderful website where the product list is growing every day and the service is tremendous. They offer such a wide range I think it's probably time they called themselves something else in case anyone thinks that all they offer is hair products. They don't and if you haven't visited them before go there now.

Regarding nail polishes and treatments the philosophy is much the same as hair products although there are far fewer ranges. It's best to know which colours you like in advance of buying online as the colour charts are not usually very accurate, but if you use Jessica, Opi, Essie or Darielle, which are quite hard to buy in the shops, you'll probably want to start ordering here. They can often be less expensive as well.

Beauty Accessories

More and more importance is being put on 'having the right make-up brushes' and other tools to assist with your perfect makeup. Sometimes there just isn't the time to do things as you would like (when you're just about to dash out of the door and you're late) and sometimes you have those extra few minutes when you'd like to experiment.

Check the major brands for their accessories and you can be horrified at what you can be expected to spend, however, there are some very good ranges online, from brushes to tweezers and powerful hair dryers and you'll find them all below.

Sites to Visit

www.beverlybeaute.com

Once you've taken a good look here you may well decide to order your nail products from this US based retailer. They stock the full range of Jessica, Opi, Essie, Seche and Creative plus less well known brands Star Nail, Qtica and Gena and everything at a very good discount. You can also order from the Thalgo range of Marine Algae and plant based products here. Delivery is fast and there's a standard charge of £3 but don't forget you may have to pay duty.

Site Usability:	★★★★★	Based:	US
Product Range:	★★★★★	Express Delivery Option?	(UK) No
Price Range:	Luxury/Medium/<u>Very Good Value</u>	Gift Wrapping Option?	No
Delivery Area:	Worldwide	Returns Procedure:	Down to you

www.ferobeauty.com

Buying high quality makeup brushes can be an expensive business. On this unsophisticated but not overpriced website there's a professional range of brushes, wallets and holders, manicure and pedicure tools, beauty kits, waxing systems and Mavala nail enamels. Be slightly careful what you buy here as some of the items are strictly for professionals. Delivery is to the UK only and free when you spend over £50.

Site Usability:	★★★	Based:	UK
Product Range:	★★★	Express Delivery Option?	(UK) No
Price Range:	Luxury/<u>Medium</u>/Very Good Value	Gift Wrapping Option?	No
Delivery Area:	UK	Returns Procedure:	Down to you

www.hqhair.com

If you haven't used it already you should really try this fun and incredibly useful website, where along with funky beauty products and jewellery (and absolutely everything you could need for your hair including Blax, Nexxus and Paul Mitchell products), you'll also discover Anya Hindmarch, Kate Spade and Lulu Guinness exquisite cosmetic bags, (perfect for presents and also for treats) also lots of beauty accessories including high quality makeup and hair brushes.

Site Usability:	★★★★★	Based:	UK
Product Range:	★★★★★	Express Delivery Option?	(UK) No
Price Range:	Luxury/Medium/Very Good Value	Gift Wrapping Option?	No
Delivery Area:	Worldwide	Returns Procedure:	Down to you

www.jasonshankey.co.uk

If you're a fan of GHD, Fudge or Tigi hair products this is the place for you. There's also a phenomenal range of excellent products on this site from hair care and hair appliances to nail care, slimming products, men's grooming and hangover cures. They're also excellent for appliances – they claim to sell the most powerful hair dryer on the market although it's not always in stock, as well as a very good choice of men's hair products.

Site Usability:	★★★★	Based:	UK
Product Range:	★★★★	Express Delivery Option?	(UK) Yes
Price Range:	Luxury/Medium/Very Good Value	Gift Wrapping Option?	Yes
Delivery Area:	Worldwide	Returns Procedure:	Down to you

www.kaven.co.uk

This site offers skincare from Guerlain, Decleor, and Guinot plus St Tropez self-tanning products and the full range of Jessica nail care although the colours are hard to see if you're not sure exactly which one you want. This is a quick and easy site to order from with detail and pictures of each and every item. Guerlain makeup is also available. If you have any queries you can call them and they're always delighted to help.

Site Usability:	★★★★	Based:	UK
Product Range:	★★★★	Express Delivery Option?	(UK) No
Price Range:	Luxury/Medium/Very Good Value	Gift Wrapping Option?	No
Delivery Area:	Worldwide	Returns Procedure:	Down to you

www.lookfantastic.com

Here's a marvellous selection of hair care products from well-known brands such as Kerastase, Paul Mitchell, Tigi and Redken, plus nailcare by Essie, Opi, Jessica and Nailtiques. In the Beauty Accessories section they offer straighteners, dryers, brushes and clippers by GHD, Babyliss, T3 and Icon and if you haven't discovered ghd ceramic brushes yet you can order them here. Try them, they're excellent. Provided you join their club you can take advantage of the very good discounts on offer.

Site Usability:	★★★★	Based:	UK
Product Range:	★★★★★	Express Delivery Option?	(UK) Yes
Price Range:	Luxury/Medium/Very Good Value	Gift Wrapping Option?	No
Delivery Area:	Worldwide	Returns Procedure:	Down to you

www.nailsbymail.co.uk

Calling themselves 'The UK's leading nail boutique' (and why not?) with products by Essie and Seche (and if you haven't yet tried the truly marvellous Seche Vite quick dry yet you should) together with colours, treatments, files and buffers this is an excellent well priced site for all the elements necessary for keeping your nails in top shape. If you need any advice you can give them a call and their Nail Technicians will be happy to help.

Site Usability:	★★★★	Based:	UK
Product Range:	★★★★★	Express Delivery Option?	(UK) No
Price Range:	Luxury/<u>Medium</u>/Very Good Value	Gift Wrapping Option?	No
Delivery Area:	UK	Returns Procedure:	Down to you

www.nailsinc.com

If you've visited the US you'll know that there are several nail bars in each and every shopping mall no matter how big or small and much of the time you don't even have to book, you can just walk in on a whim. The UK has taken a long time to catch up but now with Nails Inc you can visit one of their 35 locations in the UK for an excellent, speedy manicure and you can also buy their products online, from high quality treatments and gift sets to their outlet store offering goodies for less.

Site Usability:	★★★	Based:	UK
Product Range:	★★★	Express Delivery Option?	(UK) No
Price Range:	Luxury/<u>Medium</u>/Very Good Value	Gift Wrapping Option?	No
Delivery Area:	UK	Returns Procedure:	Down to you

www.saloneasy.com

This is the place to find your professional standard hairdryer by Parlux (they're really excellent and not overpriced), hair straighteners and stylers and a wide range of hair brushes. This site is aimed at the professional so there are a wide range of salon products that you almost certainly won't be interested in but the prices for the dryers and brushes are some of the best you'll find and the service is speedy.

Site Usability:	★★★	Based:	UK
Product Range:	★★★★	Express Delivery Option?	(UK) No
Price Range:	Luxury/<u>Medium</u>/Very Good Value	Gift Wrapping Option?	No
Delivery Area:	UK	Returns Procedure:	Down to you

www.salonlines.co.uk

Here's another hair product website offering a very good range of Schwarzcopf hair care products plus Tigi and Joico, GHD straighteners and ceramic brushes, and loads of other beauty products including specialist hair treatments and some grooming products. You can go to their advice section and find out about how to deal with specific problems or you can email their expert and ask for help. They're happy to ship all over the world, offer an express delivery option and bulk shipping discount.

Site Usability:	★★★★	Based:	UK
Product Range:	★★★★	Express Delivery Option?	(UK) Yes
Price Range:	Luxury/<u>Medium</u>/Very Good Value	Gift Wrapping Option?	No
Delivery Area:	Worldwide	Returns Procedure:	Down to you

www.screenface.com

The next time you want to buy a new set of makeup brushes have a good look here before you rush off and spend hundreds of pounds on some of the major brands. The selection is huge and very well priced and you can also buy makeup bags and cases, professional makeup and tweezerman products. Some of the pictures are not very clear (if they're there at all) but you can send off for their catalogue.

Site Usability:	★★★	Based:	UK
Product Range:	★★★★	Express Delivery Option?	(UK) No
Price Range:	Luxury/Medium/<u>Very Good Value</u>	Gift Wrapping Option?	No
Delivery Area:	UK	Returns Procedure:	Down to you

Chapter 26

Healthcare and Contact Lenses

What are you looking for? Do you just want to stock up with your basic healthcare products such as antihistamines and aspirin? Or do you want the latest in vitamins and sports supplements to keep your energy levels high enough so that you can go shopping? You'll find everything online, all the above plus prescription medicines as well, frequently at lower prices than at your local pharmacy.

Contact Lenses are a growing area of online retailing and the competition to get you away from your local supplier is huge. You will find really good savings here for most lenses, up to a third off what you're paying outside, so really consider ordering your replacement lenses online provided they're a standard prescription.

If (or when) you start ordering your lenses online you will probably be asked to pay a fee for a sight check and new prescription from the Opthalmologist who was charging you the original inflated prices. Provided your prescriptions are lasting a while and your eyes aren't changing too much it's very much worth your while to go down this route.

Prescriptions are another area you can consider getting filled online, particularly for drugs such as the malaria drug Malarone, where you cannot get them on the NHS (unless in an exceptional case). Here again you can make huge savings against what you'd pay in your local chemist. Do a test and see. Get an online price for whatever you're needing from one of the sites recommended below and then phone up your local chemist. You'll be surprised.

Your chemist will almost certainly tell you that there are lots of non bona fide online pharmacies who are not offering you the real thing and yes, there are. If in doubt call the online pharmacy and ask to check that they're members of the Royal Pharmaceutical Society of Great Britain. Check their membership if you want to. Then order from them.

Sites to Visit

www.auravita.com

Claiming to stock over 20,000 products (phew) you'll find everything here from Nurofen to eyelash curlers, homeopathy remedies, health foods and drinks and sport supplements and vitamins. There's also a wide choice of cosmetics including Elizabeth Arden, Kanebo, Clarins, Lancôme, Christian Dior lipstick and nail polish and Max Factor. It's a confusing website to go round, so make use of the Brand search and Store Guide facilities near the top of the Home Page.

Site Usability:	★★★	Based:	UK
Product Range:	★★★★★	Express Delivery Option?	(UK) No
Price Range:	Luxury/Medium/Very Good Value	Gift Wrapping Option?	No
Delivery Area:	Worldwide	Returns Procedure:	Down to you

www.bs4health.com

The B & S House of Health takes itself extremely seriously, with a mission statement that sets out exactly what it is trying to do – offer you very high quality vitamins and supplements from sources that it has found to be totally reliable. Click on each area and you get a full list of subsections describing exactly what you'll find and what the products are for, which then links through to each individual product and the buying facility. This is an excellent, clear and informative website.

Site Usability:	★★★★	Based:	UK
Product Range:	★★★★	Express Delivery Option?	(UK) No
Price Range:	Luxury/Medium/Very Good Value	Gift Wrapping Option?	No
Delivery Area:	Worldwide	Returns Procedure:	Down to you

www.chemistdirect.co.uk

Chemist Direct operates out of London and is a member of the National Pharmaceutical Association. There's a wide range of products here from vitamins and health supplements, baby products, toiletries, holiday and sun care. They're also happy to fulfil your prescriptions for you, either private or NHS and their prices are excellent (always check against an offline chemist if you're not sure about the price). You send payment to them online and your prescription by post after which they'll immediately despatch your order to you.

Site Usability:	★★★★	Based:	UK	
Product Range:	★★★★	Express Delivery Option?	(UK) Yes	
Price Range:	Luxury/Medium/Very Good Value	Gift Wrapping Option?	No	
Delivery Area:	UK	Returns Procedure:	Down to you	

www.contactsdirect.co.uk

Here's another contact lens retailer trying to get your business away from your local supplier and they should certainly be considered. Remember that when you do order your contacts online and you need a check-up or a new prescription you'll probably have to pay a fee. Even so you'll save lots of money by buying online (and having done this already, I know). The prices are keen here and you can expect a speedy service.

Site Usability:	★★★★★	Based:	UK	
Product Range:	★★★★	Express Delivery Option?	(UK) No	
Price Range:	Luxury/Medium/Very Good Value	Gift Wrapping Option?	No	
Delivery Area:	UK	Returns Procedure:	Free	

www.goldshield.co.uk

As well as all the vitamins and supplements you would expect from a health food store, here you can also buy food and snacks, such as assortments of fruit and nuts, crystalised ginger, dried fruit, pistachios and pumpkin seeds and everything for making your own yoghurt, plus not quite so 'healthy' (but very tempting) snacks including chocolate coated ginger and brazils. There's lots of information on all the different sections here plus health books.

Site Usability:	★★★★	Based:	UK	
Product Range:	★★★★	Express Delivery Option?	(UK) No	
Price Range:	Luxury/Medium/Very Good Value	Gift Wrapping Option?	No	
Delivery Area:	Worldwide	Returns Procedure:	Free	

www.goodnessdirect.co.uk

There's really a vast range here with 3000+ health foods, vitamins and items selected for those with special dietary needs. You can search for foods that are dairy free, gluten free, wheat free, yeast free and low fat plus organic fruit, vegetables (in a selection of boxed choices), fish and meat. You'll also find frozen and chilled foods, so you can do your complete shopping here. Don't be worried by the amount of choice, the website is very easy to get round and order from.

Site Usability:	★★★★	Based:	UK	
Product Range:	★★★★★	Express Delivery Option?	(UK) No	
Price Range:	Luxury/Medium/Very Good Value	Gift Wrapping Option?	No	
Delivery Area:	UK	Returns Procedure:	Down to you	

www.hollandandbarrett.com

This famous name health supplement and information retailer has a simple and easy to use website, offering products within sections such as Sports Nutrition, Digestive Aids, Weight Management and Women's Products. You do really need to know what you're looking for, as you'll only find out the details on each individual product when you click on it, however, the order system is very simple so if you want something specific then have a look here.

Site Usability:	★★★		Based:	UK
Product Range:	★★★★		Express Delivery Option?	(UK) No
Price Range:	Luxury/<u>Medium</u>/Very Good Value		Gift Wrapping Option?	No
Delivery Area:	Worldwide		Returns Procedure:	Down to you

www.lensway.co.uk

If you're still buying your contact lenses from a standard retailer you really need to consider changing to buying online, as the competition for your business is extremely fierce and you can usually save at least a third of the normal price (if not more). At Lensway you can buy your contact lenses online for standard prescription lenses at very good prices, from daily to monthly lenses by Johnson & Johnson, Acuvue, Bausch and Lomb and others.

Site Usability:	★★★★		Based:	Holland
Product Range:	★★★★★		Express Delivery Option?	(UK) No but fast delivery is automatic
Price Range:	Luxury/<u>Medium</u>/Very Good Value		Gift Wrapping Option?	No
Delivery Area:	Worldwide		Returns Procedure:	Down to you

www.marnys.com

On this website you can find organic products such as Muesli, toasted sesame seeds, brown lentils, texturised soya, flax seeds, pumpkin and sunflower seeds as well as salt crystal lamps. There's also a wide range of supplements, vitamins and minerals divided into sections such as Royal Jelly, Korean Ginseng and Bee Pollen, as specific products and Weight Control, Cardiovascular System and Hormonal System as areas.

Site Usability:	★★★★		Based:	Spain
Product Range:	★★★★★		Express Delivery Option?	(UK) No but fast delivery is automatic
Price Range:	Luxury/<u>Medium</u>/Very Good Value		Gift Wrapping Option?	No
Delivery Area:	Worldwide		Returns Procedure:	Down to you

www.pharmacy2u.co.uk

All your regular medicines and healthcare essentials are available on this site plus plenty of advice and suggestions. If you can't be bothered or don't have the time to go out to the chemist then this is definitely the site for you. It's very clear and well laid out and I doubt if there would be anything you couldn't find. You can also arrange for your prescriptions to be filled. They are members of the Royal Pharmaceutical Society of Great Britain and the National Pharmaceutical Association.

Site Usability:	★★★★★	Based:	UK
Product Range:	★★★★★	Express Delivery Option?	(UK) No
Price Range:	Luxury/Medium/Very Good Value	Gift Wrapping Option?	No
Delivery Area:	Worldwide for most products	Returns Procedure:	Down to you

www.thefitmap.com

Do you really want to know how fit you are (and do something about it)? *Thefitmap.com* gives you loads of information on where to find a personal trainer, diet and fitness news and health club reviews, and if you really want to get going click to subscribe on the Fitness Training Planner and get your own schedule against which you can then plot your success (or ????). This is maybe not quite the same as having your personal trainer banging on the door to take you through your paces but certainly an incentive worth trying out.

Site Usability:	★★★★★	Based:	UK
Product Range:	N/A	Express Delivery Option?	(UK) N/A
Price Range:	N/A	Gift Wrapping Option?	N/A
Delivery Area:	N/A	Returns Procedure:	N/A

www.travelpharm.com

TravelPharm is an independent private pharmacy and a member of the National Pharmaceutical Association. You can buy first aid and medical kits, total sun block, travel sickness tablets, water purification tablets and flight socks on this well designed website. As a registered pharmacy they can also provide you with pharmacy-only medication such as malaria tablets and they offer up-to-the-minute details of vaccinations and anti-malarial requirements for your destination as a free of charge service.

Site Usability:	★★★★★	Based:	UK
Product Range:	★★★★★	Express Delivery Option?	(UK) No
Price Range:	Luxury/Medium/Very Good Value	Gift Wrapping Option?	No
Delivery Area:	UK	Returns Procedure:	Down to you

You'll also find healthcare products at the following websites

Website Address	You'll find them in
www.boots.com	Skincare and Cosmetics
www.garden.co.uk	Skincare and Cosmetics

Chapter 27

Natural Beauty

I have to confess that I'm a brand name fragrance and skincare person and not a natural product one although I'm sure that many of you are. When I was researching for this chapter I was amazed at the really beautifully presented websites I found (not always of course, but you only get to see the ones I approved of) and the enormity of the range of products available.

Some of these have been sourced from around the world and I definitely hadn't heard of them before and you may well not have either. However, the love and care that has been put into bringing them before you and the amount of information that you'll be given on each and every one makes this a paradise for anyone who likes natural beauty products. I'm sure you'll find something here.

An area where I'm definitely tempted is aromatherapy, because some of the products, the fruit scented essences, naturally fragranced soaps (and fizzing soap bombs) and candles sound like perfect antidotes to the stresses of our everyday lives (children, husbands, dogs, work, mess, clutter – you know what I'm talking about) and browsing round the specialist websites was full of far too many opportunities to buy (no I'm not going to tell you if I did or not).

One thing I'm certain of. If you spend very long here, you'll be tempted too.

Sites to Visit

www.airandwater.co.uk

Here you can discover the properties of essential oils with their natural soaps, beauty products, aromatherapy boxes, carrier and massage oils, enhance your home with oil burners, incense, resins, candles and vaporisers and find Bach flower remedies and the Rescue Remedy range of herbal supplements. Their suppliers include Edom Health and Beauty products, Meadows Aromatherapy and Arran Aromatics.

Site Usability:	★★★★	Based:	UK
Product Range:	★★★★	Express Delivery Option?	(UK) Yes
Price Range:	Luxury/Medium/Very Good Value	Gift Wrapping Option?	No
Delivery Area:	EU	Returns Procedure:	Down to you

www.baldwins.co.uk

G. Baldwin & Co is London's oldest and most established Herbalist and if you pay a visit to their shop you'll find that it still has a nostalgic atmosphere of stepping back in time, with wooden floors, high old fashioned counters and shelves stacked with herbs, oils and ointments. You can shop online from the complete ranges of both Bach Flower Remedies and the Australian Bush Flower Essences, their own brand aromatherapy oils, natural soaps, creams and bath accessories and herbs, seeds, roots and dried flowers.

Site Usability:	★★★★	Based:	UK
Product Range:	★★★★	Express Delivery Option?	(UK) Yes
Price Range:	Luxury/Medium/Very Good Value	Gift Wrapping Option?	No
Delivery Area:	Worldwide	Returns Procedure:	Down to you

www.beauty-republic.com

Beauty Republic sources natural beauty secrets from all over the World and they offer a range of specialised products such as Black Palm Natural Soap, Hi Shine hair products, Lullaby Lavender, Kosmea natural skin care and Rainforest Remedies. For each and every product they tell you what it does, what's in it and how to use it, so if you've never come across it before you may well be tempted to give it a try.

Site Usability:	★★★★★	Based:	UK
Product Range:	★★★★	Express Delivery Option?	(UK) Yes
Price Range:	Luxury/Medium/Very Good Value	Gift Wrapping Option?	Yes
Delivery Area:	Worldwide	Returns Procedure:	Down to you

www.freshsoapdeli.com

The handmade soap deli is a speciality soap, bath and body company producing a therapeutic range of products using high quality essential oils, tailor-made fragrances and herbal extracts to create a range which includes 'freshly cut off the block' soaps, wonderful Lemon Sherbert, Cherry and Lavender bath bombes, Mango Body Butter, Strawberry Body Polish and gifts such as the Tutti Frutti Soap Kebab. You'll definitely have fun choosing here.

Site Usability:	★★★★		Based:	UK
Product Range:	★★★		Express Delivery Option?	(UK) No
Price Range:	Luxury/Medium/Very Good Value		Gift Wrapping Option?	No
Delivery Area:	EU		Returns Procedure:	Down to you

www.highlandsoaps.com

On this really attractive website you'll find a wide range of handmade soaps from the Highlands of Scotland, beautifully packaged and with names like May Chang and Lime, and Rosehip and Patchouli. Alternatively there's Mango Butter, Wild Nettle and Heather and exfoliating soaps with natural loofah (I'll definitely be trying one of those!). They offer bath bombes, body crème and luxurious hand wash plus gift boxes and bath accessories and their services include overseas shipping and gift wrapping.

Site Usability:	★★★★★		Based:	UK
Product Range:	★★★		Express Delivery Option?	(UK) No
Price Range:	Luxury/Medium/Very Good Value		Gift Wrapping Option?	Yes
Delivery Area:	Worldwide		Returns Procedure:	Down to you

www.loccitane.com

L'Occitane is another brand you're sure to have heard of, offering products ranging from personal care to home fragrance and all manufactured in traditional ways using natural ingredients, primarily from Provence. The range includes fragrance, body and hand care, bath and shower products, skin care, hair care and home fragrance with Verbena Harvest, Eau d'Ambre, Lavender, Oranger and Green Tea forming the bases for Eau de Toilette, soaps, hand creams, shower gels and shampoos.

Site Usability:	★★★★★		Based:	UK
Product Range:	★★★★★		Express Delivery Option?	(UK) No
Price Range:	Luxury/Medium/Very Good Value		Gift Wrapping Option?	Yes
Delivery Area:	Worldwide		Returns Procedure:	Down to you

www.naturalcollection.com

All the products on this website are seriously natural, from fair trade laundry baskets to organic cotton bed linen. They also have a Personal Care selection which includes brands such as Organic Options (natural soaps), Faith in Nature (aromatherapy body care), Barefoot Botanicals (skin and body care) and lots of natural pampering products and gift ideas. In their Wellbeing section you can order Sage Organics vitamins and minerals and Bath Indulgence Spa sets.

Site Usability:	★★★★★	Based:	UK
Product Range:	★★★★★	Express Delivery Option?	(UK) Yes
Price Range:	Luxury/Medium/Very Good Value	Gift Wrapping Option?	No
Delivery Area:	Worldwide	Returns Procedure:	Down to you

www.nealsyardremedies.com

This is probably one aromatherapy and herbal remedy retailer you have heard of. From the first shop located in Neal's Yard in the heart of London's Covent Garden, Neal's Yard Remedies has grown into one of the country's leading natural health retailers and on their attractive website you can buy a wide range of their products, from aromatherapy, body care, luxurious bath products and homeopathic remedies plus attractively packaged gift sets.

Site Usability:	★★★★★	Based:	UK
Product Range:	★★★★	Express Delivery Option?	(UK) Yes
Price Range:	Luxury/Medium/Very Good Value	Gift Wrapping Option?	No
Delivery Area:	Worldwide	Returns Procedure:	Down to you

www.pendle-aromatics.co.uk

All the aromatherapy products here are made by hand by a qualified aromatherapist and contain only high quality, therapeutic grade essential oils and gentle ingredients. They offer gorgeous bath treats, massage oils and skincare including moisturisers, cleansers and toners as well as everything you need (and lots of information) to make your own aromatherapy products from carrier oils to blending bottles.

Site Usability:	★★★	Based:	UK
Product Range:	★★★★	Express Delivery Option?	(UK) No
Price Range:	Luxury/Medium/Very Good Value	Gift Wrapping Option?	No
Delivery Area:	UK	Returns Procedure:	Down to you

www.potions.org.uk

Potions & Possibilities produce natural toiletries and aromatherapy products, ranging from soaps and bath oils to restorative balms and creams. Everything is blended and created using the highest quality essential oils, and you can find their award winning products in Bloomingdales (in the US) and Fenwicks in the UK among other stores and of course online. Resist if you can or choose from bath sizzlers, bath and shower gels, shampoos, fragrance and gift collections.

Site Usability:	★★★★	Based:	UK
Product Range:	★★★	Express Delivery Option?	(UK) Yes
Price Range:	Luxury/Medium/Very Good Value	Gift Wrapping Option?	No
Delivery Area:	Worldwide	Returns Procedure:	Down to you

www.primrose-aromatherapy.co.uk

This attractively laid out website is just about aromatherapy (rather than offering you lots of other products as well) and the selection of Essential Oils is huge, with pictures of the fruits, flowers and herbs themselves rather than dinky little bottles. For each product there's a great deal of information, on the properties and how to use them. They will ship all over the world and you need to contact them if you want courier delivery.

Site Usability:	★★★★	Based:	UK
Product Range:	★★★	Express Delivery Option?	(UK) Yes
Price Range:	Luxury/Medium/Very Good Value	Gift Wrapping Option?	No
Delivery Area:	Worldwide	Returns Procedure:	Down to you

www.rose-apothecary.co.uk

Here's a natural beauty website with a difference, as it offers lots of their own, different, really prettily packaged products such as Rose Petal Bath and Shower Creme, Lavender Shampoo and luxurious gift boxes plus J & E Atkinson fragrances, I Coloniali, Rice and Segreti Mediterranei, Yardley English Lavender, 4711 Cologne and Soir de Paris. Their Aromatherapy products, remedy oils and creams and massage oils are all blended in house.

Site Usability:	★★★★	Based:	UK
Product Range:	★★★★	Express Delivery Option?	(UK) No
Price Range:	Luxury/Medium/Very Good Value	Gift Wrapping Option?	No
Delivery Area:	Worldwide	Returns Procedure:	Down to you

www.youraromatherapy.co.uk

This is a really clear and modern aromatherapy website, where you can immediately see all the products on offer, including essential and massage oils, aromatherapy kits, candles and accessories, vaporisers and ionisers and body care for all the family. They have a very good gift section and an attractive selection of candles.

Site Usability:	★★★★★	Based:	UK
Product Range:	★★★★	Express Delivery Option?	(UK) No
Price Range:	Luxury/Medium/Very Good Value	Gift Wrapping Option?	No
Delivery Area:	Worldwide	Returns Procedure:	Down to you

Chapter 28

The Beauty Specialists

I f you're not into the 'superbrand' beauty products but prefer something a bit out of the ordinary, or there's a special product or brand that you've been using for some time that's hard to find on the high street, then you should take a look here, where you'll find brands such as Dermalogica, Eve Lom, Decleor, Dermablend, Liz Earle and Dr Sebagh.

At the end of the day it's what works for you and your skin. Most of these brands are those that you will have come across in beauty salons both here and overseas and of course that's what's so great about the internet, you can now find them without any trouble. But: And there is a 'but' here. Most of these products are also quite expensive. Some are very expensive. Before you invest heavily ask for a sample, or buy the smallest size pot, just to make sure that you like the results.

No doubt you've guessed that I'm speaking from experience here and in the past I've bought into a new product range (partially because I like the sound of it and partially because I like the packaging), and then really not used it properly and even (horrors) ended up throwing it away. You definitely don't want to go there.

Even so there is a really marvellous choice here and you can find almost every product you've ever heard of. It's just another trial of temptation. Sorry.

Your siteguide.com password is SG001. Please use this as the media code when subscribing for your free year's login.

Sites to Visit

www.beautyexpert.co.uk

Here you'll find beauty products by Caudalie, Aromatherapy Associates, Fudge, L'Occitane, NV Perricone, Phytomer and Ren, plus lots more. Most of these are not ranges that you'll find in the shops, but specialist products from salons and spas. There's lots of specialist advice on the Advice Line run by beauty therapists if you should have a query, and an excellent selection of starter kits if you want to try a new product.

Site Usability:	★★★★	Based:	UK
Product Range:	★★★	Express Delivery Option?	(UK) Yes
Price Range:	Luxury/Medium/Very Good Value	Gift Wrapping Option?	Yes
Delivery Area:	Worldwide	Returns Procedure:	Down to you

www.beautyflash.co.uk

Beauty Flash offer the full range from Dermalogica, including masques and moisturisers, specialist treatments and treatment foundations (although you really need to know your colour before you buy these), spa body products and sun care. They have the Skin Doctors range of professional strength skincare (with lots of information and advice), Fake Bake and St Tropez tanning products, Air Stockings and Dermablend Cover Creme.

Site Usability:	★★★★	Based:	UK
Product Range:	★★★★	Express Delivery Option?	(UK) No
Price Range:	Luxury/Medium/Very Good Value	Gift Wrapping Option?	No
Delivery Area:	UK	Returns Procedure:	Down to you

www.beautyxposure.com

Beauty Xposure is a Dermalogica skin care salon based in Hertfordshire, and on their clear and cleanly designed website they offer three ranges for you to buy online: Dermalogica skin care system, Fake Bake (a really great fake tan that will last up to a week and was recently voted best self tanner in the New York Times) and the Nailtiques nail care system. If you're not sure which Dermalogica products you should order just fill in their questionnaire and they'll give you lots of advice.

Site Usability:	★★★★	Based:	UK
Product Range:	★★★	Express Delivery Option?	(UK) No
Price Range:	Luxury/Medium/Very Good Value	Gift Wrapping Option?	Yes
Delivery Area:	UK	Returns Procedure:	Down to you

www.espaonline.com

ESPA was created to bring together the best of ancient and modern therapies with the finest quality ingredients and skin care advances. This is a lovely light and modern website offering their famous range of aromatherapy products from specific beauty treatments to bath and body products and luxury gifts, with everything formulated from the highest quality organically grown plants. So if you're feeling stressed, this would definitely be a good place to start.

Site Usability:	★★★★★	Based:	UK
Product Range:	★★★★	Express Delivery Option?	(UK) No
Price Range:	Luxury/<u>Medium</u>/Very Good Value	Gift Wrapping Option?	No
Delivery Area:	Worldwide	Returns Procedure:	Down to you

www.evelom.co.uk

This is surely one of the most famous names in modern skincare, based on Eve Lom's belief that the best skincare is quite simply total cleansing using natural products and her famous polishing cloth. You may not be able to get to her for a personal facial but at least now you can find her products to buy online. The range is small and definitely not cheap but you'll know that you're buying the very best and you can order from anywhere in the World.

Site Usability:	★★★★	Based:	UK
Product Range:	★★★	Express Delivery Option?	(UK) No
Price Range:	<u>Luxury</u>/Medium/Very Good Value	Gift Wrapping Option?	No
Delivery Area:	Worldwide	Returns Procedure:	Down to you

www.lizearle.com

Liz Earle has a beautiful website offering her 'Naturally Active Skincare' – a pampering range of skin, body and sun care products. She's particularly well known for her cleanse and polish hot cloth cleanser and well priced but excellent special treatments and moisturisers. Shimmer products for body and lips, Vital Aromatherapy Oils and travel mini-kits from the wide range are just some of the temptations on offer and the lovely packaging is an extra bonus.

Site Usability:	★★★★	Based:	UK
Product Range:	★★★★	Express Delivery Option?	(UK) Yes
Price Range:	Luxury/Medium/<u>Very Good Value</u>	Gift Wrapping Option?	Yes, everything is beautifully packaged
Delivery Area:	Worldwide	Returns Procedure:	Down to you

www.philosophy.com

You can find a very good selection of these products at *www.hqhair.com* but if you want to choose from the complete Philosophy range then you need to visit their US based website and order from them. Although the range appears whimsical, with its childish pictures and lighthearted wording, there are groundbreaking cleansers and peels here and really excellent moisturisers and anti-ageing treatments. Also bath and body essentials, fab cosmetics and very good beauty accessories.

Site Usability:	★★★★★		Based:	US
Product Range:	★★★★★		Express Delivery Option?	(UK) No
Price Range:	Luxury/Medium/Very Good Value		Gift Wrapping Option?	Yes
Delivery Area:	Worldwide		Returns Procedure:	Down to you

www.salonskincare.com

Some of the brands you'll find here such as Elemis, Decleor, Gatineau and Phytomer are not hard to find on the web and others, such as luxury skincare brand Carita, Baxter of California, Max Benjamin (candles) and MD Formulations are not readily available. Couple this with the extremely well thought out design of this website and this becomes an essential beauty destination if you like salon brand products. You can also buy Dermalogica, Fake Bake, Molton Brown and Nailtiques here plus Klein-Becker Strivectin SD, the stretch mark turned anti-wrinkle wonder cream.

Site Usability:	★★★★★		Based:	UK
Product Range:	★★★★★		Express Delivery Option?	(UK) Yes
Price Range:	Luxury/Medium/Very Good Value		Gift Wrapping Option?	No
Delivery Area:	Worldwide		Returns Procedure:	Down to you

www.thebeautyroom.com

You may well have come across the French salon brands Gatineau, Phytomer and Mary Cohr (or perhaps you haven't), but on this website you can order from the full ranges of skincare including anti-ageing creams, cleansers, toners, moisturisers and exfoliators plus the Mary Cohr/Masters Colours extensive range of cosmetics. These are expensive products and this website will work best for those who have already tried them, although there's lots of information and advice if you want to invest in a new range.

Site Usability:	★★★★		Based:	UK
Product Range:	★★★		Express Delivery Option?	(UK) Yes
Price Range:	Luxury/Medium/Very Good Value		Gift Wrapping Option?	No
Delivery Area:	No		Returns Procedure:	Down to you

www.thisworks.com

Here you'll find soothing, natural and gently scented products for bath and body with unusual names such as Energy Bank or Deep Calm Bath and Shower Oil, Muscle Therapy and Enjoy Really Rich Lotion or Hot Stone Essences, and all have been created by Vogue beauty expert Kathy Phillips. The collection also includes bath and shower gels, moisturisers, lovely gift ideas and an irresistible travel pouch designed by Orla Kiely containing eight miniature This Works products.

Site Usability:	★★★★	Based:	UK
Product Range:	★★★	Express Delivery Option?	(UK) No
Price Range:	Luxury/<u>Medium</u>/Very Good Value	Gift Wrapping Option?	Yes
Delivery Area:	Worldwide	Returns Procedure:	Down to you

www.timetospa.com

Time to Spa offers Elemis face and body products, La Therapie solutions for acne, scarring and hyper-pigmentation and Steiner Haircare. This is not a retailer so much as a beauty salon, where you can register with them for an online consultation by one of their team of therapists on your beauty regimen, find out about food and fitness for health and have your beauty questions answered. If you purchase from their online shop you'll find lots of gift ideas, excellent Elemis travel collections and gift wrapping.

Site Usability:	★★★★	Based:	UK
Product Range:	★★★	Express Delivery Option?	(UK) Yes
Price Range:	Luxury/Medium/Very Good Value	Gift Wrapping Option?	Yes
Delivery Area:	Worldwide	Returns Procedure:	Down to you

Also check out these websites for specialist beauty products

Website Address	You'll find it in
www.spacenk.co.uk	Skincare and Cosmetics, Fragrance etc
www.jomalone.co.uk	Skincare and Cosmetics, Fragrance etc

Chapter 29

Travel Products

I'm one of those people who likes to keep a well organised bag packed and ready for the moment someone comes along who wants to whisk me off to the Bahamas (is anyone listening out there)?

I'm also one of those people who wants to travel light and always fails miserably, taking far too many clothes that I don't wear ('in case' clothes, you know the sort) but I am really, really good in the travel skincare, cosmetics and spa products department.

Firstly, of course, you need a really good travel wash bag with compartments that you can hang up so whether you're staying just for one night or for a fortnight you have everything at the ready. Take a look at *www.hqhair.com* and *www.zpm.com* where you'll find a good selection. Then I want to be able to take either miniatures of my favourite products or something different and special that's available in small sizes (and needless to say I frequently take both).

There's a very good selection of retailers here who offer travel sized selections of everything from skincare to bath and body products. Get your bag packed now.

Sites to Visit

www.arranaromatics.com

Click on the 'Travel Size' button on the menu here and you'll immediately be taken to a range of their best selling products, packaged up into essential 50ml travel sizes. The prices here are extremely reasonable so you can order your favourites and experiment with a few new products as well. You'll also find travel sets and gift boxes within the different ranges.

Site Usability:	★★★★★	Based:	UK
Product Range:	★★★★	Express Delivery Option?	(UK) Yes
Price Range:	Luxury/Medium/Very Good Value	Gift Wrapping Option?	No
Delivery Area:	Worldwide	Returns Procedure:	Down to you

www.crabtree-evelyn.co.uk

Well known and sold throughout the World, Crabtree & Evelyn offer a wide range of bath, body and spa products from classic fragrances such as Lily of the Valley to the ultra modern La Source. As well as the large size versions you'll also find travel sized sets of all the major fragrances, perfect for your next trip away and also very good as small gifts.

Site Usability:	★★★★★	Based:	UK
Product Range:	★★★★★	Express Delivery Option?	(UK) No
Price Range:	Luxury/Medium/Very Good Value	Gift Wrapping Option?	No
Delivery Area:	Worldwide	Returns Procedure:	Down to you

www.lizearle.com

Liz Earle has cleverly packaged her skincare products into kits perfect for travelling, with names such as The Holiday Beauty Essentials Kit and Mini Bodycare Kit, so not only can you try out her products if you haven't used them before, but you can also pack them up easily and take them away with you.

Site Usability:	★★★★	Based:	UK
Product Range:	★★★★	Express Delivery Option?	(UK) Yes
Price Range:	Luxury/Medium/Very Good Value	Gift Wrapping Option?	Yes, everything is beautifully packaged
Delivery Area:	Worldwide	Returns Procedure:	Down to you

www.jomalone.co.uk

As well as the irresistible products you'll find on her website you can also buy her indispensable travel sets, exquisitely packaged in cream or black. They're available in several different sizes, from the perfect In Flight Travel Bag, which contains everything you could need on board, to the Ultimate Travel Bag, which you customise with your essential products.

Site Usability:	★★★★★	Based:	UK
Product Range:	★★★★★	Express Delivery Option?	(UK) Yes
Price Range:	Luxury/Medium/Very Good Value	Gift Wrapping Option?	Yes
Delivery Area:	Worldwide	Returns Procedure:	Down to you

www.loccitane.com

Here's another collection of fragrance, bath and body products where there's a really comprehensive range of travel sized products, from their mini pure Shea Butter to their Orange Leaves Eau de Cologne. Often they have offers where if you buy several products you can choose an extra one for free. Their gorgeous soaps come in mini versions too which are perfect for travel or for guests.

Site Usability:	★★★★★	Based:	UK
Product Range:	★★★★★	Express Delivery Option?	(UK) No
Price Range:	Luxury/Medium/Very Good Value	Gift Wrapping Option?	Yes
Delivery Area:	Worldwide	Returns Procedure:	Down to you

www.moltonbrown.co.uk

Molton Brown's travel sets vary from the Extravagant set which contains full sized bottles in an elegant zip bag, to the New Age Traveller, a luxurious take-anywhere leather bag containing ten scaled down products for skin, body and hair and which is far more suited to trips away, in my mind. The trouble is that I'd want to take several of their shower gels as well. More packing problems.

Site Usability:	★★★★★	Based:	UK
Product Range:	★★★★★	Express Delivery Option?	(UK) No
Price Range:	Luxury/Medium/Very Good Value	Gift Wrapping Option?	Yes
Delivery Area:	Worldwide	Returns Procedure:	Down to you

www.mujionline.co.uk

You must have heard of Muji, the Japanese based company offering functional and marvellous value products for the home and office including stationery, storage solutions, cookware, bags, luggage and accessories. Did you also know that you can, on their online store, also order from their excellent range of tiny spray, flip top and screw top bottles waiting to be filled with your favourite products? Nylon vanity cases and their own hair and body care ranges are available as well.

Site Usability:	★★★★★	Based:	UK
Product Range:	★★★★★	Express Delivery Option?	(UK) No
Price Range:	Luxury/Medium/Very Good Value	Gift Wrapping Option?	No
Delivery Area:	Worldwide	Returns Procedure:	Down to you

www.penhaligons.co.uk

You need to pick the fragrance of your choice and click through to see if they do a travel version. Kits included are for Bluebell, Lily of the Valley and Quercus for her and Blenheim Bouquet for him, and they all contain Eau de Toilette, soap, shower gel and shampoo with really beautiful packaging, so they'd be great for gifts as well.

Site Usability:	★★★★★	Based:	
Product Range:	★★★★★	Express Delivery Option?	(UK) Yes
Price Range:	Luxury/Medium/Very Good Value	Gift Wrapping Option?	Automatic
Delivery Area:	Worldwide	Returns Procedure:	Down to you

Section 5

At
Home

Here you'll find lots of ideas for your home, from gorgeous home accessories – pillows and throws, lamps and mirrors, to pretty bed linen for grownups and children, bathrobes and towels, unusual tableware and loads of gift possibilities on just about every website. Whereas five years ago you would only find a very small selection of home products available on the internet, now there's almost too much choice. The best websites are beautifully photographed and even offer you roomsets from which to pick your accessories.

If you think of the time it would take you to see as much as you can see in an hour online you'll probably faint with horror. You'd have to spend hours and hours, looking at a blinding array of things, most of which you probably wouldn't like, rather than being able to click onto the next product, or the next website, in a matter of seconds.

However, I've already said that there are far too many websites. There are loads and loads offering you cheap deals. Really cheap deals for really cheap products, which you may well not be happy with. But if what you really want is not to have to wade through the cheap deal websites and be taken straight to the best, the chic and the stylish, modern or traditional, where you will find value for money but also real quality from retailers who know what they're doing, then you've come to the right place.

A great deal of time has been spent on your behalf checking out the 'At Home' websites and editing out those which don't fit the shopaholic's criterion of beautiful, 'must have them now' products at lots of different price levels but always with the emphasis on quality.

When you see something you like don't hesitate to call the retailer and ask for more details, after all, you may not have heard of his company before, or may not know the products too well. A good retailer, on or offline, is waiting to help you, to give you advice and help you make the right decisions. If they can't be bothered then definitely don't buy from them.

I just need to mention *www.johnlewis.com* here. They offer just about everything for the home and their website is stylish and easy to use (but only delivers to the UK at present). I've resisted including them in every section here but don't forget to check them out as well when you're buying for the home (or gifts, or flowers). I've used their website many a time and always received exactly the product I wanted, exactly when I expected to, and you can't possibly ask for more than that (and no, they're not paying me to say that, I just thought they deserved a special mention).

Chapter 30

In the Bedroom

odern or old fashioned, minimalist or full of your favourite pictures and bits and pieces, colourful, all in white or in modern neutral tones, which do you prefer? Probably you're already established with your interior design and just want to add a few things. A new bedspread perhaps or mirror, or do you want a complete change from your flowery bed linen? As well as accessories many of these websites offer small pieces of furniture, such as bedside and coffee tables, all in their own particular style.

There are places here where you can spend what amounts to a small fortune on your new bedlinen, and others offering very high quality at reasonable prices so you can choose what you want to do. There are also some fabulous designs to choose from, such as Paisley and Toile de Jouey and the simplest and most stylish of elegant neutrals.

Then there are the throws and bedspreads in everything from snugly fleece to supersoft (and super priced) cashmere, plus lots of other accessories to tune into whichever look you've decided to go for. As colours in particular have improved to such an extent online over the past couple of years, you can, when looking at a website such as *www.designersguild.co.uk*, get a real feel for what you'll be ordering and what it will look like which of course makes choosing so much easier.

You'll definitely enjoy going through the websites below, some are particularly beautifully designed and just make you want to buy straight away, such as *thewhitecompany.co.uk*. I always have a problem when I'm checking that one out. I find everything completely irresistible.

Bedlinen and Accessories

Sites to Visit

www.baer-ingram.com

Baer and Ingram design and print their own exclusive fabrics which you can order online. The collection includes florals, Toile de Jouey, patchwork, polka dots and stripes in a choice of colourways. You'll also find some lovely gifts and home accessories such as lighting, painted furniture, tablelinen and gifts for tinies. You can order most of their products online but if you want something made to order, such as blinds, headboards, curtains or cushions you need to give them a call.

Site Usability:	★★★★	Based:	UK
Product Range:	★★★★	Express Delivery Option?	(UK) No
Price Range:	Luxury/Medium/Very Good Value	Gift Wrapping Option?	No
Delivery Area:	Worldwide	Returns Procedure:	Down to you

www.biju.co.uk

Luxurious bathrobes and towels, cashmere blankets (at a faint inducing price) and throws and a wonderful collection of table linen, Missoni tableware, mats and trays, are just some of the items you can choose from on this treasure trove of a website, where they also offer enchanting children's bedding and bedroom accessories. There's so much here you need to have time for a good browse. They also offer a personalisation embroidery service on their bathrobes and towels to help you create totally individual gifts.

Site Usability:	★★★★	Based:	UK
Product Range:	★★★★	Express Delivery Option?	(UK) No
Price Range:	Luxury/Medium/Very Good Value	Gift Wrapping Option?	No
Delivery Area:	Worldwide	Returns Procedure:	Down to you

www.cathkidston.co.uk

Cath Kidston started her company over ten years ago in a small shop in Notting Hill, selling second-hand furniture and vintage fabrics. She soon began to design her own fabric and wallpaper, creating signature floral prints which have come to stand for her unique look. On her colourful website you'll see some really pretty and different bedlinen and bedspreads with pattern names such as 'New Bubbles' and 'Vintage Posy' plus crochet blankets and even sleeping bags.

Site Usability:	★★★★	Based:	UK
Product Range:	★★★★	Express Delivery Option?	(UK) Yes
Price Range:	Luxury/Medium/Very Good Value	Gift Wrapping Option?	Yes
Delivery Area:	Worldwide	Returns Procedure:	Down to you

www.designersguild.com

You'll find Tricia Guild's gorgeously coloured bedlinen here both for grown ups and children, plus very different towels, bedspreads and throws, small leather goods and Fragrant Home from Designers Guild – a beautiful collection of home fragrance and luxury body products. If you haven't come across Designers Guild until now but you like pretty, colourful designs then take a look here.

Site Usability:	★★★★★	Based:	UK
Product Range:	★★★★	Express Delivery Option?	(UK) Yes
Price Range:	Luxury/Medium/Very Good Value	Gift Wrapping Option?	Yes
Delivery Area:	UK	Returns Procedure:	Down to you

www.dibor.co.uk

Dibor is an independent UK based company offering continental style furniture, accessories and gifts. For your bedroom they have a selection of delightful French-inspired hand painted furniture and accessories including cupboards, chests of drawers and pretty bedside tables. There's also a selection of bedlinen in pure linen and linen and cotton although they don't offer this all year round.

Site Usability:	★★★	Based:	UK
Product Range:	★★★	Express Delivery Option?	(UK) Yes
Price Range:	Luxury/<u>Medium</u>/Very Good Value	Gift Wrapping Option?	No
Delivery Area:	Worldwide	Returns Procedure:	Down to you

www.maisoncollection.com

Maison offer a really pretty collection of plain and patterned high quality and traditionally styled bedlinen and bedspreads with detailing such as embroidery, hemstitching and lace edging. For some of the designs you'll find accessories such as lavender bags, tissue box holders and laundry bags. There's also a very feminine choice of gifts such as lace covered clothes hangers and fine linen guest towels plus lovely children's bedlinen.

Site Usability:	★★★★	Based:	UK
Product Range:	★★★★	Express Delivery Option?	(UK) Yes
Price Range:	Luxury/<u>Medium</u>/Very Good Value	Gift Wrapping Option?	No
Delivery Area:	Worldwide	Returns Procedure:	Down to you

www.monogrammedlinenshop.co.uk

For the past 25 years The Monogrammed Linen Shop has provided classical and contemporary household linens to customers from all over the world. They only use the most beautiful laces and embroideries together with the finest cottons, linens, and silks to produce luxurious bedlinen, table linen and nightwear. They also offer perfect ideas for gifts for all occasions and offer an exquisite babywear collection going up to age 4. Their monogramming service rarely takes more than ten working days.

Site Usability:	★★★★	Based:	UK
Product Range:	★★★★	Express Delivery Option?	(UK) No
Price Range:	Luxury/Medium/Very Good Value	Gift Wrapping Option?	No
Delivery Area:	Worldwide	Returns Procedure:	Down to you

www.peacockblue.co.uk

Choose from simple stylish floral jacquard in pale blue or pink, classic gingham or woven check in a wide range of colours or their enchanting children's range, everything here is beautifully photographed and if you're looking for some new ideas this would be a great place to have a look round. Discover too their unusual quilts, blankets, bedspreads and throws, fluffy towels and wide range of contemporary bathroom accessories.

Site Usability:	★★★★	Based:	UK
Product Range:	★★★	Express Delivery Option?	(UK) Yes
Price Range:	Luxury/Medium/Very Good Value	Gift Wrapping Option?	No
Delivery Area:	Worldwide	Returns Procedure:	Down to you

www.reallylindabarker.co.uk

Click on 'Sleeping' on this busy website and you'll find a small but prettily edited range of bedlinen and bedspreads, throws, cushions, lamps and porcelain and attractive bedroom furniture. Everything is designed to work together in a very attractive, light and modern style which is 'reallylindabarker' and all in her modern, natural style. In the 'Living' section there are lamps, mirrors, cushions, clocks and storage ideas for the rest of your home.

Site Usability:	★★★★★	Based:	UK
Product Range:	★★★	Express Delivery Option?	(UK) Yes
Price Range:	Luxury/Medium/Very Good Value	Gift Wrapping Option?	No
Delivery Area:	Worldwide but phone if delivery is for overseas	Returns Procedure:	Down to you

www.thelaundry.co.uk

The Laundry's exclusive collection covers everything from bedwear to bedlinen, linen cupboard accessories to laundry room essentials and everything in between. Their philosophy is to blend contemporary with vintage to create a highly individual look. This is not a large range but something quite unusual, take their pretty zinnia print and mix it with their spot printed pure cotton and you'll get the idea.

Site Usability:	★★★★	Based:	UK
Product Range:	★★★	Express Delivery Option?	(UK) No
Price Range:	Luxury/Medium/Very Good Value	Gift Wrapping Option?	No
Delivery Area:	Worldwide but phone if delivery is for overseas	Returns Procedure:	Down to you

www.thewhitecompany.com

Here's absolutely everything you need for stylish bedrooms, with a collection of beautifully made contemporary bed linen (think white, cream, natural and pale blue) and luxurious throws and blankets from cashmere to quilted velvet in colours such as pebble, willow, chocolate and taupe. They also offer luxury duvets and pillows and bedroom accessories such as rugs, mirrors and toiletries. There are lots of ideas for the rest of your home as well, plus lounge wear, gorgeous toiletries and candles and other gifts.

Site Usability:	★★★★★	Based:	UK
Product Range:	★★★★★	Express Delivery Option?	(UK) Yes
Price Range:	Luxury/Medium/Very Good Value	Gift Wrapping Option?	Yes
Delivery Area:	Worldwide	Returns Procedure:	Down to you

www.volgalinen.co.uk

The Volga Linen Company is a family run, British company that sells an exquisite collection of pure linen from Russia. The collection consists of table linen, bedlinen, ready to hang curtains and a children's range and accessories. They produce plain weaves, fabric with drawn thread work embroidery, damasks, and richly coloured Paisleys. Also take a look at their new clothing range online.

Site Usability:	★★★★	Based:	UK
Product Range:	★★★	Express Delivery Option?	(UK) No
Price Range:	Luxury/Medium/Very Good Value	Gift Wrapping Option?	No
Delivery Area:	Worldwide	Returns Procedure:	Down to you

Chapter 31

Bath Time

I f bathroom accessories seem an odd thing for the shopaholic to be considering then think again. You can go and order lots of gorgeous spa products to create your oasis of calm. You can buy the most luxurious towels you can find in your perfect colours. But if your bathroom doesn't really reflect your taste and style you won't enjoy them as much as you should.

I'm not saying you should rush out and buy a new bath. But you can easily create a new atmosphere with just a few accessories, get rid of your china loo roll holder and soap dish and replace with modern tinted glass and steel (if that's your taste) and add a few matching shelves to show off your shower gels and potions rather than stuffing them into a cupboard or round the edge of the bath.

Or go for a Hamptons effect with white painted cabinets and blue and white towels. You'll be surprised at how much change in atmosphere you can effect with just a few new ideas.

These websites are full of ideas for your bathroom. When you find a look you like take a look at your own bathroom and see if you can't make it just a little more your perfect haven. Then when you've done that you can go to *www.jomalone.co.uk*, *www.kennethturner.co.uk* or *www.moltonbrown.com* and go for broke.

Sites to Visit

www.christy-towels.com

The Christy at home website is really beautifully designed, clean, clear and modern and definitely makes you want to buy. Don't think of Christy just for towels, although there's a wide colour range to choose from, but look also at their high quality bedlinen in mostly neutral shades and cotton blends and extras including robes, cushions, throws and contemporary bathroom accessories.

Site Usability:	★★★★	Express Delivery Option?	(UK) No
Product Range:	★★★	Gift Wrapping Option?	No
Price Range:	Luxury/Medium/Very Good Value	Based:	UK
Delivery Area:	UK	Returns Procedure:	Down to you

www.heals.co.uk

I'm sure you'll have heard of this famous store on Tottenham Court Road in London, famous for their contemporary styling for furniture and accessories throughout the home, most of which are exclusive to Heals. Shelves, cup holders, shower curtains, towel rails and medicine cabinets are just some of the items you can buy here alongside bathroom storage, toiletries, towels and robes.

Site Usability:	★★★★★	Based:	UK
Product Range:	★★★★★	Express Delivery Option?	(UK) No
Price Range:	Luxury/Medium/Very Good Value	Gift Wrapping Option?	No
Delivery Area:	UK	Returns Procedure:	Down to you

www.thecotswoldco.com

If your idea of the perfect country bathroom is the one with the old fashioned bath and the white painted traditionally styled cupboards and shelves (with deep blue and white towels), then this is the place to go. In the bathroom department on this extremely quick and well laid out website there are rattan storage chests and laundry baskets and a full range of small accessories.

Site Usability:	★★★★★	Based:	UK
Product Range:	★★★★	Express Delivery Option?	(UK) No
Price Range:	Luxury/Medium/Very Good Value	Gift Wrapping Option?	No
Delivery Area:	UK	Returns Procedure:	Free furniture collection service

www.theholdingcompany.co.uk

If you've suddenly decided that it's time you went for the tidy, well organised look you'll definitely need this website, where you'll find every type of storage for the home, including for the bathroom, laundry baskets, hooks (yes they're actually for hanging your robe on rather than dumping it on the floor), trolleys, corner shelves and shaving mirrors (not storage but hey). Chic and clever storage for everywhere you can think of, in fact. The only problem is you'll have to get everyone else to use it as well.

Site Usability:	★★★★	Based:	UK
Product Range:	★★★★★	Express Delivery Option?	(UK) No
Price Range:	Luxury/Medium/Very Good Value	Gift Wrapping Option?	No
Delivery Area:	UK	Returns Procedure:	Down to you

www.towels.co.uk

This is an offshoot of excellent home accessories website *Biju.co.uk*, where you can find a really attractively photographed range of bathrobes, from the expensive hand made English variety to simple well priced waffle robes (and children's bathrobes), towels in a wide selection of colours and textures and other tempting bathroom treats. It's a very well laid out website with easy access to all the information you could need.

Site Usability:	★★★★	Based:	UK
Product Range:	★★★★	Express Delivery Option?	(UK) No
Price Range:	Luxury/Medium/Very Good Value	Gift Wrapping Option?	No
Delivery Area:	Worldwide	Returns Procedure:	Down to you

Also visit these websites for bathroom accessories

Website Address	You'll find it in
www.thewhitecompany.co.uk	In the Bedroom
www.johnlewis.com	Kitchen and Dining

Chapter 32

Living Space

Whether you call it the living room, sitting room, drawing room (old fashioned, I know), barn (as in our case), or kids tv room (every house should have one) you'll know what I mean. This is the room some people manage to keep looking beautifully uncluttered, just waiting for someone to drop in for coffee and a chat, or, as is usually the case in my house, totally cluttered with newspapers, books, dogs and children but comfortable enough to make you want to curl up on a sofa with a book.

You may like a contemporary, neutral style with shades of brown, natural and cream (that's me, but two dogs and three kids have put paid to any of those kinds of ideas) or a rich, deep coloured country look, but whatever your preferences you can find not just sofas to sink into, faux fur throws to cuddle up in and cushions to set the scene, but every kind of accessory you can think of and most of them of an extremely high quality.

You can check out the room sets at various websites such as *okadirect.co.uk* and buy just about everything you see (and some of it is really lovely) or just add a new lamp to your room to cast some new atmosphere.

This is another area that is excellent for gifts although you'll find also the specific home accessories gifts in the Gift section of this book. There were, quite frankly, too many websites to list there so have a look here as well for some alternative ideas.

Home Accessories

Sites to visit

www.atelierbypost.com

You do need to call them to order but the homewares on this website, designed by Abigail Ahern, are so different and attractive that if you like something it would be worth the effort. This is a small, very contemporary (and expensive) collection including smoky glass vases, soft pure merino throws, unusual candles, cushions, placemats and hand thrown Italian tableware. You won't find this collection anywhere else so if you're looking for something unique you may find it here.

Site Usability:	★★★★		Based:	UK
Product Range:	★★★		Express Delivery Option?	(UK) No
Price Range:	Luxury/Medium/Very Good Value		Gift Wrapping Option?	No
Delivery Area:	UK		Returns Procedure:	Down to you

www.carolinehesse.co.uk

Caroline Hesse furniture and interiors design and import specialist bespoke hardwood, Mahogany, Elm and reclaimed timber furniture. They also offer lovely and different home accessories. The furniture is all hand made by craftsmen in their workshops in South Africa, Peru, Colombia and China and the range is based on an 'East meets West' theme with classic European, Oriental and Colonial designs. They're happy to ship Worldwide and if you want an express service you need to call them.

Site Usability:	★★★★		Based:	UK
Product Range:	★★★★		Express Delivery Option?	(UK) Yes
Price Range:	Luxury/Medium/Very Good Value		Gift Wrapping Option?	No
Delivery Area:	Worldwide		Returns Procedure:	Down to you

www.casacopenhagen.com

Danish designer Theresa Bastrup Hasman has brought together a beautiful collection of cushions and soft furnishings grouped into categories with names such as Moroccan Nights, Indian Fairy Tales and Paisley Flowers. There's also a small section for children and they offer a bespoke service as well. Everything is made especially for you so you need to allow four weeks for delivery.

Site Usability:	★★★★		Based:	UK
Product Range:	★★★		Express Delivery Option?	(UK) No
Price Range:	Luxury/Medium/Very Good Value		Gift Wrapping Option?	No
Delivery Area:	Worldwide		Returns Procedure:	Down to you

www.chelseatextiles.com

Chelsea Textiles re-creates antique fabrics, cushion designs and furnishing accessories with patterns such as embroidered vines, Indo China, and Heather Voile for the fabrics, and animals (mainly dogs and cats) and insects (butterflies, dragonflies and bees) for the embroidered cushions and bags alongside gorgeous roses, florals and vines. You do have to call them or e-mail to order at present but if you're looking for a special fabric or gift you could well find it here.

Site Usability:	★★★	Based:	UK
Product Range:	★★★	Express Delivery Option?	(UK) No
Price Range:	Luxury/Medium/Very Good Value	Gift Wrapping Option?	No
Delivery Area:	Worldwide	Returns Procedure:	Down to you

www.clarissahulse.com

Ferns, pampas grass and acacia, Narnia and Magic Roundabout are just some of the designs Clarissa Hulse has created to use on cushions and wallpaper in her online store. Her colours are modern and range from neutrals, brown stone and cream to hazy purple and dark red. It's a small and very different collection but extremely attractive. Check out also the stationery collection, featuring Clarissa's designs on beautiful silk covered notebooks and photo albums and perfect for presents.

Site Usability:	★★★	Based:	UK
Product Range:	★★★	Express Delivery Option?	(UK) No
Price Range:	Luxury/Medium/Very Good Value	Gift Wrapping Option?	No
Delivery Area:	Worldwide	Returns Procedure:	Down to you

www.davidlinley.com

As you would expect, this is a really beautiful website offering you the opportunity to buy David Linley designed accessories online including frames, vases, lamps, candlesticks, home fragrance, jewellery boxes and cushions. Everything is beautifully photographed and expensive as you would expect but if you're looking for a very special gift, you might well find it here. Prices start at about £55 for his keyrings and head off upwards steeply. The packaging is gorgeous as well.

Site Usability:	★★★★★	Based:	UK
Product Range:	★★★★	Express Delivery Option?	(UK) Yes
Price Range:	Luxury/Medium/Very Good Value	Gift Wrapping Option?	No but packaging is lovely
Delivery Area:	Worldwide	Returns Procedure:	Down to you

www.elanbach.com

This is a lovely website run by a family business offering very attractive traditional Welsh fabric designs. You can buy the fabrics themselves, or made up into home accessories such as cushions, covered boxfiles and albums. Your order can take up to ten days to arrive and they're happy to ship to you anywhere in the World. Take a look at their hotel website and you'll see how the fabrics look in place.

Site Usability:	★★★★★	Based:	UK
Product Range:	★★★	Express Delivery Option?	(UK) No
Price Range:	Luxury/<u>Medium</u>/Very Good Value	Gift Wrapping Option?	No
Delivery Area:	Worldwide	Returns Procedure:	Down to you

www.grahamandgreen.co.uk

Graham & Green is a long established retailer of home and lifestyle products including candles, tableware, silk cushions, pretty etched glasses and duvet covers and quilts. They're quite hard to really categorise as the products are so widespread but if I tell you that some of their bestsellers are bevelled mirrors, Chinese lanterns, lavender scented bags and Penguin (as in the book) mugs you'll probably get the idea.

Site Usability:	★★★★	Based:	UK
Product Range:	★★★	Express Delivery Option?	(UK) Yes
Price Range:	Luxury/<u>Medium</u>/Very Good Value	Gift Wrapping Option?	No
Delivery Area:	UK	Returns Procedure:	Down to you

www.horn-trading.co.uk

Ok, so now for something totally different. Here's a Western style collection of furniture, including a cowhide and steer horn chair and cowhide shelf, soft furnishings, (yes you guessed it, cowhide covered cushions and rugs) and accessories and gifts such as bronco or cactus decorated china, western style cushions, hides, mats and cowhide bags and purses. The company is based in Battle, Sussex, but everything is sourced in the US.

Site Usability:	★★★★	Based:	UK
Product Range:	★★★	Express Delivery Option?	(UK) No
Price Range:	Luxury/<u>Medium</u>/Very Good Value	Gift Wrapping Option?	Yes
Delivery Area:	UK	Returns Procedure:	Down to you

www.in2decor.com

In2decor is a very easy to get round home accessory and gifts website where you can choose from one of the prettiest selections of traditional style cushions, Venetian glass mirrors, unusual vases and candle holders (such as the monkey nuts candle holder I'm after) and Chinese influenced porcelain. This is mainly a place to find gifts, the choice isn't enormous but what is there is very different and attractive.

Site Usability:	★★★★★	Based:	UK
Product Range:	★★★★	Express Delivery Option?	(UK) No
Price Range:	Luxury/<u>Medium</u>/Very Good Value	Gift Wrapping Option?	No
Delivery Area:	UK	Returns Procedure:	Down to you

www.interiorsathome.co.uk

This is a fabrics and interiors accessory website offering blinds, ready made curtains and tie backs plus an unexpectedly wide range of high quality fabrics, linings and trimmings. They also offer home accessories such as bedspreads, duvet covers and throws, cushions and cushion pads (for those places where they only sell you the covers) and an exceptional range of wall hangings. They offer a personal service (by email) if you want some help with your decor and they'll also try and source fabrics for you that are not included on their site.

Site Usability:	★★★★	Based:	UK
Product Range:	★★★★	Express Delivery Option?	(UK) No
Price Range:	Luxury/Medium/Very Good Value	Gift Wrapping Option?	No
Delivery Area:	UK	Returns Procedure:	Down to you

www.interiors-tides.co.uk

Driftwood pebbles, shell tie-backs and pot pourri are just a few of the delightful accessories and gifts available here, plus pretty beach-house style furniture, bathroom accessories including sponge bags, candles and soaps, kitchen and garden accessories from galvanised watering cans to ceramic measuring cups. They aim to ship everything to you within seven days and ship to the UK only.

Site Usability:	★★★★	Based:	UK
Product Range:	★★★★	Express Delivery Option?	(UK) No
Price Range:	Luxury/Medium/Very Good Value	Gift Wrapping Option?	No
Delivery Area:	UK	Returns Procedure:	Down to you

www.johnlewis.com

Needless to say you'll find all the essentials here for your kitchen and for everywhere else in your house – all the tableware and equipment you could need, fluffy towels in a huge range of colours, simple and stylish bathroom storage, modern furniture, beds and bedding and on through to mirrors and lighting, garden furniture and even flowers. This is definitely one of the best sites on the web, offering a service to match.

Site Usability:	★★★★★	Based:	UK
Product Range:	★★★★★	Express Delivery Option?	(UK) Yes
Price Range:	Luxury/Medium/Very Good Value	Gift Wrapping Option?	No
Delivery Area:	UK	Returns Procedure:	Call them to collect or return goods to store

www.lambandshirley.com

Here's simple, timeless, shaker style furniture for all the rooms in your home plus beautifully made swallowtail boxes for jewellery, sewing essentials and other storage, folk art including cards, books and 'name trains' and some unusual gift ideas. If you want overseas delivery you need to call them, they offer an express service for items in stock and aim to deliver to you within 15 days although as all the items are handmade some items may take longer to arrive.

Site Usability:	★★★★	Based:	UK
Product Range:	★★★	Express Delivery Option?	(UK) Yes
Price Range:	Luxury/<u>Medium</u>/Very Good Value	Gift Wrapping Option?	No
Delivery Area:	Worldwide but call them for overseas deliveries	Returns Procedure:	Down to you

www.lauraashley.com

If you're like me, and have always thought of Laura Ashley as a bit too flowery, then now would be a good time to take a look at their website. Alongside the clothing line, which is really quite a small collection, there is some very attractive furniture and lots of home accessory ideas, all of which you can order online. Prices go from the extremely reasonable to hand crafted cabinets at several thousand pounds. There are various roomsets to look at to gain ideas and their Design Advice service as well.

Site Usability:	★★★★	Based:	UK
Product Range:	★★★★	Express Delivery Option?	(UK) No
Price Range:	Luxury/<u>Medium</u>/Very Good Value	Gift Wrapping Option?	No
Delivery Area:	Worldwide	Returns Procedure:	Down to you in agreement with them

www.lombok.co.uk

Lombok offers high quality, stylish furniture and home accessories made from either recycled or 100% natural materials, many of which are exclusively designed and manufactured for them, so the next time you're looking for a special gift or accessory for your home, have a browse. There's a unique selection of candles and lighting, storage options, tableware, frames, cushions and vases and quilts.

Site Usability:	★★★★	Based:	UK
Product Range:	★★★★	Express Delivery Option?	(UK) No
Price Range:	Luxury/<u>Medium</u>/Very Good Value	Gift Wrapping Option?	No
Delivery Area:	Worldwide	Returns Procedure:	Down to you

www.okadirect.com

Oka has a really beautifully designed and photographed website where you'll find some inspirational ideas for your home and lovely gifts. Browse through their roomsets and pick out the individual items that would enhance your existing decor, or go for broke and buy them all. From throws, cushions, quilts and rugs to porcelain vases and elegant furniture there's a wealth of items to choose from.

Site Usability:	★★★★★	Based:	UK
Product Range:	★★★★★	Express Delivery Option?	(UK) Yes for Central London only
Price Range:	Luxury/<u>Medium</u>/Very Good Value	Gift Wrapping Option?	No
Delivery Area:	Worldwide	Returns Procedure:	Down to you

www.pier.co.uk

Based on the famous US furniture and accessories retailer Pier One Imports, everything here is attractive and well priced and you'll discover lovely gifts and accessories from all over the World. The range is very extensive; you could furnish an entire room in your house with their stylish, modern and traditional furniture or just choose from their wide selection of textiles, glassware and lighting. They're excellent for presents and bring out a special catalogue each Christmas to complement the website.

Site Usability:	★★★★★	Based:	UK
Product Range:	★★★★★	Express Delivery Option?	(UK) No
Price Range:	Luxury/Medium/Very Good Value	Gift Wrapping Option?	No
Delivery Area:	Worldwide	Returns Procedure:	Call to arrange collection or return small goods by post

www.queenshill.com

This is a family run business offering a lovely selection of fabrics, wallpapers, gifts and home accessories from brands such as Mulberry, GP and J Baker, Harlequin and Fired Earth. The selection of mouthwatering gift ideas includes Mulberry candles, pot pourri, cushions and throws and James Brindley's range of faux fur (think leopard, llama, bear and cheetah) throws, cushions and hot water bottle covers. Resist if you can. You can request free samples of fabrics to help you finalise your choice.

Site Usability:	★★★★★	Based:	
Product Range:	★★★★★	Express Delivery Option?	(UK) No
Price Range:	Luxury/Medium/Very Good Value	Gift Wrapping Option?	No
Delivery Area:	Worldwide	Returns Procedure:	Down to you

www.somersetlevels.co.uk

Somersetlevels.co.uk are a small company specialising in high quality basketware, so if you're looking for a new linen or log basket (or a dog basket for yours to chew his or her way through, and there are loads), this would be a very good place to start. As well as willow baskets made in their own workshop, they also offer an extensive range of basketware handmade by craftspeople from all across the globe, weaving materials such as rush, seagrass and cane.

Site Usability:	★★★	Based:	UK
Product Range:	★★★★	Express Delivery Option?	(UK) No
Price Range:	Luxury/Medium/Very Good Value	Gift Wrapping Option?	No
Delivery Area:	Worldwide	Returns Procedure:	Down to you

www.welch.co.uk

Robert Welch trained as a Silversmith at Birmingham College of Art. He then moved to the Royal College of Art in 1952, where he specialised exclusively in stainless steel production design. In 1965 he was awarded Royal Designer for Industry. Together with his son, William, he has designed some unusual home accessories which you can buy from their website, including candlesticks, bathroom accessories, flatware and pewter. Don't miss his hourglass salt and pepper holders.

Site Usability:	★★★★★	Express Delivery Option?	(UK) No
Product Range:	★★★	Gift Wrapping Option?	No
Price Range:	Luxury/Medium/Very Good Value	Based:	UK
Delivery Area:	Worldwide	Returns Procedure:	Down to you

Chapter 33

Kitchen and Dining

Compared to a few years ago it seems that most of us have become much less formal in the way that we entertain. Gone is the formal meal in the dining room (well it certainly has in my house, other than high days and holidays) to be replaced by something more light-hearted and relaxed. That doesn't mean it can't be pretty, elegant and/or chic, with a lot of thought put into it. It's just a different way of doing things.

The joy of this is that you can view all the different products online, whether you want to go for gleaming white or Provencal coloured table linens, modern or traditional steel or silver cutlery, chic white or patterned tableware. You don't have to spend ages walking round a large shop (or several shops) trying to choose your new china – it's easy to choose the style online and then select the pieces you want.

Where kitchen equipment and utensils are concerned the sky really is the limit. These are well thought out and incredibly well stocked websites offering everything you could possibly want for your kitchen and lots of things you wouldn't normally think of.

This is another excellent area for gifts, and particularly wedding gifts. Some of the websites offer you the opportunity of viewing the list of your friends about to get married and choosing items from it. On the other hand you may prefer to pick out something special yourself and you'll certainly find it here.

At Christmas several of the websites below will offer you special services such as gift wrapping and hopefully all of them will tell you clearly when the last day is that you can order, although my advice is to order well in advance. The best intentions of any online retailer can be totally fouled up if the courier company lets them down so please don't wait until the last minute.

Tableware and Kitchen Equipment

Sites to Visit

www.emmabridgewater.co.uk

Emma Bridgewater is well known for her high quality pottery and clever and attractive designs such as Polka Dots, Hugs and Kisses and Hearts as well as her mug collections which include dogs, cats, birds and flowers. Every season she's bringing out new products, such as cutlery, glass, preserves and teas, all with her signature script. Almost every kitchen has one or two pieces of her pottery, the only question is, can you resist the urge to collect?

Site Usability:	★★★★★	Based:	UK
Product Range:	★★★★	Express Delivery Option?	(UK) Yes
Price Range:	Luxury/Medium/Very Good Value	Gift Wrapping Option?	Yes
Delivery Area:	Worldwide	Returns Procedure:	Down to you

www.conran.com

Conran are famous for their modern, colourful and well priced furniture and accessories which you can now buy online through their website. Discover their modern take on everything from kitchen accessories, candles and soft furnishings, lighting, clocks and gifts. Oh yes, and you can book your next Conran restaurant meal here as well.

Site Usability:	★★★★★	Based:	UK
Product Range:	★★★★	Express Delivery Option?	(UK) No
Price Range:	Luxury/Medium/Very Good Value	Gift Wrapping Option?	Yes
Delivery Area:	Worldwide	Returns Procedure:	Down to you

www.cookware.co.uk

A same day despatch online cook shop offering a wide range of high quality items, including chopping boards, every kitchen utensil you can think of, pan racks and trolleys and clever storage solutions, plus bar accessories and everything for baking. There's also electrical equipment by Dualit, KitchenAid, Magimix and Krups. A great deal of care has gone into this website with lots of information and clear pictures. Well worth a browse.

Site Usability:	★★★★★	Based:	UK
Product Range:	★★★★★	Express Delivery Option?	(UK) Yes
Price Range:	Luxury/Medium/Very Good Value	Gift Wrapping Option?	No
Delivery Area:	UK	Returns Procedure:	Down to you

www.cucinadirect.co.uk

Here's another excellent retailer offering everything for the kitchen beautifully displayed, including knives, pots and pans, bar tools, glasses and serving dishes, picnic equipment, housekeeping items and a gift selection. You'll also find a small but very high quality range of electrical appliances, with Dualit toasters and kettles and KitchenAid mixers just a couple of the items you can order to be shipped to anywhere in the world.

Site Usability:	★★★★★	Based:	UK
Product Range:	★★★★	Express Delivery Option?	(UK) Yes
Price Range:	Luxury/<u>Medium</u>/Very Good Value	Gift Wrapping Option?	Yes
Delivery Area:	Worldwide	Returns Procedure:	Down to you

www.davidmellordesign.com

David Mellor, Royal Designer for Industry, has an international reputation as designer, manufacturer and shopkeeper. Born in Sheffield, he has always specialised in metalwork and has often been described as 'the cutlery king'. On his website there's a selection of his modern stainless steel cutlery, plus contemporary high quality glass and tableware, kitchen tools and equipment.

Site Usability:	★★★★★	Based:	UK
Product Range:	★★★★	Express Delivery Option?	(UK) Yes
Price Range:	<u>Luxury/Medium</u>/Very Good Value	Gift Wrapping Option?	Yes
Delivery Area:	Worldwide	Returns Procedure:	Down to you

www.dartington.co.uk

From bowls and vases, to ice buckets, decanters, jugs and glassware Dartington have created the modern options to match contemporary design in your home or to make excellent gifts (particularly for wedding presents). The prices are reasonable and you can be certain that anything you order will be very well made. They'll deliver to you anywhere in the world (7–14 days for overseas) and faster within the UK.

Site Usability:	★★★★★	Based:	UK
Product Range:	★★★	Express Delivery Option?	(UK) No
Price Range:	Luxury/<u>Medium</u>/Very Good Value	Gift Wrapping Option?	No
Delivery Area:	Worldwide	Returns Procedure:	Down to you

www.diningstore.co.uk

You'll find some quite different products on this website, such as the ZapCap bottle opener, Escali Cibo nutritional scale and CaddyO bottle chiller alongside their designer kitchen and tableware with collections from Eva Solo, Cuisinox Elysee, Le Creuset, Mauviel, Couzon and Jura. This is not the normal kitchen and cookware selection so have a look round, you're certain to discover something very different as well as some great gifts for the enthusiastic cook.

Site Usability:	★★★★	Based:	UK
Product Range:	★★★	Express Delivery Option?	(UK) No
Price Range:	Luxury/Medium/Very Good Value	Gift Wrapping Option?	No
Delivery Area:	Europe	Returns Procedure:	Down to you

www.divertimenti.co.uk

This famous London based cookery equipment site offers over 5000 items, from hand painted tableware including decorated and coloured pottery from France, a really comprehensive range of kitchen essentials including knives, boards and bakeware, plus Italian products (parmesan graters and ravioli trays) copper bowls and pans, children's baking sets, wedding gift service, knife sharpening and copper retinning. This has always been and still remains one of the best kitchen and dining shops around.

Site Usability:	★★★★	Based:	UK
Product Range:	★★★★	Express Delivery Option?	(UK) No
Price Range:	Luxury/Medium/Very Good Value	Gift Wrapping Option?	No
Delivery Area:	Worldwide	Returns Procedure:	Down to you

www.dualit.com

If you know you like the brand, and you'd like to choose from the complete range (rather than the edited range you'll find on some other websites) then you should visit this site. Dualit are surely the best known manufacturers of high quality toasters, and they also sell kettles, hand mixers, coffee grinders and scales, all to the highest specifications. You can buy spare parts and accessories for all their equipment here as well which are usually hard to find elsewhere.

Site Usability:	★★★★	Based:	UK
Product Range:	★★★	Express Delivery Option?	(UK) No
Price Range:	Luxury/Medium/Very Good Value	Gift Wrapping Option?	No
Delivery Area:	UK	Returns Procedure:	Down to you

www.evertrading.co.uk

After twelve years of supplying interior design shops with gorgeous home accessories Evertrading have opened their own online shop, where you can buy their range of elegant and contemporary hand engraved glassware, chenille and faux fur throws, pretty cushions, modern cutlery and unusual storage suggestions. Their plain and coloured glassware in a variety of styles is definitely the main part of the collection and you could find some very lovely gifts, including wedding gifts here.

Site Usability:	★★★★	Based:	UK
Product Range:	★★★	Express Delivery Option?	(UK) No
Price Range:	Luxury/Medium/Very Good Value	Gift Wrapping Option?	No
Delivery Area:	Worldwide	Returns Procedure:	Down to you

www.finetable.co.uk

FineTable offer a unique selection of linen and design-led dining accessories from across Europe from companies large and small, including unusual candles and candlesticks (with names such as single tangle and 'tangelarbra'), Volga table linen, Carrol Boyes cheese knives and Julien Macdonald glass. Most items are available by Mail Order but you have to phone or email to place your order.

Site Usability:	★★★	Based:	UK
Product Range:	★★★	Express Delivery Option?	(UK) No
Price Range:	Luxury/Medium/Very Good Value	Gift Wrapping Option?	No
Delivery Area:	UK	Returns Procedure:	Down to you

www.french-brand.com

This is a France based retailer offering you all those home accessories you saw on your last trip but weren't able to sneak into your suitcase. Gorgeous and colourful table linen from Les Olivades and Jaquard Francais (and lots more), quilted cushions by Souleido and toiletries and home fragrance by Manuel Canovas and Jardin Secret are just some of the things you can order online. There's also a fantastic range of bedlinen by designers such as Descamps and colourful beach towels as well.

Site Usability:	★★★★	Based:	UK
Product Range:	★★★★★	Express Delivery Option?	(UK) No
Price Range:	Luxury/Medium/Very Good Value	Gift Wrapping Option?	No
Delivery Area:	Worldwide	Returns Procedure:	Down to you.

www.lakelandlimited.co.uk

You've probably already heard of this marvellous colourful, fun and innovative kitchen collection. There's a huge range on offer, regularly updated, with something for just about every occasion and every room in the house. You'll find every kind of kitchen utensil plus boards and storage solutions, foils, cleaning products and waste bags and a whole host of other useful and original products. There are lots of ideas for eating outside and picnics as well, plus foodie gifts at Christmas. Have a browse.

Site Usability:	★★★★★	Based:	UK
Product Range:	★★★★★	Express Delivery Option?	(UK) Yes
Price Range:	Luxury/Medium/Very Good Value	Gift Wrapping Option?	No
Delivery Area:	Worldwide	Returns Procedure:	Down to you

www.purpleandfinelinen.co.uk

At Purple and Fine Linen their pure linen tablecloths, placemats, napkins and runners are designed to offer a look of timeless luxury and simple elegance. As well as traditional white and ivory you can also choose from their range in deep chilli red and damson (purple), which would be lovely for Christmas. These are definitely investment table linens and very beautiful.

Site Usability:	★★★★★	Based:	UK
Product Range:	★★★	Express Delivery Option?	(UK) Yes
Price Range:	Luxury/Medium/Very Good Value	Gift Wrapping Option?	No
Delivery Area:	Worldwide	Returns Procedure:	Down to you

www.silvernutmeg.com

An A–Z of high quality kitchen equipment, with professional quality cookware, kettles, knives, pasta makers, toasters, pancake pans, workstations and bread making machines being just a few from brands such as Cuisinart, Gaggia and Magimix. You can also take a look through their home interiors section for candles, rugs, floor cushions and planters. The pictures are very clear although you do have to click on a basic list first to get to them.

Site Usability:	★★★★	Based:	UK
Product Range:	★★★★★	Express Delivery Option?	(UK) No
Price Range:	Luxury/Medium/Very Good Value	Gift Wrapping Option?	No
Delivery Area:	Worldwide	Returns Procedure:	Down to you

www.smallislandtrader.com

Small Island Trader is an excellent company (with an excellent website) offering not only china and glass from a wide range of designers and manufacturers but also kitchen equipment from juicers and steamers to copper and Le Creuset pots and pans, Sabatier knives, baking trays, and the Eva Solo's range of kitchen and living products. Needless to say they can't carry everything they offer in stock and delivery time is very much dependent on what you order. Allow at least 28 days.

Site Usability:	★★★★★	Based:	UK
Product Range:	★★★★★	Express Delivery Option?	(UK) No
Price Range:	Luxury/Medium/Very Good Value	Gift Wrapping Option?	No
Delivery Area:	Worldwide	Returns Procedure:	Down to you

www.tainpottery.co.uk

If you've paid a visit to the Scottish Highlands recently you'll certainly have come across this really attractive, country style hand painted pottery, depicting fish and fruit designs on warm and atmospheric backgrounds. You can find some lovely gifts here or put together a complete dinner service for yourself and you can be sure that what you buy is very special and different. They're happy to ship all over the world and you need to allow at least 7 days in the UK for your order to arrive.

Site Usability:	★★★★	Based:	UK
Product Range:	★★★	Express Delivery Option?	(UK) No
Price Range:	Luxury/Medium/Very Good Value	Gift Wrapping Option?	No
Delivery Area:	Worldwide	Returns Procedure:	Down to you

www.thecookingshop.co.uk

There are a lot of kitchen equipment shops online offering you every tool and gadget you can think of but this one is particularly well designed and easy to use. You can select from an excellent range of pots, pans, bakeware and other kitchen equipment plus some unusual tableware including an Eastern dining section with chopsticks, mats, tableware and accessories. They also offer recipe suggestions, household hints and tips and decorative ideas for the table.

Site Usability:	★★★★★	Based:	
Product Range:	★★★★	Express Delivery Option?	(UK) No
Price Range:	Luxury/Medium/Very Good Value	Gift Wrapping Option?	No
Delivery Area:	Worldwide	Returns Procedure:	Down to you

www.thecookskitchen.com

A vast selection of products is available on this attractively designed site which promises to despatch just about all of its products to you anywhere in the World. Coffee makers, butchers blocks, knives, recipe books, saucepans and basic kitchenware are just a few of the items available. In their country kitchen department you'll find old fashioned enamelware, farmhouse crockery and traditional style kettles to sit on your Aga.

Site Usability:	★★★★★	Based:	UK
Product Range:	★★★★★	Express Delivery Option?	(UK) No
Price Range:	Luxury/Medium/Very Good Value	Gift Wrapping Option?	Yes
Delivery Area:	Worldwide	Returns Procedure:	Down to you

www.thefrenchhouse.net

As you would expect, everything here is from France; from tableware, linen and cutlery, to toiletries by Christian Lenart and Savon de Marseilles and elegant Anduze garden pots. Also a selection of pretty bedlinen in traditional French designs such as Toile de Jouy, Fleurs de Champs and Monogram. The descriptions and information about every item are clear and well written and everything is beautifully photographed. This website only delivers to the UK other than by special arrangement.

Site Usability:	★★★★	Based:	UK
Product Range:	★★★	Express Delivery Option?	(UK) No
Price Range:	Luxury/Medium/Very Good Value	Gift Wrapping Option?	No
Delivery Area:	UK	Returns Procedure:	Down to you

Also visit these websites for kitchen and dining accessories

Website Address	You'll find it in
www.heals.co.uk	Bath Time
www.johnlewis.com	Bath Time
www.thewhitecompany.co.uk	In the Bedroom

Appliances and Accessories (plus TV and Hi-Fi)

Don't even think of buying anything from one of the websites below without making sure that you're getting a good deal. They're all desperately trying to compete for your business and seem on the surface to be offering better and better prices. Maybe they are but a lot of it seems too good to be true.

Always choose the model that you want first, (and if you want to see the latest models go to the manufacturers' website) and then type in the description into the search bar at *www.kelkoo.co.uk* or *www.uk.shopping.com.* You'll then find a number of stores selling exactly the same thing. It may well be that you go back to your original store to purchase even if there's a very slight difference in the price because you know the name, or you've dealt with them before. What almost certainly will amaze you is the disparity in the prices offered and you may well be able to make a good saving.

Also when buying large appliances or equipment you have to take other things into account. How much will you be charged for delivery? Will they take away your old appliance? And all the packaging rubbish? How long will you have to wait for delivery? Will they actually bring the appliance into your house (and up the stairs if necessary) and install it for you?

These may sound like some over the top questions but believe me they're not and they all need to be answered before you buy. Don't, whatever you do, wait to ask until afterwards. Then they've got you and it could be too late. Get everything you need confirmed by email and then place your order. Please.

You'll notice that I've included tv and hi-fi electricals here, because most of the large electrical kitchen appliance retailers offer these as well. In terms of pricing, the same applies to all these products – choose your model then compare prices and ask all the questions first.

Electrical Appliances and Accessories (including TV and Hi-Fi)

Sites to Visit

www.buyersandsellersonline.co.uk

When it comes to buying electrical appliances you want to be sure to get the best price you can and a reliable service. Buyers and Sellers have been in business since 1954 and certainly offer very keen prices on all top names such as Admiral, Neff, Miele, Siemens and Rangemaster and specialise in American makes of fridges and washing machines. Make sure you check out their prices if you're looking for something new for your kitchen.

Site Usability:	★★★★		Based:	UK
Product Range:	★★★★		Express Delivery Option?	(UK)
Price Range:	Luxury/Medium/Very Good Value		Gift Wrapping Option?	N/A
Delivery Area:	UK		Returns Procedure:	Discuss with them

www.dabs.com

Dabs are simply huge, with an enormous choice of products for computing, home entertainment, in car products (including the dreaded in car theatre system that they can all fight over) and photo and video. When you're comparing prices Dabs will almost always come up with a very good one, if not the cheapest. They're extremely reliable and their delivery is far cheaper than on most sites.

Site Usability:	★★★★★	Based:	UK
Product Range:	★★★★★	Express Delivery Option?	(UK) Yes
Price Range:	Luxury/Medium/Very Good Value	Gift Wrapping Option?	N/A
Delivery Area:	UK	Returns Procedure:	Down to you

www.electricshop.com

At electricshop you'll find two main ranges, domestic appliances for kitchen and laundry including a comprehensive range of American fridges with built in ice makers and computing, photographic and audio visual products such as plasma screen TVs, Panasonic and Sony cameras and camcorders, Sony laptops and portable audio. They also have appliance spares for kitchen and laundry, vacuum bags, light bulbs and AV leads and offer free delivery within the UK.

Site Usability:	★★★★	Based:	UK
Product Range:	★★★★★	Express Delivery Option?	(UK)
Price Range:	Luxury/Medium/Very Good Value	Gift Wrapping Option?	N/A
Delivery Area:	UK	Returns Procedure:	Discuss with them

www.pantheronline.co.uk

Based in London, this company specialises in the sale of top brand high technology consumer electronics, domestic appliances, photographic equipment and communications. You can buy just about everything for the kitchen including coffee makers and washing machines, all you need for your home cinema including plasma tvs and dvd recorders (as opposed to just players) a small range of Hi Fi and digital cameras by Olympus, Panasonic and Sony.

Site Usability:	★★★★★	Based:	UK
Product Range:	★★★★	Express Delivery	No
Price Range:	Luxury/Medium/Very Good Value	Gift Wrapping Option?	N/A
Delivery Area:	UK	Returns Procedure:	Discuss with them

www.qed-uk.com

This is another electrical retailer appearing to offer you just about every product under the sun and on an uncluttered and clear website. On the household side there are washing machines and dryers, vacuum cleaners, fridges, freezers, ovens, dishwashers and small appliances by manufacturers such as

Miele, Bosch and AEG. There's also home Cinema and Hi Fi equipment by Phillips, Panasonic and loads more plus computers and accessories by Acer, Apple, HP, IBM and Sony.

Site Usability:	★★★★	Based:	UK
Product Range:	★★★★	Express Delivery Option?	(UK) No
Price Range:	Luxury/Medium/Very Good Value	Gift Wrapping Option?	N/A
Delivery Area:	UK	Returns Procedure:	Discuss with them

www.thedac.co.uk

The Discount Appliance Centre claim to have the largest selection of 'Free Standing' and 'Built In' appliances: The company catchphrase is 'Names you recognize, prices you won't' and with leading brands such as AEG Bosch, Miele, Siemens, Neff and Zanussi if you're looking for an electrical appliance you should certainly check out the prices here. They also have Rangemaster range cookers, American style refrigeration and Siemens top of the range washing machines.

Site Usability:	★★★★★	Based:	UK
Product Range:	★★★★★	Express Delivery Option?	(UK) No
Price Range:	Luxury/Medium/Very Good Value	Gift Wrapping Option?	N/A
Delivery Area:	UK	Returns Procedure:	Discuss with them

Essential Appliance Accessory Websites

www.vacuumbags2u.co.uk

This may sound like a very boring website but if you regularly have to go to the shops to buy your replacement vacuum bags (and who wants to do that?) this will make your life easier. All types of bags for just about every make of vacuum cleaner are available here and delivery is extremely quick and efficient.

Site Usability:	★★★★	Based:	UK
Product Range:	★★★★	Express Delivery Option?	(UK) No
Price Range:	Luxury/Medium/Very Good Value	Gift Wrapping Option?	N/A
Delivery Area:	UK	Returns Procedure:	Discuss with them

www.gbbulbs.co.uk

For light bulbs look no further than this website when you want to stock up and order using their easy selector which also shows you clearly the different types of bulb fittings. You'll find every type of light bulb from incandescent, to halogen, photo optic, fluorescent, energy saving and high intensity alongside sunbed tubes and daylight bulbs. They offer a 24/48 hour National Delivery service.

Site Usability:	★★★★	Based:	UK
Product Range:	★★★★★	Express Delivery Option?	(UK) Yes
Price Range:	Luxury/Medium/Very Good Value	Gift Wrapping Option?	N/A
Delivery Area:	UK	Returns Procedure:	Discuss with them

www.electricshop.com

They're already mentioned above but they also need to be kept in mind here for their wide range of appliance spares and accessories for kitchen and laundry. They offer vacuum bags, light bulbs, leads, laundry and kitchen appliance spares and accessories and offer free delivery within the UK.

Site Usability:	★★★★	Based:	UK
Product Range:	★★★★★	Express Delivery Option?	(UK)
Price Range:	Luxury/<u>Medium</u>/Very Good Value	Gift Wrapping Option?	
Delivery Area:	UK	Returns Procedure:	Discuss with them

Also check at *www.johnlewis.com* for kitchen appliances and accessories

Section 6

Food and Drink

Now here's an area that's perfect for shopping online. Just think of all that time saved not having to go to the shops to buy your food. I do come across some people who prefer to go and do it themselves, (out in the car, drive to the supermarket, load that trolley, unload it and load it again to pay, load it in the car, drive home, unload it all then put it all away) but to do that with the services on offer I think you have to be a total masochist.

As far as supermarkets go the pricing is extremely competitive so you're not going to find a huge difference wherever you buy, after all, they're checking each other's prices all the time. Using any or all of them is incredibly simple. You just need to write your list out of all the things you buy on a regular basis, register your details, create your list online and you're away. Don't listen to anyone who says that they don't deliver on time and you don't get what you've ordered. Obviously mistakes are sometimes made but on the whole the services have improved hugely over the past couple of years and reliability levels have soared.

Once you've started buying those everyday products online you'll wonder why it took you so long to get going.

For more particular, deli style products the web is your new corner store as long as you don't want it today (you can probably have it tomorrow). The same goes for cakes, fresh fish and meat. You can get the best quality of everything. Most will deliver the next day provided you order during the week before Friday so what more could you want?

Another food area that is growing very fast is that of Organics and health foods. You can have a regular order of fruit and vegetables which will arrive at your door on your specified day from various parts of the country, totally fresh and much higher quality than you'll find at most supermarkets (and probably quite a lot less expensive) so if organic is what you want you should take a look at the sites listed here and choose the one whose type of service suits you the best.

Chapter 34

The Bakery

Buying bread online is tricky, as obviously it has to be so fresh. The best places are really the supermarkets as they'll deliver to you the next day and you can get quite a selection. You can also find freshly baked bread to order with your organic fruit and vegetables so check out these websites too. They normally sell a vast range of products along with the greengrocery and the quality is usually excellent.

Cakes are much easier so let's start with the main events of Christmas and Easter. You can find some delicious, beautifully decorated cakes online for these special occasions. They may not be as large as the ones you usually make (which is why they won't be hanging around for months and months) but they really are good. Yes you *can* see that they're bought and not home made but, and it's a big and rather unfortunate but, they can be absolutely just as good as the one granny used to make and save you loads of time.

You'll find birthday cakes too in every shape and size and with a huge choice of decorations. Not only that but if you've forgotten someone and need something sent to school or someone's house very quickly you can have that as well. You can spend a fortune here so be careful when choosing but I'll say it again, if you don't have the time, go for it.

Along side the speciality cakes you'll find all sorts of other bakery goodies such as tray bakes (try Meg Rivers' chocolate brownies – they're delicious), biscuits and other types of cakes. I think you'll be amazed at how good they are.

Sites to Visit

www.bakinboys.co.uk

There's a great deal going on on this website, but click quickly through to 'Buy Stuff' and you'll find a really great selection of flapjacks, muffins, cookies, cakes, hand cooked crisps and Belgian waffles all available in boxes or packs of twelve upwards for next day delivery. You can find nutritional information on all their products and everything is nut free. So, as they say, 'say it with flour'.

Site Usability:	★★★	Based:	UK
Product Range:	★★★	Express Delivery Option?	(UK) Yes
Price Range:	Luxury/<u>Medium</u>/Very Good Value	Gift Wrapping Option?	No
Delivery Area:	UK	Returns Procedure:	Down to you

www.bettysbypost.co.uk

At *bettysbypost.com* you can order hand decorated Christmas cakes in a variety of sizes, their family recipe Christmas pudding with fruit soaked in brandy and ale and seasonal favourites such as Christmas Tea Loaf, Pannetone and Stollen. Chocolate ginger, miniature Florentines and Peppermint Creams are just a few of the goodies on offer in their confectionery section and you'll also find lovely stocking fillers for children and preserves for the Christmas larder.

Site Usability:	★★★★★	Based:	UK
Product Range:	★★★★	Express Delivery Option?	(UK) No
Price Range:	Luxury/<u>Medium</u>/Very Good Value	Gift Wrapping Option?	No
Delivery Area:	Worldwide	Returns Procedure:	Down to you

www.botham.co.uk

Here you'll find a simple collection of cakes for Christmas and other occasions which you can personalise with your own message or buy un-piped. All cakes are hand decorated and iced so they ask you to give them plenty of notice. They do, however, keep a short order iced fruit cake, piped with Happy Birthday for you to buy by quick delivery. You may well be tempted by the plum bread, biscuits and preserves on this website as well.

Site Usability:	★★★	Based:	UK
Product Range:	★★★	Express Delivery Option?	(UK) No
Price Range:	Luxury/<u>Medium</u>/Very Good Value	Gift Wrapping Option?	No
Delivery Area:	Worldwide	Returns Procedure:	Down to you

www.caketoppers.co.uk

On this website you can order a birthday cake to be sent for next day delivery (just in case you've forgotten to get one ready in time), send your own photo to be used on a cake, order a Christmas cake to be sent to anywhere in mainland UK and choose from traditional sponge and iced fruit cakes to be sent on the date of your choosing. They also offer mini decorated cupcakes and shortbread with your choice of photo.

Site Usability:	★★★★	Based:	UK
Product Range:	★★★	Express Delivery Option?	(UK) Yes
Price Range:	Luxury/Medium/Very Good Value	Gift Wrapping Option?	No
Delivery Area:	UK	Returns Procedure:	Down to you

www.homefayrelimited.co.uk

Specialists at producing cakes, chutneys and jams for events such as farmers markets, Home Fayre are now offering you the opportunity of buying their wonderful looking and extremely well priced products from home (so the next time you have a tea party you can really fool someone). Their every day cakes include chocolate, cinnamon and raisin, coffee and walnut and they also offer birthday and Christmas cakes. You can also buy Tipsy Strawberry and Plum and Ginger jams and totally naughty sweets such as fudge, nut crunch and coconut ice.

Site Usability:	★★★★	Based:	UK
Product Range:	★★★	Express Delivery Option?	(UK) No
Price Range:	Luxury/Medium/Very Good Value	Gift Wrapping Option?	No
Delivery Area:	UK	Returns Procedure:	Down to you

www.jane-asher.co.uk

I'm sure you've heard of Jane Asher, actress, film star, writer, lifestyle expert and cake designer extraordinaire, but did you also know that you could buy some of her marvellous cakes online? Well now you do. Just click through to her website and her Mail Order cake section and you'll find a choice of about forty different designs for all sorts of different occasions. You can choose from three sizes of cake and sponge or fruit filling. UK delivery only, and you need to allow up to ten days for your cake to arrive.

Site Usability:	★★★★★	Based:	UK
Product Range:	★★★★	Express Delivery Option?	(UK) No
Price Range:	Luxury/Medium/Very Good Value	Gift Wrapping Option?	No
Delivery Area:	UK	Returns Procedure:	Down to you

www.megrivers.com

An extremely tempting website offering 'home made' beautifully decorated cakes, biscuits and traybakes (flapjacks, chocolate brownies and the like). Their traditional fruit cake is extremely good and is made well in advance and if you can't be bothered to bake yourself definitely shop here. Having ordered from them several times myself I can assure you that everyone who tastes their products will be delighted and their service is excellent. Overseas delivery by request.

Site Usability:	★★★★★	Based:	UK
Product Range:	★★★	Express Delivery Option?	(UK) No
Price Range:	Luxury/<u>Medium</u>/Very Good Value	Gift Wrapping Option?	Yes
Delivery Area:	UK and overseas by request	Returns Procedure:	Down to you

www.need-a-cake.co.uk

This family run cake company will send out most of their cakes to you anywhere in the UK. Because they have so many designs you need to call them to order and confirm prices. They also offer a good range of cake making accessories, such as cake tins and forcing bags, if you do want to make your own. Their Christmas cakes appear on their website from the end of October so check back if you want to take a look at these.

Site Usability:	★★★	Based:	UK
Product Range:	★★★	Express Delivery Option?	(UK) No
Price Range:	Luxury/<u>Medium</u>/Very Good Value	Gift Wrapping Option?	No
Delivery Area:	UK	Returns Procedure:	Down to you

www.theorganiccakecompany.co.uk

There isn't a huge selection here, but when you read about their chocolate cake, made with a fresh cream and rum ganache containing 36% chocolate and their New England home style carrot and walnut cake with its lemon cream cheese topping, if you're anything like me you'll want to have a taste. You buy them as slices, cakes or large traybakes and you need to call or email them to order. All cakes are despatched by next day courier.

Site Usability:	★★★	Based:	UK
Product Range:	★★★	Express Delivery Option?	(UK) Yes
Price Range:	Luxury/<u>Medium</u>/Very Good Value	Gift Wrapping Option?	No
Delivery Area:	UK	Returns Procedure:	Down to you

www.thecakestore.com

The Cake Store offers a range of cakes of different sizes and decorations and for different types of occasion including, of course, Christmas. Prices include delivery and you need to allow 7–10 days for your order to arrive. Every cake is hand crafted and specially made for you from their choice of fun and different designs and they also offer beautiful wedding cakes. At time of writing most are only available for within the M25.

Site Usability:	★★★	Based:	UK
Product Range:	★★★★	Express Delivery Option?	(UK) No
Price Range:	<u>Luxury</u>/Medium/Very Good Value	Gift Wrapping Option?	No
Delivery Area:	UK	Returns Procedure:	Down to you

Chapter 35

The Butcher

$\mathcal{A}$lthough once you've sampled the joys of online supermarket shopping you may be tempted to order your fish and meat there too my advice is simple. Don't before you've checked out the alternatives here.

What the World Wide Web has done for food shopping is this: On the one hand you don't have to go out to pick/pack/load/unload and unpack anything any more unless you really, really want to. It's also put you in touch with an incredible number of suppliers of goods all over the country you would otherwise never have had a way of getting to.

Fresh meat is a very good example. You can order from Devon, Scotland or even further away and have your order delivered the following day. The difference in quality, taste and range in what you can buy online from what was available before is simply enormous and you should take advantage of it.

I'm not saying that you should give up your local butcher; certainly not if he gives you a good service and has high quality meat. But if you want something different that he wouldn't normally supply, or he's very expensive then take a look at what's here and give it a go.

Meat is excellent for sending out as it can be vacuum packed and you can either use it straight away or put it in your freezer. If you want to go to town you can buy Aberdeen Angus steaks, wild venison and all manner of exotic treats, ready prepared to put in your oven.

Sites to Visit

www.blackface.co.uk

Heather bred Blackface lamb, organic lamb, haggis, iron age pork, oven ready grouse, partridge and bronze turkeys are all available to order online on this site based in Scotland. Note that deliveries and availability depend on seasonality and you may have to wait for some products. Delivery is free and if you want to order your Christmas turkey from them this year they'll send them out by carrier to you a few days before Christmas.

Site Usability:	★★★★		Based:	UK
Product Range:	★★★		Express Delivery Option?	(UK) No
Price Range:	Luxury/Medium/Very Good Value		Gift Wrapping Option?	
Delivery Area:	UK		Returns Procedure:	

www.broughs.com

On Broughs unsophisticated website you can buy, amongst other things, excellent good value beef and award winning sausages. Here are just some of the awards they've won, which they're keen (and rightly so) to tell you about: Britain's Best Pork Sausage, Venison red wine sausage – Gold 'Q Butcher' Award, Birkdale Traditional Sausage – Gold Star & trophy and they've also been voted one of the top three small butchers in the UK.

Site Usability:	★★★		Based:	UK
Product Range:	★★★★		Express Delivery Option?	(UK) No
Price Range:	Luxury/Medium/Very Good Value		Gift Wrapping Option?	
Delivery Area:	UK		Returns Procedure:	

www.donaldrussell.com

This is a superb website from an excellent butcher, beautifully photographed and laid out and extremely tempting. You can buy just about every type of meat here, from goose and game (in season) to pork, beef and lamb plus natural fish and seafood. Most of the pictures show the products as you'd like them to arrive on your plate and you can either buy from their ready prepared dishes such as Salmon en Croute or Bolognese sauce or you can follow their excellent recipes.

Site Usability:	★★★★★		Based:	UK
Product Range:	★★★★★		Express Delivery Option?	(UK) No
Price Range:	Luxury/Medium/Very Good Value		Gift Wrapping Option?	No
Delivery Area:	UK		Returns Procedure:	Down to you

www.eversfieldorganic.co.uk

Eversfield Organic is an 850 acre organic farm nestling deep in the heart of the West Devon countryside and farmed to the highest Soil Association standards. Aberdeen Angus Beef, Romney Marsh sheep and Large Black pigs are prepared in the traditional manner by their professional butchers, guaranteeing extremely tasty and tender cuts of meat.

Site Usability:	★★★★★	Based:	UK
Product Range:	★★★★	Express Delivery Option?	(UK) No
Price Range:	Luxury/Medium/Very Good Value	Gift Wrapping Option?	No
Delivery Area:	UK	Returns Procedure:	Down to you

www.freshfood.co.uk

This is a prizewinning nationwide delivery service of organic and wild harvested foods, and the best way for you to buy from them is to join their box scheme, where you take out a weekly subscription to one or several of their selections. Of course you can cancel this at any time. There is fresh produce such as fruit and veg, meat, fish, game, smoked products, wine and bread - plus lots of recipe ideas. From wild Scottish Salmon to pizzas, if it's organic it'll be here.

Site Usability:	★★★★	Based:	UK
Product Range:	★★★★	Express Delivery Option?	(UK) No
Price Range:	Luxury/Medium/Very Good Value	Gift Wrapping Option?	No
Delivery Area:	UK	Returns Procedure:	Down to you

www.griffithsbutchers.co.uk

This butcher is based in Somerset and offers next day delivery on a selection of meat boxes, with names such as Winter Warmer (steak and kidney and stewing steak), Christmas Hamper pack with (yes you guessed it) a 7kg turkey, bacon, chipolatas and honey roast ham and Family Gold pack, with Somerset beef and chicken supremes. They also offer seasonal game, barbecue meats and home made sausages.

Site Usability:	★★★	Based:	UK
Product Range:	★★★★	Express Delivery Option?	(UK) Yes
Price Range:	Luxury/Medium/Very Good Value	Gift Wrapping Option?	No
Delivery Area:	UK	Returns Procedure:	Down to you

www.healfarm.co.uk

You won't find a lot of pretty pictures here on this simple site offering a wide choice of beef, lamb, pork, poultry, sausages and burgers at reasonable prices, just an excellent choice and very good service. You can order your Bronze and ready stuffed turkey here and specify the size by the kilo. You'll also find a selection of recipes, advice on roasting meat and Aga cookery information.

Site Usability:	★★★★	Based:	UK
Product Range:	★★★★	Express Delivery Option?	(UK) No
Price Range:	Luxury/<u>Medium</u>/Very Good Value	Gift Wrapping Option?	No
Delivery Area:	UK	Returns Procedure:	Down to you

www.lanefarm.co.uk

Lane Farm is a family run farming business based in the Suffolk countryside, who produce a wide range of quality pork products from their own home produced pork. You can order sausages with names like Winter Warmer and Italian Spice and Garlic, stir fry pork strips, lemon and pepper steaks, and Suffolk Roast (stuffed with apricots and wrapped in bacon), plus their own, sweet cured bacon and gammon. To order you need to call, fax or email them.

Site Usability:	★★★	Based:	UK
Product Range:	★★★	Express Delivery Option?	(UK) No
Price Range:	Luxury/<u>Medium</u>/Very Good Value	Gift Wrapping Option?	No
Delivery Area:	UK	Returns Procedure:	Down to you

www.meats.co.uk

You'll find very good value meat on this website, available for next day delivery provided you order before 10 am and if you spend over £75. They offer beef, lamb, poultry, pork and game such as wood pigeon, partridge and venison plus York ham, pancetta (which is often hard to find) and black pudding. As you click on a type of meat you'll find a recipe idea alongside the excellent pictures.

Site Usability:	★★★★	Based:	UK
Product Range:	★★★★	Express Delivery Option?	(UK) No
Price Range:	Luxury/<u>Medium</u>/Very Good Value	Gift Wrapping Option?	
Delivery Area:	UK	Returns Procedure:	

www.realmeat.co.uk

The Real Meat Company supplies meat and poultry from traditional farmers with a nationwide delivery service. You can order your turkey from them for Christmas from mid-November. Their minimum order value is £35 and you can specify the day you want your delivery. Remember to allow them enough time in the run up to Christmas.

Site Usability:	★★★★	Based:	UK
Product Range:	★★★★	Express Delivery Option?	(UK) No
Price Range:	Luxury/<u>Medium</u>/Very Good Value	Gift Wrapping Option?	No
Delivery Area:	UK	Returns Procedure:	Down to you

Chapter 36

The Cheese Shop

If you're a real cheese addict you'll be delighted to know that there's almost certainly a better choice online than you could find anywhere offline (apart from, maybe, Harrods and Selfridges in London). Every type of cheese you've ever heard of is available in most cases by next day delivery. There are also cheese societies and places where you can have a 'tasting selection' sent to you every month so you can try new and different cheeses.

Some of the websites are so sophisticated they'll tell you exactly which wine you should be drinking with each cheese (and probably try and sell it to you), plus offer you excellent recipes, cheeseboard selections and introductions to unusual cheeses. Be careful though, you can spend a fortune here and delivery is quite often expensive as well.

If this all sounds a bit much then you're probably not a 'real cheese addict' and you'll be pleased to know that you can order your regular cheese through your online supermarket (and Ocado I think has the best selection). But for those of you to whom cheese is a real pleasure, you'll be in paradise.

Sites to Visit

www.cheese-board.co.uk

This is a really beautifully laid out website offering a mouthwatering array of cheese from all over Europe plus recipes for dishes such as Swiss Fondue, Baked Vacherin (try it, it's wonderful), warm goats cheese salad and Gruyere cheese straws. They also offer a small selection of wines to complement the cheeses, unusual cheese knives as gift suggestions, olive oils and Italian antipasti.

Site Usability:	★★★★★	Based:	UK
Product Range:	★★★★★	Express Delivery Option?	(UK) Yes
Price Range:	Luxury/Medium/Very Good Value	Gift Wrapping Option?	No
Delivery Area:	UK	Returns Procedure:	Down to you

www.fromages.com

Fromages.com is based as you might expect in France and ships its French cheeses all over the World in 24 hours (excluding certain countries). For a really grown up cheese board you can choose their Party Cheese Board containing their selection of ten cheeses including some well known and some you'll probably never have heard of. Alternatively you can choose your own selection from their list.

Site Usability:	★★★★★	Based:	France
Product Range:	★★★★★	Express Delivery Option?	(UK) Yes
Price Range:	Luxury/Medium/Very Good Value	Gift Wrapping Option?	No
Delivery Area:	Worldwide	Returns Procedure:	Down to you

www.teddingtoncheese.co.uk

Every type of cheese you could possibly want and some new ones you won't have tried before are offered on this easy to use site. Buy your cheese by weight from a small piece to enough to feed a large party. Their offer includes accessories for raclette and fondue plus a selection of very unusual cheese knives. You'll find a monthly cheese board selection, gifts of cheese and wine or port and delivery worldwide.

Site Usability:	★★★★★	Based:	UK
Product Range:	★★★★★	Express Delivery Option?	(UK) Yes to Mainland UK
Price Range:	Luxury/Medium/Very Good Value	Gift Wrapping Option?	No
Delivery Area:	Worldwide	Returns Procedure:	Down to you

www.paxtonandwhitfield.co.uk

This famous cheese company has a mouthwatering online shop and offers overnight delivery. You can buy speciality British, French and Italian cheeses here and join the Cheese Society to receive their special selection each month. They also sell biscuits, chutneys and pickles, York ham and pâtés, beautifully boxed cheese knives and stores, fondue sets and raclette machines.

Site Usability:	★★★★★	Based:	UK
Product Range:	★★★★	Express Delivery Option?	(UK) Yes
Price Range:	Luxury/Medium/Very Good Value	Gift Wrapping Option?	No
Delivery Area:	Worldwide	Returns Procedure:	Down to you

www.thecheesesociety.co.uk

Although you can find continental cheeses here, the vast majority of cheeses offered here are of the specialist, unpasteurised variety, which they source throughout the country. There are some excellent gift selections, with which they can include a handwritten card with your personal message. If you want to, just give them a call and they'll be delighted to give you advice on choosing old favourites and making new discoveries. Free UK delivery on orders over £20.

Site Usability:	★★★★★	Based:	UK
Product Range:	★★★★★	Express Delivery Option?	(UK) Yes
Price Range:	<u>Luxury/Medium</u>/Very Good Value	Gift Wrapping Option?	No
Delivery Area:	Worldwide	Returns Procedure:	Down to you

www.finecheese.co.uk

You'll discover a wonderful selection of cheeses here, all beautifully photographed to make them look even more tempting although the problem is that once you start ordering here you'll never be able to buy cheese at your supermarket again – it's simply not as good (usually). You can also buy Italian antipasti, Spanish Tapas and some French products here plus chocolates and nibbles.

Site Usability:	★★★★★	Based:	UK
Product Range:	★★★★★	Express Delivery Option?	(UK) Yes
Price Range:	Luxury/<u>Medium</u>/Very Good Value	Gift Wrapping Option?	No
Delivery Area:	UK	Returns Procedure:	Down to you

Chapter 37

The Fishmonger

Gone are the days when you could go down to your local town and buy all the fresh fish you might want (unless you go to the fish counter of your local supermarket). Despite the fact that we're constantly being told how healthy fish is and that we should be eating more of it, it's also harder and harder to find.

Needless to say this has presented a perfect opportunity for online shopping and you can buy wonderful fish, fresh, frozen and smoked, from places as far afield as the Highlands and Islands of Scotland and the coast of Cornwall.

Have a look round these websites and make sure you know exactly what you're ordering and how much you're paying. If you can, buy wild smoked salmon as opposed to farmed, and fresh fish as opposed to frozen, so that you have the choice of freezing your order or not. Yes, you'll probably find that it's cheaper at the supermarkets but there's a world of difference in the flavour and nothing like knowing that your fish is pretty well straight from the sea.

Sites to Visit

www.fishworks.co.uk

From their premises in Brixham they deal with fishermen in Dartmouth, Scotland, the East Coast, France, Italy and as far away as the Maldives for fresh tuna, which means that you have access to one of the widest ranges of fish and shellfish available in the UK. The selection is inevitably huge, and you can choose from shellfish such as wild caught white prawns and Pallourde Clams, fresh fish from Brixham Lemon Sole to Gilthead Bream and loads in between. There's lots of advice here too on preparation and cooking your fish.

Site Usability:	★★★	Based:	UK
Product Range:	★★★★	Express Delivery Option?	(UK) Yes
Price Range:	Luxury/Medium/Very Good Value	Gift Wrapping Option?	No
Delivery Area:	UK	Returns Procedure:	Down to you

www.foweyfish.com

Fowey fish are retail and wholesale fishmongers. Fresh supplies come into their shop every day and they operate a nationwide mail order service for fresh fish, shellfish and some specialist fine wines including the much sought after and hard to find Cloudy Bay. They despatch four days a week, Monday to Thursdays, for next day delivery all over the UK. This is a simply designed website but you know that the fish will be fresh and there's an excellent choice.

Site Usability:	★★★	Based:	UK
Product Range:	★★★★	Express Delivery Option?	(UK) No
Price Range:	Luxury/Medium/Very Good Value	Gift Wrapping Option?	No
Delivery Area:	UK	Returns Procedure:	Down to you

www.gallowaysmokehouse.co.uk

Nestling on the banks of Wigtown Bay is the Galloway Smokehouse, home of prize winning smoked salmon, trout, seafood and game all waiting for you to order online. From the simple kipper to the grand salmon a huge variety of smoked food is on offer, and both hot and cold smoked foods are available as well, such as kippers, smoked mackerel and even smoked cheese.

Site Usability:	★★★★★	Based:	UK
Product Range:	★★★★	Express Delivery Option?	(UK) Yes
Price Range:	Luxury/Medium/Very Good Value	Gift Wrapping Option?	No
Delivery Area:	Worldwide	Returns Procedure:	Down to you

www.lochfyne.com

You may well have eaten in one of their chain of seafood restaurants which are excellent and not overpriced but you may not know that you can buy a selection of their goods online, from their beautifully laid out and photographed website. They offer fresh and smoked trout and salmon, oysters, mussels and langoustine plus Glen Fyne beef, pork, lamb and venison and lots of other goodies such as pâtés and gift boxes.

Site Usability:	★★★★★	Based:	UK
Product Range:	★★★★★	Express Delivery Option?	(UK) No
Price Range:	Luxury/Medium/Very Good Value	Gift Wrapping Option?	
Delivery Area:	EU	Returns Procedure:	Down to you

www.martins-seafresh.co.uk

Buy your fresh fish direct from Cornwall on this simple website. The fish they offer includes sea bass, sea bream, brill and cod through to salmon, skate and Dover sole. There's a wide choice of shellfish as well from crevettes and Cornish lobsters to scallops and oysters and in the smoked department you'll find mussels, salmon and eel plus chicken and goose.

Site Usability:	★★★★	Based:	UK
Product Range:	★★★★★	Express Delivery Option?	(UK) Yes
Price Range:	Luxury/Medium/Very Good Value	Gift Wrapping Option?	No
Delivery Area:	UK	Returns Procedure:	Down to you

www.skye-seafood.co.uk

Isle of Skye Smokehouse is a small dedicated producer supplying traditionally smoked fish to some of the finest hotels in Scotland and now they're happy to sell to you directly online. If you didn't know it already, smoked Scottish wild salmon is completely different to the farmed variety. Once you've tried wild salmon you'll probably never look back, although it frequently costs twice as much, but it would be certainly worth it for a special treat.

Site Usability:	★★★★	Based:	UK
Product Range:	★★★	Express Delivery Option?	(UK) Yes
Price Range:	Luxury/Medium/Very Good Value	Gift Wrapping Option?	No
Delivery Area:	Worldwide	Returns Procedure:	Down to you

www.smokedsalmon.co.uk

At the Inverawe Smokehouse you'll find classic smoked salmon and trout, smoked Wild Atlantic salmon, gifts, hampers and gourmet boxes. In their deli section they offer smoked pâtés, cod's roe and salmon and lumpfish caviar. As well as the above, hiding in the 'Larder' section, you'll find beef and pies, shortbread and fruit cakes, pickles, chutneys and jellies and cheeses.

Site Usability:	★★★★	Based:	UK
Product Range:	★★★★★	Express Delivery Option?	(UK) Yes
Price Range:	Luxury/Medium/Very Good Value	Gift Wrapping Option?	No
Delivery Area:	EU	Returns Procedure:	Down to you

www.thefishsociety.co.uk

Here you can choose from over two hundred kinds of fish and seafood, delivered frozen. There's every fish you could possibly want, from organic salmon to Dover sole, turbot and tuna plus wild smoked salmon, gigantic prawns and dived scallops. They also have a range of fish recipe books and accessories such as fish kettles and claw crackers. Deliveries are twice a week on Wednesday and Friday, delivery is £5 on orders from £65-£100 and free after that.

Site Usability:	★★★★★	Based:	UK
Product Range:	★★★★★	Express Delivery Option?	(UK) No
Price Range:	Luxury/Medium/Very Good Value	Gift Wrapping Option?	No
Delivery Area:	UK	Returns Procedure:	Down to you

Chapter 38

Gourmet Food/Deli

One of the great advantages of buying food online is that you can reach out and find things that you never would have been able to buy from your local delicatessen. Hand made game pie, damson gin, soupe de poissons, Chile Man's Smokin' Satan Sauce (yes really, go look), black truffle flavoured olive oil, Belgian butter waffles and, of course, the ever famous sticky toffee pudding. They're all there to be bought in just a few seconds.

These are the best of the deli websites, with the sort of products you always wished you had just round the corner to help brighten up your everyday meals; gorgeous cheeses and tasty extras, not to mention for example the times when you actually don't want to cook; when you'd rather produce a dish of antipasti, perhaps, or perfectly prepared York ham.

Most places here will deliver to you very quickly, even next day if you need it (usually within the UK), and although you will have to pay a delivery charge the difference you'll find in being able to order online from such a wide range will easily outweigh the cost of the postage, even if you forget to consider just how long it would take you to get out there and shop, and if you could possibly find everything together, which you simply couldn't.

What about the supermarkets, do I hear you say? Well yes, you can find a lot of these products there, though possibly not as good, and if you don't want the machine sliced plastic wrapped chorizo or Parma ham but prefer the hand cut variety you have to queue, don't you? Who does queuing any more? No thanks.

The biggest problem here is not finding things but where to stop, as you'll no doubt discover for yourself.

Sites to Visit

www.carluccios.com

You may have been lucky enough to eat in one of his restaurants or to receive some of his wonderful regional Italian delicacies as a gift. Even if you haven't done either of the above, you can now buy from his beautifully presented range online, including pasta, olive oil, antipasti and confectionery. Everything is packaged beautifully with lots of information about where the product originated and what you can use it for. Buy for yourself or give it away. It's a delight, either way.

Site Usability:	★★★★★	Based:	UK
Product Range:	★★★	Express Delivery Option?	(UK) No
Price Range:	<u>Luxury</u>/<u>Medium</u>/<u>Very Good Value</u>	Gift Wrapping Option?	No
Delivery Area:	UK	Returns Procedure:	Down to you

www.caspiancaviar.co.uk

If caviar is something that you really enjoy but you can't buy the real thing where you live, then take a look at this website which offers Beluga, Oscietre and Sevruga caviar right up to 500g tins although thankfully, bearing in mind the price, you can also order their 50g tins. To go with your caviar celebration you can buy crystal caviar bowls, vodka shot glasses, horn spoons, vodka and blinis.

Site Usability:	★★★★	Based:	UK
Product Range:	★★★	Express Delivery Option?	(UK) Yes
Price Range:	<u>Luxury</u>/<u>Medium</u>/<u>Very Good Value</u>	Gift Wrapping Option?	No
Delivery Area:	EU	Returns Procedure:	Down to you

www.deliinthenook.co.uk

The Deli in the Nook is based in Leicester, and stocks a superb range of antipasti, olives, infused oils and vinegars, balsamics and extra virgin olive oils, pâté, pasta, tins and jars of authentic Italian and French produce, hand made chocs, biscuits, chutneys, salsas and sauces, preserves, nibbles, goodies and lots more, if all that wasn't enough already. They'll customise gift parcels for you together with your personalised message and aim to despatch all orders within 24 hours.

Site Usability:	★★★★	Based:	UK
Product Range:	★★★★	Express Delivery Option?	(UK) Yes
Price Range:	Luxury/<u>Medium</u>/Very Good Value	Gift Wrapping Option?	Yes
Delivery Area:	UK	Returns Procedure:	Down to you

www.elanthy.com

If your normal thought when buying olive oil is to buy Italian you should have another think. Elanthy supply (with free UK delivery) the highest quality olive oil from Greece. The service is really excellent and the prices will probably take you by surprise, particularly if, like us, you use quite a lot. You can also buy balsamic vinegar and Maldon sea salt here, plus Pommery mustard and olive oil based soaps. Give them a try.

Site Usability:	★★★★	Based:	UK
Product Range:	★★★	Express Delivery Option?	(UK) Yes
Price Range:	Luxury/Medium/Very Good Value	Gift Wrapping Option?	No
Delivery Area:	UK	Returns Procedure:	Down to you

www.esperya.com

This is an Italian website offering quick delivery throughout Europe. They offer olive oil, wine, honey, pasta, rice, desserts, charcuterie, cheeses, preserves and seafood – from all the different regions of Italy. As you click through to each product you find a wealth of information; how Pecorino cheese is made for example, where exactly it comes from and how to use it, or Navelli saffron, its history and which dishes it's best suited for. If you like Italian food this is a real paradise.

Site Usability:	★★★★★	Based:	Italy
Product Range:	★★★★	Express Delivery Option?	(UK) Yes
Price Range:	Luxury/Medium/Very Good Value	Gift Wrapping Option?	No
Delivery Area:	Europe	Returns Procedure:	Down to you

www.formanandfield.com

Forman & Field is a luxury delicatessen specialising in traditional British produce from small independent producers. There's a delicious selection of luxury cakes and puddings, smoked salmon, ham and cheeses all beautifully photographed and extremely hard to resist. Don't miss their home made, award winning fish pâtés and pies, perfect for the next time you're entertaining. They offer speedy delivery to UK, Ireland and the Channel Isles

Site Usability:	★★★★★	Based:	UK
Product Range:	★★★★★	Express Delivery Option?	(UK) Yes
Price Range:	Luxury/Medium/Very Good Value	Gift Wrapping Option?	No
Delivery Area:	UK	Returns Procedure:	Down to you

www.frenchgourmetstore.com

Here you'll discover a marvellous choice of regional gourmet products from France, all prepared according to traditional recipes and including mushrooms and truffles, mustards, oils and vinegars and gorgeous chocolates. They also have a small but excellent range of hampers and gift baskets. They're actually based in the UK, will ship to you anywhere in the World and offer an express service.

Site Usability:	★★★★★	Based:	France
Product Range:	★★★★	Express Delivery Option?	(UK) Yes
Price Range:	Luxury/Medium/Very Good Value	Gift Wrapping Option?	No
Delivery Area:	Worldwide	Returns Procedure:	Down to you

www.iberianfoods-shop.co.uk

Do you like Spanish food? If so then this is a great website to have a look around, offering a great choice of products from Spain such as Serrano Ham, Chorizo and other cured meats and fish, herbs and spices and Spanish cheese. You can also shop from their range of Tapas, and paella dishes, cookers and ingredients, plus there's a lot of information on where to find good Spanish restaurants in the UK plus a Spanish food glossary.

Site Usability:	★★★★	Based:	Spain
Product Range:	★★★★	Express Delivery Option?	(UK) No
Price Range:	Luxury/Medium/Very Good Value	Gift Wrapping Option?	No
Delivery Area:	UK	Returns Procedure:	Down to you

www.oliviers-co.com

For those who love cooking and good food and only want to use the best don't miss this wonderful site offering special olive oils (and other pantry goods). You'll discover olive oils infused with basil, lemon and chilli or pepper, mandarin and truffles plus information and advice on how to use them and which foods they complement. Also some very attractive gift selections. They'll deliver throughout Europe and you need to allow ten days for your order to arrive.

Site Usability:	★★★★★	Based:	France
Product Range:	★★★★	Express Delivery Option?	(UK) No
Price Range:	Luxury/Medium/Very Good Value	Gift Wrapping Option?	No
Delivery Area:	Europe	Returns Procedure:	Down to you

www.provender.net

The essential deli, based in South Petherton, offering everything you would expect to find, from cheeses, bacon, salami and pâté to tea, coffee, mustards, chutneys and biscuits and a wide choice in between. The service is really excellent and their prices are good as well when you compare them with other delicatessens, either online or offline. They also have some foodie gift ideas here and lots of suggestions for your Christmas table.

Site Usability:	★★★★	Based:	UK
Product Range:	★★★★★	Express Delivery Option?	(UK) No
Price Range:	Luxury/Medium/Very Good Value	Gift Wrapping Option?	No
Delivery Area:	Worldwide for most products	Returns Procedure:	Down to you

www.savoria.com

A website run by obviously passionate 'foodies' offering you the very best from all over Italy, including cheese, meat, pasta, olive oil and antipasti. There's lots of friendly information about each product and which part of the country it comes from plus suggestions for use. Delivery comes to you direct from

Italy – orders placed by Sunday night are delivered by the end of the following week. They'll deliver to most EU countries.

Site Usability:	★★★★★	Based:	UK
Product Range:	★★★★★	Express Delivery Option?	(UK) No
Price Range:	<u>Luxury</u>/<u>Medium</u>/<u>Very Good Value</u>	Gift Wrapping Option?	No
Delivery Area:	EU	Returns Procedure:	Down to you

www.stickytoffeepudding.net

For lovers of sticky toffee pudding this must surely be the most effortless way of getting hold of some and you'll be buying it from the World famous Cartmel Village Shop in Cumbria. Strangely at a time when websites are trying to offer you everything and more the Sticky Toffee Pudding (plus sauce of course) is the only product available here. Try some. Forget that 'a moment on the lips means a lifetime on the hips' and buy the largest size for 9–10 people (if you can bear to share it) for £13.75 including postage

Site Usability:	★★★★	Based:	UK
Product Range:	★★	Express Delivery Option?	(UK) No
Price Range:	Luxury/<u>Medium</u>/Very Good Value	Gift Wrapping Option?	No
Delivery Area:	Worldwide	Returns Procedure:	Down to you

www.valvonacrolla-online.co.uk

Valvona & Crolla is an independent family business based in Edinburgh, specialising in gourmet Italian products plus their excellent range of good value, quality Italian wines from artisan producers and progressive co-operatives. In 2005 they won the Which award for the Italian Specialist Wine Merchant so if you're fond of Italian wines take a good look at their collection. In their wonderful deli you'll find a wide choice including prosciutto and pancetta, cheeses, smoked salmon and all your larder essentials.

Site Usability:	★★★	Based:	UK
Product Range:	★★★★	Express Delivery Option?	(UK) Yes
Price Range:	<u>Luxury</u>/<u>Medium</u>/<u>Very Good Value</u>	Gift Wrapping Option?	No
Delivery Area:	UK	Returns Procedure:	Down to you

www.windsorfarmshop.co.uk

Order your wild boar or Duchy chicken liver pâté here as just a couple of the mouthwatering options from their delicatessen department, plus a wide variety of meat, fish, dairy, bakery and other products Nothing here is inexpensive but everything is really excellent quality. They don't deliver everything to everywhere in the UK (particularly their bakery items) and they only stock fresh food in the correct season so before you get your hopes up, check exactly what's available to you.

Site Usability:	★★★★★	Based:	UK
Product Range:	★★★★	Express Delivery Option?	(UK) No
Price Range:	<u>Luxury/Medium</u>/Very Good Value	Gift Wrapping Option?	No
Delivery Area:	UK or local depending on the item.	Returns Procedure:	Down to you

Chapter 39

Organics Online

O
rganic food is expensive, there's no doubt. If you go into your local supermarket you'll be horrified at the difference in price between the organic and non-organic fruit and vegetables; I was, anyway.

You may or may not believe that organic foods are better for you and contain more vitamins and minerals. You may or may not think that they taste better. What you can be certain of is that they won't have been treated with chemicals and won't have been genetically modified. In the case of meat and dairy products you'll know that they're almost certainly healthier.

At this point you may be moving on. However, if you are interested in organic products you should pay a visit to the excellent websites listed below, where you can find a wide range on offer, including fruit and vegetables, meat and dairy products, bread, remedies and loads more. Some of these websites will offer you box schemes, where you take a certain box-sized delivery each week and others a complete range of products you can select from.

In the end whether or not you want everything to be organic the choice is yours and made much, much easier by the internet and steadily improving home delivery services. Whereas just a very few years ago you had to buy what was locally available, now you don't, you can go almost totally organic with ease.

Sites to Visit

www.abel-cole.co.uk

Abel & Cole deliver delicious boxes of fresh organic fruit and veg, organic meat, sustainably sourced fish and loads of other ethically produced foods, buying as much as possible from UK farms. They offer regular selection boxes of fresh produce, and providing you live in the South of England then you can order all of their other food and drink too, including locally baked bread. For those who live outside the main area they offer two selections of organic fruit and vegetables.

Site Usability:	★★★★	Based:	UK
Product Range:	★★★	Express Delivery Option?	(UK) No
Price Range:	Luxury/<u>Medium</u>/Very Good Value	Gift Wrapping Option?	No
Delivery Area:	UK	Returns Procedure:	Down to you

www.caleyco.com

Caledonian Foods represent a collective of top quality Scottish suppliers and aims to bring you real fresh food, full of flavour, of the highest quality with complete traceability and provenance. With a network of over 100 independent food producers all their food is fresh, free range, organic and wild. You can select from meat and game, fish and shellfish such as oysters, smoked salmon and hand dived scallops, cheeses, desserts and truffles, wines, whiskies and gifts.

Site Usability:	★★★★★	Based:	Scotland
Product Range:	★★★★	Express Delivery Option?	(UK) No
Price Range:	Luxury/<u>Medium</u>/Very Good Value	Gift Wrapping Option?	No
Delivery Area:	UK	Returns Procedure:	Down to you

www.freshfood.co.uk

This is a prize winning nationwide delivery service of organic and wild harvested foods, and the best way for you to buy from them is to join their box scheme, where you take out a weekly subscription to one or several of their selections. Of course you can cancel this at any time. There's fresh produce such as fruit and veg, meat, fish, game, smoked products, wine and bread, plus lots of recipe ideas. From wild Scottish Salmon to pizzas, if it's organic it'll be here.

Site Usability:	★★★	Based:	UK
Product Range:	★★★★	Express Delivery Option?	(UK) No
Price Range:	Luxury/<u>Medium</u>/Very Good Value	Gift Wrapping Option?	No
Delivery Area:	UK	Returns Procedure:	Down to you

www.goodnessdirect.co.uk

There's really a vast range here with 3000+ health foods, vitamins and items selected for those with special dietary needs. You can search for foods that are dairy free, gluten free, wheat free, yeast free and low fat plus organic fruit, vegetables (in a selection of boxed choices), fish and meat. You'll also find frozen and chilled foods, so you can do your complete shopping here. Don't be worried by the amount of choice, the website is very easy to get round and order from.

Site Usability:	★★★★	Based:	UK
Product Range:	★★★★★	Express Delivery Option?	(UK) No
Price Range:	Luxury/Medium/Very Good Value	Gift Wrapping Option?	No
Delivery Area:	UK	Returns Procedure:	Down to you

www.graigfarm.co.uk

Now in its 19th year, Graig Farm Organics is an award winning pioneer of organic meats and other organic foods in the UK. The range is now very extensive, and includes meat (organic beef, lamb, mutton, pork, chicken and turkey, as well as local game and goat meat), ready meals, fish, baby food, dairy, bread, groceries, vegetables and fruit, soups and salads, alcoholic drinks, a gluten-free range, and even pet food, plus herbal remedies and essential oils.

Site Usability:	★★★★	Based:	UK
Product Range:	★★★★	Express Delivery Option?	(UK) No
Price Range:	Luxury/Medium/Very Good Value	Gift Wrapping Option?	No
Delivery Area:	UK	Returns Procedure:	Down to you

www.organics-4u.co.uk

Organics4u supply top quality organic vegetables, fruit and dry goods direct to your home or place of work anywhere in the UK. Their fruit and vegetables are delivered in boxes of different sizes, and you can choose to have them delivered, weekly, fortnightly or monthly. They also offer dry goods boxes, containing items such as pasta, spices, pulses and oil although you can buy these products separately if you want to.

Site Usability:	★★★★	Based:	UK
Product Range:	★★★	Express Delivery Option?	(UK) No
Price Range:	Luxury/Medium/Very Good Value	Gift Wrapping Option?	No
Delivery Area:	UK	Returns Procedure:	Down to you

www.riverford.co.uk

Riverford Organic Vegetables is situated along the Dart Valley in Devon and delivers fresh organic vegetable boxes direct from the farm to homes across the South of the UK. They started organic vegetable production in 1987 and have become one of the country's largest independent growers, certified by the Soil Association. Simply enter your postcode to check that they deliver to your area (and find out which day) then select which of their fruit and vegetable boxes is most suitable for you.

Site Usability:	★★★★	Based:	UK
Product Range:	★★★★	Express Delivery Option?	(UK) No
Price Range:	Luxury/Medium/Very Good Value	Gift Wrapping Option?	No
Delivery Area:	UK (South)	Returns Procedure:	Down to you

Chapter 40

Speciality Foods, Herbs and Spices

Not only can you buy just about every type of speciality food online from Japanese to Mexican, but you can read up about them, find recipes for each and every one, have them quickly and efficiently delivered and be cooking up a Thai storm in no time (or you can go down to your local Thai takeaway and cheat, as I probably would).

All these websites are offering you much more than ingredients, and they're all run by food enthusiasts, so the next time you're feeling adventurous you can go for it. Be a bit careful of those selling you hot sauces and chillies. If they say 'hot' they probably mean 'burn the roof of your mouth off hot' – much hotter than you can find in a supermarket. Other than that, enjoy.

You can also find excellent places to buy herbs and spices here, from your regular stocks of sea salt and black peppercorns to an enormous range of spices for all sorts of cooking. These are often less expensive than your supermarket spices and of much higher quality, however they will mostly arrive in little plastic bags so you need to keep your original containers.

Sites to Visit

www.bartspicesdirect.co.uk

Bart is a well known name for herbs and spices, and now you can visit their online food hall and buy everything in just a few clicks. They offer a very good range, including their basic collection, plus spice blends such as Creole and Cajun seasoning, coconut and chillies and Thai and fish sauces. You can also dip into their deli and find Amarillo chillies and chilli flakes, curry powder and Harissa paste, saffron and star anise.

Site Usability:	★★★★	Based:	UK
Product Range:	★★★	Express Delivery Option?	(UK) No
Price Range:	Luxury/<u>Medium</u>/Very Good Value	Gift Wrapping Option?	No
Delivery Area:	UK	Returns Procedure:	Down to you

www.coolchile.com

Did you know that the Mexicans have been cooking with chiles/chillies for over 7000 years, and that they name their chillies lovingly according to their shape or taste? Ancho chiles (wide) are named because of their broad shoulders and have a sweet fruity flavour, Piquin chiles (little flea) are blisteringly hot and flea shaped. Chipotle chiles on the other hand are spicy jalapenos that have been smoked to a deep richness and Habanero chiles (from Havana) are deliciously fruity and viciously hot. On this website you can buy all these and more, including tortillas, Mexican oregano and chocolate plus their own range of sauces and salsas.

Site Usability:	★★★★	Based:	UK
Product Range:	★★★	Express Delivery Option?	(UK) No
Price Range:	Luxury/<u>Medium</u>/Very Good Value	Gift Wrapping Option?	No
Delivery Area:	Europe	Returns Procedure:	Down to you

www.culpeper.co.uk

Founded in 1927 by herbalist and writer Hilda Leyel, Culpeper is now the oldest chain of herbal shops in the UK. There's a diverse range of products on their website including candles and skincare, as well as the mainstream range of herbs and spices, sauces, chutneys and mustards. Oh yes, and if you have a sweet tooth, you'll also find Culpeper sweets, honeys and preserves. This is a really attractive website and they'll deliver to you Worldwide.

Site Usability:	★★★★★	Based:	UK
Product Range:	★★★★	Express Delivery Option?	(UK) Yes
Price Range:	Luxury/<u>Medium</u>/Very Good Value	Gift Wrapping Option?	No
Delivery Area:	Worldwide	Returns Procedure:	Down to you

www.hot-headz.com

If you like your dishes to be spiced up and you like the unusual on your table then take a look at this site offering hot everything from sauces, salsas and 'pepperphernalia'. Try 'Ass Kickin' Peach Rum Salsa' or 'Crazy Charlie' marinade and stirfry. Be warned, their 'Mega Death' sauce must be diluted. Don't even think of trying it without and don't think it'll be fun to play a trick on someone and get them to try this neat. It can burn your mouth. Seriously.

Site Usability:	★★★	Based:	UK	
Product Range:	★★★	Express Delivery Option?	(UK) No	
Price Range:	Luxury/<u>Medium</u>/Very Good Value	Gift Wrapping Option?	No	
Delivery Area:	UK	Returns Procedure:	Down to you	

www.japanesekitchen.co.uk

The Japanese Kitchen is based in The Japanese Culture Shop in London and for your next Sushi Party you should definitely take a look at their online shop, where you'll discover all the essential ingredients of Japanese cuisine. These include Miso Pastes, Sushi ingredients, Udon & Soba Noodles, Panko Breadcrumbs, Mirin, Pickles, Ginger, Green Teas, Confectionery, Rice Crackers, Seaweeds, Soy Sauces, & Wasabi. It may be simpler to visit your nearest Yo Sushi but far more fun to make your own.

Site Usability:	★★★★	Based:	UK	
Product Range:	★★★★	Express Delivery Option?	(UK) No	
Price Range:	Luxury/<u>Medium</u>/Very Good Value	Gift Wrapping Option?	No	
Delivery Area:	Worldwide	Returns Procedure:	Down to you	

www.natco-online.com

If you're fond of Indian food and you already cook it yourself or you'd like to try, then take a look at this brightly coloured website specialising in everything for Indian cuisine, including spices and chutneys, curry mixes and curry kits and all types of speciality Indian groceries. They also give some simple curry recipes to complement the curry kits they offer and you can click through their links page to find more recipes and information.

Site Usability:	★★★	Based:	UK	
Product Range:	★★★★	Express Delivery Option?	(UK) No	
Price Range:	Luxury/<u>Medium</u>/Very Good Value	Gift Wrapping Option?	No	
Delivery Area:	Worldwide	Returns Procedure:	Down to you	

www.thespiceshop.co.uk

The Spice Shop offers a range of over 2,500 herbs and spices - one of the widest available in the UK. Many chefs and famous TV cooks frequent the shop and draw upon owner Birgit Erath's skills as a source of inspiration and recipe ideas. To make life easy, they have put together a number of spice bundles that relate to TV cooks and their programmes. So if you are following Delia Smith or Jamie Oliver at the moment then in the Celebrity Cooks section you can order all the recommended spices in one easy package.

Site Usability:	★★★★	Based:	UK
Product Range:	★★★	Express Delivery Option?	(UK) No
Price Range:	Luxury/Medium/Very Good Value	Gift Wrapping Option?	No
Delivery Area:	Worldwide	Returns Procedure:	Down to you

www.saltpepper.co.uk

What's really special about this website, other than the friendly way in which it all comes across, is the amount of information given on every item it sells. That's not to say that there's too much, but everything is written by someone who obviously not only knows their products, but also enjoys using them. So, you'll find salts and peppers, a wide choice of mills, pestles and mortars plus herbs and spices, spice grinders, spice boxes and gift sets.

Site Usability:	★★★★	Based:	UK
Product Range:	★★★★	Express Delivery Option?	(UK) Yes
Price Range:	Luxury/Medium/Very Good Value	Gift Wrapping Option?	Yes
Delivery Area:	UK	Returns Procedure:	Down to you

www.simplyspice.co.uk

Here's one of the widest ranges of authentic Indian foods and spices you can find online, including appetisers and snacks, beans and lentils, chutneys, curry pastes and sauces, Masalas and curry mixes, nuts and dried fruit, oils and ghee, pickles, rice and flour, sweets and desserts. So the next time you consider giving an Indian themed dinner party take a good look round here. This is a very well laid out website with lots of information about Indian culture as well.

Site Usability:	★★★★	Based:	UK
Product Range:	★★★★	Express Delivery Option?	(UK) No
Price Range:	Luxury/Medium/Very Good Value	Gift Wrapping Option?	No
Delivery Area:	UK	Returns Procedure:	Down to you

www.steenbergs.co.uk

This is a really attractive website offering a wide choice of organic salts and peppers, herbs and spices, from succulent vanilla to the heady Herbs de Provence. Most of the herbs and spices are offered in three or four different sizes of jars but if you want a specially large quantity, of their highest quality Tellicherri Garbled Extra Bold black peppercorns for example, then just send them an email or call them. There's also a small selection of Fairtrade tea here and accessories such as unusual salt and pepper mills.

Site Usability:	★★★★★	Based:	UK
Product Range:	★★★	Express Delivery Option?	(UK) Yes
Price Range:	Luxury/Medium/Very Good Value	Gift Wrapping Option?	No
Delivery Area:	Worldwide	Returns Procedure:	Down to you

www.spice-master.com

There's a great selection of herbs and spices from around the World here, where you're best to know what you're looking for and use their search facility if you want to find something quickly. There are dried herbs and spices, pickles, chutneys and pastes, specific areas for Thai, Malay and Chinese foods and spices, fresh chillies, garlic and ginger, all types of salts and peppers and nuts, pulses and lentils. I'll say it again. You really need to know what you want and then search. You'll see why.

Site Usability:	★★★★	Based:	UK
Product Range:	★★★★★	Express Delivery Option?	(UK) Yes
Price Range:	Luxury/Medium/Very Good Value	Gift Wrapping Option?	No
Delivery Area:	Worldwide	Returns Procedure:	Down to you

www.spicesofindia.co.uk

Everything you'd expect here for great Indian cooking, including an excellent choice of (well photographed) pulses and lentils, pickles and chutneys, appetisers, drinks and beverages. They also offer kitchen and tableware such as balti dishes and pickle servers plus gift baskets such as The Pickle Basket and Delux Indian Spice Basket. One of the great things about this website is the amount of information, plus their constantly updated recipe section.

Site Usability:	★★★★	Based:	UK
Product Range:	★★★★★	Express Delivery Option?	(UK) No
Price Range:	Luxury/Medium/Very Good Value	Gift Wrapping Option?	No
Delivery Area:	Worldwide	Returns Procedure:	Down to you

www.wingyip.co.uk

You've probably already tasted their ingredients in your local Chinese restaurant and now you can buy everything you need to create the perfect Chinese meal at home. Select from their sauces, seasonings and condiments, rice and noodles and tinned and preserved foods and buy from their selection of well priced steamers and woks, Chinese tableware and cookbooks. You can also use their Easy Shop to take you straight to the most popular items (as there really is a lot to choose from).

Site Usability:	★★★★	Based:	UK
Product Range:	★★★★	Express Delivery Option?	(UK) Yes
Price Range:	Luxury/Medium/Very Good Value	Gift Wrapping Option?	No
Delivery Area:	Worldwide	Returns Procedure:	Down to you

Chapter 41

Supermarkets

Don't listen to anyone who tells you that UK supermarket shopping online is impossible; that they never deliver on time and that you don't get what you've ordered. The people who tell you that will not have ordered very often and probably gave up before the supermarkets got their act together. They certainly have now. They're almost always totally reliable and the service is fantastic. How did we ever live without it?

All of the supermarkets are now offering you help in getting started online. By far the most important thing is to get your list straight which will then become your 'favourites' shopping list online and you can re-order from it each time you shop. You can also add to it whenever you want to. Once you've done that the weekly shop becomes extremely fast and you'll never go out to do it again.

Deciding on which supermarket you want to go to will depend on the following:

Do you have a particular favourite, which you'd rather use anyway?

Do they deliver in your area?

What kind of service are you looking for?

It really depends on what kind of service you want. Tesco delivers in two-hour slots and you can usually order for the next day. If anyone's going to be less expensive they will, definitely with their own brand. You can gain Air Miles with Tesco, which is great. The downside is that you have to pay for delivery.

Ocado offers free delivery on orders over £75 (at time of writing) and delivers in one-hour slots, and despite their (my opinion) annoying radio ads their service really is friendly and excellent and they totally deserve their success. They have very good fresh goods although they're not always the cheapest but then quality really never is.

Sainsbury is fighting to catch up online and if it's your favourite offline supermarket (where I think they're excellent) you may well want to go there. You'll find good service. At time of writing they're offering free delivery all day Tuesday, Wednesday and Thursday.

These are the sites to visit – they all only deliver in the UK.

www.ocado.com
www.sainsbury.co.uk
www.tesco.com

Note that Tesco is also trying to sell you everything else as well, from books, dvds and flowers to mobile phones. Start with the groceries. The service is great.

Chapter 42

Tea and Coffee

Some people don't drink coffee, or if they do they drink it very, very weak (I'm one of them, I have to admit). Others are quite simply addicts and the numerous Starbucks and Costa (to name but two) coffee places springing up (or that have sprung up) everywhere are feeding this addiction.

Add to that the advances in home coffee making machines – although I'm not sure that cappuccino makers really live up to their expectations (from the frothy point of view) unless they're of the incredibly expensive practically restaurant quality variety – and you can understand why coffee is on the way up.

You really need to know your beans here if you're going to make the most out of these websites, as there's a huge variety. If in doubt email the retailer you like the look of the best and ask for a recommendation to suit your requirements. They're all incredibly knowledgeable and will certainly be delighted to point you in the right direction. The same applies with coffee machines as the choice, again, is enormous and you can spend whatever you want.

If you're a lover of very good tea you'll also find that here, so you can sip your Lapsang Souching, Earl Grey or Camomile in tranquillity, knowing that it's the very best.

Sites to Visit

www.drury.uk.com

Drury have over sixty years experience in blending fine quality teas and roasting the world's finest gourmet coffees. Established in central London in 1936, they remain a family-owned business and supply a huge variety of coffee, both beans and ground. They also offer espresso machines, coffee makers and accessories and are waiting to offer you advice. You can choose from an extensive range of leaf teas and tea bags including black, green, herbal or flavoured and from the finest English Breakfast to aromatic Earl Grey and Lapsang.

Site Usability:	★★★	Based:	UK	
Product Range:	★★★★	Express Delivery Option?	(UK) No	
Price Range:	Luxury/<u>Medium</u>/Very Good Value	Gift Wrapping Option?	No	
Delivery Area:	UK	Returns Procedure:	Down to you	

www.fortnumandmason.com

With its famous name and lovely packaging anything from Fortnum and Mason is a pleasure to buy and receive. Their website now offers tea, coffee, hampers, confectionery, ham and cheeses to name but a few and most items can be delivered all over the World. Don't expect anything to be cheap, here we're talking about real luxury but don't let that put you off. The teas and coffees are beautifully packaged and so make great gifts as well.

Site Usability:	★★★★	Based:	UK	
Product Range:	★★★★	Express Delivery Option?	(UK) No	
Price Range:	<u>Luxury</u>/Medium/Very Good Value	Gift Wrapping Option?	No	
Delivery Area:	Worldwide	Returns Procedure:	Down to you	

www.hasbean.co.uk

If you'd like to be sure that your coffee beans have been specifically roasted for you then buy here, as your coffee will arrive with the 'roasted on' date so you can be sure it'll be extra fresh. There's a wide variety of coffee available here, from Jamaican Blue Mountain Top to Brazil CO2 Decaffeinated plus every type of coffee maker, grinder and pot you can think of, and a great deal of information on which coffee to buy if you're not sure. This is a wonderful website for real coffee enthusiasts.

Site Usability:	★★★★	Based:	UK	
Product Range:	★★★★★	Express Delivery Option?	(UK) No	
Price Range:	Luxury/<u>Medium</u>/Very Good Value	Gift Wrapping Option?	No	
Delivery Area:	Worldwide	Returns Procedure:	Down to you	

www.nespresso.com

If you've already bought one of the coffee machines that takes the Nespresso capsules, or if you're thinking of buying one, this is the place you can buy both and you'll need to order your replacement capsules here as well. It sounds a nuisance but it couldn't be easier. They're based in Beauchamp Place in London and will deliver to you extremely fast. There's a very good selection of coffees from the very strong to decaf (and strong decaf) plus a selection of accessories.

Site Usability:	★★★★★	Based:	
Product Range:	★★★	Express Delivery Option?	(UK) Yes
Price Range:	Luxury/Medium/Very Good Value	Gift Wrapping Option?	No
Delivery Area:	Worldwide	Returns Procedure:	Down to you

www.realcoffee.co.uk

The original founders of the Roast & Post Coffee Company were in the coffee business for over 150 years and owned coffee trading companies and estates in Kenya, Tanzania and Uganda, so now they're using the knowledge and expertise perfected over three generations in roasting and blending the finest coffees in the world. You can buy organic and fairtrade coffees here as well as their blended and premium collections, and obtain lots of information about each one. Tea and coffee making equipment is available here too.

Site Usability:	★★★★	Based:	UK
Product Range:	★★★★	Express Delivery Option?	(UK) Yes
Price Range:	Luxury/Medium/Very Good Value	Gift Wrapping Option?	No
Delivery Area:	Worldwide	Returns Procedure:	Down to you

www.thebeanshop.com

With its clear, well photographed website and excellent selection of coffee, tea and hardware this is a very good place to come to order your next cup. There's a lot of information about all the different ranges plus clear roast/body/acidity/strength ratings so you can see straight away what you're buying. You can also buy espresso machines, coffee grinders, tea pots, milk frothers and unusual (and humorous) mugs and cups.

Site Usability:	★★★★★	Based:	UK
Product Range:	★★★★	Express Delivery Option?	(UK) Yes
Price Range:	Luxury/Medium/Very Good Value	Gift Wrapping Option?	No
Delivery Area:	Worldwide	Returns Procedure:	Down to you

www.whittard.co.uk

Famous for fine tea and coffee since 1886, Whittard of Chelsea offers a wide range of teas and coffees (choose from Monsoon Malabar, Old Brown Java and Very Very Berry Fruit Infusion) and also offers instant flavoured cappuccinos plus coffee and tea gifts. They have a very high quality hot chocolate to order here and you'll also find machines, grinders, roasters and cafetières, accessories and equipment spares as well as very attractive ceramics, fine bone china and seasonal hampers.

Site Usability:	★★★★	Based:	UK
Product Range:	★★★★	Express Delivery Option?	(UK) No
Price Range:	Luxury/Medium/Very Good Value	Gift Wrapping Option?	No
Delivery Area:	Worldwide	Returns Procedure:	Down to you

Chapter 43

Wine, Champagne and Spirits

You're probably thinking, when you compare the number of sites here to those under Tea and Coffee, that this is an area that I prefer. Well, I have to admit you'd be correct. I'd take a glass of champagne over a cup of strong coffee any day.

It's also an area that's growing extremely fast online, with an enormous amount of choice and very high quality service. In terms of competition, if Majestic (UK) stock it, it'll almost certainly be cheaper there, so if you know what you want and you're prepared to buy a dozen bottles check there first.

Also if you know what you want do use the wine price comparison website *www.wine-searcher.com*. I advise you to register for the pro-version as more sites will be listed, not just those that are paying to be there. Type in the particular wine you're looking for, choose your vintage and you'll find all the places you can buy that wine. Do note, however, that these prices do not include VAT, nor do they include any special deals that an outlet such as Majestic may be running so check those too.

Just to wet your appetite take Veuve Cliquot Yellow Label champagne. The lowest price at time of writing is £19.91 and the highest nearly £26. Quite a difference, don't you think?

There are so many wine merchants now online that it would not be possible to list them all (they'd deserve a separate book). Here are some that I consider the best in terms of choice and service. If you don't find what you want, or you'd like more choice, click through to *wine-searcher.com* and you'll discover just about everyone who's selling the type of wine you're looking for. At the same time don't forget to take a look at the wine offers from the supermarkets which are frequently excellent.

Sites to Visit

www.armit.co.uk

This is a young and enthusiastic wine merchant, based in West London, who sell their wines across the world to private individuals, top restaurants and traders alike. They offer a lot of information and advice on their website and they suggest that you create a wish list based on this from which they can place their orders. Their website is particularly easy on the eye so you'll almost certainly enjoy having a look around.

Site Usability:	★★★★★	Based:	UK
Product Range:	★★★★	Express Delivery Option?	(UK) No
Price Range:	Luxury/<u>Medium</u>/Very Good Value	Gift Wrapping Option?	No
Delivery Area:	Worldwide	Returns Procedure:	Down to you

www.ballsbrothers.co.uk

Balls Brothers is a long established business, having shipped and traded wines for over 150 years. You'll discover a handpicked selection of over four hundred wines here, and you can be sure that everything has been carefully chosen from the least expensive (reds starting at around £4.50 a bottle) right up to Chateaux Palmer Margaux at over £100. The search facility is quite difficult to use as you can't see the complete list so just input the type or colour of wine you're looking for and you'll get a selection.

Site Usability:	★★★	Based:	UK
Product Range:	★★★★	Express Delivery Option?	(UK) No
Price Range:	<u>Luxury/Medium</u>/Very Good Value	Gift Wrapping Option?	No
Delivery Area:	Worldwide	Returns Procedure:	Down to you

www.bbr.com

Berry Bros. & Rudd is Britain's oldest wine and spirit merchant, having traded from the same shop for over 300 years. Today members of the Berry and Rudd families continue to own and manage the family-run wine merchant. Their website is a surprisingly busy one. You can not only find out about the wines you should be drinking now but you can also start a BBR Cellar Plan, use their Wedding List services and join their Wine Club.

Site Usability:	★★★★★	Based:	UK
Product Range:	★★★★★	Express Delivery Option?	(UK) Yes
Price Range:	<u>Luxury/Medium</u>/Very Good Value	Gift Wrapping Option?	No
Delivery Area:	Worldwide	Returns Procedure:	Down to you

www.cambridgewine.com

This is a really beautifully designed website from a Cambridge based independent wine merchant and a site that's a pleasure to browse through. You can choose by category and by country, select from their mixed cases and promotional offers and take advantages of their gift and En Primeur services. It's the perfect website if you want one that isn't too busy and where it's very easy to place your order.

Site Usability:	★★★★★	Based:	UK
Product Range:	★★★★★	Express Delivery Option?	(UK) No
Price Range:	Luxury/Medium/Very Good Value	Gift Wrapping Option?	Yes
Delivery Area:	UK	Returns Procedure:	Down to you

www.champagnewarehouse.co.uk

Here is an attractive website from a retailer established just four years ago, to offer personally selected, top quality champagnes throughout the UK. You can buy your champagne by the bottle, six pack or case and prices start at around £14.00 a bottle. They also offer tasting cases containing two different champagnes. The selection of champagnes changes from month to month as their orders arrive.

Site Usability:	★★★★	Based:	UK
Product Range:	★★★	Express Delivery Option?	(UK) No
Price Range:	Luxury/Medium/Very Good Value	Gift Wrapping Option?	No
Delivery Area:	UK	Returns Procedure:	Down to you

www.everywine.co.uk

Everywine is a wine retailer combining an excellent search facility, wines from the reasonably priced to the extremely expensive and some very good deals as well. You do need to buy by the case here, if you want a mixed case then you just click through to their sister site at *www.booths-wine.co.uk*. This is another award winning wine merchant as they won the International Wine Challenge Regional Wine Merchant of the Year 2005.

Site Usability:	★★★★	Based:	UK
Product Range:	★★★★★	Express Delivery Option?	(UK) No
Price Range:	Luxury/Medium/Very Good Value	Gift Wrapping Option?	No
Delivery Area:	UK	Returns Procedure:	Down to you

www.laithwaites.co.uk

Laithwaites are an excellent, family run online (and offline) wine merchant with a really personal and efficient service and a very good choice at all price ranges. They offer wines and champagnes, mixed cases, a wide range of fortified wines and spirits and there's also a clever food matching service plus all the other options you would expect including bin ends, mixed case offers and wine plans.

Site Usability:	★★★★★	Based:	UK
Product Range:	★★★★	Express Delivery Option?	(UK) No
Price Range:	Luxury/Medium/Very Good Value	Gift Wrapping Option?	No
Delivery Area:	UK	Returns Procedure:	Down to you

www.laywheeler.co.uk

Based in Colchester and specialising in Bordeaux and Burgundy, Lay and Wheeler are also agents for wine producers in Australia, California, South Africa and other areas. There's a wide range of wine on offer on this busy website plus assistance if you need it. You can choose from their current offers or the full wine list, use their gift service, view the tastings programme and find out about their Bin Club and Wine Discovery Club as well.

Site Usability:	★★★★	Based:	UK	
Product Range:	★★★★	Express Delivery Option?	(UK) No	
Price Range:	Luxury/Medium/Very Good Value	Gift Wrapping Option?	No	
Delivery Area:	UK	Returns Procedure:	Down to you	

www.majestic.co.uk

You've definitely heard of Majestic, but have you tried their online ordering service, which takes away all the hassle of having to go there, load up and then carry everything from your car when you get home? Not only do they make ordering really easy and offer the best prices on bulk orders, but your nearest branch will give you a call once you've placed your order and bring it to you exactly when you want it. You can order right up to Christmas too.

Site Usability:	★★★★★	Based:	UK
Product Range:	★★★★★	Express Delivery Option?	(UK) Yes if you request it by phone
Price Range:	Luxury/Medium/Very Good Value	Gift Wrapping Option?	No
Delivery Area:	UK	Returns Procedure:	Down to you

www.oddbins.co.uk

The main difference between buying from Oddbins or buying from Majestic is that at Oddbins you don't have to buy twelve bottles and you can still take advantage of lots of their special offers. So if you just want a couple of bottles at a good price (or even two bottles of their Batard Montrachet at £84 each) you should take a look here. It's a cheerful, colourful and easy to get round website and you can also use their weddings and party services.

Site Usability:	★★★★★	Based:	UK
Product Range:	★★★★★	Express Delivery Option?	(UK) No
Price Range:	Luxury/Medium/Very Good Value	Gift Wrapping Option?	No
Delivery Area:	UK	Returns Procedure:	Down to you

www.tanners-wines.co.uk

You'll find a comprehensive range of wine, champagne, liqueurs and spirits on this clear and well laid out site. Tanners are a traditional style wine merchant with a calm style (very different from the 'full on' style of Majestic and Oddbins), offering an excellent service and reasonable prices plus lots of advice and information about everything on offer. So you may not always find the cheapest deals here, but you'll certainly enjoy buying from them.

Site Usability:	★★★★★		Based:	UK
Product Range:	★★★★		Express Delivery Option?	(UK) No
Price Range:	Luxury/Medium/Very Good Value		Gift Wrapping Option?	No
Delivery Area:	UK		Returns Procedure:	Down to you

www.thewhiskyexchange.com

Although you can buy blended and some single malt whiskies from just about every supermarket and wine merchant, if you want a really good selection of specialist whisky you need to have a look here. They offer a very good range from the reasonably priced to the not so reasonably priced and include help and advice for the drinker, collector and the investor. Their list of single malts is amazing and prices go up to (don't faint) over £2000 but of course there are plenty between £20 and £25.

Site Usability:	★★★★★		Based:	UK
Product Range:	★★★★★		Express Delivery Option?	(UK) No
Price Range:	Luxury/Medium/Very Good Value		Gift Wrapping Option?	No
Delivery Area:	Worldwide		Returns Procedure:	Down to you

www.whiskyshop.com

Shop for your malt whisky here by area (if you really know what you're doing) and choose from Speyside, Highland, Islands and Islay. Alternatively choose from their top ten whiskies or simply enter the brand you're looking for. Don't forget to compare prices to make sure that you're getting the best deal, particularly if you're buying something expensive. There is a good range, from Macallan 1951 at £1,500 and Glenfarclas 30 year old at £93 to more regular varieties (and prices).

Site Usability:	★★★★		Based:	UK
Product Range:	★★★★		Express Delivery Option?	(UK) Yes
Price Range:	Luxury/Medium/Very Good Value		Gift Wrapping Option?	No
Delivery Area:	Worldwide		Returns Procedure:	Down to you

www.wine-searcher.com

Looking for a particular vintage of Pomerol? Or just Oyster Bay Chardonnay? With prices differing by as much as 40% you need this fantastic worldwide wine comparison website if you're considering buying more than a single bottle of wine. Do register for the pro-version to get all the benefits.

There are literally hundreds of wine merchants online all over the world and it's simply not possible to list all the good ones. Wine-searcher will take you to many you've never heard of so take a good look at the sites you visit, make sure they're secure, compare the prices and enjoy.

The Gift Shop – Or can you bear to give it away?

The web is the most perfect place to buy gifts. The only real problem for shopaholics is that it's too easy to slip something in for yourself along the way as you're browsing through the enormous choice online. Just a small box of Jo Malone soaps, perhaps, or that sleeveless roll neck cashmere you've been wanting for so, so long.

Don't worry, you deserve it I'm sure. Anyway, with all the time and money you save by not traipsing round the shops buying all those presents, drinking all those cappuccinos and paying for all that parking (or train tickets) you've probably earned it anyway.

You'll find the major gift and gadget sites here offering loads of ideas for things useful, decorative and not so useful. For children, of course, the web makes gift shopping so much easier. No more having to carry large boxes back from the shops of Lego or Micro Machines. If you're looking for something in particular, a hard to find quick selling toy, for example, the web's your best place. Forget about trawling round or phoning up the shops to try and find it. A few clicks and you'll be there, even if you have to import it from abroad.

Many of the websites listed will gift wrap and despatch for you to anywhere in the world and some retailers, such as Penhaligon, Links of London, Jo Malone and Tiffany have gorgeous, luxury packaging as standard which is wonderful when you're getting them to send something out for you.

Don't forget that you'll not only find great gifts here but also throughout the Guide in each section. There are far too many wonderful present giving opportunities to list them all again here, so if you're looking for cashmere, or modern jewellery, or bath and body products to name just a few possibilities, browse through the relevant chapters as well.

Having said all that I've selected for this section a collection of retailers who really make gift giving easier for you. Their products are lovely and their service speedy. So you can just choose from here or look right through. It's entirely up to you.

Chapter 44

Send those Cards and Balloons

Cards are available online for every type of occasion. You can either order e-cards, where what you're sending will arrive by email or cards and balloons by post. Sometimes the e-cards can be very good indeed but you need to make sure that the recipient often opens their email otherwise it'll be entirely wasted. Being someone who lives and breathes (well practically) by email, I find it hard to believe that there are still people who don't use it all the time but I gather there are.

Alternatively you can order single cards by post, where the card company will write your message and send it out for you and frequently here the postage is included in the price. They say the postage is free but who's kidding who? It's still an excellent service. Alternatively just order your cards by the pack or box, fill them in and send them all out yourself. So much better than standing bemused in a card shop wondering which to pick and then giving up when you don't see anything you really like.

There are also loads of websites offering to send balloons out for you and they're usually very good with a reliable service. I've just included two that I've tried and tested and I know through experience that if you want to send Good Luck, Get Well, or Congratulations to someone, particularly a younger person, they're always welcome and raise a smile.

I've included the site address for the Royal Mail as you can now buy your stamps online. You have to order quite a number so it may well only work for you around Christmas time but it certainly saves a visit to the Post Office, a personal hate of mine. You can buy your Christmas and special edition stamps online too, or use their SmartStamp system and print your own postage.

With the reminder services that most of the card sites offer, you can put away the Birthday book you so often forget to open and get email reminders in good time. Of course you don't have to order a card from the company sending you the reminder, but the choice is yours and you'll never forget those important dates again.

Sites to Visit

www.balloonstation.com

If you want to escape from the traditional and you want to surprise someone then why not send a balloon in a box, which you can send with your personal message or anonymously? The large box arrives and when opened out floats a huge balloon with Happy Birthday or Good Luck (or whatever occasion you're aiming at) printed on it.

Site Usability:	★★★★	Based:	UK
Product Range:	★★★	Express Delivery Option?	(UK) Yes
Price Range:	Luxury/<u>Medium</u>/Very Good Value	Gift Wrapping Option?	N/A
Delivery Area:	UK	Returns Procedure:	N/A

www.charitycards.co.uk

On this site there are some lovely cards for every single type of occasion plus thank-you cards and luxury Christmas cards, Advent calendars and stocking fillers (for girls). You can also order your printed Christmas cards here and if you buy ten or more cards shipping is free. When you're ordering your Christmas cards you can buy books of Christmas stamps at the checkout.

Site Usability:	★★★★★	Based:	UK
Product Range:	★★★★★	Express Delivery Option?	(UK) Yes
Price Range:	Luxury/<u>Medium</u>/Very Good Value	Gift Wrapping Option?	N/A
Delivery Area:	Worldwide	Returns Procedure:	N/A

www.clintoncards.co.uk

Here you can order a card for a wide selection of occasions, to be sent to you to send to the recipient, or for Clinton to personalise on your behalf. You can also use their reminder service for future birthdays and anniversaries. It's quite an attractive and unusual website, with links to other gift websites on the home page and information about who did what on the day you've chosen to visit the site.

Site Usability:	★★★★★	Based:	UK
Product Range:	★★★★	Express Delivery Option?	(UK) Yes
Price Range:	Luxury/<u>Medium</u>/Very Good Value	Gift Wrapping Option?	N/A
Delivery Area:	Worldwide	Returns Procedure:	N/A

www.moonpig.com

There are more than enough cards here for whenever you might need them and they'll personalise them for you and send them out within 24 hours. It's a very good site, quick and easy to get round with some excellent cards for birthdays where you can change the name and date to that of the recipient. They really are very funny (provided you want funny) and there's everything else as well. They also offer a very good and reliable service.

Site Usability:	★★★★★	Based:	UK
Product Range:	★★★★★	Express Delivery Option?	(UK) Yes
Price Range:	Luxury/Medium/Very Good Value	Gift Wrapping Option?	N/A
Delivery Area:	Worldwide	Returns Procedure:	N/A

www.royalmail.com

Go to their 'Buy Online' section and order your books of stamps here (or your Special Editions or ready stamped envelopes). You do have to order quite a lot of stamps but it's the easiest way if you're going to be posting a lot of mail in the near future. Alternatively download 'SmartStamp', which allows you to print your postage directly onto your envelopes from your own printer.

Site Usability:	★★★★★	Based:	UK
Product Range:	★★★★★	Express Delivery Option?	(UK) Yes
Price Range:	N/A	Gift Wrapping Option?	N/A
Delivery Area:	UK	Returns Procedure:	N/A

www.sharpcards.com

Cards for anniversaries, weddings, Easter, Valentines, birthdays or Christmas with handwritten greetings and sent out for you. They also have a very good address book and reminder service, so you won't ever forget that birthday or anniversary again and this is one of the best parts of the website. The site is very clear and easy to use but the range of cards is not as large as on some others so have a look round at several before choosing.

Site Usability:	★★★★★	Based:	UK
Product Range:	★★★★	Express Delivery Option?	(UK) Yes
Price Range:	Luxury/Medium/Very Good Value	Gift Wrapping Option?	N/A
Delivery Area:	Worldwide	Returns Procedure:	N/A

www.skyhi.co.uk

Sky Hi balloons will deliver anything from a single balloon in a box with your message to a huge bouquet of balloons. They also offer a same day delivery service which, although expensive, can be a lifesaver if you've forgotten an important event and want to make a statement. They're very reliable too, which is essential if you're going for the last minute panic send, and you'll find balloons here for just about every type of occasion.

Site Usability:	★★★★	Based:	UK
Product Range:	★★★★	Express Delivery Option?	(UK) Yes
Price Range:	Luxury/Medium/Very Good Value	Gift Wrapping Option?	N/A
Delivery Area:	UK	Returns Procedure:	N/A

Chapter 45

Chocolates for Chocoholics

I'm not sure that I need to say very much about buying chocolates online. All the websites listed below offer an excellent service, some try to offer you loads of other gifts and goodies alongside the chocolates (although I've never been sure why anyone would want to send a teddy with chocolates but apparently they do), and some just offer you absolutely mouthwatering selections of sweet things.

There is a wide range of prices here so set a budget in your mind before you go browsing or you'll almost certainly overspend and after all, we are talking about chocolates here (maybe I don't really understand this chocoholics thing, sorry, the shopaholic version I'm totally in line with).

You'll find everything from top brand name chocolates and truffles from producers such as Godiva, Leonidas, Ackerman and Charbonel and Walker and the better priced selections from Thorntons and Groovy Chocolate. Both taste and price will depend on the quality of the cocoa used, and if you really love chocolate you should certainly join the Chocolate Tasting Club at *hotelchocolat.com* to make sure that you get to try everything too and don't just give them away.

If you'd like more information about what you're buying and why the costs are so different, click through to *chocolatetradingco.com* and their 'chocolate knowledge' section where there's a wealth of information on the history of chocolate and what makes special, high priced chocolate special. It really is quite interesting and you probably won't ever want to buy or send cheap chocolate again.

Sites to Visit

www.chococo.co.uk

This is a small husband and wife-led team based in Purbeck in Dorset. Passionate about proper chocolate, they've developed their own, totally unique, award winning range of fresh chocolates in vibrant, stylish packaging. Here you'll find goodies such as Chilli Tickles and Raspberry Riots, a range of Hamper Boxes, hand-dipped organic fruits including apricots, figs and prunes, and Granny's award-winning Tablet (Scottish style fudge). Irresistible.

Site Usability:	★★★★	Based:	UK
Product Range:	★★★	Express Delivery Option?	(UK) Yes
Price Range:	Luxury/<u>Medium</u>/Very Good Value	Gift Wrapping Option?	No
Delivery Area:	Europe	Returns Procedure:	Down to you

www.chocolatebuttons.co.uk

LET YOUR CHILDREN ON THIS WEBSITE AT YOUR PERIL. From old fashioned sherbert to Toblerone, chocolate coins, novelties and gifts, jelly beans and natural candy canes this site is a cornucopia of irresistible sweets. Not only that, but you can buy in quantity here. They won't stop you from buying one bag of chocolate Victorian coins, but why not buy 30? Surely you'll find a use for them.

Site Usability:	★★★★	Based:	UK
Product Range:	★★★★	Express Delivery Option?	(UK) Yes
Price Range:	Luxury/<u>Medium</u>/Very Good Value	Gift Wrapping Option?	Yes for their gift packs
Delivery Area:	Worldwide	Returns Procedure:	Down to you

www.groovychocolate.co.uk

As well as offering boxes of chocolates you can also choose a design from their wide range to suit any occasion, and Groovy Chocolate will paint it onto a chocolate bar with the message of your choice. These are great for children who may be bored with the usual Easter egg or stocking fillers. They also offer luxury truffles and boxes of chocolates with names such as Seven Deadly Sins, chocolate beer mugs and chocolate champagne truffles and specialities for all types of occasion.

Site Usability:	★★★★★	Based:	UK
Product Range:	★★★★	Express Delivery Option?	(UK) Yes
Price Range:	Luxury/<u>Medium</u>/Very Good Value	Gift Wrapping Option?	No but beautifully presented
Delivery Area:	Worldwide	Returns Procedure:	Down to you

www.hotelchocolat.co.uk

This is a really lovely and well designed website with a large selection of beautifully packaged chocolates. Send someone a Chocogram Delux or Champagne Truffles or let them choose, and order their Seasonal Selection. They also have some unusual goodies such as Strawberries in White Chocolate, Christmas Crates and Chocolate Logs, Goody Bags and Rocky Road Slabs. Resist if you can.

Site Usability:	★★★★★	Based:	UK
Product Range:	★★★★★	Express Delivery Option?	(UK) Yes
Price Range:	<u>Luxury/Medium</u>/Very Good Value	Gift Wrapping Option?	No
Delivery Area:	Worldwide	Returns Procedure:	Down to you

www.leonidasbelgianchocolates.co.uk

For the ultimate in Belgian chocolates click through to this dedicated website and make your choice. First you choose the size of box you want to order and then choose from the chocolate menu with possibilities such as Butter Creams, General Assortment, milk or dark chocolates, Neapolitans and Liqueurs, all of which will be boxed up and despatched to wherever you choose.

Site Usability:	★★★★	Based:	UK
Product Range:	★★★	Express Delivery Option?	(UK) Yes
Price Range:	<u>Luxury/Medium</u>/Very Good Value	Gift Wrapping Option?	No
Delivery Area:	UK	Returns Procedure:	Down to you

www.chocolatetradingco.com

Here's a mouthwatering selection of chocolates, from Charbonel et Walker serious chocolate indulgences and chocoholics hampers, to funky and fun chocolates such as chocolate sardines and Jungle Crunch. They'll send out your chocolates for you with a personalised gift card and give you lots of information on how to know when you taste the best.

Site Usability:	★★★★★	Based:	UK
Product Range:	★★★★	Express Delivery Option?	(UK) Yes
Price Range:	Luxury/<u>Medium</u>/Very Good Value	Gift Wrapping Option?	Yes
Delivery Area:	UK	Returns Procedure:	Down to you

www.thehouseofchocolates.co.uk

If your taste is for the top brand chocolates such as those from Godiva and Ackerman to Charbonel et Walker and Neuhaus then this is the place for you. There's a lot to choose from – a chocolate heart box or chocolate covered crystallised ginger from Charbonel, Ackerman's luxurious truffles, luxury boxes from Godiva and Duchy of Cornwall Chocolate Mint Thins. There's quite a wide price range from the reasonable to the truly expensive and you'll also find diabetic, Kosher and dairy free chocolates as well.

Site Usability:	★★★★★	Based:	UK
Product Range:	★★★★	Express Delivery Option?	(UK) Yes
Price Range:	<u>Luxury/Medium</u>/Very Good Value	Gift Wrapping Option?	No but beautifully presented
Delivery Area:	Worldwide	Returns Procedure:	Down to you

www.thorntons.co.uk

Thorntons are ideal for Easter, Birthdays, Anniversaries and Weddings, or simply when you want to treat yourself. You can buy their delicious chocolate hampers, choose 800g of continental chocolates or one of Thorntons' classic boxes and you'll also find gifts to add such as wine, flowers and Steiff bears. As well as all of this they have a small collection of cards which they'll personalise for you and send out with your gift.

Site Usability:	★★★★★	Based:	UK
Product Range:	★★★★★	Express Delivery Option?	(UK) Yes
Price Range:	Luxury/Medium/Very Good Value	Gift Wrapping Option?	No
Delivery Area:	Worldwide for most products	Returns Procedure:	Down to you

Chapter 46

Flowers

I t's never been easier to send flowers online. Some of the very best florists have taken beautiful pictures of their specialities and placed them online for you to choose from. Names such as Jane Packer and Kenneth Turner have cleverly designed websites just waiting to entice you to order, and on some of them you may well be tempted to order something for your own home as well as to send to friends.

You can order flowers at all price levels, from very good value (from somewhere like *bunches.co.uk*) to what would seem to be extremely expensive. Thank goodness there are quite a number in the middle range probably roughly equalling what you would expect to spend in your local flower shop, say £30–£50. Needless to say the sky's the limit if you want to spend a lot. You can also, on some websites, specify in advance the date you want your flowers delivered. You'll find a particularly good and well priced service of this kind at *www.johnlewis.com* (yes really).

Happily this is an area where you can almost always get an express delivery, in most cases provided you order by mid day the day before. So the next time you forget a special occasion, wherever you are in the World, you can do something about it fast.

Sites to Visit

www.bloom.uk.com

If you're fed up of chucking out dead flowers and having to spend real money to replace them then take a look at this website, offering the new generation of silk flowers online. They are incredibly real looking in most cases (you may well have admired some in a friend's house without realising they were silk, I certainly have) and they offer all types of arrangements from Dorset cream roses and cabbages to really pretty orchids and seasonal arrangements.

Site Usability:	★★★★★	Based:	UK
Product Range:	★★★★	Express Delivery Option?	(UK) Yes
Price Range:	Luxury/Medium/Very Good Value	Gift Wrapping Option?	No
Delivery Area:	UK	Returns Procedure:	Down to you

www.bunches.co.uk

What you'll find here is really excellent value for money. There are very few florists who will offer to send out for you flowers by post for under £20 (including delivery), and although these may not be the most sophisticated of flowers if you really don't want to spend too much you certainly should have a look. They also have a luxury bouquet selection and rose bouquets and nothing is unreasonably priced. You can include the usual chocolates, teddies and mini birthday cakes.

Site Usability:	★★★★	Based:	UK
Product Range:	★★★	Express Delivery Option?	(UK) Yes
Price Range:	Luxury/Medium/Very Good Value	Gift Wrapping Option?	Automatic
Delivery Area:	UK	Returns Procedure:	N/A

www.crocus.co.uk

Crocus believe that you should know more about the flowers you give than just what they look like, so they take the trouble to tell you not only exactly what will be going into your bouquet but what each of the flowers means, such as the fact that lilies are ancient symbols of perfection, and roses are for those who deserve the best in life. It may sound a bit over the top, however it does make buying flowers much more interesting, and although there's only a small collection to choose from you'll no doubt want to visit other parts of this gardeners' paradise.

Site Usability:	★★★★★	Based:	UK
Product Range:	★★★	Express Delivery Option?	(UK) Yes
Price Range:	Luxury/Medium/Very Good Value	Gift Wrapping Option?	Automatic
Delivery Area:	UK	Returns Procedure:	N/A

www.davidaustin.com

David Austin is famous for developing new types of English Roses, with his first, 'Constance Spry', launched in 1963. On his website you can find many varieties, including Modern Hybrid Tea Roses and Floribundas, Climbing Roses, Ramblers, Modern Shrub Roses and Wild Species Roses. You'll also find his new fragrant English Roses created specially for the home. You can order his gift boxed container roses and exquisite rose bouquets here as well for UK delivery.

Site Usability:	★★★★★	Based:	UK
Product Range:	★★★★	Express Delivery Option?	(UK) Yes
Price Range:	Luxury/Medium/Very Good Value	Gift Wrapping Option?	Yes for Container Roses
Delivery Area:	Worldwide except for container roses and bouquets	Returns Procedure:	Down to you

www.designerflowers.org.uk

At Designer Flowers all the arrangements are created by their own florists and delivered direct by courier in secure boxes to London and the UK. You can also include Champagne, Belgian chocolates and soft toys and choose from their selection of occasions. Prices are not inexpensive and delivery is extra at £4.50. You can order from them for next day delivery or they'll use their network of florists if you want delivery on the same day.

Site Usability:	★★★★★	Based:	UK
Product Range:	★★★★	Express Delivery Option?	(UK) Yes
Price Range:	Luxury/Medium/Very Good Value	Gift Wrapping Option?	Automatic
Delivery Area:	UK	Returns Procedure:	N/A

www.flowergram.co.uk

On this website you can buy reasonably priced and very attractive hand tied flower bouquets. You also have the opportunity of choosing between small, medium and large size bouquets depending on how much you want to spend. All prices include delivery and if you order before mid day your choice can be delivered the same day. If you want to send flowers to someone overseas you can do this here as well.

Site Usability:	★★★★★	Based:	UK
Product Range:	★★★★	Express Delivery Option?	(UK) Yes
Price Range:	Luxury/Medium/Very Good Value	Gift Wrapping Option?	Automatic
Delivery Area:	Worldwide	Returns Procedure:	N/A

www.flowersdirect.co.uk

You'll find a good collection of hand tied and traditional bouquets here (and you can choose the size you want to send) with a same day delivery option if you order before 2pm, Monday to Saturday.

Choose one of their exotic arrangements if you want to give something a bit different with names such as Oriental Orchids and Exotic Paradise and if you want to you can include the extras such as wine and champagne, spirits, chocolates, balloons and cuddly toys.

Site Usability:	★★★★	Based:	UK
Product Range:	★★★★	Express Delivery Option?	(UK) Yes
Price Range:	Luxury/Medium/Very Good Value	Gift Wrapping Option?	Automatic
Delivery Area:	UK	Returns Procedure:	N/A

www.hayesflorist.co.uk

Well priced and attractive planters and hand tied bunches, international delivery and same day delivery are some of the services offered here. The designs are essentially modern and beautifully photographed, so you can see exactly what you're ordering, from the Heavenly Rose hand tied to the Autumn Planter or Conservatory Basket. You can include chocolates, balloons, champagne and candles with your order or select from one of their ready designed gift sets.

Site Usability:	★★★★	Based:	UK
Product Range:	★★★★	Express Delivery Option?	(UK) Yes
Price Range:	Luxury/Medium/Very Good Value	Gift Wrapping Option?	Automatic
Delivery Area:	Worldwide	Returns Procedure:	N/A

www.janepackerdelivered.com

Here are the most beautifully presented, modern flowers to send as a gift or if you want to give yourself a treat, to yourself. The range in her stores is much larger than what's offered online, but here you'll find roses, hyacinths, pink parrot tulips, orchids and mixed bouquets all presented in her unique, chic style. You can buy Jane Packer's books, fragranced bath and body gifts, champagne and chocolates and gift vouchers here as well.

Site Usability:	★★★★★	Based:	UK
Product Range:	★★★	Express Delivery Option?	(UK) Yes
Price Range:	Luxury/Medium/Very Good Value	Gift Wrapping Option?	Automatic
Delivery Area:	UK	Returns Procedure:	N/A

www.mkn.co.uk/flower/

This retailer has determinedly stayed with its techie inspired design which may well put you off at first but do persevere. They offer a lovely selection of flowers which they'll deliver the same day if you order before 1pm. The hand tied bunches are particularly pretty and modern and not overpriced. You won't find a huge choice, but what's there is very good and some arrangements are quite unusual. Also here you'll find a range of unusual mini fruit trees such as fruit and nut trees (think crab apple, pear and mulberry), ornamentals and shrubs to send as gifts.

Site Usability:	★★★	Based:	UK
Product Range:	★★★★	Express Delivery Option?	(UK) Yes
Price Range:	Luxury/<u>Medium</u>/Very Good Value	Gift Wrapping Option?	Automatic
Delivery Area:	UK	Returns Procedure:	N/A

www.serenataflowers.com

A very well designed website where you'll discover an extremely good selection of not overpriced flowers. Their selection menus are clear and easy to use – choose your flower style from contemporary, elegant or simple, your occasion from birthday, anniversary etc and colours red, white orange or green. Select the type of bouquet, the price you want to pay or the variety of flower.

Site Usability:	★★★★★	Based:	UK
Product Range:	★★★★	Express Delivery Option?	(UK) Yes
Price Range:	Luxury/<u>Medium</u>/Very Good Value	Gift Wrapping Option?	Automatic
Delivery Area:	UK	Returns Procedure:	N/A

You'll also find a very pretty selection of well priced flowers and very good service at:

www.marksandspencer.co.uk
www.johnlewis.com
www.thorntons.co.uk

Chapter 47

Pamper Someone

There are so many wonderful websites online where you can find all sorts of pampering gifts, from luxurious and unusual scented candles to pretty cosmetic bags and gorgeous bath and body products such as bath truffles, body shimmer and fragrance to beaded slippers, the softest hand made bath robes and embroidered jewellery rolls.

You'll also discover places where you can book spa days and breaks as gifts, where the retailer will send out a gift voucher and brochure for you for the place you've chosen, and the person you're giving it to just has to book in and relax (hopefully you'll get to go too).

You're unlikely to go wrong on these websites, not only are the products very attractive and frequently well priced, but the retailers themselves are some of the best at pretty packaging, express delivery and often overseas shipping, making sure that what arrives is simply a joy to receive.

You'll notice that these online retailers are mostly different from those in the Pamper Yourself section of the guide, so to make sure you really have lots of choice you should take a look at those as well.

Sites to Visit

www.ancienneambiance.com

The Ancienne Ambiance concept of antiquity-inspired luxury goods has been designed and developed by Adriana Carlucci, a graduate of the London College of Fashion with a degree in product development. She began by creating a unique collection of six glass encased candles, each featuring fragrances evocative of an ancient culture together with elegant hand-crafted packaging. You'll also discover small inserts made of authentic hand-made Egyptian papyrus which carry the description and the ancient associations of each scent used.

Site Usability:	★★★★	Based:	UK
Product Range:	★★★	Express Delivery Option?	(UK) Yes
Price Range:	Luxury/Medium/Very Good Value	Gift Wrapping Option?	Yes
Delivery Area:	Worldwide	Returns Procedure:	Down to you

www.gorgeousthingsonline.com

This is a mixture of pampering gifts, including candles by Arco, bath melts and bath truffles by Di Palomo, Nougat London Body Shimmer and moisturising soap plus pretty bathroom accessories, throws and blankets and attractive cushions. Everything is beautifully photographed and extremely tempting and nothing is overpriced.

Site Usability:	★★★★	Based:	UK
Product Range:	★★★	Express Delivery Option?	(UK) No
Price Range:	Luxury/Medium/Very Good Value	Gift Wrapping Option?	Yes
Delivery Area:	Worldwide	Returns Procedure:	Down to you

www.kiarie.co.uk

Kiarie has one of the best ranges of scented candles, by brands such as Geodosis, Kenneth Turner, Manuel Canovas, Creation Mathias, Rigaud and Millefiori – there are literally hundreds to choose from at all price levels (this site is very fast, so don't panic) and you can also choose your range by price, maker, fragrance, colour and season. Once you've made your selection you can ask them to gift wrap it for you and include a hand written message.

Site Usability:	★★★★★	Based:	UK
Product Range:	★★★★★	Express Delivery Option?	(UK) Yes
Price Range:	Luxury/Medium/Very Good Value	Gift Wrapping Option?	Yes
Delivery Area:	Worldwide	Returns Procedure:	Down to you

www.leadingspasoftheworld.com

All you need to know is when you want to go (did I say this was for a gift? I must have been mad), roughly where you want to go, i.e. which country and you're away. Use their excellent search facility to find the most luxurious spas throughout the world, where you can choose from spas with hydrotherapy, Ayurvedic spas, spas with Yoga, Pilates and Tai Chi or somewhere gorgeous to just relax and be pampered. If you are going to choose one of these as a gift, make absolutely sure you're free to go as well.

Site Usability:	★★★★★	Based:	
Product Range:	★★★★★	Express Delivery Option?	(UK)
Price Range:	Luxury/Medium/Very Good Value	Gift Wrapping Option?	
Delivery Area:	Worldwide	Returns Procedure:	

www.lessenteurs.com

Les Senteurs is a famous parfumery based in London, offering different and unusual fragrance and bath and body products and an excellent service. Brands they offer are Creed, Annick Goutal, Diptyque, E Coudray, Serge Lutens, Carons and Parfums Historique to name but a few and the ranges are split into categories, such as fragrance, bath and body and then fragrance notes, such as citrus, oriental or fruity.

Site Usability:	★★★	Based:	UK
Product Range:	★★★★	Express Delivery Option?	(UK) No
Price Range:	Luxury/Medium/Very Good Value	Gift Wrapping Option?	Yes
Delivery Area:	UK	Returns Procedure:	Down to you

www.millerharris.com

If you'd like to give someone a gorgeous fragrance or bath and body product which is not so well known, then Miller Harris may have the answer. This is a small, independent company which specialises in blending its own fragrances, which have enticing names such as Tangerine Vert, Fleur Oriental and Terre de Bois. In each one you'll find not only the Eau de Parfum, but bath and body products and candles as well.

Site Usability:	★★★★	Based:	UK
Product Range:	★★★	Express Delivery Option?	(UK) Yes
Price Range:	Luxury/Medium/Very Good Value	Gift Wrapping Option?	Yes
Delivery Area:	Worldwide	Returns Procedure:	Down to you

www.parkscandles.com

Parks Candles has an easy to get round website offering a beautiful range of scented candles in decorative containers. Three wick candles in silver bowls, perfumed candles in glass containers with silver lids and scented dinner candles in green, burgundy or cream, are just some of the selection. Delivery is excellent and the prices are less than you find in most shops.

Site Usability:	★★★★★	Based:	UK	
Product Range:	★★★	Express Delivery Option?	(UK) Automatic	
Price Range:	Luxury/Medium/Very Good Value	Gift Wrapping Option?	No	
Delivery Area:	Worldwide	Returns Procedure:	Down to you	

www.serendipbeauty.com

Next time you're looking for a pampering beauty/gift website which is also a pleasurable and relaxing shopping experience then click onto this new website. Products on offer include Burt's Bees, Cowshed, Croft + Croft, Fruits and Passion, Jane Packer, Korres, Manuel Canovas and Tocca and if that's not enough there are lots of pretty gift sets to choose from plus really cute make-up bags and wash bags by Zoe Phayre-Mudge.

Site Usability:	★★★★★	Based:	UK	
Product Range:	★★★	Express Delivery Option?	(UK) No	
Price Range:	Luxury/Medium/Very Good Value	Gift Wrapping Option?	No	
Delivery Area:	Worldwide	Returns Procedure:	Down to you	

www.spabreak.co.uk

Spa Break offer comprehensive information on luxury spas all over the UK, with plenty of advice and pictures to help you make up your mind as to which to choose. You can purchase a Gift Voucher for a specific monetary value, or you can select a voucher for a specific type of break and these can be sent to you or whoever you want, together with the relevant colour brochure. You can see exactly where each of the spas are in the UK and call for advice if you need to.

Site Usability:	★★★★★	Based:	UK	
Product Range:	★★★★	Express Delivery Option?	(UK) N/A	
Price Range:	Luxury/Medium/Very Good Value	Gift Wrapping Option?	N/A	
Delivery Area:	UK	Returns Procedure:	N/A	

www.thanksdarling.com

Yes thanks indeed, here are some wonderful pampering spa breaks and days out, mainly in the south of England, where on ordering you (or your chosen recipient) are sent an open dated voucher pack for the break you've chosen, whether it's a 'Special Chill Out Spa Break for Two' or just a 'Luxury Pamper Day'. You'll no doubt be extremely popular if you give one of these as a gift for someone and hopefully you'll be invited along.

Site Usability:	★★★★	Based:	UK	
Product Range:	★★★★	Express Delivery Option?	(UK) No	
Price Range:	Luxury/Medium/Very Good Value	Gift Wrapping Option?	N/A	
Delivery Area:	UK	Returns Procedure:	N/A	

www.truegrace.co.uk

If you want to pamper someone with something small and beautiful and you don't want to spend a fortune you should choose from the gorgeous candles here. All beautifully wrapped and in glass containers, you'll find the 'Never a Dull Day' range in pretty printed boxes with fragrances such as Vine Tomato, Stem Ginger and Hyacinth and 'As it Should Be' the slightly more simply (but equally attractively) boxed candle in thirty seven fragrances including Citrus, Cappucino and Raspberry. Try them.

Site Usability:	★★★★	Based:	UK
Product Range:	★★★★	Express Delivery Option?	(UK) No
Price Range:	Luxury/<u>Medium</u>/Very Good Value	Gift Wrapping Option?	No
Delivery Area:	Worldwide	Returns Procedure:	Down to you

www.waxandwane.co.uk

This is an unsophisticated website offering a large choice of well priced candles where the selection is almost too much, however, persevere, because if you don't want to pay the earth and you know someone (don't we all) who loves prettily packaged, good quality (and hand poured) scented candles, you will definitely find something here. Fragrances range from Cinnamon and Cashmere to Bergamot and Bay leaf, and Vanilla.

Site Usability:	★★★	Based:	UK
Product Range:	★★★★	Express Delivery Option?	(UK) No
Price Range:	Luxury/<u>Medium</u>/Very Good Value	Gift Wrapping Option?	No
Delivery Area:	Worldwide	Returns Procedure:	Down to you

www.zpm.com

If you know someone who does a lot of travelling then you'll find a perfect gift here, as ZPM specialise in really pretty and useful make-up bags – everything from small cosmetic purses to hanging weekenders, all in a range of patterns. As well as these you'll find ideas for kids and babies and some attractive laundry and kitchen accessories. There's also a gift finder by occasion or personality to make life even easier.

Site Usability:	★★★★	Based:	UK
Product Range:	★★★	Express Delivery Option?	(UK) Yes
Price Range:	Luxury/<u>Medium</u>/Very Good Value	Gift Wrapping Option?	No
Delivery Area:	Worldwide	Returns Procedure:	Down to you

Other websites to visit for pampering gifts

Website Address	You'll find them in
www.arranaromatics.com	Pamper Yourself
www.cologneandcotton.com	Pamper Yourself
www.escentual.co.uk	Pamper Yourself
www.jomalone.co.uk	Pamper Yourself
www.kennethturner.co.uk	Pamper Yourself
www.laboutiquedelartisanparfumeur.com	Pamper Yourself
www.ormondejayne.co.uk	Pamper Yourself
www.penhaligons.co.uk	Pamper Yourself
www.garden.co.uk	Pamper Yourself

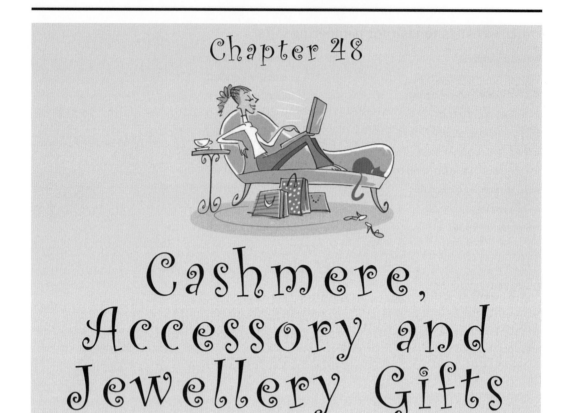

Chapter 48

Cashmere, Accessory and Jewellery Gifts

*A*lthough you can, of course, find a wide range of knitwear, accessories and jewellery in the fashion section of this Guide, sometimes it's easier just to be taken to a smaller selection of excellent websites offering not only a good choice of ideas, but also the extra services such as gift wrapping, express delivery when you need it and overseas shipping so that you can send something to that friend you don't see very often (or better still, deliver it yourself).

Accessories cover a wide range of products, needless to say, from handbags costing hundreds of pounds to high quality gloves, belts, scarves and shawls. Here's just one piece of advice. Don't buy cheap pashminas from anywhere. You'll always be disappointed.

As far as jewellery goes of course the sky's the limit and, if you are looking to spend a lot, you can take a look at the luxury websites below or the jewellery section within Fashion at a Click. I've included here websites who offer you fun and pretty jewellery, using semi-precious stones and modern designs, assuming that it's an unusual and attractive present you're after, not a ten carat diamond but hey, you can find those as well.

Sites to Visit

www.austique.co.uk

Here's a very attractive and well designed website offering a bit of everything; accessories, lingerie, Rococo chocolates, modern jewellery and unusual bathroom treats such as Limoncello Body Butter and Arnaud Chamomile and Lavender Bubble Bath. The offers change frequently depending on the season. They offer you gift wrapping, express delivery and international orders by special request.

Site Usability:	★★★★	Based:	UK
Product Range:	★★★	Express Delivery Option?	(UK) Yes
Price Range:	Luxury/<u>Medium</u>/Very Good Value	Gift Wrapping Option?	Yes
Delivery Area:	Worldwide	Returns Procedure:	Down to you

www.bootik.co.uk

On this well laid out website you'll find lots of gift ideas, from pretty, well priced jewellery set with semi-precious stones, beaded bags and attractive cosmetic bags, bath and body products, unusual cushions and tableware and a small and very different (but not so inexpensive) collection of clothes. Most of the items here can't be found elsewhere so it could be well worth having a look round.

Site Usability:	★★★	Based:	UK
Product Range:	★★★	Express Delivery Option?	(UK) Yes
Price Range:	Luxury/<u>Medium</u>/Very Good Value	Gift Wrapping Option?	Yes
Delivery Area:	Worldwide	Returns Procedure:	Down to you

www.boutiquetoyou.co.uk

This is a cross between a hip website selling hand painted Art and Sole Scholl sandals and fab maternity t-shirts to a gift site offering quite expensive jewellery (and really cheap jewellery too), aromatherapy treats, gadgets and flowers. There are departments for all sorts of occasions and in each one you'll find a wide range of products and price levels.

Site Usability:	★★★	Based:	UK
Product Range:	★★★★	Express Delivery Option?	(UK) No
Price Range:	Luxury/<u>Medium</u>/Very Good Value	Gift Wrapping Option?	Yes
Delivery Area:	Worldwide	Returns Procedure:	Down to you

www.brora.co.uk

If you gave anything from this lovely cashmere website you would definitely be in favour as the quality is really high and there are lots of lovely colours to choose from. Although this is definitely not the cheapest place to buy cashmere, they've cleverly put together a collection of gifts, starting at under £50, which include fine plain coloured and lacy knit scarves. They'll beautifully gift wrap as well.

Site Usability:	★★★★★	Based:	UK
Product Range:	★★★★	Express Delivery Option?	(UK) Yes
Price Range:	Luxury/Medium/Very Good Value	Gift Wrapping Option?	Yes
Delivery Area:	Worldwide	Returns Procedure:	Down to you

www.butlerandwilson.co.uk

Famous for their signature whimsical fashion jewellery you can now choose from a glamorous and well priced range online of necklaces, bracelets, earrings and brooches. Both costume jewellery and jewellery using semi-precious stones such as rose quartz, agate, amber and jade are available. You'll also find a range of very pretty printed and beaded handbags plus tops and skirts.

Site Usability:	★★★★	Based:	UK
Product Range:	★★★★	Express Delivery Option?	(UK) No
Price Range:	Luxury/Medium/Very Good Value	Gift Wrapping Option?	No but everything is beautifully packaged
Delivery Area:	Worldwide	Returns Procedure:	Down to you

www.caxtonlondon.com

Browse round here for a wide choice of high quality gifts, including leather travel accessories, photograph albums, address books and organisers in colours such as cerise, white, sky blue, lilac and lime. You'll also find games such as backgammon and solitaire, silver pens by Lalex and the Mont Blanc Meisterstuck range and delightful baby and christening gifts. Postage within the UK is free and they offer a free gift wrapping service as well.

Site Usability:	★★★★	Based:	UK
Product Range:	★★★★	Express Delivery Option?	(UK) No
Price Range:	Luxury/Medium/Very Good Value	Gift Wrapping Option?	Yes
Delivery Area:	Worldwide	Returns Procedure:	Down to you

www.cocoribbon.com

Calling itself London's lifestyle boutique, Coco Ribbon offers a selection of contemporary clothing by designers such as Collette Dinnigan, Rebecca Taylor and Cynthia Vincent, pretty, modern lingerie and swimwear, a small but beautiful range of handbags and jewellery plus gorgeous and unusual girly gifts and candles. There's a lot to choose from here and the range is constantly updated so you need to return regularly for another browse.

Site Usability:	★★★★	Based:	UK
Product Range:	★★★★	Express Delivery Option?	(UK) Yes
Price Range:	Luxury/Medium/Very Good Value	Gift Wrapping Option?	Yes
Delivery Area:	Worldwide	Returns Procedure:	Down to you

www.davidhampton.com

Here you'll find wallets and purses in Oak Grain leather, in colours such as aubergine, fuchsia and straw plus photo albums and frames and travel accessories, wash bags, luggage tags and even mouse mats in Oxford Hide. This is quite a small collection, but beautifully photographed (often with three or four views to each product) and with lots of detail. Many of the items can be personalised with the recipient's initials as well.

Site Usability:	★★★★	Based:	UK	
Product Range:	★★★	Express Delivery Option?	(UK) No	
Price Range:	Luxury/Medium/Very Good Value	Gift Wrapping Option?	No	
Delivery Area:	Worldwide	Returns Procedure:	Down to you	

www.fuchsiafuchsia.co.uk

For a quick one stop shop to find girly gifts this could very well be an excellent place, where you'll discover pretty fashion jewellery that won't break the bank including the collection from Les Nereides, unusual toiletries from companies such as Croft and Croft and Cheeky Chimp plus an eclectic collection of toiletries, bags, accessories and small home accessories and gifts.

Site Usability:	★★★★	Based:	UK	
Product Range:	★★★	Express Delivery Option?	(UK) Yes	
Price Range:	Luxury/Medium/Very Good Value	Gift Wrapping Option?	No	
Delivery Area:	Worldwide	Returns Procedure:	Down to you	

www.heroshop.co.uk

There are lots of places you can buy leather goods online, but very few that offer the quality and service you'll find here. It's not a huge range but a selection of classic luggage and weekenders, photo albums, home accessories, document wallets, jewellery boxes & cosmetic bags for her, wet packs for him plus shooting accessories and luxury dog leads, collars & baskets.

Site Usability:	★★★★	Based:	UK	
Product Range:	★★★	Express Delivery Option?	(UK) No	
Price Range:	Luxury/Medium/Very Good Value	Gift Wrapping Option?	No	
Delivery Area:	Worldwide	Returns Procedure:	Down to you	

www.pascal-jewellery.com

A collection of timeless stylish jewellery from a jeweller that was originally established in Liberty of London about twenty-five years ago and who you can now find in stores such as Harvey Nichols (and still Liberty). As members of the National Association of Goldsmiths you can be sure that you're buying real quality. The collection is updated at least four times a year so you can be tempted regularly and prices start at around £30.

Site Usability:	★★★★★	Based:	UK
Product Range:	★★★★	Express Delivery Option?	(UK) No
Price Range:	Luxury/Medium/Very Good Value	Gift Wrapping Option?	Yes
Delivery Area:	UK	Returns Procedure:	Down to you

www.pickett.co.uk

You probably already know of Pickett of Burlington Arcade as a retailer of superb quality leather goods, jewellery boxes, briefcases and wallets. There's a really attractive selection as well, of classic handbags, wallets and purses in pigskin, ostrich and calf and colours such as black, dark brown, beige, pink and red. Their jewellery boxes range from tiny ring boxes to superb contrast lined tiered jewel cases and gloves in a selection of leathers and colourways. You'll find umbrellas and jewellery here as well.

Site Usability:	★★★★	Based:	UK
Product Range:	★★★	Express Delivery Option?	(UK) Yes, call them
Price Range:	Luxury/Medium/Very Good Value	Gift Wrapping Option?	No but luxury packaging is standard
Delivery Area:	Worldwide	Returns Procedure:	Down to you

www.purecollection.com

Here's chic, high quality cashmere in a wide range of styles and colours and at different price levels. Check their Gift Selector, which allows you to choose price range and the person for whom you're buying and see what they come up with. Also look through their accessories, which range in price from around £50 upwards. One of the benefits of shopping here is that you can immediately see what's in stock and available to send out.

Site Usability:	★★★★★	Based:	UK
Product Range:	★★★★	Express Delivery Option?	(UK) Yes
Price Range:	Luxury/Medium/Very Good Value	Gift Wrapping Option?	Yes
Delivery Area:	Worldwide	Returns Procedure:	Free

www.thesilvershopdirect.co.uk

There's an interesting selection of well priced silver jewellery on this website, including unusual Dichronic glass jewellery which changes colour, pretty, well priced stone set pendants and earrings, a selection by Charles Rennie Mackintosh and silver jewellery set with tiny white diamonds. Everything is well priced and would make very good gifts. Delivery is free on orders over £25.

Site Usability:	★★★★	Based:	UK
Product Range:	★★★★	Express Delivery Option?	(UK) Yes
Price Range:	Luxury/Medium/Very Good Value	Gift Wrapping Option?	No
Delivery Area:	Worldwide	Returns Procedure:	Down to You

www.treasurebox.co.uk

Here you'll find a wealth of costume jewellery from Butler and Wilson, Tarina Tarantino, Angie Gooderham and Les Nereides to name just a few, with the emphasis on what's in fashion right now. You can select jewellery to go with the new season's look and they're adding in new designers all the time. This is a really fun website where there is not only a lot of choice, but also a great deal of information about the trends the pieces go with and also about the designers themselves.

Site Usability:	★★★★	Based:	UK
Product Range:	★★★★	Express Delivery Option?	(UK) Yes
Price Range:	Luxury/Medium/Very Good Value	Gift Wrapping Option?	Yes
Delivery Area:	Worldwide	Returns Procedure:	Down to you

www.zocaloalpaca.com

This is a small, fairly new online retailer, specialising in (yes you guessed it) South American Alpaca products from soft and light baby alpaca scarves to brightly coloured striped shawls and chunky wraps. The advantage here is that the products look lovely with a wide choice of colourways, the prices are very reasonable and they offer an express service plus gift wrapping, so if you want to give a pretty scarf or shawl that isn't cheap pashmina you can shop here instead.

Site Usability:	★★★★	Based:	UK
Product Range:	★★★	Express Delivery Option?	(UK) Yes
Price Range:	Luxury/Medium/Very Good Value	Gift Wrapping Option?	Yes
Delivery Area:	Worldwide	Returns Procedure:	Down to you

Chapter 49

Home and Accessory Gifts

Home accessories can mean a lot of different things, from cushions and throws, lamps, mirrors and candles to decorative pieces such as hand painted planters, wall hangings and rugs. Here are some of the best of the home accessory/gift websites, where you can find some really beautiful pieces and of course you can order them all online. You'll find lots more also in the At Home section of this book.

There is an endless choice here and the websites are becoming more and more beautifully photographed, which makes it much easier for you to choose. On some of the websites you can change the look of just about every room in your house, and on others you'll find just a few, beautifully made products which are perfect for gifts. In the same way some of these websites offer interesting and different, well priced accessories and on others the sky's the limit, so you can find excellent value or alternatively that one special piece you just can't live without (let alone give it away).

This is a great place to have a browse through to get ideas for your house, for wedding presents, for Christmas, birthdays and lots of other occasions so go and get yourself a glass of wine (or a cup of tea), sit down and relax and prepare to be astonished by what you can find.

Sites to Visit

www.alisonhenry.com

These are seriously gorgeous, modern accessories, mainly in neutral colours, which would make superb gifts for weddings and other 'important' occasions, or when you feel in the need of adding something really special to your home. There's a cut crystal fragrance bottle filled with Alison's own bath oil, pure cashmere cushions and double sided throws and other beautifully photographed objects.

Site Usability:	★★★★	Based:	UK	
Product Range:	★★★	Express Delivery Option?	(UK) No	
Price Range:	Luxury/Medium/Very Good Value	Gift Wrapping Option?	No	
Delivery Area:	UK	Returns Procedure:	Down to you	

www.angelarosedesigns.com

Angela Rose are specialists in soft furnishings and what you'll find on this website are attractive cushions of all shapes and sizes and in pretty colours with slogans such as Glamour Girl, Gone Shopping, and Who Needs Santa I've Got Grandparents (!!). There are delightful candy coloured baby cushions, cushions you can hang on the wall and luxury cushions with traditional designs. They'll also design a custom cushion for you.

Site Usability:	★★★★	Based:	UK	
Product Range:	★★★	Express Delivery Option?	(UK) No	
Price Range:	Luxury/Medium/Very Good Value	Gift Wrapping Option?	No	
Delivery Area:	Worldwide	Returns Procedure:	Down to you	

www.blondeinteriors.co.uk

Here's something a bit more unusual – Blonde Interiors offer Scandinavian designed accessories including pretty cushions, table linens and throws in soft, natural colours, modern bathroom accessories and a range of contemporary tableware in pale neutrals. There are also some lovely glass and decanters you're unlikely to find anywhere else plus an enchanting range for children comprising bed linen, tableware, storage and cushions.

Site Usability:	★★★★	Based:	UK	
Product Range:	★★★	Express Delivery Option?	(UK) No	
Price Range:	Luxury/Medium/Very Good Value	Gift Wrapping Option?	No	
Delivery Area:	Worldwide	Returns Procedure:	Down to you	

www.bombayduck.co.uk

This is a very pretty home gifts and interiors website with a wide range of ideas from their own beautifully packaged candles to candy coloured leather accessories, crystal glass chandeliers, vintage style bathroom accessories and printed cushions. There's a wealth of gift suggestions, some expensive – their gorgeous vintage style chandelier at £275 – and others extremely reasonable. They also have a special Christmas area which you can browse in season.

Site Usability:	★★★★	Based:	UK
Product Range:	★★★★	Express Delivery Option?	(UK) Yes
Price Range:	Luxury/Medium/Very Good Value	Gift Wrapping Option?	No
Delivery Area:	Worldwide	Returns Procedure:	Down to you

www.bodieandfou.com

Bodie and Fou is a home accessories company named after its co-founders, French sisters Elodie and Karine, who decided to fill a gap in the market for simple, contemporary and unique home interiors. You can buy handmade glass candlesticks, unusual table linens and accessories and a wide range of Cote Bastide home and bath products here. It's not a large range but everything is extremely beautiful and gorgeously photographed so it's well worth a browse.

Site Usability:	★★★	Based:	UK
Product Range:	★★★	Express Delivery Option?	(UK) Yes
Price Range:	Luxury/Medium/Very Good Value	Gift Wrapping Option?	No
Delivery Area:	UK	Returns Procedure:	Down to you

www.cabane.co.uk

Here's another website offering a wide selection of ideas for the home, influenced by traditional French style yet with a practical modern twist. Think of simply furnished cabins with crackling log fires, perched high on hillsides or wooden beach houses, full of light and you'll get the mood that's being created here. You'll find pretty bedspreads, cushions and blankets, Savon de Marseilles soaps and candles, colourful linen and cotton napkins and tablecloths.

Site Usability:	★★★★	Based:	UK
Product Range:	★★★★	Express Delivery Option?	(UK) Yes
Price Range:	Luxury/Medium/Very Good Value	Gift Wrapping Option?	No
Delivery Area:	Worldwide	Returns Procedure:	Down to you

www.coffeeandcream.co.uk

This is a beautifully neutral and calm website to visit, offering attractively photographed and unusual home accessories, mainly in neutral shades. Think animal print candles, faux fur throws, smoky glasses, almond coloured velvet quilts, black ceramic canisters and pale French Provencal cushions. For anyone who likes natural colours and five star chic in their home, this is the place to find it.

Site Usability:	★★★★	Based:	UK
Product Range:	★★★	Express Delivery Option?	(UK) No
Price Range:	Luxury/Medium/Very Good Value	Gift Wrapping Option?	Automatic
Delivery Area:	Worldwide	Returns Procedure:	Down to you

www.dianaforrester.co.uk

On Diana Forrester's website there's a very good choice of quite unusual gifts and decorative accessories for the home and garden mainly from France and also from other parts of the World, ranging from a cute mouse salt and pepper set to vintage style French storage jars, unusual vases and photo frames, fine porcelain and an original expresso set. You can also see pictures from Diana's shop which will definitely make you want to go there.

Site Usability:	★★★	Based:	UK	
Product Range:	★★★	Express Delivery Option?	(UK) No	
Price Range:	Luxury/<u>Medium</u>/Very Good Value	Gift Wrapping Option?	Yes	
Delivery Area:	Worldwide	Returns Procedure:	Down to you	

www.grandillusions.co.uk

There's a lot to look at on this attractive website, but it's very easy to get round and the pictures are really clear. You can choose from their ranges of reasonably priced accessories, including candelabra, storm lanterns, votive glasses and French scented candles and guest soaps plus a wide selection of small, pretty items for outdoors, from traditional watering cans, to bird feeders, glass carriers and sconces.

Site Usability:	★★★★	Based:	UK	
Product Range:	★★★★	Express Delivery Option?	(UK) No	
Price Range:	Luxury/<u>Medium</u>/Very Good Value	Gift Wrapping Option?	No	
Delivery Area:	UK	Returns Procedure:	Down to you	

www.janconstantine.com

This is a collection of hand embroidered fabric, cushions and lavender bags with themes such as Bees and Bugs, Seaside Collection, Botanical, Rose and Classic, described as 'designed for today and destined to be the heirlooms of the future'. These are unique textiles and accessories which you'll probably want to collect and you'll find extremely hard to give away, although their present giving potential is excellent.

Site Usability:	★★★★	Based:	UK	
Product Range:	★★★	Express Delivery Option?	(UK) Yes	
Price Range:	Luxury/<u>Medium</u>/Very Good Value	Gift Wrapping Option?	No	
Delivery Area:	Worldwide	Returns Procedure:	Down to you	

www.ninacampbell.com

As you would expect, the website of well known interior designer Nina Campbell is really beautifully designed. On it you can choose from a range of her home accessories, including glassware, linens, patterned lambswool throws, small items such as match strikers and pretty bon bon bowls. You can also order her stunningly packaged home fragrance collection which includes candles and room sprays.

Site Usability:	★★★★	Based:	UK
Product Range:	★★★	Express Delivery Option?	(UK) No
Price Range:	Luxury/Medium/Very Good Value	Gift Wrapping Option?	No
Delivery Area:	Worldwide	Returns Procedure:	Down to you

www.objects-of-design.com

Here you'll find British designed and made gift and home accessory ideas, with everything either being made in small runs or specially for you. There's the Penguin (as in the book) collection of mugs, Emily Readett-Bayley bookends, wonderful Ferguson's Irish Linen and Phil Atrill crystal stemware and that's just a small selection to give you an idea. You can search by product type or by supplier and create a wish list as you go. You could spend a great deal of time here and you'll find gifts for everyone.

Site Usability:	★★★★	Based:	UK
Product Range:	★★★★★	Express Delivery Option?	(UK) Yes
Price Range:	Luxury/Medium/Very Good Value	Gift Wrapping Option?	Yes
Delivery Area:	Worldwide	Returns Procedure:	Down to you

www.queenshill.com

This is a family run business offering a lovely selection of fabrics, wallpapers, gifts and home accessories from brands such as Mulberry, GP and J Baker, Harlequin and Fired Earth. Their mouth-watering gift ideas includes Mulberry candles, pot pourri, cushions and throws and James Brindley's range of faux fur throws, (think leopard, llama, bear and cheetah) cushions and hot water bottle covers. Resist if you can.

Site Usability:	★★★★	Based:	UK
Product Range:	★★★★	Express Delivery Option?	(UK) No
Price Range:	Luxury/Medium/Very Good Value	Gift Wrapping Option?	No
Delivery Area:	Worldwide	Returns Procedure:	Down to you

www.polly-online.co.uk

Whereas on some websites you have to search for information about delivery and gift wrapping, at polly-online it's all clearly laid out for you as are the items on offer so buying is far easier. There's an eclectic, contemporary collection here – unusual sculptures and modern jewellery sit side by side with funky lighting, 'sculpted' cushions and pretty, reasonably priced sets of tableware, making this a good place for wedding gifts as well as gifts for other occasions.

Site Usability:	★★★★★	Based:	UK
Product Range:	★★★	Express Delivery Option?	(UK) No
Price Range:	Luxury/Medium/Very Good Value	Gift Wrapping Option?	Yes
Delivery Area:	Worldwide	Returns Procedure:	Down to you

www.thefrenchhouse.net

Everything from France, from tableware, linen and cutlery to toiletries by Christian Lenart and Savon de Marseilles and elegant Anduze garden pots. Also a selection of pretty bedlinen in traditional French designs such as Toile de Jouy, Fleurs de Champs and Monogram. The descriptions and information about every item are clear and well written and everything is beautifully photographed.

Site Usability:	★★★★	Based:	UK	
Product Range:	★★★★	Express Delivery Option?	(UK) No	
Price Range:	Luxury/<u>Medium</u>/Very Good Value	Gift Wrapping Option?	No	
Delivery Area:	UK	Returns Procedure:	Down to you	

www.thewhitecompany.co.uk

The white company has grown to be one of the premier website shopping destinations, which should be no surprise. The site is lovely and clear and the items offered delectable. It's a great place for gifts as almost any of their products, from home accessories to toiletries, cashmere knits and baby goodies would be a pleasure to receive. Their packaging is lovely as well and they offer a special gift service.

Site Usability:	★★★★★	Based:	UK	
Product Range:	★★★★	Express Delivery Option?	(UK) Yes	
Price Range:	Luxury/<u>Medium</u>/Very Good Value	Gift Wrapping Option?	Yes	
Delivery Area:	Worldwide	Returns Procedure:	Down to you	

Also check out www.pier.co.uk for home and accessory gifts

Chapter 50

Food and Drink gifts

I've always had conflicting thoughts about hampers, considering them something that you would give if you weren't sure what else would suit, particularly for people living on their own or for friends living overseas who'd like a reminder of what we're great for (Scottish smoked salmon, for example, excellent preserves and fruit cakes, Marmite and Worcester Sauce).

While writing this section I've really had to change my mind. Yes there are loads of hamper companies offering hampers which I think are a bit mundane, and where you would do much better to put the goodies together yourself, however you won't find those here. Those listed below offer some really beautiful foodie gifts where very high quality food and drink is beautifully presented in wicker baskets or wooden boxes, with products usually specially chosen from each retailer's outlets and which just about anyone would be delighted to receive.

In some cases you can choose yourself what you want to include, from the aforesaid smoked salmon, Foie Gras, caviar, pâtés and preserves, wonderful home cooked pies and desserts, fruit baskets, olive oils and amazing cheeses and in others you take a ready assembled selection. You can spend anything from an entirely reasonable amount to a fortune.

You'll also find more suggestions in the Gourmet Food/Deli section earlier on in the Guide – so you can make a quick choice from here or have a real browse round.

Delivery is usually extremely quick on these websites and often throughout the world, although if you're buying for Christmas allow as much time as possible. It won't necessarily be the retailer's fault if something doesn't arrive on time, and the post and courier services get exceptionally overburdened, so only buy at the last minute if you have no alternative.

Sites to Visit

www.bayley-sage.co.uk

Bayley and Sage are a top quality delicatessen based in Wimbledon. On their website you can't actually visit the deli, but you can buy one of their well put together gift selections, with names like Sweet Sensation (jelly beans, chocolate brownies, mini cakes and marshmallows etc) or Gentleman's Selection (wine, coffee, marmalade, nuts and Gentlemen's Relish). Everything is very clearly photographed and the prices are reasonable.

Site Usability:	★★★★	Based:	UK
Product Range:	★★★★	Express Delivery Option?	(UK) No
Price Range:	Luxury/<u>Medium</u>/Very Good Value	Gift Wrapping Option?	No
Delivery Area:	UK	Returns Procedure:	Down to you

www.collinstreet.com/

This is a really, really bad website to visit if you're on a diet. The Collins Street Bakery is based in Texas and sells the most delicious luxury fruit cakes stuffed with fruit and nuts and pecan cakes (think Apple Cinnamon and Pineapple Pecan). Don't get too excited about the toffee, cookies and cheesecake here as those items will only ship to the US. The cakes, however, they'll ship to anywhere in the World so take care if you have a really sweet tooth.

Site Usability:	★★★★★	Based:	US
Product Range:	★★★	Express Delivery Option?	(UK) No
Price Range:	Luxury/<u>Medium</u>/Very Good Value	Gift Wrapping Option?	No
Delivery Area:	Worldwide	Returns Procedure:	Down to you

www.efoodies.co.uk

This is an extremely tempting website, where you can order the highest quality olive oil and balsamic vinegar, British and French cheese, caviar, Foie Gras, black and white truffles and truffle oil, spices, mushrooms and champagne. Everything is beautifully photographed with lots of information about every product - where it comes from and what makes it special. The prices here are good, particularly when you consider the quality of what you're buying. They offer gift vouchers as well.

Site Usability:	★★★★★	Based:	UK
Product Range:	★★★	Express Delivery Option?	(UK) Yes
Price Range:	<u>Luxury</u>/Medium/Very Good Value	Gift Wrapping Option?	No
Delivery Area:	UK	Returns Procedure:	Down to you

www.fruit-4u.com

This company will put together the most mouthwatering mix of fresh fruit and present it beautifully in a basket so that you can send it as a gift, with names such as the Exotic Fruit Basket and the Supreme Fruit Basket, both packed with perfect Class 1 seasonal fruits. You can also add cheese, wine, teddies and champagne to your selected basket.

Site Usability:	★★★★	Based:	UK
Product Range:	★★★	Express Delivery Option?	(UK) Yes
Price Range:	Luxury/Medium/Very Good Value	Gift Wrapping Option?	No
Delivery Area:	UK	Returns Procedure:	Down to you

www.gorgeous-food.co.uk

Here's a really attractive website, using traditional script and really good pictures to make you want to stay and browse. They offer a selection of hampers, from Decadence, Luxury and Indulgence to themed selections such as Afternoon Tea, Chocoholic, Spanish and Chilli Lover and for each one you not only see the filled hamper but also each individual ingredient, as well as the list of what's included. In the 'Other Goodies' section you'll find Booja Booja truffles (!), Catalan Mountain Honey and lots more.

Site Usability:	★★★★★	Based:	UK
Product Range:	★★★★	Express Delivery Option?	(UK) Yes
Price Range:	Luxury/Medium/Very Good Value	Gift Wrapping Option?	No
Delivery Area:	UK	Returns Procedure:	Down to you

www.hamper.com

Winner of the Queen's award for Enterprise for International Trade in 2003, Clearwater Hampers can deliver your choice of Hamper to just about anywhere in the World. You can create your own from their range of wines and food goodies and give you lots of tips to help you create the perfect gift, depending on the recipient. Alternatively choose from their Classic Collection where you can spend between £30 and £300. It really is a very well designed website and you should certainly find something here.

Site Usability:	★★★★★	Based:	UK
Product Range:	★★★★	Express Delivery Option?	(UK) No
Price Range:	Luxury/Medium/Very Good Value	Gift Wrapping Option?	No
Delivery Area:	Worldwide	Returns Procedure:	Down to you

www.jeroboams.co.uk

This is a seriously beautifully photographed website, from a luxury cheese specialist, deli and fine wine importer based in South Kensington. On this site you can order from their cheese selections or gifts of food and wine which include port with stilton, vodka and caviar or whisky and cheddar; choose from one of their luxury hampers or from their list of wines, champagnes and spirits. This would be an excellent place to find a gift for a real food or wine lover although it's definitely at the luxury end.

Site Usability:	★★★★	Based:	UK
Product Range:	★★★	Express Delivery Option?	(UK) No
Price Range:	Luxury/Medium/Very Good Value	Gift Wrapping Option?	No
Delivery Area:	UK	Returns Procedure:	Down to you

www.lewisandcooper.com

Lewis and Cooper are a family run business offering a marvellous selection of hampers for all tastes and price levels. You can choose one of their ready selected hampers or pick the items that you want included. Some of the more unusual items include Chatka crab, Russian caviar and quails eggs alongside the finest York ham, handmade plum puddings and Yorkshire Moors honey on the comb.

Site Usability:	★★★★★	Based:	UK
Product Range:	★★★★	Express Delivery Option?	(UK) Yes
Price Range:	Luxury/Medium/Very Good Value	Gift Wrapping Option?	No
Delivery Area:	UK	Returns Procedure:	Down to you

www.lordswines.co.uk

There's a good selection of food and wine gifts here, from the clever stacking spirit bottles (if you haven't already seen them then take a look) to more traditional ideas such as port and stilton, well priced food and drink gift boxes, wine and champagne selections and beautifully packaged hampers. Most gifts can be personalised, not just the card but the box as well, and they'll even produce a special wine or champagne bottle label for you.

Site Usability:	★★★★★	Based:	UK
Product Range:	★★★★	Express Delivery Option?	(UK) Yes
Price Range:	Luxury/Medium/Very Good Value	Gift Wrapping Option?	Yes
Delivery Area:	UK	Returns Procedure:	Down to you

www.mkn.co.uk

Get past the fact that this website is unlike any you've ever been on before. The design couldn't be more basic but the products are excellent and MKN offer hampers in all shapes and sizes, National Hampers (Scottish, Australian or New Zealand) pretty and unusual hampers for mother and baby, special occasion hampers and Tipsy hampers. The pictures are extremely clear, they offer free delivery to the UK and they'll deliver the next day if you order by 3.30pm.

Site Usability:	★★★	Based:	UK
Product Range:	★★★★★	Express Delivery Option?	(UK) Yes
Price Range:	Luxury/Medium/Very Good Value	Gift Wrapping Option?	No
Delivery Area:	Europe	Returns Procedure:	Down to you

www.mortimerandbennett.co.uk

This online deli is crammed full of speciality foods from around the world, many of which are exclusive to them. You'll find an extensive range of cheeses, breads, oil and charcuterie, as well as a selection of fun foodie gifts such as the world's most expensive jam, Italian flower jellies and gold and silver buttons. There's also panettone from Turin, extra virgin olive oil from New Zealand and biscuits from Sardinia; lots to choose from and all easy to see.

Site Usability:	★★★★★	Based:	UK
Product Range:	★★★★	Express Delivery Option?	(UK) Yes
Price Range:	Luxury/Medium/Very Good Value	Gift Wrapping Option?	No
Delivery Area:	UK	Returns Procedure:	Down to you

www.optimacompany.com

Optima specialises in making traditional willow picnic baskets and picnic accessories including picnic bags, rugs and furniture, and also have a chic, colourful 'Carnival' picnic range including a fun shocking pink polka dot basket. They combine picnic baskets with gourmet food and wines creating luxury gift hampers. Free UK mainland delivery.

Site Usability:	★★★★★	Based:	UK
Product Range:	★★★★	Express Delivery Option?	(UK) No
Price Range:	Luxury/Medium/Very Good Value	Gift Wrapping Option?	No
Delivery Area:	UK	Returns Procedure:	Down to you

www.thedrinkshop.com

Here's a selection of unusual luxury chocolate boxes from Belgian retailers Gudrun and Lassiter plus a wide choice of champagnes, wines and spirits. They also have cocktail kits for different types of drinks, gift hampers and presentation boxes so there are some very good gift ideas here (which you know will almost certainly be used). A full range of reasonably priced glassware is available by US company Anchor Hocking.

Site Usability:	★★★★	Based:	UK
Product Range:	★★★	Express Delivery Option?	(UK) Yes
Price Range:	Luxury/Medium/Very Good Value	Gift Wrapping Option?	No
Delivery Area:	Europe	Returns Procedure:	Down to you

www.thegiftgourmet.co.uk

The Gift Gourmet is an easy to get round website which offers a broad and innovative range of affordable food gift sets, containing the highest quality ingredients, and all presented within 'gift ready' packaging so that you don't have to do any more work. There's a wide range of prices, from expensive hampers at around £100 to suggestions at under £20.

Site Usability:	★★★★	Based:	UK
Product Range:	★★★	Express Delivery Option?	(UK) Yes
Price Range:	Luxury/Medium/Very Good Value	Gift Wrapping Option?	Yes
Delivery Area:	UK	Returns Procedure:	Down to you

www.villandry.com

Villandry Foodstore Restaurant & Bar is a must for all foodies in London, as it stocks a wonderful range of the finest ingredients sourced from specialist suppliers around the world such as olive oils, vinegars, wines, cheese and hams, pickles, chutneys and chocolate. You can now order a range of gift hampers online which can be delivered within 48 hours. Beautifully presented in wicker baskets and wooden boxes there's a very good range including the Italian Style Hamper, BBQ hamper and Cookie Monster hamper plus exclusive ideas for women and babies.

Site Usability:	★★★★	Based:	UK
Product Range:	★★★★	Express Delivery Option?	(UK) Yes
Price Range:	Luxury/Medium/Very Good Value	Gift Wrapping Option?	No
Delivery Area:	UK	Returns Procedure:	Down to you

www.virginiahayward.com

Established in 1984, Virginia Hayward offers a beautifully presented traditional range of gifts and hampers. They offer gifts for all seasons and events and can fulfil large corporate orders as well as individual purchases. They have a wide choice of other food and wine related gifts and a range of romantic and pampering gifts. You can choose from a named or standard delivery and they'll deliver to BFPO addresses

Site Usability:	★★★★★	Based:	UK
Product Range:	★★★★	Express Delivery Option?	(UK) Yes
Price Range:	Luxury/Medium/Very Good Value	Gift Wrapping Option?	No
Delivery Area:	UK	Returns Procedure:	Down to you

www.winedancer.com

You can, of course, just walk into your local wine merchant and buy your bottle of bubbly then and there. Or you could do something a bit different and send a bottle of Veuve Clicquot in its very own ice bucket with your personalised card, or a boxed mini bottle of Laurent Perrier with a candle and bath essence.

If you want to be really popular send a Methuselah of champagne in a wooden crate (the equivalent of eight bottles) and cross your fingers you'll be invited to share it. This is a really good selection of unusual gift ideas.

Site Usability:	★★★★	Based:	UK
Product Range:	★★★★	Express Delivery Option?	(UK) Yes
Price Range:	Luxury/Medium/Very Good Value	Gift Wrapping Option?	No
Delivery Area:	Worldwide	Returns Procedure:	Down to you

Also check out these websites for food and drink gifts

Website Address	You'll find it in
www.carluccios.com	Gourmet Food/Deli
www.formanandfield.com	Gourmet Food/Deli
www.lakelandlimited.co.uk	Tableware and Kitchen Equipment
www.francetoyourdoor.com	General Gift Stores

Chapter 51

Luxury Gifts

I f you're in a hurry and you need a really special gift for someone, (and I mean really special) come and have a look here, where the sky's the limit. Also look in the first chapter of this book; Luxury Brands Online. The brands are as you would expect, world famous, you can choose jewellery from Tiffany, Boodles and Theo Fennell, pens by Mont Blanc, Yard O'Led and Faber Castel, luxury accessories by Dalvey, fragrance by Jo Malone, home accessories by David Linley, handbags by Gucci, Mulberry and Anya Hindmarch and stationery by Smythson (and that's just mentioning a few).

Then you have just about anything from Fortnum and Mason, with their aura of luxury and beautiful packaging, plus an increasing range from Harrods online. Both websites are growing all the time and both offer an excellent service. Keep checking back as there will doubtless be more and more to select from.

Of course there are other websites in this guide where you can spend a small fortune and it wouldn't be possible to list them all here, however, these websites all offer (99.9% of the time, just hedging my bets) a really perfect service, great attention to detail and gorgeous packaging. So if you really need something extra, extra special, these are the places to visit.

Sites to Visit

www.astleyclarke.com

New online designer jewellery retailer Astley Clarke have a really lovely website, where you'll find the collections of New York and London based designers such as Coleman Douglas, Vinnie Day, Talisman Unlimited Flora Astor and Catherine Prevost, some of which are exclusive to Astley Clarke. Prices start at around £100 and then go skywards. For gorgeous gifts or treats this is the perfect place, as everything arrives beautifully gift boxed and can be gift wrapped as well. There's also a collection for brides and bridesmaids.

Site Usability:	★★★★★	Based:	UK
Product Range:	★★★★★	Express Delivery Option?	(UK) Yes
Price Range:	Luxury/Medium/Very Good Value	Gift Wrapping Option?	Yes
Delivery Area:	UK	Returns Procedure:	Down to you

www.dalvey.com

Dalvey of Scotland has created a range of elegant and useful gifts which are attractively displayed on their extremely well laid out website. Suggestions such as beautifully made leather travel clocks and business card cases, cufflinks and cufflink cases, hipflasks and binoculars are all luxuriously presented and would make really lovely presents. It is a small range but if you're looking for something for the man in your life (and it's something you know he needs or he'll use) then buy here. Most items can be engraved.

Site Usability:	★★★★★	Based:	UK
Product Range:	★★★	Express Delivery Option?	(UK) No
Price Range:	Luxury/Medium/Very Good Value	Gift Wrapping Option?	No
Delivery Area:	Worldwide	Returns Procedure:	Down to you

www.davidlinley.com

As you would expect, this is a really beautiful website offering you the opportunity to buy David Linley designed accessories online including frames, vases, lamps, candlesticks, home fragrance, jewellery boxes and cushions. Everything is beautifully photographed and expensive and there are some really gorgeous gifts here. Prices start at about £55 for his key rings.

Site Usability:	★★★★★	Based:	UK
Product Range:	★★★★	Express Delivery Option?	(UK) Yes
Price Range:	Luxury/Medium/Very Good Value	Gift Wrapping Option?	No but packaging is lovely
Delivery Area:	Worldwide	Returns Procedure:	Down to you

www.fortnumandmason.com

With its famous name and lovely packaging anything from Fortnum and Mason is a pleasure to buy and receive. On their website you can order food and drink (think foie gras, smoked salmon, caviar and champagne) with lots of Christmas specialities in season and their marvellous teas plus an eclectic range of gifts including hip flasks and albums for men, and toiletries, jewellery and accessories for women. Most items can be delivered all over the world.

Site Usability:	★★★★	Based:	UK
Product Range:	★★★★	Express Delivery Option?	(UK) No
Price Range:	Luxury/Medium/Very Good Value	Gift Wrapping Option?	No
Delivery Area:	Worldwide	Returns Procedure:	Down to you

www.harrods.com

Harrods are adding more and more products into their online store and most of them they'll ship worldwide. They include silver and glass, decorative accessories, food and drink, fashion and gorgeous bath and body products, and although of course the range is nothing like as wide as their Knightsbridge store there are some excellent gift ideas at a range of prices. Delivery takes up to two weeks and you need to allow longer for overseas orders.

Site Usability:	★★★★★	Based:	UK
Product Range:	★★★★	Express Delivery Option?	(UK) No
Price Range:	Luxury/Medium/Very Good Value	Gift Wrapping Option?	No
Delivery Area:	Worldwide	Returns Procedure:	Down to you

www.halcyon-days.co.uk

The next time you want to buy a special present for someone, to commemorate a particular event, such as a silver wedding or birthday or maybe just because you want to give something really unique, you should take a look at these exquisite ideas from Halcyon Days, where you'll find hand painted enamel boxes with designs such as The Owl and The Pussycat, Jack Vettriano paintings, Andy Warhol, sayings and quotations and museum editions plus musical boxes, jewelled boxes and clocks.

Site Usability:	★★★★	Based:	UK
Product Range:	★★★★	Express Delivery Option?	(UK) Yes
Price Range:	Luxury/Medium/Very Good Value	Gift Wrapping Option?	Yes
Delivery Area:	Worldwide	Returns Procedure:	Down to you

www.penshop.co.uk

This is a really attractive website offering one of the best selections of luxury pens including; Yard-o-led's beautiful sterling silver fountain pens, ballpoints and pencils, Faber Castell pens in wood and silver, Mont Blanc (you need to phone to order), and Porsche Design steel pens. Lamy, Rotring, Shaeffer and Waterman are also available. They aim to send out the day you order and they'll deliver worldwide. They also offer a repair service.

Site Usability:	★★★★★	Based:	UK	
Product Range:	★★★★★	Express Delivery Option?	(UK) No	
Price Range:	Luxury/Medium/Very Good Value	Gift Wrapping Option?	Yes	
Delivery Area:	Worldwide	Returns Procedure:	Down to you	

Also check out the following for luxury gifts

Website Address	You'll find them in
www.anyahindmarch.com	Luxury Brands Online
www.dunhill.com	Luxury Brands Online
www.gucci.com	Luxury Brands Online
www.jomalone.co.uk	Skincare and Cosmetics
www.smythson.com	Luxury Brands Online
www.theofennell.com	Luxury Brands Online
www.tiffany.com	Luxury Brands Online

Chapter 52

Sporting Gifts

Next time you're looking for a present for someone who plays golf, shoots (clays, preferably) or fishes, skis, sails, or scuba dives, rides horses, plays tennis, rugby, football or cricket (the list can go on and on) then take a quick look at the websites below.

These are some of the easiest people to buy gifts for because as long as you don't get something trying to be too clever, but buy something really great for their sport - even the latest book by the latest sports hero, you'll probably get it right. Banish for ever more those ideas of buying socks (did you ever?) handkerchiefs and scarves and choose something that they're going to be pleased, and slightly amazed, to receive.

These websites are divided up into types of sports, with two or more websites given for each on which you'll find loads of ideas. One of these will probably offer absolutely everything for the sport in case you know exactly what you're sporting friend wants, and the alternative will be something slightly different that you might not immediately think of. You can also drift off to *amazon.co.uk* and look the sport up there, but if you want to buy the latest book you'd better make sure they haven't bought it for themselves already.

Garden Games

Sites to Visit

www.gardengames.co.uk

Whether you're looking for trampolines, climbing frames, swings and slides, junior and full sized croquet sets, snooker and pool tables, table tennis tables, aqua slides or an old fashioned wooden sledge you'll find everything on this friendly website. All the items are very well photographed, they offer speedy UK delivery and will also ship to the USA, Canada and Spain.

Site Usability:	★★★★★	Based:	UK
Product Range:	★★★★	Express Delivery Option?	(UK) Yes
Price Range:	Luxury/<u>Medium</u>/Very Good Value	Gift Wrapping Option?	No
Delivery Area:	UK, USA, Canada and Spain	Returns Procedure:	Down to you

www.mastersgames.com

At Master's Games you'll find a wide range of traditional indoor and outdoor games made only in high quality materials, such as Chinese Checkers with a solid teak board, and a hand crafted bagatelle board. You'll also find outdoor draughts, table football, bar billiards, table tennis, roulette, croquet, rounders and bar games such as skittles, Aunt Sally and bar billiards.

Site Usability:	★★★★	Based:	UK
Product Range:	★★★★	Express Delivery Option?	(UK) Yes if you contact them
Price Range:	Luxury/<u>Medium</u>/Very Good Value	Gift Wrapping Option?	No
Delivery Area:	Worldwide	Returns Procedure:	Down to you

For the Walking and Hiking enthusiast

Sites to Visit

www.completeoutdoors.co.uk

Everything for walking, trekking, rambling, camping, climbing, and many other activities is available here, with a wide range of tents, rucksacks, sleeping bags, navigation equipment, boots, walking poles, and general camping accessories from well known brands such as Paramo, Berghaus, Brasher, Meindl, Bushbaby, Victorinox, Leki, Karrimor, Leatherman, Rohan, Nomad Medical and Regatta. There's lots more plus a good gift section.

Site Usability:	★★★★	Based:	UK
Product Range:	★★★★★	Express Delivery Option?	(UK) No
Price Range:	Luxury/<u>Medium</u>/Very Good Value	Gift Wrapping Option?	No
Delivery Area:	UK	Returns Procedure:	Down to you

www.blacks.co.uk

If you or any member of your family has ever done any camping, walking or hiking (or climbing) you'll probably already have visited Blacks, where they offer a well priced (rather than 'designer') range of clothing and accessories and good value skiwear in season. You'll find waterproof jackets and trousers, lots of fleece, tents, poles, footwear and socks and great gifts such as Cybalite torches, Kick and Huntsman knives and tools and Garmin compasses.

Site Usability:	★★★★★	Based:	UK
Product Range:	★★★★★	Express Delivery Option?	(UK) No
Price Range:	Luxury/Medium/Very Good Value	Gift Wrapping Option?	No
Delivery Area:	UK	Returns Procedure:	Down to you

For the Fisherman

Let me offer a word of caution here. Don't get carried away and start buying rods, reels or flies for your fisherman (or fisherwoman) friend. They'll no doubt be very particular about what they use and if you give them the wrong thing it'll be totally sniffed at. (And having two fishermen in my family I know about these things).

The websites below have some excellent ideas for non-specific gifts and my advice is to stick to those unless, needless to say, you've dropped clever hints and found out exactly which type of new rod he/she's hankering after and you're prepared to spend some real money. You may think they're just long sticks with some string at the end but believe me they're not and can cost hundreds of pounds (and don't ever tell him/her that you think it's just a long stick with some string at the end when you discover to your horror how much was spent on the last one). You will not be popular. Take it from me.

Sites to Visit

www.fly-fishing-tackle.co.uk

From a full range of rods and reels by manufacturers such as Snowbee, Fulling Mill, Loop and Fladen to waders, hats, caps and gloves, everything for the keen fisherman is available here. If you're looking for a gift, go past the fly tying kits unless you're sure they'll be welcome and concentrate more on fly boxes, tackle bags and rod carriers or fly tying tools, lamps and magnifiers.

Site Usability:	★★★★	Based:	UK
Product Range:	★★★★	Express Delivery Option?	(UK) Yes
Price Range:	Luxury/Medium/Very Good Value	Gift Wrapping Option?	No
Delivery Area:	Worldwide	Returns Procedure:	Down to you

www.gifts4fishing.co.uk

This is a really good website offering gifts for fishermen that don't get in the way of the rods, reels and flies. You'll find sterling silver fish cufflinks, Barbour scarves and hip flasks, humorous mugs, limited edition prints, note cards, barware, Richard Wheatley fly boxes and silk ties. They use first class post for all deliveries and ship worldwide.

Site Usability:	★★★★	Based:	UK
Product Range:	★★★	Express Delivery Option?	(UK) Yes
Price Range:	Luxury/<u>Medium</u>/Very Good Value	Gift Wrapping Option?	No
Delivery Area:	Worldwide	Returns Procedure:	Down to you

For the Golfer

This is another area where you need to take care. Don't splash out on golf clubs, the latest driver or putter (yes I do know what those are, well sort of) for example without knowing exactly what you're doing. It's far better to go for more general items for the golfer and far less likely that you'll get it wrong. At *118golf.co.uk* you'll find a wide range of gift suggestions at all price levels from golf balls to electronic swing refiners plus loads of accessories.

If you take a look round the Gleneagles luxury gift selection you could also consider their gift vouchers, provided of course that the person you're giving them to would be willing to take you along, even if you don't play golf.

Sites to Visit

www.118golf.co.uk

With its excellent delivery service, offering standard, express and Saturday delivery plus international delivery and its diverse range of products for the golfer this would be an excellent website for gifts. Check through their golf accessories where you'll find the range from Callaway and Nike, golf gadgets including swing trainers and ball retrievers, dvds and books. There's also a gift finder which offers you a selection depending on how much you want to spend.

Site Usability:	★★★★★	Based:	UK
Product Range:	★★★★★	Express Delivery Option?	(UK) Yes
Price Range:	<u>Luxury/Medium</u>/Very Good Value	Gift Wrapping Option?	No
Delivery Area:	Worldwide	Returns Procedure:	Down to you

www.gleneagles.com

I probably don't need to tell you that this is a five star hotel and championship golf course and it offers five star products in its shop. So it's expensive. But if you want something really special, then this could be a good place to visit (online, I mean). I wouldn't, personally, go for the Gleneagles embroidered clothing unless whoever you're buying the gift for had actually played there, however, take a quick look at the accessories and you may find something that'll be a success.

Site Usability:	★★★★	Based:	UK
Product Range:	★★★	Express Delivery Option?	(UK) No
Price Range:	Luxury/Medium/Very Good Value	Gift Wrapping Option?	No
Delivery Area:	Worldwide	Returns Procedure:	Down to you

www.erinhousegifts.co.uk

I had to add this one in, as this retailer not only offers a wide choice of gifts including Halcyon Days Enamels, Churchill China (which uses images painted by Sir Winston Churchill), Franz Porcelain, delightful Winnie the Pooh classics, the extraordinary Yoro pen (take a look) and pens by Swarovski but also, in their History Craft section, an attractive range of sporting gifts for the cricketer, rugby player and golfer. They're happy to deliver all over the world.

Site Usability:	★★★★	Based:	UK
Product Range:	★★★★	Express Delivery Option?	(UK) No
Price Range:	Luxury/Medium/Very Good Value	Gift Wrapping Option?	Yes
Delivery Area:	Worldwide	Returns Procedure:	Down to you

www.hattiesmart.com

Hattie Smart designs golf gloves, but not just any old golf gloves, these are designer golf gloves, made from the finest leather and available in a range of colours including pistachio, violet, fuchsia and cranberry for women and kangaroo, bay leaf and vanilla for men. All the gloves are very reasonably priced and arrive beautifully packaged so they'd be the perfect gift for your golf playing friend or relative.

Site Usability:	★★★	Based:	UK
Product Range:	★★★	Express Delivery Option?	(UK) No
Price Range:	Luxury/Medium/Very Good Value	Gift Wrapping Option?	Yes
Delivery Area:	Worldwide	Returns Procedure:	Down to you

For the Rider

You're bound to know a child that rides, has his or her own pony and is crazy about horses, probably to the exclusion of almost everything else. You may also have some adult friends who ride, every week, come rain or shine. If this is the case then you've come to the right place to find some very good horsey gift suggestions.

There are loads of horse related websites available, all offering you the complete kit, jodhpurs, jackets, gaiters, boots, hats, tack, rugs, whips, etc but these are probably not what you're looking for here.

What you want are accessories, books (boring maybe, but if it's a good one just out ...) and interesting and funny (maybe) horse related presents. The Equestrian Store is well laid out, offers everything for the horse and rider plus gift, books and dvd sections and a really excellent delivery service.

Thelwell? Well if you haven't heard of him you should have, as the master cartoonist of everything horse and riding related. The range at the Thelwell website is enormous and personally I think that unless the friend you're buying for really doesn't have a sense of humour you'd be best to start there.

Sites to Visit

www.theequestrianstore.com

This well designed and easy to get round website offers express worldwide delivery and sells just about everything for horse and rider. You'll find a comprehensive clothing section offering jodhpurs and hard hats, jackets and boots and in the horse section all you need including saddles, bridles, horse rugs and accessories. The gift, books and dvd section should give you some great ideas for gifts for the rider.

Site Usability:	★★★★	Based:	UK
Product Range:	★★★★	Express Delivery Option?	(UK) Yes
Price Range:	Luxury/Medium/Very Good Value	Gift Wrapping Option?	No
Delivery Area:	Worldwide	Returns Procedure:	Down to you

www.thelwell-horsey-gifts.com

Norman Thelwell's wonderfully funny cartoons first appeared in Punch magazine over forty years ago. His portrayals of country life, sporting pursuits and in particular horses and riders are known and loved the World over. This is not a sophisticated website with sophisticated pictures but if you know someone, whatever age, who rides or loves horses (and has a sense of humour, of course) you'll doubtless find a gift for them, from cards, diaries, gift wrap and pictures to 'get off my foot!' socks, printed t-shirts, The Riding Academy money box and cross stitch kits.

Site Usability:	★★★	Based:	UK
Product Range:	★★★★★	Express Delivery Option?	(UK) Yes
Price Range:	Luxury/Medium/Very Good Value	Gift Wrapping Option?	No
Delivery Area:	Worldwide	Returns Procedure:	Down to you

For the Rugby, Football or Cricket Enthusiast

We all know them, don't we? The ones who spend hours and hours and hours crouched in front of the television yelling 'kick it', 'get him', 'you idiot', and far worse things when watching, in particular, rugby (well they wouldn't be shouting 'kick it' or 'get him' during a cricket match, would they)?

Maybe you know someone who plays, or someone's son who plays (yes, you guessed). They tend to be complete addicts and buying a gift for them is really, really easy. Just get them the latest shirt for the team they support or a new rugby ball. You can't fail there and you'll find them and more on the websites below.

If you're looking for something for a cricketer firstly you need to find out if he's read the books about Brian Johnston, the much loved and admired (and frequently extremely funny) BBC presenter and commentator, known the World over as the voice of cricket. If he hasn't then go straight to Amazon.

Alternatively take a look at the sites below which should give you some good ideas both for adult and junior cricketers.

Sites to Visit

www.cartoonstock.com

Cartoonstock is a searchable database of over 60,000 quality gag cartoons, political cartoons, cartoon pictures and illustrations and sporting cartoons by over 290 of the world's best cartoonists. Once you've chosen your area, e.g. sporting, you just have to put the type of sport (football for example) into their search box and click 'search'. You'll then have loads of cartoons to choose from which you can add to your shopping basket and once you've done that you can choose whether you want your selected cartoon as a print, on a mug, t-shirt or mouse mat.

Site Usability:	★★★★	Based:	UK
Product Range:	★★★★★	Express Delivery Option?	(UK) No
Price Range:	Luxury/Medium/Very Good Value	Gift Wrapping Option?	No
Delivery Area:	Worldwide	Returns Procedure:	Down to you

www.kitbag.com

Kitbag is one of the best websites for football and rugby clothing, equipment and accessories. It's clear and quick to get round, has a really wide range of products and offers fast delivery. They keep well up to date with the latest kit from your favourite team and offer a full range of shoes and balls from all the top brands. As they ship Worldwide and offer European shirts there's a quick currency converter ready and waiting for you to use and you can choose from Standard, Royal Mail Special and Express delivery.

Site Usability:	★★★★★	Based:	UK
Product Range:	★★★★★	Express Delivery Option?	(UK) Yes
Price Range:	Luxury/<u>Medium</u>/Very Good Value	Gift Wrapping Option?	No
Delivery Area:	Worldwide	Returns Procedure:	Down to you

www.rugbymegastore.com

This is just as it sounds, a huge, busy website offering a total range for the rugby player, including bags, balls, team kit, books and rugby boots by brands such as Mizuno, Puma, Adidas and Nike plus team t-shirts, protection, videos and news direct from the BBC. In the gift and souvenirs section you'll find ideas such as limited edition prints and signed photos and rugby balls and World Cup souvenirs.

Site Usability:	★★★★	Based:	UK
Product Range:	★★★★★	Express Delivery Option?	(UK) No
Price Range:	Luxury/<u>Medium</u>/Very Good Value	Gift Wrapping Option?	No
Delivery Area:	UK	Returns Procedure:	Down to you

www.rugbyrelics.com

Rugby Relics are a family business based in Neath in North Wales, where you'll find the most amazing collection of rugby gifts and memorabilia. If you want to buy a gift for a rugby mad friend there's probably no better place to visit, you'll almost certainly find something from their collection of official programmes, prints and clothing or by clicking through to their sister website *rugbygifts.com*.

Site Usability:	★★★	Based:	UK
Product Range:	★★★	Express Delivery Option?	(UK) Yes
Price Range:	Luxury/<u>Medium</u>/Very Good Value	Gift Wrapping Option?	No
Delivery Area:	Worldwide	Returns Procedure:	Down to you

www.owzat-cricket.co.uk

Here are bats by Gunn and Moore, Kookaburra and Gray-Nichols plus loads of other brands, gloves, pads, kitbags, body protection, accessories and balls. This is a website obviously designed for real cricketers and they're proud of the fact that they've sold to some of the World's top players, such as Phil Defreitas, Karl Krikken and Paul Franks. You'll definitely find something for the cricketer including junior players, for whom they have an excellent range.

Site Usability:	★★★★★	Based:	UK
Product Range:	★★★★★	Express Delivery Option?	(UK) Yes
Price Range:	Luxury/<u>Medium</u>/Very Good Value	Gift Wrapping Option?	No
Delivery Area:	Europe	Returns Procedure:	Down to you

www.cricketbits.co.uk

The one stop shop for cricket novelties and gifts with best sellers such as a cricket-ball clock, cricket letter rack and a framed limited edition picture commemorating The Birth of the Ashes in 1882, showing the handwritten batting orders, scorecard and original scorers sheet. There are simply loads of ideas from the very cheap and cheerful to the not so cheap (although most things are well priced). So take a look around here for stocking fillers and attractive gifts for all ages of cricketer.

Site Usability:	★★★★	Based:	UK
Product Range:	★★★★	Express Delivery Option?	(UK) No
Price Range:	Luxury/Medium/Very Good Value	Gift Wrapping Option?	No
Delivery Area:	UK	Returns Procedure:	Down to you

For the Sailor

Most sailing enthusiasts seem to live in a totally different World, and simply don't understand why the rest of us don't want to get up early and go out on a cold day to get even more thoroughly wet and cold (and probably sea sick), and even worse to spend nights in narrow uncomfortable bunks bobbing up and down in the water.

Of course that's for the hardy English sailor, not the one used to luxurious yachts in the South of France, probably parked in the marina at the side of the local five star hotel and within spitting distance of shops such as Bvlgari, Versace and Prada.

If you know someone who's mad about sailing you may well find something at one of the websites below.

Sites to Visit

www.chandlerystore.co.uk

Musto, Henri Lloyd, and Gill are the three main brands on offer here for the sailor, including the clothing, accessories, footwear and luggage ranges. You'll also find deck shoes and chandlery, Kahuna watches, Leatherman knives, Silva compasses and charts and marine books, plus the clever Sea Shore 6 speed Marine Folding Bike which stows away on board or in the boot of your car.

Site Usability:	★★★★	Based:	UK
Product Range:	★★★★	Express Delivery Option?	(UK) No
Price Range:	Luxury/Medium/Very Good Value	Gift Wrapping Option?	No
Delivery Area:	Europe	Returns Procedure:	Down to you

www.crewclothing.co.uk

This is a really attractive and modern website with a constantly expanding range, offering all the Crew gear, from the full collection of sailing inspired clothing to lots of other choices including hard wearing footwear, faux fur jackets and gilets (resist them if you can) and excellent travel bags, gloves, hats and socks. They offer standard and next day UK delivery and same day in central London if you order by 12pm.

Site Usability:	★★★★	Based:	UK
Product Range:	★★★★	Express Delivery Option?	(UK) Yes
Price Range:	Luxury/Medium/Very Good Value	Gift Wrapping Option?	No
Delivery Area:	Worldwide	Returns Procedure:	Down to you

For the Skier or Boarder

There are lots of websites offering ski and snowboarding clothing and gear, and lots of people who are skiing mad and just can't wait for the start of the skiing season each year.

The great thing about gifts for the skier, of course, is that usually (unless they're going off to somewhere really far flung) the skiing season gets going properly immediately after Christmas, so if you know someone who's going to shortly be heading for the mountains you can buy a present that'll be really welcome and timely, from a silly hat or pompom scarf to a voucher for a new pair of high tech boots.

Sites to Visit

www.ellis-brigham.com

This is a wonderful, clearly photographed website for mountaineers and skiers, offering brands such as The North Face, Patagonia, Ice Breaker and Lowe Alpine. Every possible type of equipment is very clearly shown and there are some good sporting gift ideas as well including items by Leatherman, Victorinox, Maglite and Toollogic. In the ski section you'll find ski clothing by lots of different makes, colourful beanies and humorous ski socks plus boots and skis by all the great brands.

Site Usability:	★★★★★	Based:	UK
Product Range:	★★★★★	Express Delivery Option?	(UK) No
Price Range:	Luxury/Medium/Very Good Value	Gift Wrapping Option?	No
Delivery Area:	Worldwide	Returns Procedure:	Down to you

www.snowandrock.com

Snow and Rock are a well known retailer for skiers, snowboarders and rock climbers with a full range of equipment and clothing and accessories by brands such as Animal, Billabong, Ski Jacket, Helly Hanson, O'Neill, Quicksilver, Salomon and Oakley. There's also lots of advice on what to buy and on fit. In the gift and gadget section you'll find ideas including books and films, watches, 2 way radios, solar chargers and compasses.

Site Usability:	★★★★★	Based:	UK
Product Range:	★★★★★	Express Delivery Option?	(UK) Yes
Price Range:	Luxury/Medium/Very Good Value	Gift Wrapping Option?	No
Delivery Area:	Worldwide	Returns Procedure:	Down to you

For the Tennis or Squash Player

Tennis and squash are harder than some other sports in terms of gifts. Yes you can buy a dozen dozen tennis balls (and you'd certainly be very popular if you did) the latest book by the latest star or a Wimbledon dvd but it's definitely not easy in terms of general gadgets and accessories.

If you're looking for a special present for a tennis player then you just need to find out which new racquet they want (and probably provide a budget) and away you go, but don't guess, they'll probably want to change it. Once you know what they want you can pay a visit to one of the websites below, which surely have the most comprehensive selections of tennis racquets online and tells you a great deal about them.

Sites to Visit

www.pwp.com

Calling itself 'Europe's No 1 racquet specialist for Tennis, Squash and Badminton' you can see the reason clearly when you browse round this site. There's a great deal for the tennis player with racquets by Wilson, Dunlop, Head, Slazenger and Prince, tennis shoes, well priced tennis balls and lots of accessories including the ITP series of dvds. If you're thinking of buying a gift for a player you would need to know exactly what they want or you could, of course, buy them the huge Wilson logo umbrella.

Site Usability:	★★★★	Based:	UK
Product Range:	★★★★★	Express Delivery Option?	(UK) No
Price Range:	Luxury/Medium/Very Good Value	Gift Wrapping Option?	No
Delivery Area:	Worldwide	Returns Procedure:	Down to you

www.racquetlink.com

This is another excellent tennis website retailing racquets by Prince, Wilson, Babolat and Yonex amongst others, ball baskets and ball lobbers by Lobster, Tennis Tower and Shotmaker and everything else for the tennis player. They also have a Unique Gifts section, where you'll find things like tennis bookends, coin trays, bottle openers and letter racks and they offer Gift Certificates as well.

Site Usability:	★★★★★	Based:	UK
Product Range:	★★★★★	Express Delivery Option?	(UK) Yes
Price Range:	Luxury/Medium/Very Good Value	Gift Wrapping Option?	No
Delivery Area:	Worldwide	Returns Procedure:	Down to you

And just one more ... Rowing

I'm well aware that rowing is not considered a mainstream sport as it's not one that most people try (at least on the water). However, having had a son who spent much of his school life on the river in what looks like an incredibly unstable long narrow boat with eight other boys (including the cox) with eight of them having only one blade each, I had to recommend this website. Anyone who knows someone who rows, or is considering taking up this wet, cold sport, this one's for you.

Sites to Visit

www.rock-the-boat.co.uk

The essential website for anyone who rows. For the gear (apart from the boat and blades, of course) the absolutely essential waterproof splash tops, hoodys and jackets, the lycra (yes I know) leggings and shorts plus neckwarmers, hats and pogies (for the hands). Then there are the wonderful, funny t-shirts and tops that only those who have oarsmen in their families will understand, with slogans such as 'Ergo, Ergoing, Ergone' and 'Going Forwards Backwards'. They're all great gifts for the rower you know.

Site Usability:	★★★	Based:	UK
Product Range:	★★★	Express Delivery Option?	(UK) Yes
Price Range:	Luxury/Medium/Very Good Value	Gift Wrapping Option?	No
Delivery Area:	EU	Returns Procedure:	Down to you

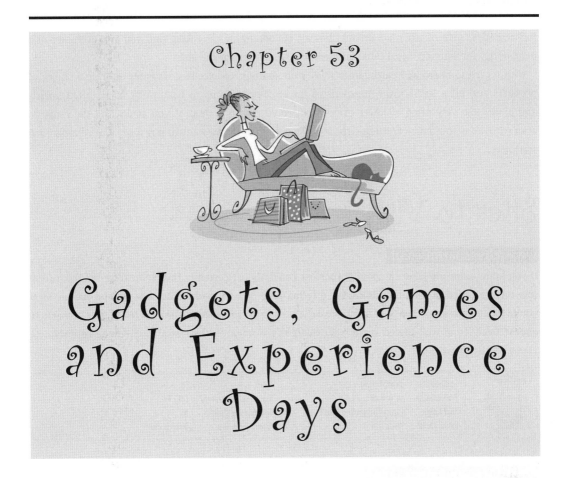

Chapter 53

Gadgets, Games and Experience Days

Although most of these gadget sites offer something for the girls let's be honest here. Most of these are boy's toys and boys days out, for boys of any age from teenagers upwards with loads of (often useless) ideas for gifts. Frequently these are gadgets that'll go straight into the cupboard or get given away. However don't despair, there are also great suggestions for gifts that will be welcomed, kept and used.

I know that if ever I do take my two teenage sons out shopping with me (something to be avoided at all costs, it's far too expensive and they never want to go where I want to go), I can safely steer them towards the doorway of any gadget and gizmo shop and leave them for hours. (That sounds dreadful, I realise but they're not young teens, but old teens, if that makes sense). They're deliriously happy and so am I. The only risk is the call on my mobile phone that tells me they've run out of money.

So take a good look at these sites. The man in your life (or your brother, son or nephew may HATE gadgets of all kinds) in which case he'll be unique and you should hang on to him. You'll save loads.

As far as days out are concerned, or 'experience days', this is a growing market and extremely popular. Do make sure that what you buy is suited to the recipient. I'm sure all these companies rejoice at the number of vouchers they send out that are paid for but never used. There are some great fun activities, such as off road driving, hot air ballooning or car racing and you can even slip in a pamper day for yourself. See, I told you there was something for the girls.

With regard to board and card games there's no shortage of excellent websites offering a choice of products and price levels, from inexpensive travel compendiums to beautifully handcrafted boards and pieces and very often at lower prices than you'd pay in a shop, if you could find the range to start with. So if your game is bridge, chess or Monopoly or if you want to buy a set to give away then start here.

Sites to Visit

www.chessbaron.co.uk

If you know someone who's a chess enthusiast you'll almost certainly find something for them from this retailer based in Taunton, Somerset offering only artisan made chess boards and pieces, so if you're looking for any other type of game you'll need to go somewhere else. There are over 100 sets to choose from, from well priced travel sets retailing for under £50 to exquisitely made rosewood or ebony sets at about £300.

Site Usability:	★★★★★	Based:	UK
Product Range:	★★★★	Express Delivery Option?	(UK) No
Price Range:	Luxury/Medium/Very Good Value	Gift Wrapping Option?	No
Delivery Area:	Worldwide	Returns Procedure:	Down to you

www.farscapegames.co.uk

You may be looking for a complete travel games compendium, or just a new reasonably priced backgammon set, whether your favourite game is Mah Jong, dominoes, Monopoly or bridge you're sure to find what you're seeking here, and that's without going to your local store and trying to decide whether you should be in the children's section or somewhere else, and finding eventually that there are only a couple of options for your chosen game.

Site Usability:	★★★★★	Based:	UK
Product Range:	★★★★	Express Delivery Option?	(UK) Yes
Price Range:	Luxury/Medium/Very Good Value	Gift Wrapping Option?	No
Delivery Area:	Worldwide	Returns Procedure:	Down to you

www.thegadgetshop.com

Browse their online catalogue for some of the funniest, coolest gadgets you can buy, with everything from the frivolous to the functional, the digital to the downright silly. You'll find Big Boy's Toys, Retro Toys, Fun Stuff, Star Wars and ipod accessories here too. They'll ship all over the world and offer an express delivery service in the UK. This is a particularly good website for mid- to older teenagers so if you've one of those to buy for take a good look round.

Site Usability:	★★★★★	Based:	UK
Product Range:	★★★★★	Express Delivery Option?	(UK) Yes
Price Range:	Luxury/Medium/Very Good Value	Gift Wrapping Option?	Yes
Delivery Area:	Worldwide	Returns Procedure:	Freepost or via their customer services department

www.greatexperiencedays.co.uk

Here if you're looking for a gift for an active person you can choose between driving a Ferrari or Porsche 996, dual control flying lessons or clay pigeon shooting (to name just a few). Alternatively you can organise a pampering day out or simply purchase an original newspaper for the special date. They'll ship (items that can be shipped, of course) anywhere in the World and offer standard or express delivery for gifts and vouchers in the UK.

Site Usability:	★★★★★	Based:	UK
Product Range:	★★★★★	Express Delivery Option?	(UK) Yes
Price Range:	Luxury/Medium/Very Good Value	Gift Wrapping Option?	Experiences arrive as a gift pack.
Delivery Area:	Worldwide	Returns Procedure:	N/A

www.iwantoneofthose.co.uk

An irresistible (and very cleverly designed) gift and gadget shop with a huge choice and a very well designed website. You can search by price or product type and there's a wide range of all levels. With excellent animation for most products you can choose from gadgets for garden, kitchen and office plus the inevitable toys and games. They offer same day delivery, free standard delivery on orders over £50 and are happy to ship to you anywhere in the World.

Site Usability:	★★★★★	Based:	UK
Product Range:	★★★★★	Express Delivery Option?	(UK) Yes
Price Range:	Luxury/Medium/Very Good Value	Gift Wrapping Option?	Yes
Delivery Area:	Worldwide	Returns Procedure:	Down to you

www.microanvica.com

Here's an online site with an offline presence in Tottenham Court Road and Selfridges, offering the latest in computers, cameras and audio equipment including ipod and all the accessories. Expect a very good choice and excellent service – they do know what they're talking about and really want to help. Being a slightly less well known retailer Micro Anvika is a very good place to look if you're trying to buy that hot new product just before Christmas.

Site Usability:	★★★★★	Based:	UK
Product Range:	★★★★	Express Delivery Option?	(UK) Yes
Price Range:	Luxury/Medium/Very Good Value	Gift Wrapping Option?	No
Delivery Area:	Worldwide	Returns Procedure:	Down to you

www.oregonscientific.co.uk

Oregon Scientific, established in the US in 1989, creates electronic products for modern lifestyles. Its innovative products are the combination of cutting-edge US technology and stylish European design. You've no doubt seen their stylish wireless weather stations and thermometers, but did you know that you can also find the World's slimmest radio controlled alarm clock or a Barbie B Book learning laptop on this irresistible website, plus loads more ideas ranging from the very reasonable to the really quite expensive.

Site Usability:	★★★★★	Based:	UK
Product Range:	★★★	Express Delivery Option?	(UK) Yes
Price Range:	Luxury/Medium/Very Good Value	Gift Wrapping Option?	No
Delivery Area:	UK	Returns Procedure:	Down to you

http://eurostore.palm.com

At this worldwide specialist in hand-held computers you can purchase a wide range of products from the newest state of the art latest compact models, to all the essential accessories to link your hand-held to your PC. As the world of hand held computers seems to develop by the day (and it seems to me you need to be something of a boffin to be able to use them properly) you'll need all the excellent information they give you here. GPS solutions and SmartPhones are available as well.

Site Usability:	★★★★★	Based:	UK
Product Range:	★★★★★	Express Delivery Option?	(UK) Yes
Price Range:	Luxury/Medium/Very Good Value	Gift Wrapping Option?	No
Delivery Area:	Worldwide	Returns Procedure:	Down to you

www.paramountzone.com

Paramount Zone offers an extensive and carefully selected choice of gadgets, games, boy's toys, bar items, sports gadgets (a good selection), mp3 players, executive items/toys, bachelor pad stuff, gift ideas, and lifestyle accessories – and these are just some of the items you'll find. The majority of UK address orders are despatched the same day for 1–2 day delivery and they're happy to deliver worldwide.

Site Usability:	★★★★	Based:	UK
Product Range:	★★★★	Express Delivery Option?	(UK) Yes
Price Range:	Luxury/Medium/Very Good Value	Gift Wrapping Option?	No
Delivery Area:	Worldwide	Returns Procedure:	Down to you

www.redletterdays.co.uk

One of the best 'Experience' day providers (and you've probably seen their brochures and packs in some of the larger stores), Red Letter Days make it easy for you to choose between flying, driving and some serious adventurers experiences. They also offer some great junior options plus body and soul pampering and luxuries such as lunch on the Orient Express. Once you've ordered what you want it will be sent out in an attractive gift pack to the recipient.

Site Usability:	★★★★★	Based:	UK
Product Range:	★★★★★	Express Delivery Option?	(UK) Yes
Price Range:	Luxury/Medium/Very Good Value	Gift Wrapping Option?	No
Delivery Area:	UK	Returns Procedure:	N/A

www.sciencemuseumstore.com

Next time you go to London pay a visit to the Science Museum, where you can take a 'Moon Walk', check out the Wild Safari or examine the Spy Car. If you can't get there you can find a number of fun and innovative products at their online shop. A rocket that flies using vinegar and baking soda to demonstrate Newton's Third Law of Motion for example, and a light that floats in mid-air as if by magic. Just two of the interesting and fun gifts you can find here.

Site Usability:	★★★★★	Based:	UK
Product Range:	★★★★	Express Delivery Option?	(UK) Yes
Price Range:	Luxury/Medium/Very Good Value	Gift Wrapping Option?	No
Delivery Area:	UK	Returns Procedure:	Down to you

www.shopping-emporium-uk.com

This is a brightly coloured unsophisticated website offering the highest quality Italian made sets for backgammon, dominoes and solitaire, bridge, roulette, poker and other games. The sets are contained in unique boxes and travel cases made of mahogany, walnut and high quality leather. This is definitely top end of the market but the prices are not unreasonable for what you're buying.

Site Usability:	★★★★	Based:	UK
Product Range:	★★★	Express Delivery Option?	(UK) No
Price Range:	Luxury/Medium/Very Good Value	Gift Wrapping Option?	No
Delivery Area:	Worldwide	Returns Procedure:	Down to you

www.trackday-gift-experiences.com

Different from most of the 'Experience' websites in that Trackday only offer driving experiences (at different venues in the South and Midlands), you can select here for the boy racer in your life (if he hasn't got a fast enough car already). Send him Rally Driving, 4 × 4 off road, Formula 1 or off in a supercar or even to learn how to manage a skid pan (excellent for everyone particularly new drivers). You order vouchers (either open or for a particular experience) and they're valid for a year.

Site Usability:	★★★★	Based:	UK
Product Range:	★★★	Express Delivery Option?	(UK) Yes
Price Range:	Luxury/Medium/Very Good Value	Gift Wrapping Option?	No
Delivery Area:	UK	Returns Procedure:	N/A

www.thesharperedge.co.uk

Originally in the mobile phone industry, this retailer branched out into up to the minute gadgets and gifts about five years ago and specialises in keeping you up to date with the latest ideas on the market. It's a really excellent gift and gadget store offering you clever and unusual gift ideas plus innovative household accessories, and a good place to look if you need a last minute present as they despatch aiming for next day delivery and offer to wrap your present as well.

Site Usability:	★★★★	Based:	UK
Product Range:	★★★★	Express Delivery Option?	(UK) Yes
Price Range:	Luxury/<u>Medium</u>/Very Good Value	Gift Wrapping Option?	Yes
Delivery Area:	Worldwide	Returns Procedure:	Down to you

Chapter 54

Cigars, Pens and Small Leather Gifts

There are just a couple of websites you need to know about here if you know someone who smokes cigars and you want to give him (presumably him) a present. They're both beautifully designed with (I'm told) a wonderful selection so if you want to give them something they'll really appreciate, you won't go wrong. Of course you don't have to buy cigars; you can also buy beautiful quality humidors, cigar cutters and leather cigar holders as well.

Pens (really high quality ones, or something slightly different), are usually a welcome gift. You may get the odd 'oh not another pen', but at least it's not as bad as 'oh not another pair of socks' and because the house pen thief is always about no one can have enough pens. Special makes include Mont Blanc, Yard O'Led and Faber Castell and you can really shell out for these although Yard O'Led in particular has come up with a lovely range of barley stamped black and silver 'Retro' pens which won't break the bank.

You'll also find innovative styles from Cross and Lamy which the younger generation seem to like (at least my children do) plus classic pens from brands such as Parker and Shaeffer. Refills, spare nibs and repairs are also to be found on these excellent sites.

On the subject of small leather gifts I'm referring to stud and jewellery boxes, cosmetic bags (I know, not for men but most of these websites offer ideas for both sexes), leather bound books, photo albums and high quality document wallets, plus those clever fold up change holders you can take on holiday with you or use at home. On some of the websites you'll find monogramming services which are usually free, plus gift wrapping, express and worldwide delivery and everything to make your life easier.

Cigars

Sites to Visit

www.simplycigars.co.uk

This is my favourite UK based website offering cigars and humidors plus some very attractive accessories and gifts, wines and spirits. The cigars are expensive as you would expect, however the site is beautifully designed with clever drop down menus and I know from experience that if you need a last minute gift for a smoker (or wine lover) they will do their utmost to get it to you on time so do have a look.

Site Usability:	★★★★★	Based:	UK
Product Range:	★★★★★	Express Delivery Option?	(UK) Yes
Price Range:	Luxury/Medium/Very Good Value	Gift Wrapping Option?	No
Delivery Area:	Worldwide	Returns Procedure:	Down to you

www.topcubans.com

Buying cigars in the UK is an extremely expensive experience particularly as you can buy from abroad and make a huge saving on superb quality products. Here is a wide choice, recommendations and advice you can trust and the delivery service is excellent. Not only that but if you're a smoker you'll be bombarded with regular special offers and even recipes to match the time of year. This is a cigar smoker's paradise.

Site Usability:	★★★★★	Based:	Switzerland
Product Range:	★★★★★	Express Delivery Option?	(UK) No
Price Range:	Luxury/Medium/Very Good Value	Gift Wrapping Option?	No
Delivery Area:	Worldwide	Returns Procedure:	Down to you

Pens and Small Leather Gifts

Sites to Visit

www.cityorg.co.uk

You may well not have heard of this excellent website, offering Filofax organisers and accessories, Cocinelle handbags, wallets and keyrings, Lo Scritto leather bound notebooks in lots of colours, Quo Vadis diaries, Paul Smith handbags and accessories, pens by Cross, Azuni jewellery, Paul Smith and Mont Blanc cufflinks, Leatherman tools and gadgets by Oregon Scientific. The website is easy to get round and the pictures large and clear. There's definitely something here for just about everyone.

Site Usability:	★★★★	Based:	UK
Product Range:	★★★★	Express Delivery Option?	(UK) Yes
Price Range:	Luxury/Medium/Very Good Value	Gift Wrapping Option?	No
Delivery Area:	Worldwide	Returns Procedure:	Down to you

www.filofax.co.uk

Your Filofax is now available in many different colours, sizes and styles; including mini, pocket, A5 and A4, black, red, pink, purple, pale blue and denim and on this website you can see each and every one, plus all the refills and accessories such as calculators and pens. Together with this you can download their address software and also buy the luxury range of Yard O'Led pens here, making this a very good website for gifts.

Site Usability:	★★★★★	Based:	UK
Product Range:	★★★	Express Delivery Option?	(UK) Yes
Price Range:	Luxury/Medium/Very Good Value	Gift Wrapping Option?	No
Delivery Area:	Worldwide	Returns Procedure:	Down to you

www.h-s.co.uk

This is a name you may well never have heard of, but Harrison and Simmonds have been in business since 1928 offering pipes, cigar humidors and accessories and luxury gifts from companies such as Dalvey. There's also a wide range of Mont Blanc pens and accessories which you need to call them to order, plus chess sets, Hunter pocket watches and shooting sticks. They're happy to ship to you anywhere in the world and if you call them for advice you'll receive excellent service.

Site Usability:	★★★★	Based:	UK
Product Range:	★★★★	Express Delivery Option?	(UK) No
Price Range:	Luxury/Medium/Very Good Value	Gift Wrapping Option?	No
Delivery Area:	Worldwide	Returns Procedure:	Down to you

www.mrpen.co.uk

Mr Pen has a clear website offering different ranges of pens, including Cross and Sheaffer plus the gorgeously packaged Mount Everest Legacy. An engraving service is available for most pens for a small charge and gift-wrapping is free. Cut glass inkwells, general cartridges and pen repairs are also available. If you're looking for a special nib then call them and you can expect a really personal service.

Site Usability:	★★★	Based:	UK
Product Range:	★★★★	Express Delivery Option?	(UK) Yes
Price Range:	Luxury/Medium/Very Good Value	Gift Wrapping Option?	Yes
Delivery Area:	Worldwide	Returns Procedure:	Down to you

www.penandpaper.co.uk

So what's different about this website, when you can find most of the same pens elsewhere? Well apart from being well laid out and offering free delivery on orders over £50 they also have a section for 'Different Pens', which certainly drew my attention. As well as the colourful Cross Morph Pens they offer a very good range of the Fisher Space Pens from lacquered Bullet Pens in bronze, black and colours such as Orange Slush and Purple Passion, Shuttle retractable pens, speciality space pens, YK3 and Zero Gravity pens.

Site Usability:	★★★★	Based:	UK
Product Range:	★★★★	Express Delivery Option?	(UK) No
Price Range:	Luxury/Medium/Very Good Value	Gift Wrapping Option?	No
Delivery Area:	Worldwide	Returns Procedure:	Down to you

www.penshop.co.uk

This is a really attractive website offering one of the best selections of luxury pens including Yard-o-Led's beautiful sterling silver fountain pens, ballpoints and pencils, Faber Castell pens in wood and silver, Mont Blanc (you need to phone to order), and Porsche Design steel pens. They also offer Lamy, Rotring, Shaeffer and Waterman, aim to send out the day you order and they'll deliver Worldwide. There's a repairs service as well.

Site Usability:	★★★★	Based:	UK
Product Range:	★★★★	Express Delivery Option?	(UK) Yes
Price Range:	Luxury/Medium/Very Good Value	Gift Wrapping Option?	No
Delivery Area:	Worldwide	Returns Procedure:	Down to you

www.peterdraper.co.uk

Offering Porsche design, Caran D'Ache and Lalex pens plus Parker, Waterman, Lamy and Cross plus Filofax organisers and pen refills, Peter Draper has an unsophisticated website but one where you can expect to find very good service – free delivery on all orders over £25 and worldwide shipping. This is the kind of retailer where, if you have a query, you can call up and speak to someone who really knows what they're talking about and can give you good advice, particularly if you're looking for a special gift.

Site Usability:	★★★	Based:	UK
Product Range:	★★★★	Express Delivery Option?	(UK) No
Price Range:	Luxury/Medium/Very Good Value	Gift Wrapping Option?	No
Delivery Area:	Worldwide	Returns Procedure:	Down to you

www.pickett.co.uk

Gloves, wallets, umbrellas, belts, briefcases and stud boxes are just some of the high quality, beautifully made men's accessories you'll find on Pickett's website. If you've ever visited one of their shops you'll know that everything is the best quality you can find and most items would make lovely gifts. Couple this with their distinctive dark green and orange packaging and excellent service and you can't go wrong, whatever you buy.

Site Usability:	★★★★	Based:	UK
Product Range:	★★★★	Express Delivery Option?	(UK) Yes
Price Range:	Luxury/Medium/Very Good Value	Gift Wrapping Option?	No but luxury packaging is standard
Delivery Area:	Worldwide	Returns Procedure:	Down to you

www.old.co.uk

Robert Old has a really attractive and easy to get round website, offering a high quality range of men's gifts and accessories including cashmere sweaters and scarves, leather gifts from cufflink boxes to travel alarm clocks, classic English briefcases and weekenders and shoes by Crockett and Jones. There's lots of clear information about each item and although standard delivery is the norm, they switch to express delivery towards Christmas.

Site Usability:	★★★★	Based:	UK
Product Range:	★★★★	Express Delivery Option?	(UK) Yes
Price Range:	Luxury/Medium/Very Good Value	Gift Wrapping Option?	No
Delivery Area:	Worldwide	Returns Procedure:	Down to you

Also check out these websites for pens and small leather gifts

Website address	You'll find them in
www.forzieri.com	Luxury brands online
www.gucci.com	Luxury brands online

Chapter 55

Gifts for the Cook and the Gardener

I think you have to be quite careful here, particularly before shelling out for a new set of pans or a garden fork, you may just make yourself quite unpopular (unless it's a very, very special garden fork, of course).

Look for gifts that are unusual, clever or particularly attractive and you'll do far better. Take Cucina Direct, for example. You'll find the normal run of the mill kitchen equipment, beautifully photographed, alongside Provencal tableware, excellent and different barware, Dualit toasters and KitchenAid mixers. So there would definitely be something for everyone.

If you're thinking of tableware choose something special to add to a collection that the person you're giving to has already, or a gift that can be used independently, such as a set of six pretty dessert plates or unusual mugs. That way they're much more likely to be kept and used rather than suffer the worst fate of unappreciated gifts and be given on to another recipient.

Gifts for the Cook

Sites to Visit

www.emmabridgewater.co.uk

Emma Bridgewater is very well known for her high quality pottery and clever and attractive designs, such as Polka Dots, Hugs and Kisses and Hearts as well as her mug collections including dogs, cats, birds and flowers. Every season she's bringing out new products, such as cutlery, glass, preserves and teas, all with her signature script. Almost every kitchen has one or two pieces of her pottery and they make really lovely gifts.

Site Usability:	★★★★★	Based:	UK
Product Range:	★★★★	Express Delivery Option?	(UK) Yes
Price Range:	Luxury/<u>Medium</u>/Very Good Value	Gift Wrapping Option?	Yes
Delivery Area:	Worldwide	Returns Procedure:	Down to you

www.cucinadirect.co.uk

Everything for the kitchen is beautifully displayed, including the highest quality knives and chopping boards, pots and pans, unusual bar tools, glasses and serving dishes, picnic equipment, general housekeeping items and a gift selection. You'll also find a small but very high quality range of kitchen electrical appliances plus their small selection of attractively packaged hampers.

Site Usability:	★★★★★	Based:	UK
Product Range:	★★★★	Express Delivery Option?	(UK) Yes
Price Range:	Luxury/<u>Medium</u>/Very Good Value	Gift Wrapping Option?	Yes
Delivery Area:	Worldwide	Returns Procedure:	Down to you

www.diningstore.co.uk

There are some quite different products on this website, such as the ZapCap bottle opener, Escali Cibo nutritional scale and CaddyO bottle chiller, alongside their designer kitchen and tableware with collections from Eva Solo (wonderful for presents), Cuisinox Elysee, Le Creuset, Mauviel, Couzon and Jura. This is not the normal kitchen and cookware selection so have a look round, you're certain to find something very different and some great gifts for the enthusiastic cook.

Site Usability:	★★★★	Based:	UK
Product Range:	★★★	Express Delivery Option?	(UK) No
Price Range:	Luxury/<u>Medium</u>/Very Good Value	Gift Wrapping Option?	No
Delivery Area:	Europe	Returns Procedure:	Down to you

www.divertimenti.co.uk

This famous London based cookery equipment site offers over 5000 items from hand painted tableware including decorated and coloured pottery from France, a really comprehensive range of kitchen essentials including knives, boards and bakeware plus Italian products (parmesan graters and ravioli trays), copper bowls and pans, children's baking sets, wedding gift service, knife sharpening and copper re-tinning. This has always been and still remains one of the best kitchen and dining shops around.

Site Usability:	★★★★	Based:	UK
Product Range:	★★★★	Express Delivery Option?	(UK) No
Price Range:	Luxury/Medium/Very Good Value	Gift Wrapping Option?	No
Delivery Area:	Worldwide	Returns Procedure:	Down to you

www.french-brand.com

This is a France based retailer offering you all those home accessories you saw on your last trip but weren't able to sneak into your suitcase. Gorgeous and colourful table linen from Les Olivades and Jaquard Francais (and lots more), quilted cushions by Souleido and toiletries and home fragrance by Manuel Canovas and Jardin Secret. There's also a fantastic range of bed linen by designers such as Descamps and colourful beach towels as well.

Site Usability:	★★★★	Based:	UK
Product Range:	★★★★★	Express Delivery Option?	(UK) No
Price Range:	Luxury/Medium/Very Good Value	Gift Wrapping Option?	No
Delivery Area:	Worldwide	Returns Procedure:	Down to you

www.smallislandtrader.com

Small Island Trader is an excellent company (with an excellent website) offering not only china and glass from a wide range of designers and manufacturers, but also a wide selection of kitchen equipment from juicers and steamers to copper and Le Creuset pots and pans, Sabatier knives, baking trays, and the Eva Solo's range of kitchen and living products. There are lots of gift ideas here. Needless to say they can't carry everything they offer in stock and delivery time is very much dependent on what you order.

Site Usability:	★★★★★	Based:	UK
Product Range:	★★★★★	Express Delivery Option?	(UK) No
Price Range:	Luxury/Medium/Very Good Value	Gift Wrapping Option?	No
Delivery Area:	Worldwide	Returns Procedure:	Down to you

Gifts for the Gardener

The gardener is even more difficult to buy for than the cook as so many of the products on offer on the garden websites seem either too mundane (forks, trowels, gloves etc) or a bit silly (a bronze garden sheep for almost £200?) but then, what do I know? I do know that a high quality pair of secateurs is always welcome as long as they're really good as is a pair of Hunter wellies (Hunter, mind, not a cheap variety) but with garden statues and ornaments you need to be careful, some people love them and some don't. Gorgeous planters, however, are excellent gifts, if heavy and expensive.

Some of the websites below offer you everything for the garden with a few gift ideas, and some specialise in unusual items 'suitable' for gardeners. You'll find lots of suggestions on both. Delivery on some of these websites seems to be rather long so if in doubt give them a call. The 28 day rule is usually just to cover them in case they don't have something in stock and you should be able to get things sent out much more quickly.

Sites to Visit

www.birstall.co.uk

Here you can buy absolutely everything for the garden and gardening enthusiast, from seeds to recliners, from barbecues to poultry houses and swimming pool lighting. There's so much product bursting out from the site that it looks a bit confusing but its well worth the effort. As far as gifts are concerned they sell high quality Felco secateurs, decorative brass Haws watering cans and Leatherman knives plus loads of other ideas.

Site Usability:	★★★★	Based:	UK
Product Range:	★★★★	Express Delivery Option?	(UK) No
Price Range:	Luxury/Medium/Very Good Value	Gift Wrapping Option?	No
Delivery Area:	Worldwide	Returns Procedure:	Down to you

www.baileys-home-garden.co.uk

Baileys offer a wonderfully eclectic mix of home and garden accessories, from pretty Welsh blankets and paint buckets to big sinks, garden lighting, Bailey's Bath Soak and Carrot Hand Cream. There are ideas for junior gardener's gifts from junior tools, watering cans and buckets (all in a gorgeous cherry red) and vintage style garden forks, pots and twine reels. To order anything on their website you need to phone them.

Site Usability:	★★★★	Based:	UK
Product Range:	★★★	Express Delivery Option?	(UK) No
Price Range:	Luxury/Medium/Very Good Value	Gift Wrapping Option?	No
Delivery Area:	UK	Returns Procedure:	Down to you

www.davidaustin.com

David Austin is famous for developing new types of English Roses, with his first, 'Constance Spry', launched in 1963. On his website you can find many varieties, including Modern Hybrid Tea Roses and Floribundas, Climbing Roses, Ramblers, Modern Shrub Roses and Wild Species Roses. You'll also find his new fragrant English Roses created specially for the home. You can order his gift boxed container roses and exquisite rose bouquets here as well for UK delivery.

Site Usability:	★★★★★		Based:	UK
Product Range:	★★★★		Express Delivery Option?	(UK) Yes
Price Range:	Luxury/Medium/Very Good Value		Gift Wrapping Option?	Yes for Container Roses
Delivery Area:	Worldwide except for container roses and bouquets		Returns Procedure:	Down to you

www.rhs.org.uk

On the Royal Horticultural Society's website you can become a member of the RHS or make someone else a member, which provides their monthly magazine, reduced entry into RHS flower shows and free entry into RHS and partner gardens. You can also order Spring bulbs from their excellent collection or click through to their online gift shop containing over 400 ideas including Burgon and Ball tools, RHS well priced and prettily packaged toiletries, games and activities, gifts for the garden and wildlife gifts such as bird feeders and bee nests.

Site Usability:	★★★★★		Based:	UK
Product Range:	★★★★		Express Delivery Option?	(UK) No
Price Range:	Luxury/Medium/Very Good Value		Gift Wrapping Option?	No but they will send some items as gifts for you
Delivery Area:	Worldwide		Returns Procedure:	Down to you

www.rkalliston.com

This is a really exceptional website offering perfect gifts for the gardener, from wasp catchers and storm lanterns to dibbers and twine, hammocks (to rest in after a hard day) and fairy vases as well as gardeners gift sets, china for alfresco dining and pretty flower baskets, and these are just a few of the eclectic collection of gardening items available here.

Site Usability:	★★★★★		Based:	UK
Product Range:	★★★★		Express Delivery Option?	(UK) Yes
Price Range:	Luxury/Medium/Very Good Value		Gift Wrapping Option?	No
Delivery Area:	Worldwide		Returns Procedure:	Down to you

www.thecuttinggarden.com

Sarah Raven specialises in teaching people how to grow flowers that can be cut and used indoors, and her first book, The Cutting Garden, won The Specialist Garden Book of the Year Award. On her colourful and attractively designed website you'll find a wonderful collection of seeds, seedlings and bulbs, her books and annual diary (a great gift) plus plenty of other ideas such as florist's scissors, flower arranging gloves and outdoor tableware and glass.

Site Usability:	★★★★	Based:	UK
Product Range:	★★★★	Express Delivery Option?	(UK) No
Price Range:	Luxury/<u>Medium</u>/Very Good Value	Gift Wrapping Option?	No
Delivery Area:	UK	Returns Procedure:	Down to you

www.thegluttonousgardener.co.uk

Beautifully packaged and hand tied with raffia, this is a wide selection of well photographed gifts for any of your friends who like to garden and eat as well. So you'll find sloe gin accompanying young sloe trees, a bottle of Macon with a white grape vine and champagne with terracotta pots planted with sage, thyme, oregano and rosemary. This really is an excellent website and something just that little bit different.

Site Usability:	★★★★★	Based:	UK
Product Range:	★★★★	Express Delivery Option?	(UK) Yes
Price Range:	Luxury/<u>Medium</u>/Very Good Value	Gift Wrapping Option?	Yes
Delivery Area:	UK	Returns Procedure:	Down to you

www.treesdirect.co.uk

Fruit and nut trees, ornamentals and aromatic, evergreen bays are just some of the unusual gift ideas you can find here. The trees are chosen for their colour, blossom, shape and size to suit all types of gardens and patios and they arrive dressed in a hessian sack tied with green garden string, planting instructions and hand written message card. You can request that your tree arrives on a specific date and if you want advice just give them a call.

Site Usability:	★★★★	Based:	UK
Product Range:	★★★★	Express Delivery Option?	(UK) Yes
Price Range:	Luxury/<u>Medium</u>/Very Good Value	Gift Wrapping Option?	No
Delivery Area:	Europe	Returns Procedure:	Down to you

Chapter 56

Tickets and Subscriptions

Gone are the days when you had to queue on the telephone to book your theatre tickets. Gone also, are the days when you could phone most theatres direct to book your favourite seats. Nowadays you're almost pushed to order online and you have to be really, really careful to ensure that you get the seats you want, and not just the ones they want to sell you.

However, for many online theatre booking systems you can see exactly what you're booking from the online seating plan and in some cases also check your seat numbers before you confirm your booking. In this way booking is much, much easier than before. This also applies to opera tickets and some concerts so you can reserve your seats with confidence.

Where there is any doubt about where you'll be sitting don't if at all possible, use that ticketing agency. Use another.

Subscriptions are totally another matter, of course, and you can book your best friend's birthday subscription to Vogue, Glamour or Vanity Fair with impunity. Nothing could be easier and the service is excellent. You can also get discounts on your annual subscriptions by checking out the codes in the advertisements in the glossies so look out for those, the discounts are really good. Don't buy an annual subscription without checking that you can get it discounted. You most likely can.

Sites to Visit

www.aloud.com

Aloud specialises in Rock and Pop Concert Tickets and the alphabetic index in the left hand column on the homepage on this website allows you to quickly choose from their Hot New Tickets or Best Seller collections. Ordering is clear and easy although they only tell you the area your seats will be in rather than the row. From their Merchandise Shop, also accessible from the Home Page, you can buy t-shirts and posters with lots of choices available to give as gifts or keep yourself.

Site Usability:	★★★★	Based:	UK	
Product Range:	★★★★★	Express Delivery Option?	(UK) No	
Price Range:	Luxury/Medium/<u>Very Good Value</u>	Gift Wrapping Option?	No	
Delivery Area:	UK	Returns Procedure:	N/A	

www.barbican.org.uk

Open 363 days a year, the Barbican presents a uniquely diverse programme of world-class performing and visual arts, encompassing all forms of classical and contemporary music, international theatre and dance and a cinema programme which blends first-run films with special themed seasons. On this website there's lots of information about all the productions, together with a ticket booking facility and you can also find out about the restaurants and bars.

Site Usability:	★★★★	Based:	UK	
Product Range:	★★★★★	Express Delivery Option?	(UK) No	
Price Range:	Luxury/<u>Medium</u>/Very Good Value	Gift Wrapping Option?	No	
Delivery Area:	UK	Returns Procedure:	N/A	

www.discountpublications.co.uk

If you'd like to give the gift of a magazine subscription then take a look at this website, where you'll find subscriptions for less, including Vogue, Vanity Fair, Tatler, Red, FHM and GQ, House and Garden, The World of Interiors and most other glossy publications available at much lower prices than you'd pay if you bought them each month. You can also send your subscription with a personalised message and gift certificate and delivery is to the UK only.

Site Usability:	★★★★	Based:	UK	
Product Range:	★★★★	Express Delivery Option?	(UK) No	
Price Range:	Luxury/<u>Medium</u>/Very Good Value	Gift Wrapping Option?	No	
Delivery Area:	UK	Returns Procedure:	N/A	

www.eno.org

It's really easy to book your tickets for the English National Opera on this modern website so you can pay a visit to their newly refurbished home in St Martin's Lane in London. You can also find out about special events such as family events and singing courses, take advantage of their special ticket offers, read reviews and learn about regional tours.

Site Usability:	★★★★		Based:	UK
Product Range:	★★★		Express Delivery Option?	(UK) No
Price Range:	Luxury/<u>Medium</u>/Very Good Value		Gift Wrapping Option?	No
Delivery Area:	UK		Returns Procedure:	N/A

www.glyndebourne.co.uk

Here's the famous opera house in the country with members being able to buy their tickets about six months in advance. Now with their new website advertising returns and other available seats it should be much easier to get there. Don't forget to take your picnic and your brolly as it rains (often) however, the new opera house offers covered trestle tables if you don't want to risk the weather but you need to get there early if you want to bag one.

Site Usability:	★★★★★		Based:	UK
Product Range:	★★★		Express Delivery Option?	(UK) No
Price Range:	<u>Luxury/Medium</u>/Very Good Value		Gift Wrapping Option?	No
Delivery Area:	UK		Returns Procedure:	N/A

www.magazine-group.co.uk

With over 400 titles on offer and some very good discounts you could find something for just about everyone here, from the sportsman (Rugby World, Dive, Inside Edge, The Angler), food and drink lover (Olive, Good Food, Decanter) home interiors enthusiast (Beautiful Homes, Elle Decoration) and fashion addict (Vogue, Harpers Bazaar and In Style). It's a really comprehensive selection and once you've placed your order you can ask them to send you a gift card to forward on to the recipient.

Site Usability:	★★★★★		Based:	UK
Product Range:	★★★★★		Express Delivery Option?	(UK) No
Price Range:	Luxury/<u>Medium</u>/Very Good Value		Gift Wrapping Option?	No
Delivery Area:	UK		Returns Procedure:	N/A

www.magazinesofamerica.com

Some magazines frankly don't travel well, you read them when you're abroad and when you bring them home they just seem somehow wrong. Personally I think it's different with some of the US publications, such as American Vogue, Glamour and House Beautiful which complement their UK counterparts. Be warned, some of the subscriptions here are extremely expensive, however delivery is included in the price.

Site Usability:	★★★★	Based:	US
Product Range:	★★★★	Express Delivery Option?	(UK) No
Price Range:	Luxury/<u>Medium</u>/Very Good Value	Gift Wrapping Option?	No
Delivery Area:	Worldwide	Returns Procedure:	N/A

www.npg.org.uk

The National Portrait Gallery houses a unique record of men and women who created – and are creating – Britain's history and culture. It holds ten major events each year such as 'Self Portrait – Renaissance to Contemporary' and 'Photographs 1850–2000'. It also holds its primary collection of over 10,000 portraits, from Gainsborough to Cecil Beaton. Pay a visit to the online shop and take out a subscription to the Gallery, or look through their selection of high quality side tied notebooks, art books, prints, mugs and gifts.

Site Usability:	★★★★	Based:	UK
Product Range:	★★★	Express Delivery Option?	(UK) No
Price Range:	Luxury/<u>Medium</u>/Very Good Value	Gift Wrapping Option?	No
Delivery Area:	Worldwide	Returns Procedure:	N/A

www.nt-online.org

The website for London's National Theatre gives full details and cast lists for all productions plus an online ticket booking facility. Find out about the restaurants as well and make your reservation for lunch or dinner and have a browse through their bookshop where you'll find books on theory, history, criticism and practical help about theatre.

Site Usability:	★★★★	Based:	UK
Product Range:	★★★	Express Delivery Option?	(UK) No
Price Range:	Luxury/<u>Medium</u>/Very Good Value	Gift Wrapping Option?	No
Delivery Area:	Worldwide	Returns Procedure:	N/A

www.royalacademy.org.uk

Treat yourself or someone special to a years membership of The Royal Academy, in its beautiful buildings just off Piccadilly. You can also buy individual tickets to the fabulous exhibitions held here, such as CHINA: The Three Emperors or Andrew Lloyd Webber's personal art collection (sorry if you missed that, it was wonderful). Alternatively pay a visit to their online shop where you'll find cards, limited edition prints, lifestyle gifts, diaries and calendars.

Site Usability:	★★★★	Based:	UK
Product Range:	★★★	Express Delivery Option?	(UK) No
Price Range:	Luxury/<u>Medium</u>/Very Good Value	Gift Wrapping Option?	No
Delivery Area:	Worldwide	Returns Procedure:	N/A

www.royalopera.org

The Royal Opera House has for some while had a really elegant website. Once you've read about the different productions and reviews you can select the one you want to see, then the date and the type of seating and when you find seats available you'll know the actual row and seat number, so you'll have no doubt at all about where you'll be sitting. Hopefully all ticket websites will offer this service soon.

Site Usability:	★★★★	Based:	UK
Product Range:	★★★	Express Delivery Option?	(UK) No
Price Range:	Luxury/Medium/Very Good Value	Gift Wrapping Option?	No
Delivery Area:	UK	Returns Procedure:	N/A

www.seetickets.com

From the X Factor Live to Billy Eliot to Bryn Terfel at Christmas you can book just about everything here, plus events such as the Good Food Show and Clothes Show Live, sporting events such as the Horse of the Year show and the Grand Prix, comedy shows and classical music performances. It's an attractive website to get round and although you can't see exactly where you'll be sitting when you order your tickets they give you a clearer idea than on some others. They also suggest places to stay.

Site Usability:	★★★★★	Based:	UK
Product Range:	★★★★★	Express Delivery Option?	(UK) No
Price Range:	Luxury/Medium/Very Good Value	Gift Wrapping Option?	No
Delivery Area:	UK	Returns Procedure:	N/A

www.subscription.co.uk

Here you'll find a vast range of titles to subscribe to, including Vogue, Vanity Fair, Tatler, Harper's Bazaar, In Style and Red plus other titles such as House and Garden, Country Living and Mother and Baby. What you won't find are the special offers available through the magazines themselves, so I suggest you buy a single issue to give you the relevant offer code as there are quite significant discounts to be found. You then quote this code when placing your order.

Site Usability:	★★★★★	Based:	UK
Product Range:	★★★★★	Express Delivery Option?	(UK) No
Price Range:	Luxury/Medium/Very Good Value	Gift Wrapping Option?	No
Delivery Area:	Worldwide	Returns Procedure:	N/A

www.ticketmaster.co.uk

Music, theatre and sport tickets are available on this – the original ticket website. Seating plans for the different venues are easy to see and tickets are quick and easy to book although **do** make sure you're happy with your seats for certain before you book. If you want standing room tickets to see Robbie Williams, seats for England v Barbarians at Twickenham or Firework and Music tickets at Hampton Court or tickets for pretty well anything else, then this is your site. Gift vouchers are on offer too, and they also have links to websites offering you travel, places to stay and eat plus 'What's On in Europe'.

Site Usability:	★★★★★	Based:	UK
Product Range:	★★★★★	Express Delivery Option?	(UK) No
Price Range:	Luxury/Medium/Very Good Value	Gift Wrapping Option?	No
Delivery Area:	UK	Returns Procedure:	N/A

Chapter 57

Books, Music and Movies

The competition for all these products online is now extremely fierce and it's all to your benefit provided you know how to get the best out of the sites. There are comparison websites for books, cds, dvds and computer games so if you're searching for something specific (such as that boxed set of the OC you've been asked for) you should check and see where you can get the best deal. Ok so this may sound time consuming but believe me it isn't once you've got the hang of it and you can save quite a lot of money.

When you're looking at what you think is a good discount, don't forget the postage. Buying cheap books is all very well but if you then have to add on an extra £1 or so you'll find you're getting back to near the original price so keep this in mind. With cds and dvds you can usually find a good price with free delivery as well.

All these sites are very addictive and you'll find yourself returning again and again and adding on just one extra book or cd. The worst thing that you can do is to give your 1-click Amazon password to one of your children. Then you're really asking for trouble. 1-click is very quick and excellent when *you're* buying books etc. It's definitely not for the kids.

Books

Books must be one of the most popular items to buy online. They're so easy to package up, you know exactly what you're ordering and everyone out there is competing for your business, so you'll probably never buy a full price book again once you've started to buy on the web (shhh I didn't say that).

The problem is frequently where to stop. Not only can you find the book you're after but loads more ideas and suggestions along the same line will suddenly pop up in front of you so that before you know what you're doing you've ordered enough books to keep you busy for months.

The book websites are also great places to buy presents. Not just the latest books on every subject under the sun. Not just the perfect present for the cricketer/golfer/cook/gardener/art lover in your life. You can also find limited editions books, books signed by the author, out of print books and first editions. You can find books in other countries and have them sent to you anywhere in the world, and you can have that first edition gift wrapped with your personalised message and sent out for you without ever having to leave your chair.

Sites to Visit

www.amazon.co.uk

At Amazon you can buy not only books but just about everything, including your new Kenwood food mixer or digital camera, baby products and tools for your garden, which can make life rather confusing. They have probably the most comprehensive range of books, music, movies and games available anywhere, frequently at the best price and their service is excellent.

Site Usability:	★★★★★	Based:	UK
Product Range:	★★★★★	Express Delivery Option?	(UK) Yes
Price Range:	Luxury/Medium/Very Good Value	Gift Wrapping Option?	Yes
Delivery Area:	Worldwide	Returns Procedure:	Down to you

www.abebooks.co.uk

This is the worldwide marketplace for rare, secondhand and out of print books. You just need to know the title or the author and if it's available it'll be found immediately. You can then narrow your search to see only first editions, or signed copies, among other options. For special gifts this would be an excellent website as you can choose from a selection of real collectors' items, alternatively you can simply track down that book you lost some years ago and always wanted to read again.

Site Usability:	★★★★★	Based:	UK
Product Range:	★★★★★	Express Delivery Option?	(UK) No
Price Range:	Luxury/Medium/Very Good Value	Gift Wrapping Option?	No
Delivery Area:	Worldwide	Returns Procedure:	Down to you

www.best-book-price.co.uk

www.bookbrain.co.uk

These are two excellent places where you can compare book prices and see who has the book you're looking for in stock to send out immediately. They're both very easy to use - not really for buying ordinary paperbacks, although you can use them for that if you want to, but when you've found a special hardback that you want to give as a gift next week and Amazon is quoting you 4-6 weeks delivery you may be able to find another bookshop who has it ready to send out, and of course you can also compare the prices from all the bookstores.

www.blackwells.co.uk

If you prefer a less busy book website then pay a visit to Blackwell's of Oxford, established in 1879 and an online store for over ten years. What you'll find here is a really excellent and more personal service with a clear path through to the various departments: Fiction, Leisure and Lifestyle, Science, Humanities, Arts, Medical, Business Finance and Law. There are some good discounts to be found and shipping is free to the UK on orders over £20.

Site Usability:	★★★★★	Based:	UK
Product Range:	★★★★★	Express Delivery Option?	(UK) Yes
Price Range:	Luxury/Medium/Very Good Value	Gift Wrapping Option?	No
Delivery Area:	Worldwide	Returns Procedure:	Down to you

www.bol.com

Next time you're looking for a new book take a quick look at *bol.com*. They don't have anything like the range of Amazon but what they do have are very good special offers, with special edition (usually small hardback) copies of brand new titles at up to 60% off the normal price. Postage and Packing are free if you order three items or more, otherwise it's just £1 and you need to register to order (so they can send you regular updates and keep your details to make your next order even quicker).

Site Usability:	★★★★★	Based:	UK
Product Range:	★★★	Express Delivery Option?	(UK) No
Price Range:	Luxury/Medium/Very Good Value	Gift Wrapping Option?	No
Delivery Area:	Worldwide	Returns Procedure:	Down to you

www.compman.co.uk

This site started off as a computer books website and has moved into general educational books and fiction. So you can buy the latest John Grisham alongside Selected Papers on Particle Image Velocimetry (help). The site is very clearly laid out and you can see exactly what's in stock or on limited availability. Some of the discounts are very good. Standard delivery is 1–2 days and is free on orders over a small amount, which varies.

Site Usability:	★★★★	Based:	UK
Product Range:	★★★	Express Delivery Option?	(UK) Yes
Price Range:	Luxury/<u>Medium</u>/Very Good Value	Gift Wrapping Option?	No
Delivery Area:	Worldwide	Returns Procedure:	Down to you

www.hatchards.co.uk

Hatchards, booksellers since 1797, is the oldest surviving bookshop in London and is now based in its luxurious quarters at 187 Piccadilly, right next door to Fortnum and Mason. Not only do they offer a very good choice of titles in hardback and paperback, from fiction, children's books, art and architecture, biography, food and wine, gardening, history and humour, but they also specialise in signed and special editions and what they call VIP's (Very Important Publications), their recommendations for the season.

Site Usability:	★★★★★	Based:	UK
Product Range:	★★★★★	Express Delivery Option?	(UK) Yes
Price Range:	<u>Luxury/Medium</u>/Very Good Value	Gift Wrapping Option?	No
Delivery Area:	Worldwide	Returns Procedure:	Down to you

www.jonkers.co.uk

Jonkers specialise in modern first editions, fine illustrated books, classic children's fiction and nineteenth century literature. So if you have a goddaughter who might appreciate a first edition of Michael Bond's Paddington Goes to Town you'll find it here, plus AA Milne, Enid Blyton, Lewis Carroll and many more. Because some of these books are very expensive and precious (up into the £1000s) you can't order online but need to phone them using their freephone number.

Site Usability:	★★★★	Based:	UK
Product Range:	★★★	Express Delivery Option?	(UK) No
Price Range:	<u>Luxury/Medium</u>/Very Good Value	Gift Wrapping Option?	No
Delivery Area:	Worldwide	Returns Procedure:	Down to you

www.thebookplace.com

If you want a new bookshop to look at you could have a browse on this very clear site, which offers an extremely wide range and shows availability as soon as you search for your book. They also have a good selection of signed copies which would make excellent gifts and you can read the weekly press reviews on the latest releases. Postage is £2.75 per single book order plus £0.50 for each additional book and note that they also offer worldwide shipping and express delivery.

Site Usability:	★★★★	Based:	UK
Product Range:	★★★★	Express Delivery Option?	(UK) Yes
Price Range:	Luxury/<u>Medium</u>/Very Good Value	Gift Wrapping Option?	Yes
Delivery Area:	Worldwide	Returns Procedure:	Down to you

www.waterstones.co.uk

You may be a bit confused when you click through to this website, to find that you've actually landed at *amazon.co.uk*. The reason for this is that cleverly, instead of trying to set up a rival online bookstore, Waterstone's have decided to combine their excellent knowledge of the latest books with Amazon's range, delivery and customer service capabilities. So here you'll find exclusive articles and recommendations from Waterstone's, plus information about store locations and events and go through to Amazon when you want to purchase.

Site Usability:	★★★★★	Based:	UK
Product Range:	★★★★★	Express Delivery Option?	(UK) Yes
Price Range:	Luxury/Medium/Very Good Value	Gift Wrapping Option?	Yes
Delivery Area:	Worldwide	Returns Procedure:	Down to you.

www.whsmith.co.uk

On W H Smith's easy on the eye website you can buy books (often at very good discounts), all the latest dvds, music and computer games plus a small selection from their stationery ranges. There's also a wide range of gift ideas, including original historic newspapers and commemorative sporting books and you can subscribe at a discount to all your favourite magazines. The difference here from a lot of book/music/games website is that it's clear and simple to get round but also has an excellent choice.

Site Usability:	★★★★★	Based:	UK
Product Range:	★★★★★	Express Delivery Option?	(UK) No
Price Range:	Luxury/Medium/Very Good Value	Gift Wrapping Option?	No
Delivery Area:	UK	Returns Procedure:	Down to you

CDs, DVDs and Computer Games

You probably already know that just about every cd, dvd and computer game is available online, very often with free postage. Like books, if you want something expensive, a boxed set or series, you should check on the price comparison websites. There are so many websites now offering cds etc that it's impossible to list them all. All the ones below are very good. Because there are so many I personally think that your selection of retailer now depends on price, delivery and stock availability and the price comparison websites give you the short cut to getting the best overall deal.

Sites to Visit

www.amazon.co.uk

Here's a fantastic selection of dvds, cds and games etc. Not only will you almost certainly find what you're looking for but you'll also get excellent recommendations for similar items. Their One Click shopping option makes it dangerously easy to order more than you intended but that notwithstanding if you like listening to music, watching dvds or playing endless games this site is definitely for you.

Site Usability:	★★★★★	Based:	UK
Product Range:	★★★★★	Express Delivery Option?	(UK) Yes
Price Range:	Luxury/Medium/Very Good Value	Gift Wrapping Option?	Yes
Delivery Area:	Worldwide	Returns Procedure:	Down to you

www.best-cd-price.co.uk

Know the cd you want to buy but want to make sure you get the best price? Use this price comparison website, which not only shows where you'll find the best deal but includes the postage details as well, so you absolutely know where you are. This website is almost unbelievably quick to use and you can use it for dvds and games as well. As an example, if you do a search on the Lord of the Rings, The Return of the King, you'll be given twelve places where you can buy it online, with prices from an amazing £7.49, to £22.49. Quite a difference, I'm sure you'll agree.

www.cdwow.com

You'll find some of the best prices around here and again this site covers all mediums from cds and dvds to computer games. Because their prices are so good it would be worth purchasing gift vouchers here as you can be sure that the recipient will get a good deal, whatever they choose to spend them on. They offer free delivery worldwide for all items and regular special offers.

Site Usability:	★★★★★	Based:	UK
Product Range:	★★★★★	Express Delivery Option?	(UK) No
Price Range:	Luxury/Medium/Very Good Value	Gift Wrapping Option?	No
Delivery Area:	Worldwide	Returns Procedure:	Down to you

www.dvdplus.co.uk

Dvd Plus sells region 2 (UK and Europe) dvds to the UK mainland only. They frequently offer up to 20% off best selling films and have some really good special offers as well, so the next time you're looking for one to buy take a look at the prices here. They're not always the cheapest, however, and before you buy you should definitely use the price comparison website below. The problem with buying dvds online is that all the offers are changing regularly and it's impossible to keep up. UK delivery is free.

Site Usability:	★★★★★	Based:	UK
Product Range:	★★★★★	Express Delivery Option?	(UK) No
Price Range:	Luxury/<u>Medium</u>/Very Good Value	Gift Wrapping Option?	Yes
Delivery Area:	Worldwide	Returns Procedure:	Down to you

www.dvdpricecheck.co.uk

If you're looking for a dvd this is the place to start as you can see what's available throughout all the World regions. With so many places to buy films online it's hard to know without spending hours, which is the best site and with different sites charging different amounts things get even worse. So here it is; the website that'll compare the worldwide prices for you. Just key in your title and region (UK is Region 2) and you'll get all the answers.

Many of the websites they offer don't charge you delivery on top so you can order from as many as you want and as often as you like. Sounds tempting? It's hard to know when to stop.

Site Usability:	★★★★★	Based:	UK
Product Range:	★★★★★	Express Delivery Option?	(UK) Yes for the UK
Price Range:	Luxury/<u>Medium</u>/Very Good Value	Gift Wrapping Option?	No
Delivery Area:	Worldwide	Returns Procedure:	Down to you

www.game.co.uk

Whether you have an Xbox 360, Gamecube, Gameboy Micro, or Sony PS3 (or whatever the latest gaming station is) you'll find a huge range of games here for all of them plus the consoles themselves and accessories. I have to be careful here as things will no doubt have moved on by the time you're reading this, so check out this site to find out what's new and hot. They also offer a reward points system (a very good idea as loyalty to game sites is thin on the ground due to the amount of competition).

www.play.com

Music, movies and games at very good prices with delivery included from this Channel Islands based website. They offer a huge range of films on dvd, cds and games for all systems plus special offers, such as two dvds for £12, 30% off specific boxed sets and 40% off a wide choice of current releases. Because delivery is included you can order individual discs as often as you want to rather than having to group orders together to save on postage.

Site Usability:	★★★★★	Based:	Channel Islands
Product Range:	★★★★★	Express Delivery Option?	(UK) No
Price Range:	Luxury/<u>Medium</u>/Very Good Value	Gift Wrapping Option?	No
Delivery Area:	Worldwide	Returns Procedure:	Down to you

www.sendit.com

The difference here, as this is yet another website offering games consoles, games, dvds and computer peripherals and software, is the service. Not only do they offer a courier service within the UK to make sure your order arrives when you need it, free UK delivery and speedy worldwide delivery but also Gift Certificates and gift wrapping on most items with which they can include your personal message – and you can even choose your wrapping paper.

Site Usability:	★★★★★	Based:	Northern Ireland
Product Range:	★★★★★	Express Delivery Option?	(UK) Yes
Price Range:	Luxury/Medium/Very Good Value	Gift Wrapping Option?	Yes
Delivery Area:	Worldwide	Returns Procedure:	Down to you

Chapter 58

Gifts for Babies

aby clothes are great fun to buy and there are lots of very good baby clothes and accessories available online. You'll find them here and in the Baby and Toddler section of this guide, so if you think you'd like to give an exquisite babygro or blanket as a present you'll find plenty of those.

There are also lots of more unusual gift suggestions, from extremely well priced hand painted mini treasure chests to heirloom quilts, silver charm bracelets and brightly coloured soft toys, plus 'baby baskets', which either come ready assembled with lots of goodies inside or where you can choose what you want to include.

There's no end of choice on the websites listed here at all price levels, so you've no excuse for forgetting your friend's son's first birthday. It's really all too easy now, particularly as most of these retailers will also gift wrap for you and deliver your gift with your personal message inside.

Sites to Visit

www.babas.uk.com

All of Babas beautiful handmade baby bedding and accessories are individually made for you and packed in their own unique calico packaging. You can choose from cot sets, crib sets and Moses baskets, sleeping bags and towels in their range of contemporary designs with names such as Noah's Ark, Teddy Triplets and Splashy Duck. Everything is really beautiful and different from what you'll find elsewhere, and perfect for baby gifts.

Site Usability:	★★★★	Based:	UK	
Product Range:	★★★	Express Delivery Option?	(UK) No	
Price Range:	Luxury/<u>Medium</u>/Very Good Value	Gift Wrapping Option?	Yes	
Delivery Area:	Worldwide	Returns Procedure:	Down to you	

www.BABYBARE.co.uk

Here's another prettily designed and easy to get round website specialising in gifts for the new baby. There are ready to send gift sets for boys and girls at a variety of price levels, china gifts such as cups and mugs, money boxes and piggy banks, soft personalised fleece pram blankets and lots more, and if you aren't keen on their own ready made sets you can put your own together and include soft toys, bath wear, sleep suits, blankets and shawls.

Site Usability:	★★★★	Based:	UK	
Product Range:	★★★	Express Delivery Option?	(UK) Yes	
Price Range:	Luxury/<u>Medium</u>/Very Good Value	Gift Wrapping Option?	Yes	
Delivery Area:	Worldwide	Returns Procedure:	Down to you	

www.babiesbaskets.com

Babiesbaskets is a retailer offering (you guessed) 'basket' gift sets for new babies and they go right up to the luxury end of the spectrum (although starting quite reasonably), with the 'Loveheart' baby basket containing a babygro, cardigan, pram shoes, fleece and photo album and the ultimate 'Fudge' baby basket offering also a cableknit blanket, hand embroidered towel and babygro and handmade photo album, with everything exquisitely packaged.

Site Usability:	★★★★	Based:	UK	
Product Range:	★★★★	Express Delivery Option?	(UK) Yes	
Price Range:	Luxury/<u>Medium</u>/Very Good Value	Gift Wrapping Option?	Yes	
Delivery Area:	Worldwide	Returns Procedure:	Down to you	

www.babycelebrate.co.uk

This is a Cheshire based, high quality baby gift website, where there are delightful gift ideas for newborn and slightly older babies with names such as Baby Play Basket and Luxury Baby on the Go. For slightly older children aged up to two, they have pretty printed cutlery sets and lunch boxes plus colourful soft and wooden toys. As everything is designed to be a gift the products are all beautifully presented so you could have them sent out direct from the retailer.

Site Usability:	★★★★	Based:	UK
Product Range:	★★★	Express Delivery Option?	(UK) Yes
Price Range:	Luxury/Medium/Very Good Value	Gift Wrapping Option?	No
Delivery Area:	Worldwide	Returns Procedure:	Down to you

www.babygiftbox.co.uk

Babygiftbox offer a really lovely range of ideas for gifts. You can choose from Welcome Home baby boxes with names such as Flower Power and Lullaby, soft lambswool, fleece and cashmere blankets and christening gifts such as silver charms, chiming spoon and hand knitted heirloom cot blanket. There's also the Yummy Mummy Gift Set to make sure that the new mum isn't forgotten.

Site Usability:	★★★★	Based:	UK
Product Range:	★★★★	Express Delivery Option?	(UK) Yes
Price Range:	Luxury/Medium/Very Good Value	Gift Wrapping Option?	Yes
Delivery Area:	UK	Returns Procedure:	Down to you

www.gltc.co.uk

A great range of gifts and ideas for babies and young children of all ages, where you can buy personalised cutlery, clocks and adventure books, baby and toddler sleeping bags, magic lanterns, colourful wall hangings and also find really clever storage ideas. There's the Squishy, Squirty Bath Book, Jungle soft toy Bowling Set and Toy House Play Mat plus loads more clever and innovative suggestions. This would be a clever place to find something really different from the normal baby gift.

Site Usability:	★★★★	Based:	UK
Product Range:	★★★★	Express Delivery Option?	(UK) Yes
Price Range:	Luxury/Medium/Very Good Value	Gift Wrapping Option?	No
Delivery Area:	Worldwide	Returns Procedure:	Down to you

www.letterbox.co.uk

Letterbox is more of a traditional toy shop, where you can buy gifts and toys for children of all ages. These include activity toys, dressing up outfits, really pretty room accessories (painted chests of drawers and fairy mobiles) and traditional games. There are also baby gifts such as personalised cushions and towels and bathrobes from ages 6-12 months upwards.

Site Usability:	★★★★	Based:	UK
Product Range:	★★★★★	Express Delivery Option?	(UK) Yes
Price Range:	Luxury/Medium/Very Good Value	Gift Wrapping Option?	No
Delivery Area:	Worldwide	Returns Procedure:	Down to you

www.littlebundlesoflove.co.uk

Here you'll find beautiful hand finished boxes in pink, blue or white containing a variety of gifts including baby clothes by Petit Bateau, baby bath time products, books and cds. For mums to be they have several options such as pretty boxes containing Arran Aromatics bath goodies plus something gorgeous for the baby. You can also buy keepsake boxes and other accessories as separate gifts.

Site Usability:	★★★★★	Based:	UK
Product Range:	★★★★	Express Delivery Option?	(UK) No
Price Range:	Luxury/Medium/Very Good Value	Gift Wrapping Option?	No
Delivery Area:	UK	Returns Procedure:	Down to you

www.nurserywindow.co.uk

Once you arrive at this website you'll find it very hard to leave. There are some seriously lovely things here for children's rooms, from unusual bedding, Moses baskets and high quality cots and furniture to gift baskets for new babies and everything is beautifully photographed. Just click on the area of their online shop you're interested in, enter, and you'll almost certainly be hooked. You can also buy matching fabric to the bed linen. Nothing is cheap but it's all beautiful quality.

Site Usability:	★★★★★	Based:	UK
Product Range:	★★★★	Express Delivery Option?	(UK) No
Price Range:	Luxury/Medium/Very Good Value	Gift Wrapping Option?	No
Delivery Area:	Worldwide but ask for postage charges	Returns Procedure:	Down to you

www.roomersgifts.com

Embroidered baby blankets, hand painted personalised toy boxes and door plaques, personalised bracelets and friendship rings plus other unique gifts for babies and children are just some of the things you'll find here. This is not a traditional baby gift website, but one where you're more likely to find something they'll love to own a bit later on, such as a named treasure box.

Site Usability:	★★★	Based:	UK
Product Range:	★★★	Express Delivery Option?	(UK) No
Price Range:	Luxury/Medium/Very Good Value	Gift Wrapping Option?	No
Delivery Area:	Worldwide	Returns Procedure:	Down to you

www.thebaby.co.uk

This is a gorgeous baby website, offering so much for babies you could totally get lost. Go past the essential equipment pages and click through to 'Getting Dressed', where you'll find enchanting babygros, sleepsuits and accessories, or to 'Baby Furniture and Accessories', offering a wide range including decorated hangers and a John Crane mouse chair or if you're feeling really generous you could choose one of Stevenson Brothers' handmade rocking horses, made to last a lifetime.

Site Usability:	★★★★	Based:	UK
Product Range:	★★★★★	Express Delivery Option?	(UK) No
Price Range:	Luxury/Medium/Very Good Value	Gift Wrapping Option?	No
Delivery Area:	Worldwide	Returns Procedure:	Down to you

Also check out these websites for babies gifts

Website Address	You'll find them in
www.thekidswindow.co.uk	Baby and Toddler Clothes
www.jojomamanbebe.co.uk	Baby and Toddler Clothes
www.mamasandpapas.co.uk	Baby and Toddler Clothes
www.thekidswindow.co.uk	Baby and Toddler Clothes
www.linksoflondon.com	Jewellery
www.tiffany.com	Jewellery
www.thewhitecompany.co.uk	In the Bedroom
www.penhaligons.co.uk	Fragrance, Bath and Body

Chapter 59

Toys, Models, Games and Magic Tricks

The web is really a great place to buy children's gifts. All the toys and games in the World are just a few clicks away, ready and waiting to be delivered to your door or directly to the recipient at great speed if you've forgotten that important date. Take a look at the gadget sites above as they do have some excellent ideas for all ages or take your pick from the sites listed here. You'll find toys for absolutely everyone from Barbie Dolls to Lego, jigsaw puzzles, remote control cars and loads more.

You can spend a fortune at the model shops, buying rockets that actually take off (and usually disappear), planes, racing cars and boats (that frequently don't get finished) plus all the paints, glues, brushes and engines (and batteries, of course, don't let's forget those) to go with. I may sound slightly jaded about all of this, it comes of having had two boys, and the end result was frequently the disappearing/unfinished variety, however their models created hours and hours of peace and calm beforehand and were therefore well worth it.

If you're a family that's into games you can buy every imaginable type, from Monopoly to dvd versions of Trivial Pursuit and of course the new ones as they come out plus Charades, Pictionary and many more.

Sites to Visit

www.activitytoysdirect.co.uk

This is an unsophisticated but extremely easy to use website where you'll find (you probably guessed) activity toys including lots of ideas for garden fun, such as netball sets, fun rides and aqua slides, swing and slide combinations, foldaway trampolines with net protection for very young children, plus the full size versions, table tennis tables and climbing frames.

Site Usability:	★★★★		Based:	UK
Product Range:	★★★		Express Delivery Option?	(UK) Yes
Price Range:	Luxury/Medium/Very Good Value		Gift Wrapping Option?	No
Delivery Area:	UK		Returns Procedure:	Down to you

www.airfix.com

Just about every boy has at some time made an airfix model (or quite usually part made and left). The joy of opening all those tiny tins of paint and spending hours making a mess and gluing bits together seems irresistible, particularly during holiday rainy days. Well here it all is online, on a very simple site, where you can order all the kits with a few clicks from a supercharged 1930 Bentley to the Tiger Moth. There's loads to choose from and they give full details for each one.

Site Usability:	★★★★★		Based:	UK
Product Range:	★★★★★		Express Delivery Option?	(UK) No
Price Range:	Luxury/Medium/Very Good Value		Gift Wrapping Option?	No
Delivery Area:	Worldwide		Returns Procedure:	Down to you

www.amazon.co.uk

If you still think of Amazon as a bookshop it's time to think again. Just click through to Toys and Kids and you'll find every toy and game you can think of. No it's not all just sitting in a large warehouse – Amazon act in a lot of cases as the conduit through which other toy shops can sell their products. What it means is that you get a fantastic choice and no fuss ordering through a retailer you know and trust.

Site Usability:	★★★★★		Based:	UK
Product Range:	★★★★★		Express Delivery Option?	(UK) Yes
Price Range:	Luxury/Medium/Very Good Value		Gift Wrapping Option?	Yes
Delivery Area:	Worldwide		Returns Procedure:	Down to you

www.dollshouse.com

Whether you're new to the world of dolls' houses or a dedicated miniaturist, the Dolls House Emporium should fill you with inspiration. The site features fully decorated dolls' houses and thousands of miniatures in colour co-ordinated room sets plus carpets and flooring, lighting and wallpapers. You can also see a selection of 1 : 12 scale dolls' houses shown open and fully furnished to give you ideas.

Site Usability:	★★★★★	Based:	UK
Product Range:	★★★★	Express Delivery Option?	(UK) No
Price Range:	Luxury/Medium/Very Good Value	Gift Wrapping Option?	No
Delivery Area:	Worldwide	Returns Procedure:	Down to you

www.hamleys.co.uk

If you've ever visited this world famous Regent Street toy emporium (I hate the word but it's the only way to describe this store) you'll know that there's a huge range of gadgets, games, soft toys, puzzles, stocking fillers and every toy you can think of at all price levels and for all ages. In fact it's a disastrous place to take more than one child at a time as there's so much to see. There's a highly edited range here on their website although the list of products on offer is growing all the time.

Site Usability:	★★★★★	Based:	UK
Product Range:	★★★★	Express Delivery Option?	(UK) No
Price Range:	Luxury/Medium/Very Good Value	Gift Wrapping Option?	No
Delivery Area:	Worldwide	Returns Procedure:	Down to you

www.hopscotchdressingup.co.uk

Hopscotch have definitely got the children's dressing up market sewn up with their lovely bright website full of dressing up box clothes for children from angels and fairies to witches and wizards, cowboys and indians to kings and queens and everything in between. There's no question that if your child has been asked to a fancy dress party and is determined to really look the part you absolutely have to visit here.

Site Usability:	★★★★★	Based:	UK
Product Range:	★★★★	Express Delivery Option?	(UK) Yes
Price Range:	Luxury/Medium/Very Good Value	Gift Wrapping Option?	No
Delivery Area:	Worldwide	Returns Procedure:	Down to you

www.lego.com

Lego kits seem to have become more and more complicated and you practically need an engineering degree to build some of them (well I never was very good at that sort of thing). Let your son on this website if you dare. Everything is brilliantly shown, including Star Wars, Lego Sports, building sets, Robotics and the very latest editions. You can take the Club tour, order the magazine or click on to the Games Page.

Site Usability:	★★★★★	Based:	UK
Product Range:	★★★★★	Express Delivery Option?	(UK) Yes
Price Range:	Luxury/Medium/Very Good Value	Gift Wrapping Option?	No
Delivery Area:	Worldwide	Returns Procedure:	Down to you

www.magictricks.co.uk

You'll find some wonderful ideas for gifts here, from the Cyclopedia of Magic, Wizard School Video and dvd, card magic sets, pub tricks (??) and the Ultimate Magic Trick Set – a compilation of some of the greatest close-up magic tricks ever invented. And this is just a very small selection of what's on offer. You can also buy Gift Vouchers and lots of their own brand products at all price levels.

Site Usability:	★★★★	Based:	UK
Product Range:	★★★★	Express Delivery Option?	(UK) No
Price Range:	Luxury/<u>Medium</u>/Very Good Value	Gift Wrapping Option?	No
Delivery Area:	Worldwide	Returns Procedure:	Down to you

www.modelhobbies.co.uk

Model Hobbies are the perfect place for the model enthusiast. They have an extremely well laid out website and offer models by over fifty different manufacturers, plus all the paints, tools and brushes you could possibly need. There are also miniature soldiers here as well. They cleverly highlight the newest kits to hit the market so that you keep coming back for more. You can buy gift vouchers as well.

Site Usability:	★★★★★	Based:	UK
Product Range:	★★★★★	Express Delivery Option?	(UK) No
Price Range:	Luxury/<u>Medium</u>/Very Good Value	Gift Wrapping Option?	No
Delivery Area:	Worldwide	Returns Procedure:	Down to you

www.modelrockets.co.uk

You can buy model cars, tanks and planes from several different websites but there are very few specialising in rockets. By rockets I mean real enthusiasts' stuff, from starter sets and ready to fly kits to competition standard models. Don't be fooled into thinking that the rockets themselves are inexpensive, by the time you've invested in the engine and all the bits and pieces you can spend a small fortune. They can give hours of fun however, until they blow themselves to bits or land on the back of a lorry, never to be seen again (yes that one happened to us).

Site Usability:	★★★★	Based:	UK
Product Range:	★★★★	Express Delivery Option?	(UK) No
Price Range:	<u>Luxury/Medium</u>/Very Good Value	Gift Wrapping Option?	No
Delivery Area:	Worldwide	Returns Procedure:	Down to you

www.sayitwithbears.co.uk

This is one of those websites that obviously started off doing one thing and then branched out, because you can not only find bears here, but labradors, elephants, rabbits, cats and dalmatians (and lots of other dogs). So if you know someone who collects soft toys or needs a feel good gift you should take a look here. Oh yes, and you can also buy lovvie bears, thank you bears and anniversary bears here as well.

Site Usability:	★★★★	Based:	UK
Product Range:	★★★★★	Express Delivery Option?	(UK) Yes
Price Range:	Luxury/Medium/Very Good Value	Gift Wrapping Option?	Yes
Delivery Area:	Worldwide	Returns Procedure:	Down to you

www.slotcity.co.uk

Slot City is one the largest independent retailers of slot cars in the UK (and Europe) and you can only buy from them online They offer the full range of Scalextric plus other brands such as Carrera from Germany and SCX from Spain – household names in their own countries but almost impossible to find here until now. You'll also find Hornby and Carrera model kits. Everything is ready for immediate delivery unless you're told otherwise on the website.

Site Usability:	★★★★	Based:	UK
Product Range:	★★★★★	Express Delivery Option?	(UK) No
Price Range:	Luxury/Medium/Very Good Value	Gift Wrapping Option?	No
Delivery Area:	All EU countries and the USA	Returns Procedure:	Down to you

www.theentertainer.com

This is one of the largest independent toy retailers in the UK with a huge range and has an excellent, easy to use website where you can search by brand, type of toy, age group or price. Once you've decided what you want to buy and registered both your address and any addresses where you want your orders despatched to, you simply select from the standard or express delivery services, give your payment details and you're done.

Site Usability:	★★★★★	Based:	UK
Product Range:	★★★★★	Express Delivery Option?	(UK) Yes
Price Range:	Luxury/Medium/Very Good Value	Gift Wrapping Option?	No
Delivery Area:	Worldwide	Returns Procedure:	Down to you

www.toysbymailorder.co.uk

Toys by Mail Order specialise in toys, gifts, games, nursery items and jigsaw puzzles for children of all ages. You can search the range of wooden toys and soft toys for baby and toddler gifts and they also stock many items for older boys and girls, plus traditional family games. They offer fast delivery, a gift wrapping service and personalised messages for special occasions. As well as all this you'll find a range of colourful soft toys for babies, plus Manhattan bootees, puppets and dolls and puzzles and games for when they're a little older.

Site Usability:	★★★★	Based:	UK
Product Range:	★★★★★	Express Delivery Option?	(UK) Yes 2 day service
Price Range:	Luxury/<u>Medium</u>/Very Good Value	Gift Wrapping Option?	No
Delivery Area:	Worldwide	Returns Procedure:	Down to you

www.toysrus.co.uk

This one you'll definitely have heard of (or seen no doubt) as the UK branch of the US toy megastore. Personally I think the shops are just too huge to cope with, so it's great that they're online although the website is one of the busiest around. There's a fantastic range of well priced toys and equipment for children of all ages including plus MultiMedia PCs, games, bikes and outdoor fun products. You can also click through to Babiesrus with its special range for the younger members of the family.

Site Usability:	★★★★	Based:	
Product Range:	★★★★★	Express Delivery Option?	(UK) No
Price Range:	Luxury/<u>Medium</u>/Very Good Value	Gift Wrapping Option?	No
Delivery Area:	UK but there are separate Canada and US websites.	Returns Procedure:	Free by Freepost or collection

Chapter 60

For the Artist, Musician or Photographer

Arts and crafts from tapestry to painting can make wonderful gifts if you know someone who enjoys doing those things. Don't bother if you're not sure, you can spend a great deal of money on something that will never be used by a non enthusiast so check first. The websites look very enticing and offer lots of information and they're absolutely excellent if you need the full kit or just replacement colours or brushes and live a way away from a good art or craft shop.

Likewise with music. You wouldn't buy a musical instrument for someone who you weren't sure was going to really appreciate it, now would you? However, if you have a musician in the family they can choose from these websites from the instruments themselves to sheet music, song books and accessories (and then of course you can pay for them).

Photography is another hobby that appeals to all ages, from the child with his first camera to the enthusiast who wants the most high tech equipment available. On these websites you'll find all the options, from really well priced and simple to use digital cameras to the very latest lenses. This is an area where it's really well worth comparing prices. If you're considering splashing out on expensive photographic equipment, I advise you to call the retailer and make sure there's a back-up service if something goes wrong.

Arts and Crafts

Sites to Visit

www.albanyhill.com

This is a lovely clear and modern website offering tapestry cushion sets by designers such as Elizabeth Bradley, Isobel Hunt and Julia Bradley. Once you click through to your designer of choice they'll tell you all about her and show you the range then, for each design, there are exact details. It's really a website for those who already know how to do needlepoint but the choice is superb and they'll ship Worldwide.

Site Usability:	★★★★★	Based:	UK
Product Range:	★★★★	Express Delivery Option?	(UK) No
Price Range:	Luxury/Medium/Very Good Value	Gift Wrapping Option?	No
Delivery Area:	Worldwide	Returns Procedure:	Down to you

www.artboxdirect.co.uk

Artboxdirect offers discount art supplies, providing artists with a wide range of art materials from Windsor & Newton and Daler Rowney. There are good discounts off the prices of all paints and brushes, pastels, sets, pads and cases. It's best if you already know which colours you want to order, although you can download the full colour charts for each range of paints should you need to. They'll deliver to you anywhere in Europe.

Site Usability:	★★★★	Based:	UK
Product Range:	★★★★	Express Delivery Option?	(UK) No
Price Range:	Luxury/Medium/Very Good Value	Gift Wrapping Option?	No
Delivery Area:	Europe	Returns Procedure:	Down to you

www.artist-supplies.co.uk

Staedtler, Derwent, Sennelier and Windsor and Newton are just a few of the brands here, on this website offering a full range of artist's materials including easels, paints (oil, acrylic or watercolour), paper and board, canvasses, brushes and folios. They also have a well stocked crafts section with calligraphy, candle making, glass painting, needlecraft and stencilling so there's something for everyone and some very good gift ideas too.

Site Usability:	★★★	Based:	UK
Product Range:	★★★★★	Express Delivery Option?	(UK) Yes
Price Range:	Luxury/Medium/Very Good Value	Gift Wrapping Option?	No
Delivery Area:	Worldwide	Returns Procedure:	Down to you

www.lawrence.co.uk

Here are grown-up artist's materials for the grown-up artist. They carry a huge range and offer a full advisory service and quick delivery; you can buy acrylics, art boards, glass paints and palettes, gold and silver leaf, papers, cards and envelopes, everything for printmaking plus storage and packaging (and loads more). You can also buy gift vouchers here for the artist in your life or choose from their suggestions.

Site Usability:	★★★★	Based:	UK	
Product Range:	★★★★★	Express Delivery Option?	(UK) No	
Price Range:	Luxury/Medium/Very Good Value	Gift Wrapping Option?	No	
Delivery Area:	Worldwide	Returns Procedure:	Down to you	

www.stencil-library.co.uk

The Stencil Library is generally accepted as being one of the world's leading stencil design companies offering over 3,500 different designs which you can order online, including traditional, modern, Indian, Shaker and children's designs, plus brushes, paint, tools for gilding and decoupage and a wide range of general stencilling supplies. This site is a must if you're thinking of stencilling anything, anywhere.

Site Usability:	★★★★	Based:	UK	
Product Range:	★★★★★	Express Delivery Option?	(UK) Yes	
Price Range:	Luxury/Medium/Very Good Value	Gift Wrapping Option?	No	
Delivery Area:	Worldwide	Returns Procedure:	Down to you	

www.yorkshireartstore.co.uk

Discover a wonderful treasure trove of artists' and craft supplies, from paints, pencils, brushes and inks, to clay, craft paper and adhesives plus fabric art and needlecraft equipment also accessories including frames, tapestry wools, stranded cotton and fantasy threads. This is not one of the most highly sophisticated websites but it's easy to get round and quick to order from. Expect a high level of service and speedy delivery and call them if you need advice.

Site Usability:	★★★★	Based:	UK
Product Range:	★★★★	Express Delivery Option?	(UK) No
Price Range:	Luxury/Medium/Very Good Value	Gift Wrapping Option?	No
Delivery Area:	UK	Returns Procedure:	Down to you

Musical Instruments and Sheet Music

Whether you're looking for a new clarinet, an acoustic guitar or a copy of Beethoven's 9th symphony you'll find it all here, with some very good prices and quick and efficient delivery.

With something as specialised as instruments you'll almost always find that the people running the sites are musicians themselves and really know their products, so if in doubt you can call for advice.

Always check all the sites for price comparison. You'll be amazed at what you find (or horrified, whichever way you look at it).

Sites to Visit

www.dawsonsonline.com

Once you arrive at this website you need to choose to begin with whether you want to go to the piano and orchestral instrument department where you'll find an excellent range including sheet music, or through to rock and hi tech, which offers electric and acoustic guitars, microphones, mixers, synthesizers and the like. It's an extremely clear and well laid out website, all prices and delivery times are very clearly shown and they carry a full range of accessories.

Site Usability:	★★★★★	Based:	UK
Product Range:	★★★★★	Express Delivery Option?	(UK) No
Price Range:	Luxury/Medium/Very Good Value	Gift Wrapping Option?	Yes
Delivery Area:	UK	Returns Procedure:	Down to you

www.musicroom.co.uk

Established in 1995, Musicroom is a global retailer, shipping products out to over 100 countries and offering one of the largest selections of sheet music, song books, books about music and tutor methods in the world. At Christmas time they offer a gift selection, including Christmas music, learning guides for different instruments, cds and instrument accessories. It really is an excellent website so if you know any young musicians do stop off here.

Site Usability:	★★★★★	Based:	UK
Product Range:	★★★★	Express Delivery Option?	(UK) No
Price Range:	Luxury/Medium/Very Good Value	Gift Wrapping Option?	No
Delivery Area:	Worldwide	Returns Procedure:	Down to you

www.signetmusic.com

This is quite a confusing site to look at probably because the range is so big, but if you're in the market for a new or second hand musical instrument you must look here as the prices can be very good. Because there's such a wide choice it's very helpful that they have a manufacturer index showing almost 100 brands so you can go easily to the make and product you're looking for. They offer online live support (which you may well need) and worldwide delivery for just about everything.

Site Usability:	★★★	Based:	UK
Product Range:	★★★★	Express Delivery Option?	(UK) Yes
Price Range:	Luxury/Medium/Very Good Value	Gift Wrapping Option?	No
Delivery Area:	Worldwide	Returns Procedure:	Down to you

www.themusiccellar.co.uk

Choose from a fantastic selection of musical instruments on this clear and easy to get round website, from clarinets to grand pianos to acoustic and electric guitars. They offer a repair service and you can buy sheet music here as well. The instruments are discounted (check the price with your local supplier and/or a price comparison website to make sure) but some of the prices look excellent. Prices for UK shipping are supplied online but you need to call them for overseas.

Site Usability:	★★★★★	Based:	UK
Product Range:	★★★★★	Express Delivery Option?	(UK) No
Price Range:	Luxury/Medium/Very Good Value	Gift Wrapping Option?	No
Delivery Area:	Worldwide	Returns Procedure:	Down to you

www.woodwindandbrass.co.uk

Woodwind and Brass have a really attractive website which draws you in to their wide range of products, including saxophones from Yanagisawa and Selmer, clarinets from Buffet, LeBlanc and Jupiter, flutes & piccolos from Trevor J James and Buffet, bass clarinets from Jupiter and Besson, and bassoons from Oscar Adler. Accessories include mouthpieces, reeds, stands, gig bags, cases and care and maintenance materials.

Site Usability:	★★★★★	Based:	UK
Product Range:	★★★★★	Express Delivery Option?	(UK) No
Price Range:	Luxury/Medium/Very Good Value	Gift Wrapping Option?	No
Delivery Area:	Worldwide	Returns Procedure:	Down to you

Cameras etc

Sites to Visit

www.cameras.co.uk

This website will certainly take you to the places where you can buy your chosen digital camera for less, but it is, first and foremost, a review and advice centre on digital photography in general and on all the new camera ranges. Once you've had a good read and selected your camera it will then give you the price comparisons for the retailers offering that specific model, and you can see some amazing differentials in price. It's a very good place to check out if you're not sure which camera you want to buy or you want to compare prices.

Site Usability:	★★★	Based:	UK
Product Range:	★★★★	Express Delivery Option?	(UK) No
Price Range:	Luxury/Medium/Very Good Value	Gift Wrapping Option?	No
Delivery Area:	UK	Returns Procedure:	Down to you in agreement with them

www.cameras2u.com

This is an excellent place to find your new camera, where you'll find all the new models at very good prices. Compare their prices on a comparison website such as *kelkoo.co.uk* and you'll find they're nearly always the lowest. There's a lot of advice on digital photography in general such as linking up with your PC and printer plus photo taking tips. Couple this with free UK next day delivery on orders over £100 placed before 1pm and this is definitely a website you should visit.

Site Usability:	★★★★	Based:	UK
Product Range:	★★★★	Express Delivery Option?	(UK) Yes
Price Range:	Luxury/Medium/Very Good Value	Gift Wrapping Option?	No
Delivery Area:	UK	Returns Procedure:	Down to you in agreement with them

www.digitalfirst.co.uk

Here you'll find cameras from all the major brand names including Pentax, Canon, Nikon, Olympus and Fuji, plus scanners and printers. It's an extremely quick and easy website to get round with clear pages and easy buying instructions. They also offer two years warranty, 3 months free helpline, a gift wrapping service and free shipping to the UK mainland.

Site Usability:	★★★★	Based:	UK
Product Range:	★★★★	Express Delivery Option?	(UK) No
Price Range:	Luxury/Medium/Very Good Value	Gift Wrapping Option?	Yes
Delivery Area:	Worldwide	Returns Procedure:	Down to you in agreement with them

www.fotosense.co.uk

Fotosense offers an excellent range of the latest cameras, plus everything you need for digital video, MP3 players, binoculars, printers and studio lighting from a list of over fifty manufacturers as well as one of the largest photographic accessory lines available in the UK. If you need advice on what to buy you can just give them a call and they'll be delighted to help. They only deliver to the UK but offer extremely fast delivery options.

Site Usability:	★★★★★	Based:	UK
Product Range:	★★★★★	Express Delivery Option?	(UK) Yes
Price Range:	Luxury/Medium/Very Good Value	Gift Wrapping Option?	No
Delivery Area:	UK	Returns Procedure:	Down to you in agreement with them

Chapter 61

General Gift Stores

On the whole I prefer to buy presents for people from specific places - partly because it's too easy to pick up presents for everyone at general gift shops and websites without putting enough thought into it and partly because I simply enjoy it much more.

Now that you have the choice of being totally masochistic and trawling round the shops laden with heavy bags or sitting down with a cup of coffee (wine) and doing all your gift shopping online, I'm not sure why you'd go to one place and expect to find all your gifts.

However, having said that, many of the gift websites below are run by dedicated gift buyers who's main aim is to find you the special, unusual, whimsical, clever and irresistible. You can also find some things here that aren't available elsewhere because they've been specially designed for this particular retailer or because they've been imported from somewhere exotic.

Anyway, the choice is yours and you can go to Jo Malone for bath and body gifts, Brora for the perfect cashmere cardigan or The Pier for embroidered cushions or you can choose from the selection below. Happy Gift Shopping.

Sites to Visit

www.boutiquetoyou.co.uk

This is a cross between a hip website selling Art and Sole Scholl sandals and fab maternity t-shirts to a gift site offering quite expensive jewellery (and really cheap jewellery), aromatherapy treats, gadgets and flowers. There are departments for all sorts of occasions and in each one you'll find a wide range of products and price levels. The service is excellent, delivery is free if you spend £75 and they'll ship worldwide.

Site Usability:	★★★★	Based:	UK
Product Range:	★★★★	Express Delivery Option?	(UK) Yes
Price Range:	Luxury/Medium/Very Good Value	Gift Wrapping Option?	No
Delivery Area:	Worldwide	Returns Procedure:	Down to you

www.coxandcox.co.uk

This pretty website is divided up into sections such as A Decorative Home, A Creative Diva, Any Excuse for a Party and Children's Corner. In each of the sections you'll find appropriate ideas such as soft furnishings and pictures, linen ribbon and coloured tissue paper, outdoor table clips and tea light holders and gumball machines and butterfly garlands. They'll send this eclectic mix to you anywhere in the world and if you want something urgently you need to call them.

Site Usability:	★★★	Based:	UK
Product Range:	★★★	Express Delivery Option?	(UK) Yes
Price Range:	Luxury/Medium/Very Good Value	Gift Wrapping Option?	No
Delivery Area:	Worldwide	Returns Procedure:	Down to you

www.erinhousegifts.co.uk

Erinhousegifts not only offers a wide choice of gifts including Halcyon Days Enamels, Churchill China (which uses images painted by Sir Winston Churchill) Franz Porcelain, delightful Winnie the Pooh classics, the extraordinary Yoro pen (take a look) and pens by Swarovski but also, in their History Craft section, an attractive range of sporting gifts for the cricketer, rugby player and golfer.

Site Usability:	★★★★	Based:	UK
Product Range:	★★★★	Express Delivery Option?	(UK) No
Price Range:	Luxury/Medium/Very Good Value	Gift Wrapping Option?	No
Delivery Area:	Worldwide	Returns Procedure:	Down to you

www.francetoyourdoor.com

Bath and body products by Chantecaille and Compagnie de Provence, specialities such as Foie Gras and terrines, oils and vinegars, sauces, chutneys, jams and chocolates and gorgeous scented candles.

Expect speedy delivery and efficient service. This website would be perfect to use all the year round and particularly good for gifts, so check it out at Christmas (although order well in advance) to find something just that little bit different.

Site Usability:	★★★★	Based:	France
Product Range:	★★★	Express Delivery Option?	(UK) No
Price Range:	Luxury/Medium/Very Good Value	Gift Wrapping Option?	No
Delivery Area:	Worldwide	Returns Procedure:	Down to you

www.giftinspiration.com

Based in Wiltshire this website claims to be the UK's leading gift delivery service. They certainly have a good selection (think The Expresso Hamper, Hot Chocolate Cup and Saucer Gift Box, Hunter leather covered flask and cups and silver Aspirin Cufflinks) and if you needed a gift in a hurry I would definitely have a look here as they offer all the right services – gift wrapping, including your personal message and express delivery.

Site Usability:	★★★	Based:	UK
Product Range:	★★★★	Express Delivery Option?	(UK) Yes
Price Range:	Luxury/Medium/Very Good Value	Gift Wrapping Option?	Yes
Delivery Area:	UK	Returns Procedure:	Down to you

www.giftstore.co.uk

Here's a good place for ideas for birthday and anniversary gifts, from flowers, chocolates and balloons to magic sets and greeting cards, which they'll personalise and send out for you. You'll also find teddygrams, personalised newspapers, Leonidas chocolates and a small selection of toys and games. Everything is well priced so this would be an excellent retailer to visit if you have a last minute panic.

Site Usability:	★★★★	Based:	UK
Product Range:	★★★★	Express Delivery Option?	(UK) Yes
Price Range:	Luxury/Medium/Very Good Value	Gift Wrapping Option?	Yes
Delivery Area:	UK	Returns Procedure:	Down to you

www.grahamandgreen.co.uk

A long established retailer of home and lifestyle products including candles, tableware, silk cushions, pretty etched glasses and duvet covers and quilts. They're quite hard to really categorise as the products are so widespread but if I tell you that some of their bestsellers are bevelled mirrors, Chinese lanterns, lavender scented hearts and Penguin (as in the book) mugs you'll probably get the idea. You'll definitely find some lovely gifts and ideas for brightening up your home here.

Site Usability:	★★★★	Based:	UK
Product Range:	★★★	Express Delivery Option?	(UK) Yes
Price Range:	Luxury/Medium/Very Good Value	Gift Wrapping Option?	No
Delivery Area:	UK	Returns Procedure:	Down to you

www.joannawood.co.uk

Interior designer Joanna Woods' selection of gifts and accessories for the home is a lovely, cleverly chosen collection including bronze candlesticks, Rigaud scented candles, silver pens and bronze detailed crystal boxes plus gorgeous hand embroidered cushions, boxed Haut Couture tableware and Villandry china in the homewares section. Delivery is usually within 3–5 days but if you need an express service just call them. They'll also gift wrap for you.

Site Usability:	★★★★	Based:	UK
Product Range:	★★★★	Express Delivery Option?	(UK) Yes
Price Range:	Luxury/Medium/Very Good Value	Gift Wrapping Option?	Yes
Delivery Area:	Worldwide	Returns Procedure:	Down to you

www.luxeliving.com

The next time you want to give something luxurious have a look round here, where you'll find gifts and accessories for the home, from cushions and mirrors to unusual ceramics and tableware, candles, notebooks and frames. It's not a huge range and it takes a while to get to the gifts (while you're listening to the music) but they offer all the right services - express delivery options, International delivery and gift wrapping and the selection will almost certainly grow.

Site Usability:	★★★	Based:	UK
Product Range:	★★★	Express Delivery Option?	(UK) Yes
Price Range:	Luxury/Medium/Very Good Value	Gift Wrapping Option?	Yes
Delivery Area:	Worldwide	Returns Procedure:	Down to you

www.notonthehighstreet.com

There's almost an impossible amount of choice here on this website acting as a marketplace for a group of small manufacturers and designers who'll supply you direct. Most of it is reasonably priced and most items are perfect for gifts. You'll find jewellery, scarves and shawls, pretty evening and day handbags, Cote Bastide and Willow bath and body products, unusual camisoles and t-shirts, albums and keepsake boxes plus a selection of home accessories.

Site Usability:	★★★	Based:	UK
Product Range:	★★★★★	Express Delivery Option?	(UK) No
Price Range:	Luxury/Medium/Very Good Value	Gift Wrapping Option?	No
Delivery Area:	UK	Returns Procedure:	Down to you

www.oliverbonas.co.uk

Voted Best Gift Retailer for 2006 this is a very well designed and easy to use website with a lovely range of products (just as you would expect). They offer some extremely well priced gifts such as jewellery and accessories, gifts for the 'domestic goddess', ideas for the garden and leather albums, notebooks and address books. Delivery is free on orders over £50 and where items are in stock they'll despatch the same day. Contact them for overseas deliveries.

Site Usability:	★★★★	Based:	UK
Product Range:	★★★	Express Delivery Option?	(UK) Yes
Price Range:	Luxury/Medium/Very Good Value	Gift Wrapping Option?	No
Delivery Area:	Worldwide	Returns Procedure:	Down to you

www.nationaltrust-shop.co.uk

Here's a real treasure trove of well priced gifts and stocking fillers such as floral notecards, chocolate éclairs in pretty boxes, humorous t-shirts and giant crosswords. You can buy Christmas cards and good value wrap and ribbon here too and take advantage of their free gift-wrapping and personalisation service. Orders may take up to 21 days as deliveries come from The National Trust's various suppliers so allow extra time.

Site Usability:	★★★★★	Based:	UK
Product Range:	★★★	Express Delivery Option?	(UK) No
Price Range:	Luxury/Medium/Very Good Value	Gift Wrapping Option?	Yes
Delivery Area:	UKI	Returns Procedure:	Down to you

www.sogifted.co.uk

So Gifted is a general gift website offering ideas for everyone including christening gifts (pretty photo albums and a christening keepsake box) weddings, educational and general gifts for young children and unusual gifts for the home and garden. You'll also find the exquisite range of Rosana and Café Paris china of beautifully boxed expresso cups, dessert plates and Haute Shoes tea for two which you'll probably want to keep for yourself.

Site Usability:	★★★	Based:	UK
Product Range:	★★★	Express Delivery Option?	(UK) Yes
Price Range:	Luxury/Medium/Very Good Value	Gift Wrapping Option?	No
Delivery Area:	Worldwide	Returns Procedure:	Down to you

www.tjklondon.com

TJK London offers a selection of classic and contemporary silver, wood and leather gifts including jewellery, cufflinks, photo albums and frames designed in-house and sterling silver marmite and jam jar lids (also really lovely glass match strikers/tea light holders with silver hallmarked collars). A bonus here is that everything is automatically gift-wrapped. For a small charge they will also engrave items for you.

Site Usability:	★★★★	Based:	UK
Product Range:	★★★	Express Delivery Option?	(UK) Yes
Price Range:	Luxury/Medium/Very Good Value	Gift Wrapping Option?	Luxury packaging is standard
Delivery Area:	Worldwide	Returns Procedure:	Down to you

Chapter 62

Emergency gift shops – the Top Ten websites

These are my personal favourites, where I can be sure to find beautifully presented gifts for just about everyone I know, with a wide ranging selection and on really clearly designed websites from retailers who I know for a fact offer a superb service.

I'm not suggesting you buy everything here, however if you need a gift in a hurry you're unlikely to go wrong and you can be sure that if you're sending something to someone without seeing it first that it'll be very high quality, beautifully packaged and it'll arrive on time.

Sites to Visit

www.aspinal.co.uk

Aspinal specialise in leather gifts and accessories, including jewellery boxes, photo albums, wedding albums, leather journals and books, handmade by skilled craftsmen using age old traditional leather and bookbinding skills. This is also an extremely quick and cleverly designed website, where you can see a wealth of ideas with just a couple of clicks. There's a wide choice of colours for all the items and enchanting baby gift ideas as well.

Site Usability:	★★★★★	Based:	UK
Product Range:	★★★★★	Express Delivery Option?	(UK) Yes
Price Range:	<u>Luxury/Medium</u>/Very Good Value	Gift Wrapping Option?	Yes
Delivery Area:	Worldwide	Returns Procedure:	Down to you

www.braybrook.com

If you're looking for a really special present then have a browse round this excellent website, offering hand made fine silver designed by British master silversmiths and where you can expect to find an extremely personal service. Prices for gifts range upwards from £65, from beautifully coloured glass and silver bowls to gorgeous designs by leading silversmiths for over £1000 and a wide selection at under £200. They offer worldwide delivery, gift wrapping and express delivery.

Site Usability:	★★★★	Based:	UK
Product Range:	★★★★★	Express Delivery Option?	(UK) Yes
Price Range:	<u>Luxury/Medium</u>/Very Good Value	Gift Wrapping Option?	Yes
Delivery Area:	Worldwide	Returns Procedure:	Down to you

www.ctshirts.co.uk

You might not automatically think of visiting this website when looking for gifts for girls (or men) but think again, it's not just a shirt catalogue (maybe they should change their name). Not only do they have one of the easiest websites to get round, but they also offer a very attractive range of high quality cashmere, both fine and luxury weight, Argyll patterned and with detailed stitching. There are some lovely stripy cashmere scarves here too. Oh yes, and lots of great shirts.

Site Usability:	★★★★★	Based:	UK
Product Range:	★★★★★	Express Delivery Option?	(UK) Yes
Price Range:	Luxury/<u>Medium</u>/Very Good Value	Gift Wrapping Option?	Yes
Delivery Area:	Worldwide	Returns Procedure:	Down to you

www.escentual.co.uk

Escentual offer one of the largest ranges of fragrance and bath and body products available in the UK, from classic brands such as Chanel, Dior, Bvlgari or Rochas to Calvin Klein, Gucci, Crabtree and Evelyn, Tisserand and I Coloniali. Delivery is free on orders over £30 and they also offer free gift wrapping if you register. The website is clean and clearly laid out, which makes it a pleasure to use. There are new products on offer all the time.

Site Usability:	★★★★★	Based:	UK
Product Range:	★★★★★	Express Delivery Option?	(UK) Yes
Price Range:	Luxury/Medium/Very Good Value	Gift Wrapping Option?	Yes
Delivery Area:	Worldwide	Returns Procedure:	Down to you

www.iwantoneofthose.com

An irresistible (and very cleverly designed) gift and gadget shop with a huge choice and a very well designed website. Search by price or product type – you'll find there's a wide range of both. The excellent animation for most products makes it easy to choose from gadgets for garden, kitchen and office plus the inevitable toys and games. They offer same day delivery, free standard delivery on orders over £50, gift wrap services and are happy to ship to you anywhere in the world.

Site Usability:	★★★★★	Based:	UK
Product Range:	★★★★★	Express Delivery Option?	(UK) Yes
Price Range:	Luxury/Medium/Very Good Value	Gift Wrapping Option?	Yes
Delivery Area:	Worldwide	Returns Procedure:	Down to you

www.kiarie.co.uk

This is one of the best ranges of scented candles, by brands such as Geodosis, Kenneth Turner, Manuel Canovas, Creation Mathias, Rigaud and Millefiori; there are literally hundreds to choose from at all price levels (this site is very fast, so don't panic) and you can also choose your range by price, maker, fragrance, colour and season. Once you've made your selection you can ask them to gift wrap it for you and include a hand written message. Then if you want you can use their express delivery service to make sure it arrives fast.

Site Usability:	★★★★★	Based:	UK
Product Range:	★★★★★	Express Delivery Option?	(UK) Yes
Price Range:	Luxury/Medium/Very Good Value	Gift Wrapping Option?	Yes
Delivery Area:	Worldwide	Returns Procedure:	Down to you

www.linksoflondon.com

Links of London are well known for an eclectic mix of jewellery in sterling silver and 18ct gold, charms and charm bracelets, cufflinks, gorgeous gifts and leather and silver accessories for your home. Inevitably each season they design a new collection of totally desirable pieces such as the 'Sweetie

Rolled Gold Bracelet', or 'Annoushka' gold and ruby charm. There are lots of lovely gift ideas here if you're looking for something special.

Site Usability:	★★★★★	Based:	UK
Product Range:	★★★★★	Express Delivery Option?	(UK) Yes
Price Range:	Luxury/Medium/Very Good Value	Gift Wrapping Option?	Yes
Delivery Area:	Worldwide	Returns Procedure:	Down to you

www.net-a-porter.com

As the ultimate online fashion retailer you might not immediately think of net-a-porter for gifts, however, if you check through their accessories section you'll find lots of possibilities, from the latest fashion jewellery by Me & Ro, Kenneth Jay Lane and Erickson Beamon, scarves by Burberry, Pucci and Chloe and must-have small leather items. Couple all this with their speedy service and lovely packaging and you have an excellent gift destination.

Site Usability:	★★★★★	Based:	UK
Product Range:	★★★★★	Express Delivery Option?	(UK) Yes
Price Range:	Luxury/Medium/Very Good Value	Gift Wrapping Option?	Yes
Delivery Area:	Worldwide	Returns Procedure:	Down to you

www.sendit.com

The difference here, as this is yet another website offering games consoles, games, dvds, computer peripherals and software is the service. Not only do they offer a courier service within the UK to make sure your order arrives when you need it, free UK delivery and speedy worldwide delivery but also Gift Certificates and gift wrapping on most items with which they can include your personal message – and you can even choose your wrapping paper.

Site Usability:	★★★★★	Based:	Northern Ireland
Product Range:	★★★★★	Express Delivery Option?	(UK) Yes
Price Range:	Luxury/Medium/Very Good Value	Gift Wrapping Option?	Yes
Delivery Area:	Worldwide	Returns Procedure:	Down to you

www.thewhitecompany.co.uk

Everything you need for stylish living and stylish gifts with a collection of beautifully made contemporary home accessories, from luxurious throws and blankets in cashmere or quilted velvet, rugs, mirrors and glassware, enchanting children's nightwear and accessories to gorgeously packaged toiletries. If you're anything like me you'll find it very hard to leave this site without buying something for yourself, whatever your original intentions were, so be warned.

Site Usability:	★★★★★	Based:	UK
Product Range:	★★★★★	Express Delivery Option?	(UK) Yes
Price Range:	Luxury/Medium/Very Good Value	Gift Wrapping Option?	Yes
Delivery Area:	Worldwide	Returns Procedure:	Down to you

Chapter 63

The One Stop Christmas Shop

Y ou may be frantically busy at Christmas and find it hard to get everything done, let alone the shopping, and not just because you have three children and a husband all clamouring to be in different places at the same time (with you, or with you driving).

You may live miles from the shops and the thought of having to go out, find somewhere to park and battle through the crowds yet again for your wrap and ribbon not to mention your Christmas cards, gifts and, most importantly, your new outfit is making you faint. Let alone the tree.

You may simply not be able this year to go out and do all your shopping. Maybe you're working round the clock, having a baby, travelling, whatever.

Of course you know what I'm going to say. For whatever reason, all or any of the above, you don't need to go out shopping this Christmas. Actually you don't need to at all. For anything. Rejoice in the extra free time to relax/get ready for a party/read a book/spend time talking to your friends.

Below you'll find websites divided into the following categories:

Christmas cakes and food (including the turkey).

The Christmas Table – candles, crackers, linens and more.

Christmas trees, decorations and lighting.

Christmas ribbon and wrap.

For the following you need to go to other places in the Guide:

You can select your presents from the gift websites above as well as having a look through some of the other more specific websites in this Guide such as Jewellery (Chapter 13), Lingerie (Chapter 10) and Fragrance, Bath and Body (Chapter 24). You'll also find other wonderful food websites in the main food section from Chapter 34.

The only thing I would say is this. The postal and courier services have improved by leaps and bounds to try and keep pace with our love of online ordering, however no one is infallible so please allow just that little bit of extra time. Yes you can have things delivered right up to Christmas and all the retailers should tell you their last ordering days very clearly but don't put these too much to the test. For peace of mind give them an extra few days (or couple of weeks) if you can, to make sure they can get their deliveries out to you on time.

After all, the whole idea of this is not just to give you all that extra choice but also to remove the stress of shopping for Christmas – you want to have some nails left to paint, after all, don't you?

Christmas Cakes and Food

Sites to Visit

www.bettysbypost.com

At *bettysbypost.com* you can order hand decorated Christmas cakes in a variety of sizes, their family recipe Christmas pudding with fruit soaked in brandy and ale and seasonal favourites such as Christmas Tea Loaf, Pannetone and Stollen. Chocolate ginger, miniature Florentines and Peppermint Creams are just a few of the goodies on offer in their confectionery section and you'll also find lovely stocking fillers for children and preserves for the Christmas larder.

Site Usability:	★★★	Based:	UK	
Product Range:	★★★	Express Delivery Option?	(UK) No	
Price Range:	Luxury/Medium/Very Good Value	Gift Wrapping Option?	No	
Delivery Area:	Worldwide	Returns Procedure:	Down to you	

www.canapeum.com

You know, those delicious little bite size nibbles that you have at drinks parties that used to be quite simple and now are more and more complicated, using ingredients such as lobster, foie gras, tapenade and pastrami. At Canapeum you just calculate how many canapes you need then choose which ones you want to order. Prices range from reasonable to quite expensive but when you think of all that fiddling in the kitchen you won't have to do at your next party, you may well think them worth a go.

Site Usability:	★★★	Based:	UK
Product Range:	★★★★	Express Delivery Option?	(UK) No
Price Range:	Luxury/Medium/Very Good Value	Gift Wrapping Option?	No
Delivery Area:	UK	Returns Procedure:	Down to you but only if there's a problem

www.christmasdinnercompany.co.uk

If you really don't have the time to order all your Christmas ingredients online and prepare your feast yourself then let The Christmas Dinner Company do everything for you. They'll select the best ingredients – a Kelly Bronze turkey, Duchy Originals stuffings and cocktail sausages, Joubere gravy, cranberry sauce and Mrs Ray's Christmas pudding and pack them off to you with ready peeled spuds, brandy butter and mince pies. Cooking guidelines, a suggested time plan and recipe leftover ideas are included too.

Site Usability:	★★★★	Based:	UK
Product Range:	★★★	Express Delivery Option?	(UK) No
Price Range:	Luxury/Medium/Very Good Value	Gift Wrapping Option?	No
Delivery Area:	UK	Returns Procedure:	Down to you but only if there's a problem

www.donaldrussell.com

This is a superb website from an excellent butcher, beautifully photographed and laid out and extremely tempting. You can buy just about every type of meat here, from free range goose and game (in season) to pork, beef and lamb plus natural fish and seafood. Most of the pictures show the products as you'd like them to arrive on your plate and you can either buy from their ready prepared dishes such as Salmon en Croute, Smoked Salmon Pâté or Bolognese sauce or you can follow their excellent recipes.

Site Usability:	★★★★★	Based:	UK
Product Range:	★★★★★	Express Delivery Option?	(UK) No
Price Range:	Luxury/Medium/Very Good Value	Gift Wrapping Option?	No
Delivery Area:	UK	Returns Procedure:	Down to you

www.formanandfield.com

Forman & Field is a luxury delicatessen specialising in traditional British produce from small independent producers. You'll find a delicious selection of luxury cakes and puddings, smoked salmon, ham and cheeses all beautifully photographed and extremely hard to resist. Don't miss their home made, award winning fish pâtés and pies, perfect for the next time you're entertaining. They offer speedy delivery to UK, Ireland and the Channel Isles

Site Usability:	★★★★★	Based:	UK
Product Range:	★★★★★	Express Delivery Option?	(UK) Yes
Price Range:	<u>Luxury/Medium</u>/Very Good Value	Gift Wrapping Option?	No
Delivery Area:	UK, Ireland, Channel Isles	Returns Procedure:	Down to you

www.frenchgourmetstore.com

Here you'll discover a marvellous selection of regional gourmet products from France, all prepared according to traditional recipes and including mushrooms and truffles, mustards, oils and vinegars and gorgeous chocolates. They also have a small but excellent range of hampers and gift baskets. They're actually based in the UK, will ship to you anywhere in the world and offer an express service.

Site Usability:	★★★★★	Based:	France
Product Range:	★★★★	Express Delivery Option?	(UK) Yes
Price Range:	<u>Luxury/Medium</u>/Very Good Value	Gift Wrapping Option?	No
Delivery Area:	Worldwide	Returns Procedure:	Down to you

www.georgieporgiespuddings.co.uk

These traditional Christmas puddings are made with all the ingredients you'd expect from the home-made variety, including currants, sultanas, raisins and orange peel, brandy, rum and spices. They're available in a choice of sizes, from a tiny one person pudding to one large enough to feed fifteen. Other puddings and desserts on offer are Cider and Apple, Orange and Cointreau, Lemon and Pimms, treacle sponge and Spotted Dick. This one's definitely not good for the diet.

Site Usability:	★★★★	Based:	UK
Product Range:	★★★	Express Delivery Option?	(UK) No
Price Range:	Luxury/<u>Medium</u>/Very Good Value	Gift Wrapping Option?	No
Delivery Area:	UK	Returns Procedure:	Down to you

www.kelly-turkeys.com

Recommended as the turkey du jour by celebrity chefs, you can order your traditionally farmed Kelly Bronze turkey directly from their website. Select your turkey by weight on their order form and it will be delivered to you, close to Christmas, in their insulated cool boxes. There are lots of recipes and advice on storing, preparing and cooking your turkey plus delicious suggestions on what to do with the leftovers.

Site Usability:	★★★★	Based:	UK
Product Range:	★★★	Express Delivery Option?	(UK) No
Price Range:	Luxury/<u>Medium</u>/Very Good Value	Gift Wrapping Option?	No
Delivery Area:	UK	Returns Procedure:	Down to you

www.lakelandlimited.co.uk

If you thought (as I always have) that Lakeland was about gifts and gizmos for the kitchen and home and clever picnic and tableware then think again. A selection of chocolates, Bay Tree Turkish Delight, Apricots in Moscato, Candied Fruits, Marrons Glacé, olive oils, jalapeno spiced nuts plus the famous Australian Celebration Cake are just some of the goodies they offer at Christmas. Couple this with Lakeland's emphasis on quality and service and you certainly won't go wrong when you place an order here.

Site Usability:	★★★★★	Based:	UK
Product Range:	★★★★★	Express Delivery Option?	(UK) Yes
Price Range:	Luxury/Medium/Very Good Value	Gift Wrapping Option?	No
Delivery Area:	Worldwide	Returns Procedure:	Down to you

www.megrivers.com

This is an extremely tempting website offering 'home made' beautifully decorated cakes, biscuits and traybakes (flapjacks, chocolate brownies and bakewells). Their traditional fruit cakes and Christmas cakes (including a chocolate Christmas cake) are lovely to look at and taste delicious (and I know, I've tried them). If you can't be bothered or don't have the time to bake yourself this Christmas definitely shop here. You won't be disappointed.

Site Usability:	★★★★★	Based:	UK
Product Range:	★★★	Express Delivery Option?	(UK) No
Price Range:	Luxury/Medium/Very Good Value	Gift Wrapping Option?	No
Delivery Area:	Worldwide	Returns Procedure:	Down to you

www.paxtonandwhitfield.co.uk

You can buy a mouthwatering selection of speciality British, French and Italian cheeses here and join the Cheese Society to receive their special selection each month. They also sell biscuits, chutneys and pickles, York ham and pâtés, beautifully boxed cheese knives and stores, fondue sets and raclette machines. This is really the place to find all the cheeses you need here for Christmas plus some excellent gifts for cheese lovers.

Site Usability:	★★★★★	Based:	UK
Product Range:	★★★★	Express Delivery Option?	(UK) Yes
Price Range:	Luxury/Medium/Very Good Value	Gift Wrapping Option?	No
Delivery Area:	Worldwide	Returns Procedure:	Down to you

www.realmeat.co.uk

The Real Meat Company supplies excellent quality meat and poultry from traditional farmers with a nationwide delivery service. You can order your turkey from them for Christmas from mid-November.

Their minimum order value is £35 and you can specify the day you want your delivery. Remember to allow them enough time in the run up to Christmas.

Site Usability:	★★★		Based:	UK
Product Range:	★★★		Express Delivery Option?	(UK) No
Price Range:	Luxury/<u>Medium</u>/Very Good Value		Gift Wrapping Option?	No
Delivery Area:	UK		Returns Procedure:	Down to you

www.thecarvedangel.com

At *thecarvedangel.com* you'll find their famous Christmas pud, which you can order in three sizes to feed up to a dozen people. All the puddings are traditionally presented in a re-usable earthenware bowl that is dishwater and microwave safe and then hand tied with a muslin cloth and ribbon with cooking instructions attached. You can buy your brandy butter here as well. Allow at least 14 days for delivery

Site Usability:	★★★★		Based:	UK
Product Range:	★★★		Express Delivery Option?	(UK) No
Price Range:	Luxury/<u>Medium</u>/Very Good Value		Gift Wrapping Option?	No
Delivery Area:	UK		Returns Procedure:	Down to you

www.thescottishgourmet.com

If you'd like someone else to do the work in the kitchen for you this Christmas (or at any other time of year, for that matter), then check out The Scottish Gourmet. They'll deliver by overnight courier such delicacies as duck with port and orange, roast salmon in filo pastry and raspberry and orange liqueur pudding plus Scottish cheeses and smoked salmon. You can browse this month's menu and order a taster pack as a gift here as well.

Site Usability:	★★★		Based:	UK
Product Range:	★★★★		Express Delivery Option?	(UK) No
Price Range:	<u>Luxury</u>/Medium/Very Good Value		Gift Wrapping Option?	No
Delivery Area:	UK		Returns Procedure:	Down to you

The Christmas Table

If yours is anything like our household, how our Christmas table looks is extremely important. It has to be richly coloured and decorated with loads of crackers and candles, and sugared almonds and gold stars scattered around. Each year I try and add something slightly different, a mirrored Indian cloth, for example or gold tealights in glittering holders but if it changes too much, there are noisy mutterings of disapproval from just about everyone.

There's a very good choice in the websites below, whether you want a completely new look or just to make a few additions to what you use already. I've not included the obvious places as they've already had several entries, however look as well at *www.johnlewis.com*, *www.thewhitecompany.co.uk* and *www.lakelandlimited.co.uk* to make sure you haven't missed anything, Lakeland in particular always has new, extremely well priced ideas.

Sites to Visit

www.candle-city.co.uk

There are lots of places you can buy candles online, but few with as comprehensive a selection as you'll find here, with a very good range of Price's dinner candles, plus Yankee Candles, Colonial, Pintail (those little tins of fragranced candles), Claremont and May and more. They'll deliver to the UK, Europe and USA although the delivery charges to the USA are steep.

Site Usability:	★★★	Based:	UK
Product Range:	★★★	Express Delivery Option?	(UK) No
Price Range:	Luxury/<u>Medium</u>/Very Good Value	Gift Wrapping Option?	No
Delivery Area:	Worldwide	Returns Procedure:	Down to you

www.festive-dresser.co.uk

There are some really different and beautifully made decorations here, including both circular and heart-shaped wreaths incorporating beads, feathers, jewels and even marabou plus the more traditional autumn foliage and berries. You'll also find exquisite table decorations – beaded and feathered napkin rings, glass decorations and candle rings and garlands to decorate your home. There are decorative ideas here not just for Christmas but perfect for summer weddings as well.

Site Usability:	★★★★	Based:	UK
Product Range:	★★★	Express Delivery Option?	(UK) No
Price Range:	Luxury/<u>Medium</u>/Very Good Value	Gift Wrapping Option?	No
Delivery Area:	UK	Returns Procedure:	Down to you

www.gocrackers.co.uk

Don't wait for the last minute to order your crackers online from this excellent website. I suggest you go for it sometime during November or you may find that your chosen design has sold out. You'll find a wide selection here from the unusual (leopard print) crackers to much more traditional red and gold, burgundy and green script and holly design. Prices range from luxury to very reasonable and there's also a wide range of high quality Christmas paper napkins to choose from.

Site Usability:	★★★★	Based:	UK
Product Range:	★★★	Express Delivery Option?	(UK) No
Price Range:	<u>Luxury/Medium</u>/Very Good Value	Gift Wrapping Option?	No
Delivery Area:	UK	Returns Procedure:	Down to you

www.justcrackers.com

Ok so this year your crackers are going to be really special (and I mean really special). Here you'll find 'couture' crackers, totally handmade and utterly luxurious. You choose your cracker design from their selection and then whatever you want to go inside from Jasmine scented bath confetti to a mother-of-pearl caviar spoon. There's something for everyone including children and the city slicker in your life, so before you even think of choosing your crackers take a look here first.

Site Usability:	★★★★	Based:	UK
Product Range:	★★★	Express Delivery Option?	(UK) No
Price Range:	Luxury/Medium/Very Good Value	Gift Wrapping Option?	No
Delivery Area:	UK	Returns Procedure:	Down to you

www.onestopcandleshop.co.uk

Here you'll find very well priced dinner candles in a wide choice of colours including gold and silver, tea lights (again available in gold and silver as well as plain and scented ranges), a huge selection of candle holders for all sizes of candles, from individual holders to multi candle sconces and some gift ideas. They offer express and standard delivery to the UK mainland so if you live in the Highlands and Islands you need to call them for delivery.

Site Usability:	★★★	Based:	UK
Product Range:	★★★	Express Delivery Option?	(UK) Yes
Price Range:	Luxury/Medium/Very Good Value	Gift Wrapping Option?	No
Delivery Area:	UK	Returns Procedure:	Down to you

www.parkscandles.com

This is quite a small website offering a beautiful range of scented candles in decorative containers, triple wick candles in silver bowls and perfumed candles in glass containers some of which would look lovely on a Christmas table. They also offer scented dinner candles in green, burgundy and cream and nothing here is overpriced. Expect speedy delivery and excellent service.

Site Usability:	★★★★	Based:	UK
Product Range:	★★★	Express Delivery Option?	(UK) Yes
Price Range:	Luxury/Medium/Very Good Value	Gift Wrapping Option?	No
Delivery Area:	Worldwide	Returns Procedure:	Down to you

www.pier.co.uk

Based on the famous US furniture and accessories retailer Pier One Imports, everything here is attractive and well priced and you'll find lovely gifts and accessories here from all over the World. At Christmas they bring out a special catalogue to complement the website so order yours early. You'll find lots of ideas for the Christmas table, from table linen, glasses and cutlery to candles and colourful napkin decorations.

Site Usability:	★★★★★	Based:	UK
Product Range:	★★★★	Express Delivery Option?	(UK) No
Price Range:	Luxury/Medium/Very Good Value	Gift Wrapping Option?	No
Delivery Area:	UK	Returns Procedure:	Down to you

www.purpleandfinelinen.co.uk

At Purple and Fine Linen their pure linen tablecloths, placemats, napkins and runners are designed to offer a look of timeless luxury and simple elegance. As well as traditional white and ivory you can also choose from their range in deep chilli red and damson (purple), which would be lovely for Christmas. These are investment linens rather than the throw away variety and very beautiful.

Site Usability:	★★★★★	Based:	UK
Product Range:	★★★	Express Delivery Option?	(UK) Yes
Price Range:	Luxury/Medium/Very Good Value	Gift Wrapping Option?	No
Delivery Area:	Worldwide	Returns Procedure:	Down to you

www.volgalinen.co.uk

Update your table linen this Christmas with the exquisite collection of Russian table linen from the Volga Linen Company. The collection consists of richly coloured Paisley, white and natural double damask and bordered linen table cloths, placements and napkins, with all tablecloths available in a selection of sizes. Nothing is inexpensive but then you shouldn't expect it to be, as you're buying the very best quality. Worldwide delivery is available.

Site Usability:	★★★★★	Based:	UK
Product Range:	★★★	Express Delivery Option?	(UK) No
Price Range:	Luxury/Medium/Very Good Value	Gift Wrapping Option?	No
Delivery Area:	Worldwide	Returns Procedure:	Down to you

Christmas Ribbon and Wrap

Sites to Visit

www.carnmeal.co.uk

This site is a must for anyone who has more than a few presents to wrap up. They specialise in a wide choice of beautiful ribbons and craft accessories for all occasions (and particularly weddings) and rather than buying those small irritating balls of gold and silver ribbon, here you can choose from wired and unwired ribbons, organzas and tartans in lots of different widths and a wide selection of colours. Most ribbons are available in 25 metre lengths.

Site Usability:	★★★	Based:	UK
Product Range:	★★★★★	Express Delivery Option?	(UK) No
Price Range:	Luxury/Medium/Very Good Value	Gift Wrapping Option?	No
Delivery Area:	Worldwide	Returns Procedure:	Down to you

www.millcrofttextiles.co.uk

Millcroft supply general haberdashery items and textiles worldwide, specialising in the bridal industry. They also have a small but lovely selection of ribbons, including taffeta, tartan and metallic lamé in lots of different colours which they show clearly. You can choose from different widths and lengths although the reels usually start at 20 metres. When you're buying these quantities, prices are inevitably much better than you'll find in the shops so buy to use throughout the year.

Site Usability:	★★★★	Based:	UK
Product Range:	★★★★	Express Delivery Option?	(UK) No
Price Range:	Luxury/Medium/Very Good Value	Gift Wrapping Option?	No
Delivery Area:	Worldwide	Returns Procedure:	Down to you

www.mjtrim.com

This is a marvellous ribbon and trimming store based in the US and they will ship worldwide. It really is well worth taking a look as not only are the prices very good but the choice is quite spectacular, including ribbons for Christmas, weddings and other occasions, plus trims such as beaded appliqué motifs (think flowers, hearts, bugs and animals), beads, feather and faux fur trims and buttons and tassels. If you're ordering from outside the US you need to fax your order and allow extra time.

Site Usability:	★★★★★	Based:	US
Product Range:	★★★★★	Express Delivery Option?	(UK) No
Price Range:	Luxury/Medium/Very Good Value	Gift Wrapping Option?	No
Delivery Area:	Worldwide	Returns Procedure:	Down to you

www.nspccshop.co.uk

You can often find some really attractive Christmas ornaments, crackers, decorations and well priced gift suggestions in the NSPCC catalogue each year and when you know that you're giving for such a good cause it makes sense to buy here. You'll also find a wide selection of Christmas Cards, excellent gift wrap, ribbons and calendars.

Site Usability:	★★★★★	Based:	UK
Product Range:	★★★★★	Express Delivery Option?	(UK) No
Price Range:	Luxury/Medium/Very Good Value	Gift Wrapping Option?	No
Delivery Area:	UK	Returns Procedure:	Down to you

379

www.nationaltrust-shop.co.uk

The National Trust shop online always has one of the best selections of high quality wrapping paper and gift tags each Christmas. When you click through to their online shop you'll find not just a wide choice of designs but you can also buy your wrap in different lengths right up to 20 metres, ideal if you've lots of gifts to organise. You'll also find crackers at a range of prices, Christmas cards and gift ideas and ordering is very quick and easy.

Site Usability:	★★★★★	Based:	UK
Product Range:	★★★★	Express Delivery Option?	(UK) No
Price Range:	Luxury/Medium/Very Good Value	Gift Wrapping Option?	No
Delivery Area:	UK	Returns Procedure:	Down to you

www.thewrappingco.com

Here's a small collection of very beautiful but quite expensive wrap, ribbon and cards which would be suitable if you have just a few presents you want to wrap superbly. They also give suggestions on which ribbon to use with which paper. The website doesn't keep its Christmas selection up all the year round so you need to visit them in October for the full range, although you can of course use them all the year round for other occasions.

Site Usability:	★★★★	Based:	UK
Product Range:	★★★	Express Delivery Option?	(UK) No
Price Range:	Luxury/Medium/Very Good Value	Gift Wrapping Option?	No
Delivery Area:	UK	Returns Procedure:	Down to you

Also check out www.johnlewis.com for Christmas ribbon and wrap

Christmas Trees, Decorations and Lighting

Sites to Visit

www.chatsworth-dec.co.uk

If you're fed up of spending a lot of money on Christmas decorations or having to go round the heaving stores to buy them then you should take a look at this website, mainly designed to supply the leisure industry but with no minimum order value; happy to sell to you too. You'll find lots of very inexpensive Christmas decorations, baubles, tinsel and the like as well as a host of other products such as party hats, novelties and lights.

Site Usability:	★★★★	Based:	UK
Product Range:	★★★★★	Express Delivery Option?	(UK) No
Price Range:	Luxury/Medium/Very Good Value	Gift Wrapping Option?	No
Delivery Area:	UK	Returns Procedure:	Down to you

www.christmastreeland.co.uk

Christmas Tree Land have a very clear site offering trees from 3ft to 45 ft and delivery to anywhere in the UK. There's a wide range of trees from Noble Firs to Norwegian Spruce and your tree will be delivered to you well in time for Christmas. They will take your order very close to Christmas but I would suggest you allow plenty of time. Delivery is by courier. You can also choose from a range of artificial trees here from the pre-lit Colorado fir to fashion trees in different colours, fibre optic trees, wreaths and decorations.

Site Usability:	★★★★	Based:	UK
Product Range:	★★★★	Express Delivery Option?	(UK) No
Price Range:	Luxury/Medium/Very Good Value	Gift Wrapping Option?	No
Delivery Area:	UK	Returns Procedure:	Discuss with them

www.grovelands.com

Grovelands are a large garden centre in Berkshire who have managed to transfer just about all their products onto their website. You'll find a wide range of Christmas trees both of the real and artificial variety, tree lights, pretty traditional ornaments from Germany and a good selection of gifts such as Victorinox cyber tools, gardeners tools and accessories, table football and compendium table games. So this could really be a one stop shop this Christmas.

Site Usability:	★★★★	Based:	UK
Product Range:	★★★★★	Express Delivery Option?	(UK) No
Price Range:	Luxury/Medium/Very Good Value	Gift Wrapping Option?	No
Delivery Area:	Worldwide	Returns Procedure:	Down to you

www.peeks.co.uk

Peeks is a family company established in 1946. Originally retailers of cards and toys, they have now developed their products to include themed party items (for occasions such as Halloween) games and other gift ideas and just about everything for Christmas including tree decorations, tinsel and garlands, artificial trees, crackers and balloons.

Site Usability:	★★★★★	Based:	UK
Product Range:	★★★★	Express Delivery Option?	(UK) No
Price Range:	Luxury/Medium/Very Good Value	Gift Wrapping Option?	No
Delivery Area:	Worldwide	Returns Procedure:	Down to you

www.xmastreesales.com

A very clear site offering just freshly cut Christmas trees, they offer free 3 day UK mainland delivery, £4.99 for next day service and you can order right up to Christmas. The choice of trees is simple with the main varieties being Norway Spruce (the traditional tree), Nordman Fir (Non Drop Needles) and Noble Fir (Slightly Scented Tree). They also give you advice on which tree to choose.

Site Usability:	★★★★	Based:	UK
Product Range:	★★★★	Express Delivery Option?	(UK) Yes
Price Range:	Luxury/Medium/Very Good Value	Gift Wrapping Option?	No
Delivery Area:	UK	Returns Procedure:	Discuss with them

www.xmastreesdirect.co.uk

There's a great deal to look at on this Christmas website, from high quality real and artificial trees, tree stands, lights, including bulb testers, transformers, motors and sensors, artificial wreaths and holly, tree baubles, a lovely selection of unusual ribbons and Christmas stockings. Delivery is to the UK only and for a very small amount extra you can use their next day courier service.

Site Usability:	★★★★	Based:	UK
Product Range:	★★★★	Express Delivery Option?	(UK) Yes
Price Range:	Luxury/Medium/Very Good Value	Gift Wrapping Option?	No
Delivery Area:	UK	Returns Procedure:	Discuss with them

Section 8
Weddings

I'm sure that you'll agree with me that there are some things here it's really difficult to buy online. Take The Dress, for example. Unless you absolutely have to, you're not going to buy your wedding dress online. You're going to want to go out and try on different dresses to find the one that's perfect for you in terms of style and fit. However, as a starting place the web can be a great help as you can showcase lots of different designers within a short space of time, look at straight styles, curvy shapes, flounces and embroidery and get a feel for prices. You can also, when you find a designer you like, find out where your nearest stockist is so you can really plan your expedition and have a much better idea of what you're looking for before you start.

This may well apply to most aspects of your wedding, depending on how busy you are and how easy it is for you to get to the shops. Whatever you decide about buying on or offline you can certainly gather a huge amount of information here which will make the overall decision process much, much easier. You can also visit all these websites at any time of day or night which will hopefully save you hours of time later on.

There are a couple of other essentials for weddings that are also quite difficult to buy online. Your florist and your cake maker will want to work with you to match your overall style from your dress and colour scheme to the size of the occasion. Having said that there are just a few really good florists and wedding cake designers who will despatch nationwide if you need them to and you'll find them listed below.

When it comes to shoes and accessories, jewellery, stationery and gifts there are lots of websites to browse through and you can order just about everything online. For pampering hair and beauty products and accessories and for lingerie, you need to go to the Health and Beauty and Lingerie sections in this guide, where you'll find an enormous amount of choice. Most of the lingerie retailers have a special section for Weddings and excellent range of sizes.

To make life easier from the start I suggest you invest in a wedding planner/file. You'll find two of the best at *www.confetti.co.uk* and *www.theweddingfile.com*. Buy one of those first and everything else will become much simpler to organise.

Chapter 64

All About The Dress

Your wedding dress will be one of the most important investments made for your wedding, whether you choose something simple and stylish, beaded, embroidered and ruffled or top of the range couture where every detail is to your individual choosing.

You can, of course go straight for a large store such as Harrods, where there's a very wide selection and lots of advice on hand and buy your dress there but if you live miles away and don't want to choose your dress without having a good look first you could browse through the websites below where you can see a wonderful, glamorous range.

These are not dresses to buy online for the main part as I've already said but they'll give you a very good idea of what's available. Some of the websites don't even give you the prices but you'll be looking at upwards of £600 for a ready made gown and into the thousands for something specially made for you.

If you find something you like here you just need to call the stockist nearest you (who you'll find on the designer's website) and enquire about price and availability which will give you a point to start from.

Most wedding dresses take quite a long time as you'll probably need some alterations and obviously longer if it's being made for you, however, some designers will work with you to produce your dress more quickly if you need it so ask when you call the stockist if this is possible.

Sites to Visit

www.alanhannah.co.uk

Marguerite Hannah has been designing wedding dresses for the past 14 years and in that time has won many awards including the Retail Bridal Association's Best Designer award in 2001, 2002, 2004 and 2005. The collection is really beautiful and embellished with modern hand crafted jewellery and hand painting as well as delicate beadwork. Fabrics include crisp silk zybeline and mikado along with the luxury of duchesse satin and lace.

Site Usability:	★★★★	Based:	UK
Product Range:	★★★★	Express Delivery Option?	(UK) N/A
Price Range:	Luxury/Medium/Very Good Value	Gift Wrapping Option?	N/A
Delivery Area:	Worldwide	Returns Procedure:	N/A

www.amandawakeley.com

The Amanda Wakeley Sposa Collection was launched in 2001 and offers a beautiful ready to wear bridal range in line with her modern and luxurious day and eveningwear. On her chic website you can preview the Sposa collection and also take a look through the main clothing and jewellery collections which give you a very good idea of her style and prices. If you like what's there check for the stockist nearest to you.

Site Usability:	★★★	Based:	UK
Product Range:	★★★★	Express Delivery Option?	(UK) N/A
Price Range:	Luxury/Medium/Very Good Value	Gift Wrapping Option?	N/A
Delivery Area:	Worldwide	Returns Procedure:	N/A

www.amandawyatt.com

Here's a gorgeous range of mid to upper priced wedding dresses shown in really clear and pretty detail. Click through to the other collection here; Charlotte Balbier, which is younger and at a slightly higher price level. You'll also find her wedding accessories. Visit the stockists' listings and you'll be able to see if there's a special event happening near you, such as a designer evening or special showing.

Site Usability:	★★★★★	Based:	UK
Product Range:	★★★★★	Express Delivery Option?	(UK) N/A
Price Range:	Luxury/Medium/Very Good Value	Gift Wrapping Option?	N/A
Delivery Area:	UK	Returns Procedure:	N/A

www.annachristina.com

Over the years Anna Christina has become one of the UK's top wedding dress designers, offering an exquisite cut and fit and very high quality workmanship. She specialises in an understated elegance which you can clearly see from the detailed pictures on the website. Once you've seen something you like you can register your email address and they'll send you a copy of the picture plus a list of stockists in your area.

Site Usability:	★★★★	Based:	UK
Product Range:	★★★	Express Delivery Option?	(UK) N/A
Price Range:	Luxury/Medium/Very Good Value	Gift Wrapping Option?	N/A
Delivery Area:	UK	Returns Procedure:	N/A

www.benjaminroberts.co.uk

Benjamin Roberts brings you gowns that are designed by young European trained designers who are encouraged to try new fabrics, silhouettes, colours and texture. The workmanship is exquisite and very high quality and prices very good with dresses generally retailing under £1000. Once you've selected the style of wedding gown you like his comprehensive stockist's directory will tell you exactly where you can find your dress.

Site Usability:	★★★★★	Based:	UK
Product Range:	★★★★★	Express Delivery Option?	(UK) N/A
Price Range:	Luxury/Medium/Very Good Value	Gift Wrapping Option?	N/A
Delivery Area:	UK	Returns Procedure:	N/A

www.brownsfashion.co.uk

Browns Bride continues the same tradition as Browns Fashion by showcasing many of the designer labels and offering a selection of the best and most beautiful dresses to be found anywhere. Some are very well known names and others not so well known, including Badgley Mischka, Emanuel Ungaro, Reem Acra and Carlos Miele. You can see the dresses clearly on their website and if you see something you like you need to call them.

Site Usability:	★★★★	Based:	UK
Product Range:	★★★★★	Express Delivery Option?	(UK) N/A
Price Range:	Luxury/Medium/Very Good Value	Gift Wrapping Option?	N/A
Delivery Area:	UK	Returns Procedure:	N/A

www.designerbridalroom.com

Here you'll find wedding dresses by Anna Christina, Ella Johannssen, Model Novias, Fabio Gritti, Caroline Castigliano and Christiana Couture, to name a few so whether you're looking for high fashion or understated style you may well find something here. They don't show a lot of the designs on the website; just enough to give you an idea of the style of each designer and their shops are in London, Birmingham, Manchester and Esher.

Site Usability:	★★★★	Based:	UK
Product Range:	★★★★	Express Delivery Option?	(UK) N/A
Price Range:	Luxury/Medium/Very Good Value	Gift Wrapping Option?	N/A
Delivery Area:	UK	Returns Procedure:	N/A

www.emptybox.co.uk

Established in 1988, The Empty Box Company first began reviving the old fashioned Edwardian Hat Box and then began to produce beautiful, handmade and pHneutral boxes after research into storage of fabrics and discussions with textile experts at The V&A. Their boxes are made specially for you with your choice of design and ribbon and you can also have your Wedding Dress Box personalised with your name and wedding date. If you're marrying abroad you'll definitely need one of these boxes to transport your dress. You can also buy accessory boxes, planners and albums, gift boxes and confetti here.

Site Usability:	★★★★		Based:	UK
Product Range:	★★★		Express Delivery Option?	(UK) No
Price Range:	Luxury/<u>Medium</u>/Very Good Value		Gift Wrapping Option?	No
Delivery Area:	Worldwide		Returns Procedure:	Down to you

www.eveningdresses.co.uk

Click through to the bridal section of this website where you can order all the dresses online and prices range from around £400 to well over £1000. You'll also find bridesmaids' dresses (which you can buy in a wide range of colours) and eveningwear in the main section of the website. They don't hold everything in stock so check with them if you want to place an order here. If they do have it, it can be delivered to you within 48 hours.

Site Usability:	★★★		Based:	UK
Product Range:	★★★★		Express Delivery Option?	(UK) Yes
Price Range:	Luxury/<u>Medium</u>/Very Good Value		Gift Wrapping Option?	No
Delivery Area:	Worldwide		Returns Procedure:	Down to you

www.helenmarina.com/index1.asp

Helen Marina's award winning bridal collections can be found in over 120 boutiques in the UK, throughout Europe and as far as Australia and America. She has three collections under her name, The Helen Marina and Infinity Collections; using silk, satin, organza and crepe with beading and embroidery and the Oceana Collection, specifically designed with weddings abroad and civil ceremonies in mind.

Site Usability:	★★★★		Based:	UK
Product Range:	★★★★		Express Delivery Option?	(UK) N/A
Price Range:	<u>Luxury</u>/<u>Medium</u>/Very Good Value		Gift Wrapping Option?	N/A
Delivery Area:	Worldwide		Returns Procedure:	N/A

www.justbrides.co.uk

You may think that buying a wedding dress online would be really difficult. Well let's just say that for some reason you can't go out and choose your dress and you'd like to be able to find one online and have it sent to you. On this website you can do just that, as not only do they offer a selection of gowns all with corset style tops which make fitting much easier, but you can also choose the fabric, skirt style and silk colour here and use their advice service to help you with all the details.

Site Usability:	★★★★	Based:	UK
Product Range:	★★★★	Express Delivery Option?	(UK) No
Price Range:	Luxury/Medium/Very Good Value	Gift Wrapping Option?	N/A
Delivery Area:	Worldwide	Returns Procedure:	N/A

www.justinalexanderbridal.com

This is a collection of glamorous, extravagantly gorgeous wedding gowns which you can find at stockists throughout the World. The gowns incorporate high levels of craftsmanship and are made of the finest fabrics: pure silk, rich satins, soft laces and hand crafted beading as well as glittering Swarovski crystals. The corsetry is based on original Victorian patterns and techniques. The pictures are really beautiful but unfortunately they don't show the prices, however you can click through to the stockists list to find the one nearest you.

Site Usability:	★★★★	Based:	UK
Product Range:	★★★★	Express Delivery Option?	(UK) N/A
Price Range:	Luxury/Medium/Very Good Value	Gift Wrapping Option?	N/A
Delivery Area:	Worldwide	Returns Procedure:	N/A

www.louellabridal.co.uk

Louella are based in Leeds and in their shop and on their website you can see a dazzling choice of bridal gowns, including collections by Pronovias, Jenny Packham and Kate Sherford. They don't advise that you buy gowns without fittings (although there is an ordering facility) so if you can get to their shop it would be a good place to visit. They also offer tiaras, hair pieces, jewellery, shoes and bags, all of which you can order online.

Site Usability:	★★★	Based:	UK
Product Range:	★★★★	Express Delivery Option?	(UK) No
Price Range:	Luxury/Medium/Very Good Value	Gift Wrapping Option?	No
Delivery Area:	UK	Returns Procedure:	Down to you

www.philipalepley.com

Philipa Lepley has been creating beautiful wedding dresses for over twenty years, combining femininity and simplicity with enormous attention to fine detail such as embroidery, colour and flowers. When you look through the gallery of pictures on her website you'll immediately see that here are some of the most unique wedding dresses available. To see the collection properly you need to visit her Fulham Road showroom where you'll find over eighty samples to choose from.

Site Usability:	★★★★	Based:	UK
Product Range:	★★★★	Express Delivery Option?	(UK) N/A
Price Range:	Luxury/Medium/Very Good Value	Gift Wrapping Option?	N/A
Delivery Area:	UK	Returns Procedure:	N/A

www.pronovias.com

Pronovias is a Spanish bridal wear company specialising in top of the range and couture wedding dresses by designers such as Elis Saab, Emanuel Ungaro, Badgley Mischka and Hannibal Laguna. On their stylish website you can look at their elegantly photographed online catalogues plus their cocktailwear, and find out where your nearest stockist is wherever you are in the world. This is a very large range so not all stockists will carry the full collection.

Site Usability:	★★★★★	Based:	Spain
Product Range:	★★★★★	Express Delivery Option?	(UK) N/A
Price Range:	Luxury/Medium/Very Good Value	Gift Wrapping Option?	N/A
Delivery Area:	Worldwide	Returns Procedure:	N/A

www.stewartparvin.com

Stewart Parvin trained at the Edinburgh College of Art and went on to work with other designers before establishing his own studio. From day and eveningwear he launched his wedding collection which now includes couture and diffusion ranges and is available worldwide. He designs everything from his studio, working with a small team and using only the most luxurious fabrics and creative embroiderers and seamstresses to create unique, elegant designs.

Site Usability:	★★★★★	Based:	UK
Product Range:	★★★★	Express Delivery Option?	(UK) N/A
Price Range:	Luxury/Medium/Very Good Value	Gift Wrapping Option?	N/A
Delivery Area:	Worldwide	Returns Procedure:	N/A

www.suzanneneville.com

Having studied at the London College of Fashion, Suzanne Neville went on to win the British Bridal Awards ('New Designer' and 'Traditionally Classic') in her first year of working under her own name. Her client list now includes celebrities and brides in media, film and television. Her dresses are hand crafted using contemporary couture techniques and on her website you'll find her Classic, Deco and Renaissance ranges with stylish photography and close-up detail.

Site Usability:	★★★★★	Based:	UK
Product Range:	★★★★	Express Delivery Option?	(UK) N/A
Price Range:	Luxury/Medium/Very Good Value	Gift Wrapping Option?	N/A
Delivery Area:	From Stockist, UK only	Returns Procedure:	N/A

Chapter 65

Accessories and Hats

his is where the fun really starts. So you've chosen your dress, and if you went to buy it from a large bridal boutique you may well have bought everything else to go with it, from a hat, feathered comb or tiara to gloves, a faux fur stole, your shoes and special jewellery.

Alternatively you may have decided to wait until your dress is ready before you choose everything else, so you can see how it looks all together with your dress fitting perfectly.

Either way there are lots of other accessories you're going to need and not just for your wedding but for your rehearsal dinner (if you're having one) your going away outfit and for your honeymoon.

On the websites below you can find a selection of hats, headwear, veils and sumptuous shawls in the softest faux fur, silk organza and velvet lined with satin. Many of the designers will customise your hat or headpiece to your specification so that it matches in with the theme of your dress and some will deliver to you anywhere in the world.

Sites to Visit

www.annabelleashton.com

This is a really excellent bridal accessories boutique, offering high quality hats and headpieces, shoes by Filippa Scott and Rainbow, silk scarves and bags, flowergirl jewellery and keepsake boxes, wedding ring cushions and even honeymoon flip flops and t-shirts. Some of the hats would be perfect for the mother of the bride and a few are available in a range of colours. They're happy to ship worldwide.

Site Usability:	★★★★	Based:	UK
Product Range:	★★★★	Express Delivery Option?	(UK) No
Price Range:	Luxury/Medium/Very Good Value	Gift Wrapping Option?	No
Delivery Area:	Worldwide	Returns Procedure:	Down to you

www.baileytomlin.com

Bailey Tomlin hats are designed to look special, make a statement and reflect the wearer's personality. They're sold at Harrods, Selfridges and Saks 5th Avenue and they've also created hats for Jean Muir, Caroline Charles and Mulberry. The collection is gorgeously fun, modern and different and if you see something you like on this website you can call them to place an order or have one of their hats customised to match your outfit.

Site Usability:	★★★★	Based:	UK
Product Range:	★★★	Express Delivery Option?	(UK) No
Price Range:	Luxury/Medium/Very Good Value	Gift Wrapping Option?	No
Delivery Area:	UK	Returns Procedure:	Down to you

www.blossom.co.uk

The accessory shop at Blossom is based near Farnham in Surrey, and offers a collection of over 300 tiaras, plus shoes, veils, silk accessories and jewellery. Their online store carries a highly edited selection of the range but it's still well worth looking at if you can't get to their shop, with gorgeous tiaras, pretty jewellery sets, jewelled hairpins, feathered and beaded combs and enchanting little tiaras for bridesmaids.

Site Usability:	★★★★★	Based:	UK
Product Range:	★★★★★	Express Delivery Option?	(UK) No
Price Range:	Luxury/Medium/Very Good Value	Gift Wrapping Option?	No
Delivery Area:	Worldwide	Returns Procedure:	Down to you

www.hatsandthat.com

If you want to choose a hat or striking headpiece to wear on your wedding day, here's one of the places where you can select from a range online. You need to click through to Ladies Occasion and Wedding

Hats or Hair Accessories and choose from the selection at different price ranges. There are some really pretty ones here and they offer a helpful measuring guide to make sure you get the right size.

Site Usability:	★★★★	Based:	UK
Product Range:	★★★	Express Delivery Option?	(UK) No
Price Range:	<u>Luxury</u>/Medium/Very Good Value	Gift Wrapping Option?	No
Delivery Area:	UK	Returns Procedure:	Down to you

www.hatsnstuff.co.uk

This is an unusual and pretty collection of tiny hats and hair pieces using silk flowers, feathers, quills and net that can all be made to match your dress or going away outfit. The prices are very reasonable, particularly when you take into account that each piece is specially made for you. You can hire hats here as well and you'll also find really high quality pashminas made from Scottish cashmere. You need to contact them by phone or email to place an order.

Site Usability:	★★★	Based:	UK
Product Range:	★★★★	Express Delivery Option?	(UK) N/A
Price Range:	Luxury/<u>Medium</u>/Very Good Value	Gift Wrapping Option?	N/A
Delivery Area:	UK	Returns Procedure:	N/A

www.jameslock.co.uk

Click through to Couture Hats and you'll find a small collection of beautiful hats designed by Sylvia Fletcher, who creates two collections a year and offers a made to order service, so fabrics can be matched or dyed to tone with your dress or outfit. All prices are on application only so expect them to be high. They prefer to fit you personally at their St James's Street premises but offer a measuring guide as well and will ship worldwide. High quality top hats for men are available here too.

Site Usability:	★★★★	Based:	UK
Product Range:	★★★	Express Delivery Option?	(UK) N/A
Price Range:	<u>Luxury</u>/Medium/Very Good Value	Gift Wrapping Option?	N/A
Delivery Area:	Worldwide	Returns Procedure:	N/A

www.siggihats.co.uk

Here you'll find unusual hats and hair pieces designed by Siegfried Hesbacher (known as Siggi), who sold his first collection of cocktail hats to Harvey Nichols in 1982 and has never looked back. He designs Florentine straw hats with luxurious trimmings, beautiful head pieces with silk flowers and feathers and his gorgeous couture hats which are hand blocked and finished and individually trimmed.

Site Usability:	★★★★	Based:	UK
Product Range:	★★★★	Express Delivery Option?	(UK) N/A
Price Range:	<u>Luxury</u>/Medium/Very Good Value	Gift Wrapping Option?	N/A
Delivery Area:	Worldwide	Returns Procedure:	N/A

www.wonderfulwraps.co.uk

Established for over ten years, Wonderful Wraps has featured major UK retail outlets such as Harrods, Selfridges and Harvey Nichols in London and Saks Fifth Avenue and Neiman Marcus in the US. They offer a collection of sumptuous velvets, silk organzas, chiffons and tulles, satins, faux furs, marabous and other luxury wraps, stoles and capes. To place your order you need to call them.

Site Usability:	★★★★	Based:	UK
Product Range:	★★★★	Express Delivery Option?	(UK) N/A
Price Range:	Luxury/Medium/Very Good Value	Gift Wrapping Option?	N/A
Delivery Area:	Worldwide	Returns Procedure:	Down to you

Also check www.justbrides.co.uk for wedding accessories

Chapter 66

Bridesmaids and Flowergirls

$\mathcal{A}$ re you having tiny little flower girls and page boys to follow along behind you or the early teen version who'll be really sensitive about whatever you ask them to wear? Alternatively you may be inviting a friend to be your Maid of Honour and you may want to have a combination of all three – tinies, teens and older friend.

On the websites below you'll find a small selection of dresses which you can order online plus lots of ideas for shoes and accessories for bridesmaids of all ages, shapes and sizes.

Sites to Visit

www.bridesmaidsdirect.co.uk

This Somerset based manufacturer offers you a choice of bridesmaids dresses which you can order online for tiny and more grown up bridesmaids. The pictures are not the greatest but some of the designs are very pretty and made up in fabrics such as satin back crepe and silk dupion. I suggest that before you even think of ordering you should ask for a fabric swatch, particularly if you want to order a colour they haven't used for their main photograph.

Site Usability:	★★★	Based:	UK
Product Range:	★★★★	Express Delivery Option?	(UK) N/A
Price Range:	Luxury/Medium/Very Good Value	Gift Wrapping Option?	N/A
Delivery Area:	Worldwide	Returns Procedure:	N/A

www.jlmeurope.co.uk

There's a lot to see here, so be prepared to spend some time. There are three ranges here for bridesmaids of all ages, from enchanting little flowergirls' dresses in pretty soft colours to chic and sophisticated dresses for older bridesmaids that'll definitely be worn more than once. You can view the whole range here plus colour swatches for each style online right down to ribbon swatches, order their brochure and find out where your nearest stockist is.

Site Usability:	★★★★★	Based:	UK
Product Range:	★★★★★	Express Delivery Option?	(UK) N/A
Price Range:	Luxury/Medium/Very Good Value	Gift Wrapping Option?	N/A
Delivery Area:	Worldwide	Returns Procedure:	N/A

www.katepennington.co.uk

Kate Pennington Designs specialise in hand decorating Bridal and Bridesmaid shoes. Using their extensive range of trimmings they'll decorate your shoes to complement the theme and design of your dress. You can see lots of the styles on her website and then you need to contact her about a month before your wedding to confirm the style and sizes you want to order, and if you can you should send her a photo of your dress plus a fabric swatch which can be incorporated into the shoes.

Site Usability:	★★★★	Based:	UK
Product Range:	★★★	Express Delivery Option?	(UK) N/A
Price Range:	Luxury/Medium/Very Good Value	Gift Wrapping Option?	N/A
Delivery Area:	UK	Returns Procedure:	N/A

www.littlebevan.co.uk

Little Bevan offers clothes for girls, boys and tinies as flowergirls, bridesmaids and pageboys. The prices will differ according to the fabric you choose and how much detail there is involved in the design. There are also lots of accessory options here such as sashes, petticoats, wraps and shoes to match the dresses. For boys there are waistcoats (in silk, velvet or cord), trousers and breeches, shirts and jackets.

Site Usability:	★★★★	Based:	UK
Product Range:	★★★★	Express Delivery Option?	(UK) N/A
Price Range:	Luxury/Medium/Very Good Value	Gift Wrapping Option?	N/A
Delivery Area:	UK	Returns Procedure:	N/A

www.my-wedding-wishes.co.uk

Here you'll find a very good choice of wedding shoes for brides, bridesmaids and pages from designers such as Diane Hassell, Gabriella & Lucido, Else and Paradox, some of which are very well priced and some quite expensive so it's well worth spending some time looking round. They also offer wedding petticoats. If you send them a swatch of the fabric of your dress they'll dye your shoes to match. Patent leather men's shoes are available here as well.

Site Usability:	★★★★★	Based:	UK
Product Range:	★★★★★	Express Delivery Option?	(UK) N/A
Price Range:	Luxury/Medium/Very Good Value	Gift Wrapping Option?	N/A
Delivery Area:	UK	Returns Procedure:	Down to you

www.themagpieandthewardrobe.co.uk

The Magpie and the Wardrobe is a small London based firm specialising in making beautiful things from antique and vintage treasures sourced in England and France. If you're looking for special treats for your flowergirls this could be the perfect place as you'll find really pretty and colourful vintage style bracelets, necklaces and earrings decorated with tiny charms, lovebirds and flowers.

Site Usability:	★★★	Based:	UK
Product Range:	★★★	Express Delivery Option?	(UK) No
Price Range:	Luxury/Medium/Very Good Value	Gift Wrapping Option?	N/A
Delivery Area:	Worldwide	Returns Procedure:	Down to you

www.theirnibs.com

There are enchanting dresses for little girls here aged 2–8 including white or dusty pink net and voile 'tutu' dresses and 50's style sash tied dresses covered with gorgeous roses. For a fairytale tiny there's their pink netting dress with hand stitched, hand sewn flowers. All would be perfect for a summer wedding. There are lots of other, more casual clothes here for boys and girls as well.

Site Usability:	★★★★	Based:	UK
Product Range:	★★★	Express Delivery Option?	(UK) No
Price Range:	Luxury/Medium/Very Good Value	Gift Wrapping Option?	N/A
Delivery Area:	Worldwide	Returns Procedure:	Down to you

Also check out these websites for bridesmaids and flowergirls

Website Address	You'll find it in:
www.blossom.co.uk	Accessories and Hats
www.eveningdresses.co.uk	All About The Dress
www.lovesmelovesmeknot.co.uk	Flowers and Confetti
www.tinytreats.co.uk	Shoes

Chapter 67

Flowers and Confetti

Second to your dress, flowers are the least likely thing you're going to buy online, so I'm not going to pretend and introduce you to lots of online florists.

There are a few here for you to look at (and a couple you can order from if you want to) but if you don't know a really good local florist you can go (again) to *www.confetti.com* and look a few up in their supplier directory. Many of them have pictures showing you their style and some have websites you can visit which will give you even more information.

Regarding confetti and the throwing thereof. Wherever you're getting married you need to know if it's allowed as some churches and other venues simply don't permit confetti of any sort to be thrown and others allow certain types only. If it's not allowed or if there's a specific rule make sure that your guests are aware of it (maybe by a note or line included with the invitation). That way they won't splash out on something they can't use.

Sites to Visit

www.confettidirect.co.uk

Charles Hudson's Wyke Manor estate is the British centre for real flower confetti and every year he plants an original design in a 10-acre field. He is in the Guinness Book of Records and his 2004 Delphinium Union Jack was pictured from the air by the national press and TV. For his real petal collection, flower heads, rose petals, sunflowers and lavender are included as are a variety of different packaging ideas.

Site Usability:	★★★★★	Based:	UK
Product Range:	★★★★	Express Delivery Option?	(UK) No
Price Range:	Luxury/<u>Medium</u>/Very Good Value	Gift Wrapping Option?	No
Delivery Area:	Worldwide	Returns Procedure:	Down to you

www.foreverandeverpetals.com

Forever and ever specialises in supplying beautiful biodegradable, freeze dried, rose petals and rosebuds, with each rose being hand selected and carefully preserved to the highest quality to retain its shape and form. There's a really lovely selection here, all beautifully photographed and you can order online, making sure that you allow two to three months for delivery. They also offer favour boxes and organza, rose trimmed bags and rose petal potpourri.

Site Usability:	★★★★★	Based:	UK
Product Range:	★★★★	Express Delivery Option?	(UK) No
Price Range:	Luxury/<u>Medium</u>/Very Good Value	Gift Wrapping Option?	No
Delivery Area:	UK	Returns Procedure:	Down to you

www.jgmd.co.uk

Juliette At Home's pretty website has a wedding range of fabric and paper flowers in a variety of colours, unusual table decorations such as beads and glass faceted flowers, scripted glass candles and bespoke candles personalised for you. They also offer little luxuries and gifts such as colourful Julian MacDonald candles, beaded glass lanterns, leaf lights from Thailand and vintage, embroidered lavender and soap bags, so if you want to steer away from the norm to something a little different you may find it here.

Site Usability:	★★★★	Based:	UK
Product Range:	★★★	Express Delivery Option?	(UK) No
Price Range:	Luxury/<u>Medium</u>/Very Good Value	Gift Wrapping Option?	No
Delivery Area:	Worldwide	Returns Procedure:	Down to you

www.kennethturner.com

Kenneth Turner is famous for his exceptional floral designs throughout the World. If you'd like to have them design your wedding flowers you'll first need to call them to arrange a consultation before you can place your order. Needless to say if you order flowers here you'll be paying for 'designer quality' bouquets and arrangements but you'll also be certain of having something really special on your wedding day.

Site Usability:	★★★	Based:	UK
Product Range:	★★★★★	Express Delivery Option?	(UK) No
Price Range:	Luxury/Medium/Very Good Value	Gift Wrapping Option?	N/A
Delivery Area:	Worldwide	Returns Procedure:	N/A

www.lovesmelovesmeknot.co.uk

This is a pretty website offering bridesmaid's accessories including jewellery, hair decorations and handbags, freeze dried confetti and dried rose buds, ideas for gifts and favours and decorations for the table and elsewhere such as daisy hearts, orchid blossoms, butterfly garlands and napkin ties. There's a wide selection to choose from and everything is beautifully photographed in clear detail.

Site Usability:	★★★★★	Based:	UK
Product Range:	★★★★★	Express Delivery Option?	(UK)
Price Range:	Luxury/Medium/Very Good Value	Gift Wrapping Option?	N/A
Delivery Area:	Worldwide	Returns Procedure:	N/A

www.miraflores.org.uk

Miraflores deliver brides wedding bouquets, bridesmaids' bouquets, buttonholes and matching table arrangements to all addresses in England and Wales and they've designed two simple and beautiful selections to deliver to you featuring pink or white roses. If you want any other types of flowers you need to contact them by phone or email. Place your order at least two weeks before your wedding and the flowers will be delivered the day before.

Site Usability:	★★★★	Based:	UK
Product Range:	★★★	Express Delivery Option?	(UK) No
Price Range:	Luxury/Medium/Very Good Value	Gift Wrapping Option?	N/A
Delivery Area:	UK	Returns Procedure:	N/A

www.rainbowweddingflowers.co.uk

It may be that you live somewhere that makes it difficult to have real flowers on your wedding day; you're getting married abroad, or you would just rather have something that will last. If so then you should take a look at the wedding flower portfolio here, where all the designs are created from silk flowers but at the same time are almost unbelievably real looking. There are also designs for bridesmaids, buttonholes, corsages and receptions.

Site Usability:	★★★★	Based:	UK
Product Range:	★★★★	Express Delivery Option?	(UK) No
Price Range:	Luxury/Medium/Very Good Value	Gift Wrapping Option?	No
Delivery Area:	Worldwide	Returns Procedure:	N/A

www.realflowers.co.uk

The Real Flower Company will deliver beautiful wedding bouquets, church and reception flowers wherever you need them in the UK, so if you live somewhere that makes it difficult for you to order the flowers of your choice then call them on 0870 403 6548 and ask to speak to their wedding expert, Karen Watson. You need to do this once you have chosen your dress and know what colour scheme you are looking for.

Site Usability:	★★★★	Based:	UK
Product Range:	★★★★	Express Delivery Option?	(UK) No
Price Range:	Luxury/Medium/Very Good Value	Gift Wrapping Option?	N/A
Delivery Area:	UK	Returns Procedure:	N/A

www.trulymadlydeeply.biz

You'll find freeze dried rose petal confetti here in gorgeous colours plus peony, delphinium and hydrangea petals and aromatic lavender grains. Choose from tiny sequinned straw or organza petal bags, envelopes or cones, plus freeze dried rose buds and silk orchid blossoms to scatter on the table along with rose scatter lights and pretty candle surrounds. You can even order a Swarovski crystal encrusted 'Just Married' t-shirt here in white, black or fuchsia.

Site Usability:	★★★★★	Based:	UK
Product Range:	★★★★	Express Delivery Option?	(UK) No
Price Range:	Luxury/Medium/Very Good Value	Gift Wrapping Option?	N/A
Delivery Area:	Worldwide	Returns Procedure:	Down to you

Chapter 68

Gifts and Wedding Lists

Every one of your guests will want to give you something special and that they hope they'll be remembered for and I'm speaking from experience here, both as a bride and a wedding gift giver.

This can make things really difficult if you're having a very big wedding as several hundred individual items, some of which you almost certainly won't like, will be really irritating. First you have to thank for them, then you have to work out what to do with them if they simply don't work for you. Hopefully you can exchange some of them for what you do want.

I've included here websites where you can set up your wedding list online to make your life really easy, with clear lists and very good photographs of each and every item and also others where you can find individual gifts for wedding goers to look, where there are some really lovely and unusual ideas for presents.

Sites to Visit

www.albumania.com

Here's a website where you can find a totally unique kind of present. At Albumania you design your own photo album, box file, guest book, wine book, address book or diary. You just download a photograph (digitally), choose the colour of binding and ribbon, all online and then you can see exactly what the cover of your book will look like. While you're ordering you have the option of adding extra pages and adding a ribbon tied card with your personal message. All the books are gift boxed and take about two weeks.

Site Usability:	★★★★★	Based:	UK
Product Range:	★★★	Express Delivery Option?	(UK) No
Price Range:	Luxury/<u>Medium</u>/Very Good Value	Gift Wrapping Option?	No
Delivery Area:	Worldwide	Returns Procedure:	Down to you

www.culinaryconcepts.co.uk

Going round the shops looking for a different wedding gift (when you don't want to buy into the Wedding List) is sometimes very difficult, because classic gifts may well clash with what's already been chosen. Here you'll find some new and clever design ideas including unusual cheese knives and servers, hammered stainless steel bowls and plates and table accessories such as hammered sugar and olive bowls, wine buckets and vases.

Site Usability:	★★★★	Based:	UK
Product Range:	★★★★	Express Delivery Option?	(UK) No
Price Range:	Luxury/<u>Medium</u>/Very Good Value	Gift Wrapping Option?	No
Delivery Area:	Worldwide	Returns Procedure:	Down to you

www.harrods.com

Harrods are adding more and more products into their online store and most of them they'll ship worldwide. They include silver and glass, decorative accessories, food and drink and gorgeous bedlinen and although of course the range is nothing like as wide as their Knightsbridge store there are some excellent gift ideas here at a range of prices. Delivery takes up to two weeks and you need to allow longer for overseas orders.

Site Usability:	★★★★	Based:	UK
Product Range:	★★★★★	Express Delivery Option?	(UK) No
Price Range:	Luxury/<u>Medium</u>/Very Good Value	Gift Wrapping Option?	No but standard packaging is excellent
Delivery Area:	Worldwide	Returns Procedure:	Down to you

www.heals.co.uk

Heals is famous for its Tottenham Court Road store in London and the modern/retro styling for all the products you'll find there. Just register with them and you can set up your gift list online or if you want, in store with the help of one of their personal shopping consultants. Before you register take a look around the store website to make sure their style is for you. Once you've set up your list you can publish it yourself online or ask them to do it for you.

Site Usability:	★★★★★	Based:	UK	
Product Range:	★★★★★	Express Delivery Option?	(UK) No	
Price Range:	Luxury/<u>Medium</u>/Very Good Value	Gift Wrapping Option?	No	
Delivery Area:	UK	Returns Procedure:	Down to you	

www.jbsilverware.co.uk

There's a very wide range of silver gifts here, from inexpensive silver plate to lovely sterling silver hallmarked pieces. Prices go from around £20 to £500 so you have a lot to choose from, including traditional sterling Armarda (their spelling) dishes and tumbler cups to contemporary glass and silver ice buckets, candlesticks and bowls. They offer an engraving service, express delivery (you need to call them for this) and they'll ship worldwide.

Site Usability:	★★★★	Based:	UK	
Product Range:	★★★★★	Express Delivery Option?	(UK) Yes	
Price Range:	Luxury/<u>Medium</u>/Very Good Value	Gift Wrapping Option?	No	
Delivery Area:	Worldwide	Returns Procedure:	Down to you	

www.johnlewisgiftlist.com

I'm sure that you won't be surprised to learn that John Lewis has one of the most popular wedding list services in the country. With its huge range of products at different price levels and the excellent service it offers this would be a very good place to set up your list (or part of your list, obviously you don't have to have it all in one place). You can register either online or at your local store but you need to actually select the items for your list in store, after which it can all be handled online.

Site Usability:	★★★★★	Based:	UK	
Product Range:	★★★★★	Express Delivery Option?	(UK) No	
Price Range:	Luxury/<u>Medium</u>/Very Good Value	Gift Wrapping Option?	No	
Delivery Area:	UK	Returns Procedure:	In store or they'll collect	

www.laywheeler.com

Lay and Wheeler offer a traditional and personal wedding list service whether you'd prefer to be given wine to drink immediately or looking to start a cellar plan. Their wines can be viewed online and once you've made your selection, the list can be set up and despatched either by post or via e-mail. Use their sales team before you set up your list for advice on all aspects of selecting wines and contact them by email at weddings@laywheeler.com, or by calling 01473 313260.

Site Usability:	★★★★	Based:	UK
Product Range:	★★★	Express Delivery Option?	(UK) Yes
Price Range:	Luxury/Medium/Very Good Value	Gift Wrapping Option?	
Delivery Area:	UK	Returns Procedure:	

www.onslowandridley.co.uk

Unlike a lot of wedding list suppliers, Onslow and Ridley offer free delivery of your gifts throughout the UK. To start with they'll send you a copy of their 'memory jogger'. This is a list of everything you may want to consider putting in your wedding list. They'll then give you as much or as little help as you want in compiling your wedding list. They are based in Scotland, which may or not be perfect for you to visit. If not you can call them and ask that they send their brochures out to you so you can see if you'd like to keep your list with them.

Site Usability:	★★★★	Based:	UK
Product Range:	★★★★★	Express Delivery Option?	(UK) No
Price Range:	Luxury/Medium/Very Good Value	Gift Wrapping Option?	
Delivery Area:	UK	Returns Procedure:	

www.silvercompany.co.uk

You'll find some very traditional sterling silver gift ideas here plus some more unusual items, such as their Olympia silver and crystal candlesticks, glass and silver match strikers and churn wood and silver salt and pepper mills. Almost anything here would make a perfect wedding present although with some of the different ideas you're less likely to clash with a formal wedding list. Many of the pieces can be engraved as well.

Site Usability:	★★★★	Based:	UK
Product Range:	★★★★	Express Delivery Option?	(UK) Yes
Price Range:	Luxury/Medium/Very Good Value	Gift Wrapping Option?	Yes
Delivery Area:	Worldwide	Returns Procedure:	Down to you

www.theolivegrove.co.uk

The Olive Grove online was established in May 2000, and is home to an expanding range of beautiful interior and garden accessories from a number of independent designers alongside leading brands such as Mulberry Home. If you're looking for a slightly unusual wedding gift you would do well to have a look round here, where you can choose from iron candlesticks, glass ice buckets, slate cheeseboards and Mulberry's gorgeous cushions and willow baskets.

Site Usability:	★★★★	Based:	UK
Product Range:	★★★★★	Express Delivery Option?	(UK) Yes
Price Range:	Luxury/Medium/Very Good Value	Gift Wrapping Option?	Yes
Delivery Area:	Europe	Returns Procedure:	Down to you

www.wedding.co.uk

At Wedding List Services you have the option of visiting one of their two South London showrooms, where you can use their advisors to help you compile your list from a huge range of brands such as Bridgewater, Alessi, Christophle, Jasper Conran, Lalique and William Yeoward. You can, alternatively compile your list online from their fully illustrated selection if you're unable to visit them and they'll help you make sure you don't end up with too much of one thing and not enough of another.

Site Usability:	★★★★★	Based:	UK
Product Range:	★★★★★	Express Delivery Option?	(UK) No
Price Range:	Luxury/Medium/Very Good Value	Gift Wrapping Option?	No
Delivery Area:	UK	Returns Procedure:	Down to you

www.weddingshop.com

The Wedding Shop have selected over 250 suppliers from which you can compile your Wedding List, including Rosenthal, Villeroy and Boch, Arthur Price, Gaggia, Dualit, Mulberry Home, Bodum, Sabatier, Baccarat and Edinburgh Crystal. You need to make an appointment with them at one of their London showrooms and then after that everything can be handled online, with your guests being able to purchase online and you being able to view the gifts selected at any time.

Site Usability:	★★★★	Based:	UK
Product Range:	★★★★★	Express Delivery Option?	(UK) No
Price Range:	Luxury/Medium/Very Good Value	Gift Wrapping Option?	No
Delivery Area:	UK	Returns Procedure:	Down to you

www.weddingpresentsdirect.co.uk

Wedding Presents Direct offer a very personal wedding list service. To start with you need to visit one of their showrooms, either in Battersea, London, or West Harling, Norfolk and for both you need to make an appointment. Once you've selected your list, with as much help and advice as you want, they endeavour to provide you with a copy of it within just a couple of days. After you've made sure you're happy with the list your guests can purchase from it online or by phone or email.

Site Usability:	★★★	Based:	UK
Product Range:	★★★★	Express Delivery Option?	(UK) No
Price Range:	Luxury/Medium/Very Good Value	Gift Wrapping Option?	No
Delivery Area:	Worldwide	Returns Procedure:	Down to you

www.wrapit.co.uk

This is a wedding list service that claims to offer the choice and affordability of a department store, the personal service of a specialist wedding shop and the convenience of the web. They offer over 350 brands – ranging from favourite tabletop and kitchenware brands to designer home furnishing and unusual gift ideas. You'll be allocated a personal consultant who you can meet at one of their showrooms or contact by phone or email and you can set up and manage your list totally online through their clear, well photographed website.

Site Usability:	★★★★★	Based:	UK
Product Range:	★★★★★	Express Delivery Option?	(UK) No
Price Range:	Luxury/Medium/Very Good Value	Gift Wrapping Option?	No
Delivery Area:	UK	Returns Procedure:	Down to you

Chapter 69

Invitations and Stationery

This is an area you really can cover online as the choice is enormous and you're unlikely to find such a range anywhere else without spending a great deal of time and trouble.

Whatever your style you'll almost certainly find something you like, whether you're looking for modern invitations and orders of service, the highest quality card with traditional script or hand tied scrolls in high quality boxes. You need to spend a bit of time visiting the different websites and checking out the designs and prices until you bring it down to the two or three who match your budget and style, and all the printers and designers need a specific amount of time, particularly if you're going for something like a hand made scroll.

The other huge advantage of choosing your invitations online is of course that if you're extremely busy you're not limited to the working hours of stores, printers and designers. This is one of the things you can do as a couple, in the evening or at a weekend with a glass of wine in your hand and no interference or unwanted suggestions from anyone else. Marvellous.

Sites to Visit

www.brideandgroomdirect.co.uk

Here you can choose from a wide range of gift ideas, guest books, bookmarks, cake boxes, envelope seals, favours, keepsake books and photo albums. You can also use their invitation service where you select the style and quantity you need, then just follow the on-screen instructions for your personal details, wording styles, typeface and ink colours. There are some really pretty designs here from beautifully ribbon tied invites to simple and elegant.

Site Usability:	★★★★★	Based:	UK
Product Range:	★★★★★	Express Delivery Option?	(UK) No
Price Range:	Luxury/Medium/Very Good Value	Gift Wrapping Option?	N/A
Delivery Area:	Worldwide delivery on request	Returns Procedure:	N/A

www.dreaminvites.co.uk

Choose your style first here from Elegant, Romantic or Modern. Once you've picked a design you like you can see how it translates from the Invitation to the Order of Service, Menu, Reply card and Thank You card. You can either choose your own wording right the way through or click through to their General Information section to find ideas for traditional and modern wording and fonts. You can't pay online but need to send them your payment once you've completed your online order.

Site Usability:	★★★★★	Based:	UK
Product Range:	★★★★	Express Delivery Option?	(UK) Yes
Price Range:	Luxury/Medium/Very Good Value	Gift Wrapping Option?	N/A
Delivery Area:	Worldwide on request	Returns Procedure:	N/A

www.giftcorporation.com

This is a collection of beautiful personalised candles for all occasions. For weddings, once you've chosen your design (and there's a wide choice), you give them your names and the date of your wedding as well as, for some candles, a photograph and/or a poem that you'd like included. You need to allow at least three weeks for your candles to arrive and they deliver all over the World.

Site Usability:	★★★★★	Based:	UK
Product Range:	★★★★★	Express Delivery Option?	(UK) No
Price Range:	Luxury/Medium/Very Good Value	Gift Wrapping Option?	No
Delivery Area:	Worldwide	Returns Procedure:	Down to you

www.libertyandfred.com

All the stationery here is assembled and finished by hand, using Italian papers, parchment inserts, tissue-lined envelopes and organza ribbons, so if you like something you see here you'll have to allow a little more time for it to be delivered. You'll find simple, classic and timeless designs for everything from invitations and Save the Date cards to Orders of Service and place cards. You may find this quite a confusing website to go round (I did) but persevere as the designs are lovely.

Site Usability:	★★★	Based:	UK
Product Range:	★★★	Express Delivery Option?	(UK) No
Price Range:	Luxury/Medium/Very Good Value	Gift Wrapping Option?	N/A
Delivery Area:	Worldwide delivery on request	Returns Procedure:	N/A

www.thanksthanks.co.uk

Thank you letters are such an important part of occasions such as weddings, although the whole idea of writing to loads of people may be rather daunting. This company has a novel way of helping you out, as they produce bespoke thank you cards and envelopes, where you can include your own picture. For best results email your picture to them or send it on a cd.

Site Usability:	★★★★	Based:	UK
Product Range:	★★★	Express Delivery Option?	(UK) No
Price Range:	Luxury/Medium/Very Good Value	Gift Wrapping Option?	N/A
Delivery Area:	UK	Returns Procedure:	N/A

www.thealternativeinvite.co.uk

The Alternative Invite Company specialises in unique and individual wedding stationery and invitations which are created using a variety of textured cards and materials. They offer each design as part of a coordinated range. Once you've selected your design you choose your typeface and either use one of their suggested wordings or give them your own. You can order RSVP cards and pre-printed thank you cards here as well (I'm not sure about these).

Site Usability:	★★★★	Based:	UK
Product Range:	★★★	Express Delivery Option?	(UK) No
Price Range:	Luxury/Medium/Very Good Value	Gift Wrapping Option?	N/A
Delivery Area:	UK	Returns Procedure:	N/A

www.letterpress.co.uk/

The Letter Press specialises in traditional high quality wedding stationery, offering a full service, covering engagement announcements, wedding and evening invitations, reply cards, orders of service, menus, place cards and thank you cards. Their designs are based on simple classical styles, which the customer can either adopt as they are or use as a starting point for their own designs. They're able to add or adapt any of the features shown on their website, using decorative motifs, borders or ribbons to different ink or typefaces.

Site Usability:	★★★★★	Based:	UK
Product Range:	★★★★★	Express Delivery Option?	(UK) No
Price Range:	Luxury/Medium/Very Good Value	Gift Wrapping Option?	N/A
Delivery Area:	UK	Returns Procedure:	N/A

www.thesilvernutmeg.com

For beautiful and elegant wedding stationery this is a very good place to visit as there's a wide range of attractively crafted invitations, note cards, response sets and thank you cards. You're clearly able to select different styles, ink colours and fonts and browse through their wide collection of traditional and unusual designs. You need to call or email them to discuss ordering your stationery. There are other wedding accessories available here as well.

Site Usability:	★★★★	Based:	UK
Product Range:	★★★★	Express Delivery Option?	(UK) No
Price Range:	Luxury/Medium/Very Good Value	Gift Wrapping Option?	N/A
Delivery Area:	Europe	Returns Procedure:	N/A

www.theweddingfile.com

The Wedding File is a beautifully designed, covetable yet practical, loose-leaf A5 planner for anyone who is organising a wedding. It contains over 200 pages divided into seventeen clear sections that cover every conceivable detail including budgets, flowers, checklists and table plans to help you make sure the wedding day runs as smoothly as possible. You may want to buy one for yourself or if you know someone who's getting married in the near future this would make a really lovely gift.

Site Usability:	★★★	Based:	UK
Product Range:	★★★	Express Delivery Option?	(UK) No
Price Range:	Luxury/Medium/Very Good Value	Gift Wrapping Option?	No
Delivery Area:	Worldwide	Returns Procedure:	Down to you

www.theweddinginvitation.co.uk

The Wedding Invitation website offers exclusive designs by Heather Marten who has been involved in product and packaging design, advertising, public relations and interior design. She's used her experience to create this really attractive mid to luxury priced range which is constantly being updated. Take a look through the different designs where you'll find a wealth of detail and send off for their brochure where you'll find more ideas plus different fonts and styles. You can't order directly online, just download their form on the website and post it to them.

Site Usability:	★★★	Based:	UK
Product Range:	★★★★	Express Delivery Option?	(UK) No
Price Range:	Luxury/Medium/Very Good Value	Gift Wrapping Option?	N/A
Delivery Area:	UK	Returns Procedure:	N/A

www.weddingcardprinters.co.uk

If you're fed up with looking at loads of (sometimes very expensive) stationery options for your wedding just take the time to click round here, where you can select the style you like from this very simple website, choose your wording from the options they give you and edit as much as you want until you're completely happy. Select several designs to compare and then place your order online. Expect to wait about seven days. There's no brochure or samples available but everything is very clearly photographed.

Site Usability:	★★★★★	Based:	UK	
Product Range:	★★★	Express Delivery Option?	(UK) No	
Price Range:	Luxury/<u>Medium</u>/Very Good Value	Gift Wrapping Option?	N/A	
Delivery Area:	UK	Returns Procedure:	N/A	

www.weddinginvitesonline.com

This is a range of contemporary wedding stationery and once you've selected the style you're interested in you're taken immediately to the very clear page showing you your different options, from invitations, to Orders of Service and thank you cards all with the same theme. You can see a selection of wedding hymns here and ask for sample cards to be sent to you. Deliveries will take from between five to seven days (UK).

Site Usability:	★★★★★	Based:	UK	
Product Range:	★★★★★	Express Delivery Option?	(UK) No but they're quite quick	
Price Range:	Luxury/<u>Medium</u>/Very Good Value	Gift Wrapping Option?	N/A	
Delivery Area:	Worldwide.	Returns Procedure:	N/A	

www.whole-caboodle.co.uk/

The Whole Caboodle Design Company offers you high quality handmade stationery for invitations, reply cards, menus, place cards, favours and thank you cards, boxed handmade scrolls in exquisite designs and lovely contemporary designs. This is very much the top end of the range for invitations etc so expect to pay more here, but if you want something absolutely unique and special you must take a look. There's lots of help as well on wording and fonts and you need to allow four weeks for your order to arrive.

Site Usability:	★★★★★	Based:	UK	
Product Range:	★★★★★	Express Delivery Option?	(UK) No	
Price Range:	<u>Luxury</u>/Medium/Very Good Value	Gift Wrapping Option?	N/A	
Delivery Area:	UK	Returns Procedure:	N/A	

Chapter 70

Jewellery

What type of jewellery are you looking for? Something for yourself? Something for gifts for your bridesmaids? Something really beautiful and expensive or something simple to wear with your dress to highlight your best features?

In terms of wedding jewellery you may well already have what you want to wear. You may have inherited something or been lent some special family jewellery or you may have a favourite pearl necklace and earrings.

On the websites here you'll find a wide range of primarily inexpensive jewellery – jewellery to accessorize your dress and jewellery for your bridesmaids. There are also some really beautiful tiaras, some of which are not so inexpensive but absolutely gorgeous and hard to resist.

Sites to Visit

www.andrewprince.co.uk

Andrew Prince has designed jewellery for well known celebrities and was also commissioned in 2002 by the Victoria and Albert museum to design a unique collection of costume jewellery to accompany their 'Tiaras Past and Present Exhibition'. He uses only the finest Swarovski crystal and Signity zirconia in the beautiful collection you'll find here, of tiaras and chokers, necklaces, earrings and brooches. You need to call or email to order and allow 4–6 weeks.

Site Usability:	★★★★★	Based:	UK	
Product Range:	★★★★	Express Delivery Option?	(UK) No	
Price Range:	Luxury/Medium/Very Good Value	Gift Wrapping Option?	No	
Delivery Area:	Worldwide	Returns Procedure:	Down to you	

www.kellyspence.co.uk

Art and design graduate Kelly Spence has been designing wedding jewellery since 1999. Each piece is made by hand and combines Swarovski crystals, faux/freshwater pearls and semi-precious stones and you'll be encouraged to be part of the designing process by contributing ideas for customisation if you choose to buy from her. Tiaras, delicate crowns and coronets, unusual hair pins and feathered combs are just some of the items you'll find here, plus a small collection of jewellery and wedding veils.

Site Usability:	★★★★	Based:	UK	
Product Range:	★★★	Express Delivery Option?	(UK) No	
Price Range:	Luxury/Medium/Very Good Value	Gift Wrapping Option?	No	
Delivery Area:	Worldwide	Returns Procedure:	Down to you	

www.miamasrijewellery.co.uk

This is an exquisite collection of individually handcrafted jewellery and tiaras created and designed by Mia. You can order a 'ready to wear' piece from her current portfolio, choose one of the existing stunning pieces and have it customised to your personal style, or become involved in the creation of a totally unique piece designed just for you. Her clients are not only brides-to-be looking for something unique and different, but include celebrities such as Natalie Imbruglia. As each piece is made to order you need to allow between four and six weeks for delivery.

Site Usability:	★★★★	Based:	UK	
Product Range:	★★★	Express Delivery Option?	(UK) No	
Price Range:	Luxury/Medium/Very Good Value	Gift Wrapping Option?	No	
Delivery Area:	Worldwide	Returns Procedure:	Down to you	

www.swarovski.com

Take a look at Swarovski's couture range of jewellery for sparkling, signature (and extremely expensive) pieces, such as their Art Nouveau inspired Abberation Earrings with their matching limited edition shoulder bag woven with crystal beads and pearls, or the Angelique bracelet set with multi coloured crystals. For something a little more reasonable click through to Jewellery and Accessories where they offer necklaces, earrings and bracelets plus really pretty evening/wedding bags. They also have a small but beautiful choice of tiaras. They'll gift wrap for you and deliver Worldwide.

Site Usability:	★★★★★	Based:	UK
Product Range:	★★★★★	Express Delivery Option?	(UK) No
Price Range:	Luxury/Medium/Very Good Value	Gift Wrapping Option?	Yes
Delivery Area:	Worldwide	Returns Procedure:	Down to you

www.theaccessoryboutique.com

This is a really stylishly designed website offering you, as they put it, 'everything bar the dress'. So you can choose from their range of shoes by Paradox, Filippa Scott, G&L and Benjamin Adams (don't worry if you don't know these names, there are some really pretty styles here at all price ranges) jewellery and hair clips, and silk and beaded handbags (plus Hollywood Fashion Tape and comfort shoe pads). If you want your shoes dyed a specific shade they'll do that for you and they offer small and large sizes as well.

Site Usability:	★★★★★	Based:	UK
Product Range:	★★★★★	Express Delivery Option?	(UK) Yes
Price Range:	Luxury/Medium/Very Good Value	Gift Wrapping Option?	Yes
Delivery Area:	Worldwide	Returns Procedure:	Down to you

www.tombodama.com

Freshwater pearls, amethysts, crystal beads and Venetian glass are just some of the ingredients in this collection of wedding and occasion jewellery, including tiaras, bridal and evening earrings and bracelets. Each piece is hand made to order and delivery takes up to three weeks for most items, or six weeks for tiaras, so be sure you allow plenty of time although they promise to try and help if you need something urgently.

Site Usability:	★★★	Based:	UK
Product Range:	★★★★	Express Delivery Option?	(UK) No
Price Range:	Luxury/Medium/Very Good Value	Gift Wrapping Option?	No
Delivery Area:	Worldwide	Returns Procedure:	Down to you

Also check out the following websites for wedding jewellery

Website Address	You'll find it in
www.butlerandwilson.com	Jewellery
www.green-frederick.co.uk	Jewellery
www.brownsfashion.com	Luxury Brands Online
www.blossom.co.uk	Accessories and Hats
www.louellabridal.co.uk	About the Dress
www.tinytreats.co.uk	Shoes (Wedding)

Chapter 71

Shoes

Wonderful, glamorous shoes. Glitzy strappy beaded shoes with killer heels. Flat silk hand embroidered ballet pumps. Palest pink satin shoes with bows on the back or sexy diamante embellished ivory satin sling backs. The choice is yours and it's a really, really wide choice.

There are several ranges that you'll come across more than once and these are the most popular UK designers. Prices range from the hundreds to extremely good value so take your time to look through.

There are also a couple of websites here based in the US. Don't be scared of buying your shoes here as shoe sizes are pretty standard and provided you use their conversion chart (or if in doubt go to *www.onlineconversion.com* clothing and shoes) you should be fine. Some of the US ranges are really lovely, particularly Stuart Weitzman and Vera Wang so it's well worth having a look.

A few of the websites here will dye your shoes to match your dress and incorporate specific beading and embroidery which is an excellent service to take advantage of.

Sites to Visit

www.bellissimabridalshoes.com

This US based website offers a wide choice of really lovely designer wedding shoes (and matching handbags) by names such as Stuart Weitzman, Vera Wang, Cynthia Rowley and Kenneth Cole. You will have to pay extra for shipping and duty so don't expect to make any great savings, but this is an opportunity to choose special and different shoes for your wedding which you can't find anywhere else. Don't forget that you'll be buying in US shoe sizes so go to the size charts at the back of this book to check your size.

Site Usability:	★★★★★	Based:	US
Product Range:	★★★★★	Express Delivery Option?	(UK) No
Price Range:	Luxury/Medium/Very Good Value	Gift Wrapping Option?	No
Delivery Area:	Worldwide	Returns Procedure:	Down to you

www.filigree.co.uk

All the shoes on this website are extremely well shown so that you can see different views. This is a very good selection of 100 plus designs with prices ranging from £65 up to £200. Many of the shoes can be decorated, beaded, appliquéd with silver, gold and bronze threads, pearls, crystals and semi-precious stones to create totally individual designs in harmony with your overall theme. They will also cover shoes you've bought elsewhere in your exact bridal fabric. You can download their order form or call to place your order.

Site Usability:	★★★★	Based:	UK
Product Range:	★★★★★	Express Delivery Option?	(UK) No
Price Range:	Luxury/Medium/Very Good Value	Gift Wrapping Option?	No
Delivery Area:	UK	Returns Procedure:	Down to you

www.flukefootwear.com

This website is just about shoes and there's quite a range to click through, from the simplest satin sling back to lovely beading and embroidery. This is an unsophisticated website and you have to use their order form to place your order but they have some unusual and very attractive designs on offer. They'll also make shoes to order for you so you should call them if this is a service you'd like to take advantage of.

Site Usability:	★★★	Based:	UK
Product Range:	★★★★★	Express Delivery Option?	(UK) No
Price Range:	Luxury/Medium/Very Good Value	Gift Wrapping Option?	No
Delivery Area:	UK	Returns Procedure:	Down to you

www.katepennington.co.uk

Kate Pennington Designs specialise in hand decorating Bridal and Bridesmaid shoes. Using their extensive range of trimmings they'll decorate your shoes to complement the theme and design of your dress. You can see lots of the styles on her website and then you need to contact her about a month before your wedding to confirm the style and sizes you want to order, and if you can you should send her a photo of your dress plus a fabric swatch which can be incorporated into the shoes.

Site Usability:	★★★★	Based:	UK
Product Range:	★★★	Express Delivery Option?	(UK) No
Price Range:	Luxury/Medium/Very Good Value	Gift Wrapping Option?	No
Delivery Area:	UK	Returns Procedure:	Down to you

www.my-wedding-wishes.co.uk

Here you'll find a very good choice of wedding shoes from designers such as Diane Hassell, Gabriella & Lucido, Else and Paradox, some which are very well priced and some quite expensive so it's well worth spending some time here. They also offer wedding petticoats and affordable adult bridesmaids' shoes plus black patent leather men's shoes. If you send them a swatch of fabric they'll dye your shoes to match and they deliver only to the UK.

Site Usability:	★★★★★	Based:	UK
Product Range:	★★★★★	Express Delivery Option?	(UK) No
Price Range:	Luxury/Medium/Very Good Value	Gift Wrapping Option?	No
Delivery Area:	UK	Returns Procedure:	Down to you

www.shannonbrittshoes.com

There are some really chic bridal shoes on this US based website (who promise speedy delivery to the UK) and many of them are limited editions so you know you'll be the only one wearing them here. My favourites are their stitched embroidered and absolutely gorgeous ballet flats which would be perfect if you're tall and want to be comfortable all day. In their Store Info section you'll find an excellent conversion chart from US to European sizes.

Site Usability:	★★★★	Based:	US
Product Range:	★★★	Express Delivery Option?	(UK) No
Price Range:	Luxury/Medium/Very Good Value	Gift Wrapping Option?	No
Delivery Area:	Worldwide	Returns Procedure:	Down to you

www.tinytreats.co.uk

You'll find here several wedding shoe designers you can order online, including Paradox and Filippa Scott plus the complete range from Diane Hassall, from her collection of hand beaded shoes to the well priced diffusion and leather collections. You can buy pretty bridesmaids shoes here from a child's size five as well as sparkling tiaras and jewellery set with Swarovski crystals, handbags, gloves and ribbons.

Site Usability:	★★★★★	Based:	UK
Product Range:	★★★★★	Express Delivery Option?	(UK) No
Price Range:	Luxury/<u>Medium</u>/Very Good Value	Gift Wrapping Option?	No
Delivery Area:	UK	Returns Procedure:	Down to you

Also visit these websites for wedding shoes

Website Address	You'll find them in
www.theaccessoryboutique.com	Jewellery
www.louellabridal.co.uk	All About The Dress
www.ginashoes.com	Shoes to Party In
www.faith.co.uk	Shoes to Party In
www.justbrides.co.uk	About the Dress

Chapter 72

Wedding Cakes and Favours

You can choose and order your wedding cake online if you want to and this will work very well if you want something really different from what you're offered locally (unless you live in London, of course, where the choice is incredible). However, and it's a big however, you will probably have to pay quite a lot for delivery if you're miles away from your cake designer.

So think about this, and if you find a cake from somewhere a bit further afield, try to arrange for one of your guests to collect it for you the day before and bring it that day if at all possible (you don't want to be worrying about your cake arriving or not on your wedding day). Also choose a cake that doesn't need to be assembled with tiers and stands but that can be collected as it will be served. In that way your choice will widen considerably.

There are some really gorgeous cakes here with very unusual designs and a huge range of prices. There's also one website where you can buy miniature wedding cakes, either to replace the large variety – but then how do you cut a mini cake with style? – or to send to the guests and relatives who can't make it on the day which I think is an excellent idea.

There are also lots of ideas for favours here, or those little gifts you can give to your guests that make the table look very pretty and again you can spend any amount you want.

In any case it's all here for you to browse through and choose from, and the idea of having it all online is to make the whole process more fun and easier to manage than it would be if you had to choose everything in the shops when you're short of time.

Sites to Visit

www.aweddinglessordinary.co.uk

A Wedding Less Ordinary offer an unusual collection of favours and ideas for your wedding table, including themed favours with categories such as beach, butterfly, floral and hearts, and under each category there's a wide choice of prices and designs. They specialise too in the prettiest favour packaging, personalised ribbon and embossed tags and they'll deliver to you worldwide although you need to email them for costs for posting overseas.

Site Usability:	★★★★★	Based:	UK
Product Range:	★★★★★	Express Delivery Option?	(UK) N/A
Price Range:	Luxury/Medium/Very Good Value	Gift Wrapping Option?	N/A
Delivery Area:	Worldwide	Returns Procedure:	N/A

www.classiccakes.co.uk

Classic Cakes offers choices of wedding cakes to suit all tastes from the traditional royal iced Victorian style to the ultra modern fairy tale wedding castle. All the cakes are designed and hand crafted by the owner of Classic Cakes, Laraine Petworth and can be delivered throughout the UK. You can see a very good selection on the website and choose from rich fruit, genoese or chocolate which can be covered with sugarpaste or chocolate fudge.

Site Usability:	★★★★★	Based:	UK
Product Range:	★★★★★	Express Delivery Option?	(UK) N/A
Price Range:	Luxury/Medium/Very Good Value	Gift Wrapping Option?	N/A
Delivery Area:	UK	Returns Procedure:	N/A

www.lindacalvert.co.uk

Linda Calvert creates the most exquisite wedding cakes, decorated to the theme, style and colours of your choice. On her website you can see a selection of her designs and either choose from those or call her to discuss your ideas and request a brochure. She will deliver to anywhere in the UK but London and the Home Counties will have the lowest delivery charges. She asks that you order six months in advance but will help you with a rush order if she can.

Site Usability:	★★★★	Based:	UK
Product Range:	★★★★	Express Delivery Option?	(UK) N/A
Price Range:	Luxury/Medium/Very Good Value	Gift Wrapping Option?	N/A
Delivery Area:	UK	Returns Procedure:	N/A

www.littlevenicecakecompany.co.uk

If you want to order a really, really special cake for your wedding (and you're not too far from London) you should visit the Little Venice Cake Company's website and have a look at the amazing creations on show. These are wedding cake designers to the stars, and you should expect the prices to be high accordingly, however it is a quite exceptional collection and definitely merits its wonderful reputation, press coverage and star studded clientele.

Site Usability:	★★★★	Based:	UK
Product Range:	★★★★★	Express Delivery Option?	(UK) N/A
Price Range:	Luxury/Medium/Very Good Value	Gift Wrapping Option?	N/A
Delivery Area:	UK	Returns Procedure:	N/A

www.maisiefantasie.co.uk

There's a really pretty range of wedding cakes here, designed by May Clee-Cadman, who studied Art and Design history graduating with an honours degree in 2000. After training with one of London's most prestigious wedding cake designers, May founded Maisie Fantasie in 2003. Designs range from the contemporary to the traditional, using a variety of flavours. They prefer you to have a personal consultation as each cake is totally made for you and they'll send your cake to you anywhere in Europe.

Site Usability:	★★★★★	Based:	UK
Product Range:	★★★★★	Express Delivery Option?	(UK) N/A
Price Range:	Luxury/Medium/Very Good Value	Gift Wrapping Option?	N/A
Delivery Area:	Europe	Returns Procedure:	N/A

www.rainbowsugarcraft.co.uk

Don't be put off by the fact that this cake maker states that they only deliver to the North of England when you click through to Wedding Cakes. If you ask them they'll actually deliver to you anywhere in the UK and they have an absolutely gorgeous range of top quality cakes, whether you want floral embellishment, a novelty design, chocolate cake or traditional tiers. You can see everything very clearly here and they'll despatch your cake by personal courier.

Site Usability:	★★★★★	Based:	UK
Product Range:	★★★★★	Express Delivery Option?	(UK) N/A
Price Range:	Luxury/Medium/Very Good Value	Gift Wrapping Option?	N/A
Delivery Area:	UK	Returns Procedure:	N/A

www.savoirdesign.com

Celebrity pastry chef, Eric Lanard offers a service from the most spectacular chocolate creation or a 5ft croquembouche to a glamorous fifties-style iced tiered cake. You need to visit him in his production kitchen in south west London for an initial consultation and then he'll deliver to you as far north as Cambridge and down to the south coast. They also offer pretty ribbon tied bags and boxes full of sugared almonds, chocolates or French iced macaroons and gorgeous little candles with name tags.

Site Usability:	★★★	Based:	UK	
Product Range:	★★★★	Express Delivery Option?	(UK) N/A	
Price Range:	Luxury/Medium/Very Good Value	Gift Wrapping Option?	N/A	
Delivery Area:	UK	Returns Procedure:	N/A	

www.securecakestore.com

You can order from this website if you live within the M25 and they have an excellent selection of wedding (and other occasion) cakes to choose from, from beautiful tiered traditional cakes to chocolate wedding cakes and fun designs. You need to place your order as early as possible and at least six weeks before your wedding, for delivery the day before.

Site Usability:	★★★★	Based:	UK	
Product Range:	★★★★	Express Delivery Option?	(UK) N/A	
Price Range:	Luxury/Medium/Very Good Value	Gift Wrapping Option?	N/A	
Delivery Area:	UK	Returns Procedure:	N/A	

www.littlecakes.co.uk

The Little Wedding Cake Company offers a creative and cost-effective alternative to the more traditional wedding cake with individual, miniature cakes made from high quality ingredients. You have the option to have them personalised and presented in hand made boxes and they'll last for up to six months, so you can give them as favours and gifts to those unable to come to your wedding or use them to replace a larger cake.

Site Usability:	★★★★	Based:	UK	
Product Range:	★★★	Express Delivery Option?	(UK) N/A	
Price Range:	Luxury/Medium/Very Good Value	Gift Wrapping Option?	N/A	
Delivery Area:	Worldwide	Returns Procedure:	N/A	

www.toogoodtoeat.co.uk

With over 20 years experience, Too Good To Eat specialises in creating unique wedding cakes specially for you. You can choose your cake by visiting their showroom or selecting from their picture gallery and calling them for specific requirements. They will ship anywhere in the World although delivery costs will be greater the further away you are from them.

Site Usability:	★★★★★	Based:	UK	
Product Range:	★★★★★	Express Delivery Option?	(UK) N/A	
Price Range:	Luxury/Medium/Very Good Value	Gift Wrapping Option?	N/A	
Delivery Area:	Worldwide	Returns Procedure:	N/A	

Travel Made Easy

This is not pretending to be a travel guide – there are plenty of other people who are expert at telling you where to go and visit, where to stay and eat out and how to get the best package deal, however, as a travel addict and having been asked many times about the best places online to book flights, car hire, ferry crossings and the like I decided to include this information so that if you don't want to use one of the large travel companies but want to make your own arrangements, which can a) be more fun and b) sometimes be better priced, then you could just look here and find the best booking websites all together.

There are other excellent travel services websites online, for checking how many dollars you'll get for your pounds, ordering foreign currency online, buying travel health insurance and how to make it easy to pay the dreaded London Congestion Charge. You'll find them all here, plus indispensable mapping and driving direction websites for wherever you are, or plan to visit, in the World.

Chapter 73

Essential Travel Websites

Currency Conversions

www.thomascook.com

This is a huge travel website, offering excellent deals on holidays all over the World, plus airport hotels, airport parking and other assistance. Wherever you're going and whether or not you've booked through Thomas Cook you could try out their foreign currency ordering service. Not only will you get extremely good rates but you can pay using your credit card and receive your currency at no extra charge by express courier the next day. It certainly beats standing in the queue at the bank.

www.xe.com

Don't go anywhere without using this website to check on how much you should be getting for your pounds and pence. You can convert any kind of currency into another instantly and even if you're going to order your currency elsewhere online or go down to the bank you should check the rate you're getting here as well. Just go to the Home Page, scroll down to the XE Quick Currency Converter and you're away.

Driving Directions

www.getamap.co.uk

This is a really speedy website containing all the Ordinance Survey maps. You just click on the area of the UK you want a map for then click again to get as close as you want. You can also search for maps anywhere in the UK simply by entering the place name, full postcode or National Grid reference – and print the maps or copy them for use on your personal or business web site. Buy maps online here too from detailed explorer maps to historical maps showing you how your town looked a hundred years ago.

www.maporama.co.uk

Here's a very easy way to find a route from one place to another with clear directions and zoom in features and this works for just about anywhere in the World. You can also see exactly where major airports are throughout the World with maps which you can zoom in on, send by email, export to your PDA or print out and use their quick links to maps of New York, Chicago, Los Angeles, London, San Francisco and Hong Kong.

www.multimap.co.uk

Multimap.com is one of Europe's most popular mapping websites, offering a range of free, useful services including street-level maps of the United Kingdom, Europe, and the US, road maps of the world, door-to-door travel directions, aerial photographs and lots of local information.

www.streetmap.co.uk

If you're looking for a particular road or street then this site will provide clear and detailed maps of exactly where you want to be. It's a simple website and although it seems to be also trying to offer you lots of other services what you really want to do here is type in the postcode, street name or even telephone dialling code and what you'll get is an excellent, clear street map without any of the frills.

www.viamichelin.com

Via Michelin will help you with all your European travel planning by giving you driving directions, across countries, to anywhere you want. You just key in your starting point and your destination and it'll tell you exactly how to get there, no matter how many borders you're crossing. It'll give you hotels and restaurants on the way and even tell you how much the tolls are going to be.

Motoring in London

www.cclondon.com

Use this site to register your car for the congestion charge and then don't, don't, don't forget to pay it when you drive into London. Although it's a complete nuisance this is by far the easiest way of paying and you can book days, weeks and months ahead. You can also get set up to use SMS text messaging so that you can pay from your mobile phone. You can also now pay the day after you've travelled into London.

Traffic Information

www.theaa.com

Go to the main AA site and click on Traffic News. Key in the area and road you're interested in and you'll get comprehensive information about what's going on (some of which you probably won't want to hear). Roadworks, delays, accidents – it's all there, giving you a chance to change your route. You can also visit the AA main website from here.

Chapter 74

Car Hire, Ferries, Trains and Planes – Book them all online and get the best deals

Car Hire – Here and Abroad

www.avis.co.uk

Avis have an extremely efficient online system for choosing your pick-up point and selecting your car just about anywhere in the world. You can also sign up for their Premium Service which means they keep all your details so you don't have to queue each time you pick up your car.

www.budget.com

If you're travelling to the USA always check the prices at *www.budget.com* for countrywide car hire as they often have some very good deals and special offers. With full descriptions of the types of car you can hire (number of passengers, amount of luggage) you can be certain that what will be waiting for you is what you've been expecting and in my experience their staff are some of the most helpful you'll come across.

www.hertz.co.uk

Fly to any airport in the world and pick up the car of your choice at your prearranged price. Check for locations for picking up and dropping off. With so many different destinations you need to make sure that you know whether you're going to have to pay extra taxes and insurances (and other charges) before you go (particularly for the USA) so make sure you read the small print.

Other car hire websites you may want to take a look at:

www.alamo.com

www.europcar.co.uk

www.nationalcar.co.uk

Ferries and Eurotunnel

www.brittanyferries.co.uk

If you want to take your car to Caen, St Malo, Roscoff or Santander then this is the site to use to book your journey. Book early to ensure you get the cabin of your choice and really early if you're planning to go in the holiday season. You'll find clear route guides and timetables here and you can combine your crossing with one of their holiday offers for self-catering and hotel accommodation throughout France and Spain.

www.condorferries.co.uk

Condor Ferries giant high-speed sea-cat sails from Poole and Weymouth to St Malo via Jersey or Guernsey. The company also runs a conventional five hour ferry crossing service for those who want to take a large vehicle or motor-home across. This is much the fastest way to get to St Malo but only runs during spring and summer months as the sea-cat does not suit rough seas.

www.eurotunnel.com

Eurotunnel will take you and your car from Folkestone to Calais and make the crossing in just 35 minutes. If you're slightly late for your train you can usually get onto the next one (except in peak times) as they leave every 20 minutes. A word of warning: Don't forget your roofbox is on top when you drive towards the train. It's really not a good idea.

www.ferries.org

Ferryprice promises to find you the cheapest current fare from a variety of major ferry operators including P & O, Stena Line, Sea France and Brittany Ferries. Sometimes this works and sometimes it doesn't because the ferry operators have special offers in very short timescales so check here and then go to the main operator's website and check there too.

www.hoverspeed.co.uk

Forget the old smelly noisy hovercraft. The new breed of Seacat is a fast, sleek machine that travels at high speed to Calais or on the longer crossing over to Dieppe from Newhaven. If you're going to Le Havre or in that direction you definitely want to try this route as it saves you a lot of time and miles. Beware though. There's very little food on board so take your picnic with you.

www.irishferries.com

Taking you from Holyhead and Pembroke across to Dublin and Rosslare and then on down to Cherbourg and Roscoff, Irish Ferries offer you an extremely modern fleet including Ulysses, the World's largest car ferry. There's lots of information on this website about timetables and fares, on board shopping and upgrades to their Club class and (yes you guessed it) offers for holidays in Ireland.

www.wightlink.co.uk

Wightlink Isle of Wight Ferries operates a round-the-clock service between the English mainland and the Isle of Wight. They run every day of the year on three routes across the Solent and sail up to 230 times a day so if you want to cross over to the Isle of Wight, with or without your car, this is the place for you.

www.poferries.com

P&O and Stena Line combined to offer ferry crossings to and from the South to Calais, Le Havre, Cherbourg and Bilbao plus Zebrugge and Rotterdam from Hull and across the Irish Sea. Register your car details to make the site even quicker to use. You can book online and if you're thinking of using another website to make your booking with P & O check the price here before you do so as you'll often find excellent special offers at certain times of the year.

www.superfast.com

Superfast Ferries offer you a high quality service whether you're travelling between Italy and Greece, between Finland and Germany, or between Scotland and Belgium. You can download their Booking Request Form and fax it back to them or book online.

Flight Information

www.baa.com

The British Airports Authority website provides real time arrival and departure information for all UK airports together with excellent car parking information, travel insurance and a foreign currency ordering service. You can book Executive Lounge passes here whatever cabin you're flying in and checkout the shop and restaurant listings for your airport and terminal. This is a great site to use before you fly and if you're meeting someone.

Take the Train – anywhere in Europe

www.eurostar.com

Eurostar will take you to Paris or Lille at high speed and will also connect you to over 100 destinations across Europe. There are special offers on the site and information about new connections plus City Guides for Brussels. Always check the Eurostar site prices before booking it through anyone else, however there are very often good rates for upgrades to first class on websites such as *www.driveline.co.uk* and *www.leisuredirection.co.uk*.

www.nationalrail.com

There's a great deal going on on this website, from train and coach ticket information for anywhere in the UK, times, fare types, luggage allowances and online booking to ferry crossings and the seemingly inevitable plane tickets, hotels and theatres. The train and coach service in particular is really excellent and easy to use.

www.raileurope.co.uk.

This is the place to book your Eurostar, TGV and high speed rail travel right across Europe. If you're a skiing or snowboarding fan you'll also be able to book the snow trains which take you from Waterloo right into the heart of the French Alps. If you want to make your journey in the summertime easier and put your car on the train all the way from Calais down to Nice or Narbonne you'll find all the information about French Motorail here as well. You can check on the interactive map at *www.raileurope.com* (US based) to decide on the route you want to take, then use the online booking service here to get you there.

Chapter 75

General Travel Planning

www.dontforgetyourtoothbrush.com

I don't know about you, but every time I make out the holiday packing list I leave something off. Well now there's no excuse. On this clever website you'll be able to tick off every possible item for lots of different types of holiday. You just check the boxes and print off your list.

www.frommers.com

If you're planning a trip to the USA you'll need this website. US based Frommers are experts on trips within the USA (and throughout the world), helping you with hotels, flights, cars and cruises. One of the best things about this site is that you don't need to know much about the country when you start, they offer you a wealth of information. Once you've decided on a City or place to visit you can find out about nightlife, restaurants, shopping, walking tours, activities and everything else you can possibly think of.

www.viamichelin.com

Via Michelin will help you with all your European travel planning, whether you want to find a restaurant in Paris, a road map of Zurich or a hotel in Milan. This is the online version of the famous Red Guides but unlike the Red Guides, where the road maps are extremely limited (the town maps are excellent) here you just key in your starting point and your destination and it'll tell you exactly how to get there, no matter how many borders you're crossing. You can find hotels and restaurants on the way and even how much the tolls are going to be.

The All-In-One Travel Websites

www.ebookers.co.uk

www.expedia.co.uk

www.lastminute.com

www.travelocity.co.uk

On all these major travel websites you can compare flight prices for different airlines for anywhere in the World and book your hotels and car hire at the same time (sometimes making some good savings), so to get a general idea of what you're going to be looking at pricewise, check on one (or two) of these first.

You'll also find that you can book absolutely everything else as well, from car hire to hotels, theatre tickets, rugby matches abroad and restaurants. If you need it they'll probably already have thought of it for you.

Always check flight prices with the individual airline of your choice as well – you may find a better deal (not always, but sometimes) and you may get offered flight times that suit you better, after all, the cheapest flights here will be out of peak times and the combinations are usually fixed.

You'll find in particular that *www.ebookers.co.uk* can be very good for flight upgrades, *www.expedia.co.uk* has the best hotel guide for anywhere in the World, *www.lastminute.com* gives you more flexibility on flight times and more add-ons, such as theatres and restaurants and *www.travelocity.co.uk* will let you know when your flight comes down in price.

Where flights only are concerned all the airlines are competing heavily with the cut price carriers such as *www.easyjet.com*, *www.ryanair.com* and *www.flybmi.com* (or *www.bmibaby.com*). These are not normally listed at the all in one travel websites and frequently have really good prices (particularly if you book early enough, so don't forget to check them out).

Section 10

Useful Information –
The Essential Websites

These are the websites where you're not actually looking for things to buy in most cases but where you'll find loads and loads of useful information for just about everything; for renewing your passport or getting a visa, for having your clothes altered and converting kilos into pounds; where to quickly look up people's telephone numbers and addresses and find that final word for your crossword. So every time you think 'I need to look up' and 'find out' just take a quick look here.

There are also some websites you can buy from that don't fall into the fashion/beauty/lifestyle areas that we all know and love but that are totally essential. I'm talking about boring office supplies such as computer paper, ink cartridges and basic pens, markers and rulers.

Listen well, all you who have children who constantly (and usually at the last minute) say they HAVE to go to Staples/PC World/WH Smiths as a matter of urgency to get their TOTALLY NECESSARY supplies, including a horrendously expensive new fountain pen as the one they lent to their best friend doesn't work any more. Tell them, in advance, that you're not doing that trip anymore. Get them to make a list of what they need or let them at your computer to fill their basket which you can then edit and get everything delivered. You'll be amazed at how much money you'll save. I have three children. I know these things.

Anyway, back to the useful information. Take a good look round and you'll find some 'Little Helpers' you didn't even know existed. I know that you're used to lots of suggestions within each Chapter and Section and in most cases below you'll only find one, that'll be because you really don't need a choice in this case and the website has been personally tested by yours truly more than once.

Chapter 76

Essential Services

Alterations Service

www.allalts.co.uk

Unless you're one of those lucky people who fits everything (and I certainly don't), if your trousers or skirt needs shortening, or the sleeves on a jacket turning up, then just post the clothes pinned as you want them to Allalts' Leicester head office with the correct amount from the clear online price list and very reasonable return postage, and they will return them to you altered to your specification within approximately seven days.

BT, Directory Enquiries and Yellow Pages

www.bt.com

Provided you have enough information this site will, through its directory enquiries link, provide you with telephone number, full addresses and postcodes for people and business anywhere in the UK. You can also get UK and International Dialling Codes and a great deal of other information including online billing, reporting and tracking faults and help with moving your phone number if you're changing address.

Book Search

www.bookfinder.com

The next time you see a book somewhere, decide to order it and find it's out of print, go immediately to *bookfinder.com*. Here you can search for all books, whether in print or not, and you'll be taken to lots of different places to buy, some of which may well be offering your (reasonably priced) book for a horrendous amount and some where you can purchase at near to the original asking price. It's an excellent website so give it a try.

China Search

www.chinasearch.co.uk

If you're looking for a particular piece of china, or want to add to a set that's no longer in production (or like me, need to replace six dessert plates that you broke in one shot), then register with ChinaSearch and they'll try and find it for you. It's incredibly easy, you just look up your pattern and then fill in their online form with all the details of what you're looking for and how they can reach you. And it works.

Citizens Advice Bureau

www.adviceguide.org.uk

This is definitely not the most exciting of websites, and one which maybe you'll never have cause to visit but if you want any information on benefits, housing and employment, plus civil and consumer issues you'll find it all here, right up to date. It also tells you who to contact if you need further help and how to make a small claim in the courts should you need to, plus there are loads of fact sheets you can print off.

Conversion Tables

www.onlineconversion.com

You know that moment when you want to change miles into kilometres, inches into metres, or ounces into grams, or when you're using that marvellous cookbook you picked up in Williams Sonoma in the US and don't have a clue about the difference between a US teaspoon and the UK version. Well on this useful website you can convert just about anything including temperature, speed, volume, weight and fuel consumption plus some more unusual options such as light years to Astronomical units and gram-force to micronewtons (sorry, I don't have a clue either).

General Office and Stationery Supplies

www.euroffice.co.uk

This is an excellent place to look for your essential pen and paper supplies and computer essentials –

they say that they offer the cheapest prices going but always check and compare. It's a very busy website with a huge range of products, so it's always better to shop here when you know exactly what you want to try and avoid getting sidetracked.

www.staples.co.uk

Buy all your stationery and computer requirements quickly and easily online, with everything from files to office furniture, high quality writing paper and the best priced copy paper. Once you've created your list you can store it so make sure that you order the right toner cartridge for your printer each time without having to look for it. This is also an excellent place for school supplies.

Online Dictionary and Thesaurus

www.askoxford.com

You can search the Compact Oxford Dictionary, The Concise Dictionary of First Names and The Little Oxford Dictionary of Quotations here. Find out about and order all the books published by the Oxford University Press or sign up for a free trial of the Oxford desktop One Click dictionary. It's quite a busy website to use but the search facility is excellent.

www.dictionary.com

The next time you're doing a crossword, playing Scrabble (I know, I know, you're not allowed dictionaries here, but every once in a while to check something up you'll need one) don't bother to go through the book version but go on to this fantastic website where you'll find every word and every spelling for every word plus alternatives for every word. American and UK spelling is given in each case.

Online Encyclopedia

www.wikipedia.org

Started in 2001, Wikipedia has rapidly grown into the largest reference website on the Internet. The content of Wikipedia is free, written collaboratively by people from all around the world. This website is a wiki, which means that anyone with access to an Internet-connected computer can edit, correct, or improve information throughout the encyclopedia. There are over 1.15 million articles in English alone.

Passport and Visa Service

www.visaservice.co.uk

Visaservice is a visa/passport processing agency based in London, UK. They will process (from online application forms) applications for UK residents, visitors to the UK and residents from other countries. With an extensive visa information database, agency facilities at most London consulates and access to all major courier and transport facilities, they can process visas for most nationalities to destinations around the world, including those where representation is outside the UK. You can also obtain a copy of a birth, marriage, adoption or death certificate here.

Royal Mail Services

www.royalmail.com

Go to their 'Buy Online' section and order your books of stamps here (or your Special Editions, ready stamped envelopes or personalised stamps). You do have to order quite a lot of stamps but it's the easiest way if you're going to be posting lots of mail in the near future. You can also find the package and letter weights and costs table here for the UK and overseas and look up addresses and postcodes.

Weather Reports

www.weather.co.uk

Although you can never be sure of the weather forecast (putting it mildly) and definitely don't totally rely on what you read here (as the situation can change so easily) you can at least get some idea of what is expected for the next ten days, hour by hour if you want and for anywhere in the World.

Chapter 77

To Buy or Not to Buy? All the essential information you need about buying online

Buying online can be so easy, addictive even. You can choose from products from all over the World. A range far greater than anything you could possibly find elsewhere and it's easy to get completely carried away.

Here are the important things you need to know before you buy. Just keep them in your mind before you start ordering and you should have no problems. Happy shopping.

Before you buy

It's always preferable to buy from a retailer you already know, however, there are new and excellent shopping websites springing up all the time and you'll find them particularly when you're using the price comparison websites *www.kelkoo.co.uk* and *www.uk.shopping.com*. If you find a website offering the particular product you're looking for at a very good price you may well want to purchase. Just use the checklist below for added security before you hand over your details.

A word of warning: There are lots of online retailers offering replica products which you may well not want. Make sure that you're purchasing an original product. If the price is really too good to be true be extra cautious and check the retailer out: Call them. Ask if they're selling the original branded product you're looking for. Any doubts at all? Don't do it. I don't want to use the word unscrupulous here as it's not always applicable. If the fact that it's a replica is clear in the wording then you'll know what you're doing. If it's not ...

- Make sure that the retailer's full address is available on its website; you'll usually find this under 'Contact Us'. If it's not there ask them for it before you buy. You need this information for any retailer, anywhere in the world.
- Make sure you're getting the best deal before you order – see the next chapter on Comparison Websites.
- The retailer's web address should start https:// before you enter any payment details. The 's' means that it's a secure website.
- Look out for the padlock at the foot of the screen when you're buying so that you know your credit card details are secure.
- Don't send your credit card details by email.
- Don't send any sensitive personal information by email unless you know exactly who it's going to.
- Pay by credit card once you've decided to purchase, which will give you more protection if something should go wrong. Preferably never pay by cheque or cash.
- If you don't know the retailer, check if they have a 'Privacy Statement', which may be hidden in their Terms and Conditions. This will tell you what they'll do with your information once you've purchased. Ever wondered why you've started to get so much junk mail? Well it's usually because someone has collected your details and then they've sold this information either to another retailer, or to a List Broker who again will be selling it on. My advice is *never* to tick the box which allows a retailer to pass your information to 'other retailers in whose products you may be interested'. You have been warned.
- Check for satisfaction and product guarantees before you order. A retailer who offers you a no questions asked money back guarantee is much easier to deal with if something should go wrong.
- Make sure that you can return the goods if you don't want them and what the returns policy is: i.e. how long do you have to make up your mind?
- Note that some websites, particularly those offering designer watches online, are not able to offer you the manufacturer's guarantee. Make sure you're happy with the arrangements they do offer if you're tempted to buy.

- Don't give any information that isn't necessary to the purchase. You're buying a book, for goodness sake. Why do they need to know your age and how many children you have??

Comparison Websites and how to use them

If you've read through this book you'll already know how strongly I feel about these websites, where you can find the best prices for almost everything. However they're best for electrical equipment, computers, cameras and everything photographic plus books, dvds, cds and games and I would repeat that you do need to know exactly what you're looking for. You can't just type in 'Camera', or 'Fridge'. You need to know the exact model and have done your homework (research) first.

So go to a dedicated product website where they offer you full specifications and advice for the type of product you want. Research an offline magazine, such as 'What Camera' (if you're looking for a camera, of course), look at some of the excellent photographic websites for the latest models and information or subscribe to Which, either online at *www.which.co.uk* or offline through Which Magazine, where thousands of products are reviewed and they'll give you their opinion of the best on the market. This is great if you know the product you want but you don't know exactly which one to buy and you want an independent assessment.

With regard to books, cds and dvds etc there are other websites than Amazon (I know, it's an amazing thought, but there are). You can often find other editions, speedy delivery and very good prices on different websites so it's worth having a look just to make sure before you spend.

There are also lots of other price comparison websites. These are the ones I always use and find the best so rather than giving you a huge choice I've just selected a small number to make things easy.

General comparison websites

www.uk.shopping.com

The next time you're looking for a new washing machine, or mobile phone, or camera, click straight through to this excellent price comparison website. If you haven't given them an exact specification of the product you want (and as I've said it's better if you can) you'll get a list of all the possible options and the relevant websites plus website reviews. Make your choice and then you can compare prices on the one you want and you'll get all the information you need to decide from price (of course), stock availability, delivery charge and site rating. You then just have to click through to buy from their preferred retailer or wherever you choose.

www.kelkoo.co.uk

With Kelkoo you really do need to know the exact specification of what you're looking for to get the best results, as you don't get a defined product list offering you everything containing your initial search criteria but a mixture of relevant products. If you specify exactly what you want you'll get all those products at the top of the page with prices, site ratings, descriptions and delivery costs.

Food and wine price check sites

www.tesco.com/pricecheck

Believe it or not Tesco offers you the opportunity of pitching its own prices against those of Sainsbury, Morrisons and Asda although it's not always the cheapest (but of course they're doing it to show you that they usually are). You can compare the prices of most of your general groceries right down to the basics but it's most useful when you want to buy booze. For example, at time of writing I'm checking on a 75cl bottle of Talisker Malt Whisky. Tesco's price is £19.97 and Sainsbury's is £25.99. Quite a difference, I'm sure you'll agree.

www.winesearcher.com

Looking for a particular vintage of Pomerol or just Oyster Bay Chardonnay? With prices differing by as much as 40% you need this site if you're considering buying more than a single bottle of wine. Do register for the pro-version to get all the benefits and they'll search for you throughout the World if you want. Bear in mind that the prices you're given don't include VAT, nor do they take into account any special offers that retailers such as Majestic may have going at any time so you should check those as well.

Books, games, cd and dvd price check

www.bookbrain.co.uk

www.best-book-price.co.uk

These are two excellent places where you can compare book prices and see who has the book you're looking for in stock to send out immediately. They're both very easy to use – not really for buying ordinary paperbacks, although you can use them for that if you want to, but when you've found a special hardback that you want to give as a gift next week, you're being quoted 4–6 weeks delivery, you may be able to find another bookshop who has it ready to send out with the added benefit that you can also compare the prices from all the bookstores.

www.best-cd-price.co.uk

Know the cd you want to buy but want to make sure you get the best price? Use this price comparison website, which not only shows where you'll find the best deal but includes the postage details as well so you absolutely know where you are. This website is almost unbelievably quick to use and you can use it for dvds and games as well. As an example, if you do a search on the Lord of the Rings, The Return of the King, you'll be given twelve places where you can buy it online, with prices from an amazing £7.49, to £22.49. Quite a difference, I'm sure you'll agree.

www.dvdpricecheck.co.uk

If you're looking for a particular dvd this is the place to start and you can see what's available throughout all the world regions. With so many places to buy dvds online it's hard to know, without spending hours, which is the best site and with different sites charging different amounts things get even worse. So here it is, the website that'll compare the worldwide prices for you. Just key in your title and region (UK is Region 2) and you'll get all the answers.

Many of the websites they offer don't charge you delivery on top so you can order from as many as you want and as often as you like. Sounds tempting? It's hard to know when to stop.

www.uk.gamestracker.com

However much you may dislike those extremely noisy (and often horrifically violent) computer games, you won't want your precious ones spending more of their not so hard earned pocket money than they need to. If you want to get them the latest game for Christmas or they want to choose one themselves then send them to Games Tracker, where you/they can compare the prices with all the retailers for any specific game and get the deal of the moment.

Internet Auctions

You may feel really tempted by some of the items you can find on auction websites, and in particular Ebay. But bear in mind the following as it can be extremely risky.

You may well be buying from a private seller and so you won't really know who you're dealing with or where they're based. Find out before you commit.

You have fewer rights when you buy from a private seller. Although the goods must be 'by law' as stated, a seller who is not acting as a business is not covered by the rules on satisfactory quality and fitness for purchase.

If you have a problem, it could be harder to put right than if you bought from a shop although some auction websites do offer complaints resolution processes and anti-fraud guarantees. If you're going to use an auction website, make sure that it's one of these. Ebay, whose Safety Centre (click at the foot of the page at *www.ebay.co.uk*), is excellent is definitely one of the best auction sites to buy from.

Top Tips:

- Check the feedback about the seller on the auction site and send an email query to the seller who should welcome your enquiry.
- Know exactly what you're buying, including the normal retail price. As I've said before, if the price seems too good to be true, it usually is. Check the authenticity of any antique or collectible.
- Use a credit card to pay through a secure website, which gives you the most protection if there's a problem.
- Don't up your bid in the last few minutes unless you know exactly what you are doing. You may well find yourself being tempted to go outside your range in the excitement of the last minute bidding (yes you guessed, that's happened to me).

- Read the small print. Make sure you know if postage and insurance are included in the price. Is the seller based in the same country as you? What action should you take if something goes wrong?
- Remember that this can be a risky way to buy so be very, very careful. That's not to say don't do it, just make sure you know what you're doing first.

Once you've bought

- Very quickly after you've made your purchase you should receive email confirmation about your buy including all necessary purchase details – order number, date, details of the goods you've ordered and purchase price, plus in most cases a link back to the website you've ordered from.
- You are entitled to a 'cooling off' period (usually seven days), during which you can cancel your order without any reason and receive a full refund.
- You're also entitled to a full refund if the goods or services are not provided by the date you agreed. If you didn't agree a date, then you are entitled to a refund if the goods or services are not provided within 28 days.
- Keep an email and paper folder into which you can save all relevant information about your online purchases. Call it something like 'Web Orders Outstanding'. Whittle it down to just the confirmation email with the order number and purchase details once you've received you're order and you're happy. There's truly nothing more infuriating than not having the right information if something goes wrong later.
- Note that the above entitlements do not apply to financial services such as insurance or banking, online auctions, or purchases involving the sale of land.

If Something Goes Wrong

If something goes wrong, and you've paid by credit card, you may have a claim not only against the supplier of the goods, but also the credit card issuer.

This applies to goods or services (and deposits) costing more than £100 but less than £30,000 and does not apply to debit or charge cards.

Contact the retailer with the problem initially by email and make sure you quote the order number and any other necessary details.

If you do not get a satisfactory result to your complaint you can contact *www.consumerdirect.gov.uk* (for the UK) or call them on 08454 040506 for what to do next. If your problem is with a retailer based in Australia, Canada, Denmark, Finland, Hungary, Mexico, New Zealand, Norway, South Korea, Sweden, Switzerland or the USA you can click through to *www.econsumer.gov*, a joint project of consumer protection agencies from 20 nations for help.

If (horrors) you find that someone has used your credit card information without your authorisation, contact your card issuer immediately. You can cancel the payment and your card company must arrange for your account to be re-credited in full.

Quick Main Brand Fashion and Beauty Directory

Please note this is a main brand list only and is not fully comprehensive of all brands offered by each online retailer, as retailers' brand lists change from season to season.

Fashion Fix – Fashion Brands

Brand	Website Address	Chapter	Page
Abercrombie	www.abercrombie.com	Shop America	44
Agnes B	www.agnesb.com	General Fashion Online	23
Alberta Feretti	www.net-a-porter.com	Luxury Brands Online	14, 63, 69, 98, 369
Alexander McQueen	www.brownsfashion.com	Luxury Brands Online	11, 417
	www.net-a-porter.com	Luxury Brands Online	14, 63, 69, 98, 369
Alfred Sung	www.eveningdresses.co.uk	General Fashion Online	24, 388, 398
Allegra Hicks	www.allegrahicks.com	Luxury Brands Online	10
American Eagle	www.ae.com	Shop America	44
Anna Sui	www.net-a-porter.com	Luxury Brands Online	14, 63, 69, 98, 369
Ann Louise Roswald	www.my-wardrobe.com	The Boutiques	20
APC	www.apc.fr	General Fashion Online	23

Azzeding Alaia	www.brownsfashion.com	Luxury Brands Online	11, 417
Balenciaga	www.brownsfashion.com	Luxury Brands Online	11, 417
Ben Sherman	www.jeans-direct.com	General Fashion Online	35
Bench	www.w1style.co.uk	Shop The High Street	55
Betty Jackson	www.shopatanna.com	The Boutiques	21
Biba	www.little-london.com	The Boutiques	20
Billabong	www.w1style.co.uk	Shop The High Street	55
Cesare Paciotti	www.lineafashion.com	Luxury Brands Online	13, 63
Juicy Couture,	www.lineafashion.com	Luxury Brands Online	13, 63
Blumarine	www.lineafashion.com	Luxury Brands Online	13, 63
Rock and Republic	www.lineafashion.com	Luxury Brands Online	13, 63
Bottega Veneta	www.net-a-porter.com	Luxury Brands Online	14, 63, 69, 98, 369
	www.matchesfashion.com	Luxury Brands Online	13
Brooks Brothers	www.brooksbrothers.com	Shop America	45
Brora	www.brora.co.uk	Knitwear	30, 279
Burberry Prorsum	www.net-a-porter.com	Luxury Brands Online	14, 63, 69, 98, 369
C & C California	www.goclothing.com	Shop America	45
	www.brownsfashion.com	Luxury Brands Online	11, 417
Cacharel	www.net-a-porter.com	Luxury Brands Online	14, 63, 69, 98, 369
	www.my-wardrobe.com	The Boutiques	20
Calvin Klein	www.net-a-porter.com	Luxury Brands Online	14, 63, 69, 98, 369
Calvin Klein Jeans	www.little-london.com	The Boutiques	20
Catherine Malandrino	www.goclothing.com	Shop America	45
Celine	www.lineafashion.com	Luxury Brands Online	13, 63
Chip and Pepper	www.goclothing.com	Shop America	45
Chloe	www.net-a-porter.com	Luxury Brands Online	14, 63, 69, 98, 369
	www.matchesfashion.com	Luxury Brands Online	13
Christian Dior	www.brownsfashion.com	Luxury Brands Online	11, 417
Citizens of Humanity	www.goclothing.com	Shop America	45
Clements Ribeiro	www.net-a-porter.com	Luxury Brands Online	14, 63, 69, 98, 369
Diane von Furstenberg	www.brownsfashion.com	Luxury Brands Online	11, 417
	www.dvflondon.com	Luxury Brands Online	11
	www.net-a-porter.com	Luxury Brands Online	14, 63, 69, 98, 369
Diesel	www.jeans-direct.com	General Fashion Online	35
	www.w1style.co.uk	Shop The High Street	55
Dolce & Gabbana	www.brownsfashion.com	Luxury Brands Online	11, 417
	www.matchesfashion.com	Luxury Brands Online	13
Dries Van Noten	www.brownsfashion.com	Luxury Brands Online	11, 417
Earl Jean	www.shopbop.com	Shop America	46
Eddie Baur	www.eddiebaur.com	Tall and Plus Size Clothing	39, 42, 45
Eddie Baur	www.eddiebaur.com	Shop America	39, 42, 45
Emilio Pucci	www.net-a-porter.com	Luxury Brands Online	14, 63, 69, 98, 369
Erickson Beamon	www.net-a-porter.com	Luxury Brands Online	14, 63, 69, 98, 369
Escada	www.escada.com	Luxury Brands Online	11
Etro	www.brownsfashion.com	Luxury Brands Online	11, 417
	www.lineafashion.com	Luxury Brands Online	13, 63

Evisu	www.evisu.com	General Fashion Online	24
FCUK	www.w1style.co.uk	Shop The High Street	55
Fendi	www.brownsfashion.com	Luxury Brands Online	11, 417
French Connection	www.fcukbuymail.co.uk	Shop The High Street	34, 144
Frostfench	www.my-wardrobe.com	The Boutiques	20
Gharani Strok	www.shopatanna.com	The Boutiques	21
	www.lineafashion.com	Luxury Brands Online	13, 63
	www.my-wardrobe.com	The Boutiques	20
Hugo Boss	www.little-london.com	The Boutiques	20
Issa London	www.brownsfashion.com	Luxury Brands Online	11, 417
	www.shopatanna.com	The Boutiques	21
	www.little-london.com	The Boutiques	20
J&M Davidson	www.net-a-porter.com	Luxury Brands Online	14, 63, 69, 98, 369
Jeans Paul Gaultier	www.goclothing.com	Shop America	45
Jil Sander	www.brownsfashion.com	Luxury Brands Online	11, 417
Jimmy Choo	www.net-a-porter.com	Luxury Brands Online	14, 63, 69, 98, 369
John Smedley	www.johnsmedley.com	Knitwear	31
Joseph	www.little-london.com	The Boutiques	20
Judith Leiber	www.net-a-porter.com	Luxury Brands Online	14, 63, 69, 98, 369
Juicy Couture,	www.lineafashion.com	Luxury Brands Online	13, 63
	www.net-a-porter.com	Luxury Brands Online	14, 63, 69, 98, 369
	www.shopbop.com	Shop America	46
Kate Spade	www.net-a-porter.com	Luxury Brands Online	14, 63, 69, 98, 369
Kenneth Jay Lane	www.net-a-porter.com	Luxury Brands Online	14, 63, 69, 98, 369
	www.shopbop.com	Shop America	46
Lainey Keogh	www.brownsfashion.com	Luxury Brands Online	11, 417
Lands End	www.landsend.co.uk	General Fashion Online	25, 42
Lanvin	www.matchesfashion.com	Luxury Brands Online	13
Levi	www.jeans-direct.com	Shop The High Street	35
Lilly Pulitzer	www.goclothing.com	Shop America	45
LL Bean	www.llbean.com	Tall and Plus Size Clothing	39, 42, 46
	www.llbean.com	Shop America	39, 42, 46
Luella	www.brownsfashion.com	Luxury Brands Online	11, 417
	www.little-london.com	The Boutiques	20
	www.net-a-porter.com	Luxury Brands Online	14, 63, 69, 98, 369
Lulu Guinness	www.luluguinness.com	Luxury Brands Online	13, 63
Mango	www.mango.com	Shop The High Street	35, 144
Marc by Marc Jacobs	www.shopbop.com	Shop America	46
Marc by Marc Jacobs Shoes	www.shopbop.com	Shop America	46
Marc Jacobs	www.net-a-porter.com	Luxury Brands Online	14, 63, 69, 98, 369
	www.matchesfashion.com	Luxury Brands Online	13
Marlene Birger	www.shopatanna.com	The Boutiques	21
Marni	www.brownsfashion.com	Luxury Brands Online	11, 417
	www.net-a-porter.com	Luxury Brands Online	14, 63, 69, 98, 369
Matthew Williamson	www.brownsfashion.com	Luxury Brands Online	11, 417
	www.net-a-porter.com	Luxury Brands Online	14, 63, 69, 98, 369

Max Mara	www.little-london.com	The Boutiques	20
Michael Kors	www.net-a-porter.com	Luxury Brands Online	14, 63, 69, 98, 369
Miss Selfridge	www.missselfridge.co.uk	Shop The High Street	36
Miss Sixty	www.w1style.co.uk	Shop The High Street	55
Missoni	www.brownsfashion.com	Luxury Brands Online	11, 417
	www.lineafashion.com	Luxury Brands Online	13, 63
	www.matchesfashion.com	Luxury Brands Online	13
	www.net-a-porter.com	Luxury Brands Online	14, 63, 69, 98, 369
Miu Miu	www.net-a-porter.com	Luxury Brands Online	14, 63, 69, 98, 369
Monsoon	www.monsoon.co.uk	Shop The High Street	36, 140
	www.net-a-porter.com	Luxury Brands Online	14, 63, 69, 98, 369
Moschino Jeans	www.goclothing.com	Shop America	45
Mulberry	www.net-a-porter.com	Luxury Brands Online	14, 63, 69, 98, 369
N Peal	www.npealworks.com	Knitwear	32
Nanette Lepore	www.goclothing.com	Shop America	45
Narciso Rodruigez	www.net-a-porter.com	Luxury Brands Online	14, 63, 69, 98, 369
Nicole Farhi	www.shopatanna.com	The Boutiques	21
O'Neill	www.w1style.co.uk	Shop The High Street	55
Orla Kiely	www.shopatanna.com	The Boutiques	21
Orvis	www.orvis.co.uk	General Fashion Online	26, 114
Paige Denim	www.shopbop.com	Shop America	46
Paper Denim and Cloth	www.shopbop.com	Shop America	46
Paul and Joe	www.shopbop.com	Shop America	46
	www.my-wardrobe.com	The Boutiques	20
Paul Frank	www.goclothing.com	Shop America	45
Paul Smith	www.brownsfashion.com	Luxury Brands Online	11, 417
	www.net-a-porter.com	Luxury Brands Online	14, 63, 69, 98, 369
	www.paulsmith.co.uk	Luxury Brands Online	15, 18, 69
Principles	www.principles.co.uk	Shop The High Street	36, 42
	www.principles.co.uk	Tall and Plus Size Clothing	36, 42
Pucci	www.brownsfashion.com	Luxury Brands Online	11, 417
Quicksilver	www.w1style.co.uk	Shop The High Street	55
Rebecca Taylor	www.shopbop.com	Shop America	46
River Island	www.riverisland.co.uk	Shop The High Street	37, 144
Roberto Cavalli	www.brownsfashion.com	Luxury Brands Online	11, 417
Roland Mouret	www.brownsfashion.com	Luxury Brands Online	11, 417
	www.net-a-porter.com	Luxury Brands Online	14, 63, 69, 98, 369
Roxy	www.w1style.co.uk	Shop The High Street	55
Sass and Bide	www.shopbop.com	Shop America	46
	www.my-wardrobe.com	The Boutiques	20
Seven for All Mankind	www.net-a-porter.com	Luxury Brands Online	14, 63, 69, 98, 369
	www.goclothing.com	Shop America	45
	www.my-wardrobe.com	The Boutiques	20
Shirin Guild	www.brownsfashion.com	Luxury Brands Online	11, 417
Sun and Sand	www.sunandsand.co.uk	General Fashion Online	26
Stella McCartney	www.matchesfashion.com	Luxury Brands Online	13

Ted Baker	www.tedbaker.co.uk	Shop The High Street	37
Temperley	www.lineafashion.com	Luxury Brands Online	13, 63
	www.net-a-porter.com	Luxury Brands Online	14, 63, 69, 98, 369
Theory	www.shopbop.com	Shop America	46
Thomas Pink	www.thomaspink.co.uk	Men only – shirts & accessories	108
Toast	www.toastbypost.co.uk	General Fashion Online	27
Tocca	www.my-wardrobe.com	The Boutiques	20
Tods	www.lineafashion.com	Luxury Brands Online	13, 63
Top Shop	www.topshop.co.uk	Shop The High Street	37, 143
Vera Wang	www.net-a-porter.com	Luxury Brands Online	14, 63, 69, 98, 369
Wallis	www.wallis-fashion.com	Shop The High Street	38, 42
	www.wallis-fashion.com	Tall and Plus Size Clothing	38, 42
Warehouse	www.warehouse.co.uk	Shop The High Street	38
Wrangler	www.jeans-direct.com	General Fashion Online	35
Wrangler 47	www.shopbop.com	Shop America	46
Zac Posen	www.net-a-porter.com	Luxury Brands Online	14, 63, 69, 98, 369

Fashion Fix – Sportswear Brands – All Appear in The Sportswear Option

Brand	Website Address	Chapter	Page
Adidas	www.jdsports.co.uk	The Sportswear Option	52
Amor Lux	www.wildlifeonline.com	The Sportswear Option	55
Animal	www.extremepie.com	The Sportswear Option	51, 142
Billabong	www.extremepie.com	The Sportswear Option	51, 142
Crew Clothing	www.crewclothing.co.uk	The Sportswear Option	51, 310
Dockers	www.wildlifeonline.com	The Sportswear Option	55
Kipling	www.wildlifeonline.com	The Sportswear Option	55
Lacoste	www.jdsports.co.uk	The Sportswear Option	52
Musto	www.wildlifeonline.com	The Sportswear Option	000
Nike	www.jdsports.co.uk	The Sportswear Option	52
O'Neill	www.extremepie.com	The Sportswear Option	51, 142
Puma	www.jdsports.co.uk	The Sportswear Option	52
	www.puma.com	The Sportswear Option	52
Quicksilver	www.extremepie.com	The Sportswear Option	51, 142
Reebok	www.jdsports.co.uk	The Sportswear Option	52
Sebago	www.wildlifeonline.com	The Sportswear Option	55
Sweaty Betty	www.sweatybetty.com	The Sportswear Option	54
Vans	www.extremepie.com	The Sportswear Option	51, 142

Fashion Fix – Lingerie – All Appear in Lingerie

Brand	Website Address	Page
Agent Provocateur	www.agentprovocateur.com	71
Aristoc	www.figleaves.com	52, 74, 80, 85
	www.tightsplease.co.uk	78
Aubade	www.barenecessities.co.uk	71, 80
	www.the-lingerie-company.co.uk	77, 80

Berlie	www.figleaves.com	52, 74, 80, 85
Betsey Johnson	www.figleaves.com	52, 74, 80, 85
Calvin Klein	www.figleaves.com	52, 74, 80, 85
Chantelle	www.figleaves.com	52, 74, 80, 85
Charnos	www.figleaves.com	52, 74, 80, 85
	www.the-lingerie-company.co.uk	77, 80
	www.tightsplease.co.uk	78
D&G	www.figleaves.com	52, 74, 80, 85
DKNY	www.figleaves.com	52, 74, 80, 85
Dolce & Gabbana Intimo	www.figleaves.com	52, 74, 80, 85
Elle Macpherson	www.figleaves.com	52, 74, 80, 85
Fantasie	www.figleaves.com	52, 74, 80, 85
	www.barenecessities.co.uk	71, 80
	www.bravissimo.com	72, 80
Freya	www.bravissimo.com	72, 80
Gideon Oberson	www.swimwearboutique.com	47, 80
Gossard	www.figleaves.com	52, 74, 80, 85
	www.the-lingerie-company.co.uk	77, 80
Gottex	www.figleaves.com	52, 74, 80, 85
	www.swimwearboutique.com	47, 80
Hanro	www.figleaves.com	52, 74, 80, 85
Janet Reger	www.figleaves.com	52, 74, 80, 85
La Perla	www.figleaves.com	52, 74, 80, 85
	www.glamonweb.co.uk	75
Lejaby	www.figleaves.com	52, 74, 80, 85
	www.barenecessities.co.uk	71, 80
Melissa Obadash	www.figleaves.com	52, 74, 80, 85
Panache	www.bravissimo.com	72, 80
Playtex	www.figleaves.com	52, 74, 80, 85
Pretty Polly	www.figleaves.com	52, 74, 80, 85
	www.tightsplease.co.uk	78
Rigby and Peller	www.figleaves.com	52, 74, 80, 85
	www.rigbyandpeller.com	76
Spanx	www.figleaves.com	52, 74, 80, 85
Warners	www.the-lingerie-company.co.uk	77, 80
Wolford	www.figleaves.com	52, 74, 80, 85
	www.wolfordboutiquelondon.com	78
Wonderbra	www.figleaves.com	52, 74, 80, 85

Fashion Fix – Shoes and Accessories

Brand	Website Address	Chapter	Page
Anya Hindmarch	www.anyahindmarch.com	Luxury Brands Online	10, 63, 300
Bill Amberg	www.billamberg.com	Handbag Addicts Only	59
Bluemarine	www.parallelshoes.com	Shoes to Party In	67
Carvela	www.kurtgeiger.com	Shoes to Party In	66

Christian Louboutin	www.net-a-porter.com	Shoes to Party In	14, 63, 69, 98, 369
	www.matchesfashion.com	Luxury Brands Online	13
Dolce & Gabbana	www.forzieri.com	Luxury Brands Online	12, 63, 117, 118, 323
Emma Hope	www.kurtgeiger.com	Shoes to Party In	66
	www.vivaladiva.com	Shoes to Party In	69
Faith	www.faith.co.uk	Shoes to Party In	65, 421
Fendi	www.forzieri.com	Luxury Brands Online	12, 63, 117, 118, 323
Francesco Biasia	www.parallelshoes.com	Shoes to Party In	67
Gianfranco Ferre	www.forzieri.com	Handbag Addicts Only	12, 63, 117, 118, 323
Gina	www.gina.co.uk	Luxury Brands Online	000
Gucci	www.forzieri.com	Luxury Brands Online	12, 63, 117, 118, 323
	www.gucci.com/uk	Luxury Brands Online	69
J&M Davidson	www.jandmdavidson.com	Handbag Addicts Only	60
Kurt Geiger	www.kurtgeiger.com	Shoes to Party In	66
LK Bennett	www.vivaladiva.com	Shoes to Party In	69
Louis Vuitton	www.louisvuitton.com	Luxury Brands Online	13
Lulu Guinness	www.luluguinness.com	Luxury Brands Online	13, 63
Maloles	www.vivaladiva.com	Shoes to Party In	69
Miu Miu	www.forzieri.com	Luxury Brands Online	12, 63, 117, 118, 323
Mulberry	www.mulberry.com	Luxury Brands Online	14, 63
Orla Kiely	www.orlakiely.com	Handbag Addicts Only	61
Osprey	www.osprey-london.co.uk	Handbag Addicts Only	62
Pickett	www.pickett.co.uk	Handbag Addicts Only	63
Pierre Hardy	www.net-a-porter.com	Shoes to Party In	14, 63, 69, 98, 369
Pollini	www.parallelshoes.com	Shoes to Party In	67
Sergio Rossi	www.vivaladiva.com	Shoes to Party In	69
Skechers	www.vivaladiva.com	Shoes to Party In	69
Stella McCartney	www.net-a-porter.com	Shoes to Party In	14, 63, 69, 98, 369
Stuart Weitzman	www.stuartweitzman.com	Shop America	47, 69
Tanner Krolle	www.tannerkrolle.co.uk	Luxury Brands Online	15, 63
Timberland	www.vivaladiva.com	Shoes to Party In	000
Uggs	www.ugsandkisses.co.uk	Shoes to Party In	68
Valentino	www.net-a-porter.com	Shoes to Party In	14, 63, 69, 98, 369

Fashion Fix

Brand	Website Address	Chapter	Page
Angie Gooderham	www.treasurebox.co.uk	Jewellery and Watches	97, 283
Boodles	www.boodles.co.uk	Luxury Brands Online	10, 98
Butler and Wilson	www.accessoriesonline.co.uk	Jewellery and Watches	91
Butler and Wilson	www.butlerandwilson.co.uk	Jewellery and Watches	92, 280
Dinny Hall	www.dinnyhall.com	Jewellery and Watches	92
Les Nereides	www.accessoriesonline.co.uk	Jewellery and Watches	91
Links of London	www.linksoflondon.com	Jewellery and Watches	94, 348, 368
Mikimoto	www.mikimoto-store.co.uk	Luxury Brands Online	14, 98
Izabel Camille	www.tictocsnrocks.co.uk	Jewellery and Watches	97
Pilgrim	www.tictocsnrocks.co.uk	Jewellery and Watches	97

Swarovski	*www.swarovski.com*	Jewellery and Watches	96, 416
Tarina Tarantino	*www.treasurebox.co.uk*	Jewellery and Watches	97, 283
Theo Fennell	*www.theofennell.com*	Luxury Brands Online	16, 98, 300
Tiffany	*www.tiffany.com*	Luxury Brands Online	16, 98, 300, 348
Flora Astor	*www.astleyclarke.com*	Jewellery and Watches	91, 298
Vinnie Day	*www.astleyclarke.com*	Jewellery and Watches	91, 298
Vinnie Day	*www.manjoh.com*	Jewellery and Watches	94
Catherine Prevost	*www.astleyclarke.com*	Jewellery and Watches	91, 298
Coleman Douglas	*www.astleyclarke.com*	Jewellery and Watches	91, 298
Les Nereides	*www.manjoh.com*	Jewellery and Watches	94
Izabel Camille	*www.manjoh.com*	Jewellery and Watches	94
Toft & Thurmer	*www.manjoh.com*	Jewellery and Watches	94
Tomoki Furusawa	*www.manjoh.com*	Jewellery and Watches	94
Kirsten Goss	*www.kirstengoss.com*	Jewellery and Watches	93
Pascal	*www.pascal-jewellery.com*	Jewellery and Watches	95, 281
Van Peterson	*www.vanpeterson.com*	Jewellery and Watches	97

Men Only – Clothes and Accessories

Brand	Website Address	Chapter	Page
Animal	*www.extremepie.com*	Shop the High Street	51, 142
Austin Reed	*www.austinreed.co.uk*	Suits Etc	111
Barker	*www.shoesdirect.co.uk*	Accessories	119
Ben Sherman	*www.theclothesstore.com*	Suits Etc	116
	www.jeans-direct.co.uk	Shop the High Street	35
Bench	*www.w1style.co.uk*	Shop the High Street	55
Brooks Brothers	*www.brooksbrothers.com*	Suits Etc	45
Burberry London	*www.theclothesstore.com*	Suits Etc	116
Burton	*www.burtonmenswear.co.uk*	Shop the High Street	000
Dalvey	*www.h-s.co.uk*	Accessories	321
Diesel	*www.jeans-direct.co.uk*	Shop the High Street	35
Dolce & Gabbana	*www.forzieri.com*	Briefcases, Bags and Small Leathers	12, 63, 117, 118, 323
Duchamp	*www.duchamp.co.uk*	Shirts and Accessories	106
Dunhill	*www.dunhill.com*	Briefcases, Bags and Small Leathers	11, 120, 300
Element	*www.w1style.co.uk*	Shop the High Street	55
Firetrap	*www.w1style.co.uk*	Shop the High Street	55
Fred Perry	*www.theclothesstore.com*	Suits Etc	116
French Connection	*www.fcukbuymail.co.uk*	Shop the High Street	34, 144
Gianfranco Ferre	*www.forzieri.com*	Briefcases, Bags and Small Leathers	12, 63, 117, 118, 323
Hackett	*www.hackett.co.uk*	Suits Etc	112
Hilditch and Key	*www.hilditchandkey.co.uk*	Shirts and Accessories	107
Lacoste	*www.theclothesstore.com*	Suits Etc	116
Levi	*www.jeans-direct.co.uk*	Shop the High Street	35
Loake	*www.shoesdirect.co.uk*	Accessories	119
Mont Blanc	*www.h-s.co.uk*	Accessories	321
Moss Bros	*www.mossdirect.co.uk*	Suits Etc	113
Mulberry	*www.mulberry.com*	Briefcases, Bags and Small Leathers	14, 63

O'Neill	www.extremepie.com	Shop the High Street	51, 142
Pickett	www.pickett.co.uk	Briefcases, Bags and Small Leathers	119, 282, 323
Quicksilver	www.extremepie.com	Shop the High Street	51, 142
Ripcurl	www.w1style.co.uk	Shop the High Street	55
Rockport	www.shoesdirect.co.uk	Accessories	119
Roxy	www.extremepie.com	Shop the High Street	51, 142
Smythson	www.smythson.com	Briefcases, Bags and Small Leathers	120
Stone Island	www.stoneisland.co.uk	Suits Etc	116
Ted Baker	www.tedbaker.co.uk	Shop the High Street	37
Thomas Pink	www.thomaspink.com	Shirts and Accessories	108
Top Shop	www.topman.co.uk	Shop the High Street	143
Versace	www.forzieri.com	Briefcases, Bags and Small Leathers	12, 63, 117, 118, 323
Wrangler	www.jeans-direct.co.uk	Shop the High Street	35

Men Only – Toiletries – All Appear in Men's Toiletries

Brand	Website Address	Page
American Crew	www.carterandbond.co.uk	121
	www.jasonshankey.co.uk	121, 123, 162
Calvin Klein	www.escentual.co.uk	124, 155, 277, 368
Caswell Massey	www.1001beautysecrets.com	122
Crabtree and Evelyn	www.carterandbond.co.uk	121
D R Harris	www.theenglishshavingcompany.co.uk	121, 123
Edwin Jagger	www.theenglishshavingcompany.co.uk	121, 123
Floris	www.carterandbond.co.uk	121
Geezers	www.jasonshankey.co.uk	121, 123, 162
Geo F Trumper	www.carterandbond.co.uk	121
	www.trumpers.com	123
GHD	www.jasonshankey.co.uk	121, 123, 162
Gucci	www.escentual.co.uk	124, 155, 277, 368
Hugo Boss	www.escentual.co.uk	124, 155, 277, 368
Kent	www.aehobbs.com	122
Lab Series	www.mankind.co.uk	123
Lacoste	www.escentual.co.uk	124, 155, 277, 368
Mason and Pearson	www.aehobbs.com	122
Molton Brown	www.carterandbond.co.uk	121
	www.theenglishshavingcompany.co.uk	121, 123
Penhaligons	www.penhaligons.co.uk	124, 157, 183, 277, 348
Phytomer	www.mankind.co.uk	123
Roger et Gallet	www.woodruffs.co.uk	124, 159
Tommy Hilfiger	www.escentual.co.uk	124, 155, 277, 368
Truefitt and Hill	www.aehobbs.com	122
	www.mankind.co.uk	123
Woods of Windsor	www.aehobbs.com	122

Pamper Yourself

Brand	Website Address	Chapter	Page
Acqua di Parma	www.hqhair.com	Hair, Nails and Beauty Accessories	146, 151, 161, 177, 180
Air Stockings	www.beautyflash.co.uk	The Beauty Specialists	176
Annick Goutal	www.beautybase.com	Skincare and Cosmetics	152
Anya Hindmarch	www.hqhair.com	Hair, Nails and Beauty Accessories	146, 151, 161, 177, 180
Aromatherapy Associates	www.bathandunwind.com	Skincare and Cosmetics	152
Bare Essentuals	www.hqhair.com	Hair, Nails and Beauty Accessories	146, 151, 161, 177, 180
Benefit	www.boots.com	Skincare and Cosmetics	124, 151, 154, 169
	www.benefitcosmetics.com	Skincare and Cosmetics	153
Bliss	www.blisslondon.co.uk	Skincare and Cosmetics	153
Bloom	www.hqhair.com	Hair, Nails and Beauty Accessories	146, 151, 161, 177, 180
Boucheron	www.beautybase.com	Skincare and Cosmetics	152
Burberry	www.escentual.co.uk	Skincare and Cosmetics	155
Burts Bees	www.bathandunwind.com	Skincare and Cosmetics	152
Bvlgari	www.garden.co.uk	Skincare and Cosmetics	124, 151, 155, 169, 277
Calvin Klein	www.garden.co.uk	Skincare and Cosmetics	124, 151, 155, 169, 277
Carita	www.salonskincare.com	The Beauty Specialists	178
Carolina Herrera	www.beautybase.com	Skincare and Cosmetics	152
Cath Collins	www.cologneandcotton.com	Skincare and Cosmetics	277
	www.woodruffs.co.uk	Skincare and Cosmetics	124, 159
Caudalie	www.garden.co.uk	Skincare and Cosmetics	124, 151, 155, 169, 277
Chanel	www.boots.com	Skincare and Cosmetics	124, 151, 154, 169
	www.garden.co.uk	Skincare and Cosmetics	124, 151, 155, 169, 277
Clarins	www.beautybase.com	Skincare and Cosmetics	152
	www.boots.com	Skincare and Cosmetics	124, 151, 154, 169
	www.garden.co.uk	Skincare and Cosmetics	124, 151, 155, 169, 277
	www.powderpuff.net	Skincare and Cosmetics	158
Clinique	www.boots.com	Skincare and Cosmetics	124, 151, 154, 169
	www.garden.co.uk	Skincare and Cosmetics	124, 151, 155, 169, 277
Clinique	www.powderpuff.net	Skincare and Cosmetics	158
Compagnie de Provence	www.cologneandcotton.com	Skincare and Cosmetics	277
Cote Bastide	www.cologneandcotton.com	Skincare and Cosmetics	277
Crabtree & Evelyn	www.crabtree-evelyn.co.uk	Skincare and Cosmetics	154, 181
	www.woodruffs.co.uk	Skincare and Cosmetics	124, 159
Darphin	www.spacenk.co.uk	Skincare and Cosmetics	151, 158, 179

Here's a general guide to the clothing size conversions between the US, Europe and the UK. If you need size conversions for other specific countries, or other types of conversions go to *www.onlineconversion.com/clothing.htm* where you'll find them all.

To be as sure as possible that you're ordering the right size, check the actual retailer's size chart against your own measurements and note that a UK 12 is sometimes a US 8 and sometimes a 10 so it really pays to make sure.

Clothing size conversions

Women

US	UK	France	Germany	Italy
6	8	36	34	40
8	10	38	36	42
10	12	40	38	44
12	14	42	40	46
14	16	44	42	48
16	18	46	44	50
18	20	50	46	52

Men

US	UK	EU		US	UK	EU
32	32	42		42	42	52
34	34	44		44	44	54
36	36	46		46	46	56
38	38	48		48	48	58
40	40	50				